OXFORD EARLY CHRISTIAN STUDIES

General Editors

GILLIAN CLARK   ANDREW LOUTH

THE OXFORD EARLY CHRISTIAN STUDIES series includes scholarly volumes on the thought and history of the early Christian centuries. Covering a wide range of Greek, Latin, and Oriental sources, the books are of interest to theologians, ancient historians, and specialists in the classical and Jewish worlds.

Titles in the series include:

The Letters of Jerome

Asceticism, Biblical Exegesis, and the
Construction of Christian Authority
in Late Antiquity

ANDREW CAIN

OXFORD
UNIVERSITY PRESS

This book has been printed digitally and produced in a standard specification
in order to ensure its continuing availability

OXFORD
UNIVERSITY PRESS

Great Clarendon Street, Oxford OX2 6DP

Oxford University Press is a department of the University of Oxford.
It furthers the University's objective of excellence in research, scholarship,
and education by publishing worldwide in

Oxford New York

Auckland Cape Town Dar es Salaam Hong Kong Karachi
Kuala Lumpur Madrid Melbourne Mexico City Nairobi
New Delhi Shanghai Taipei Toronto
With offices in
Argentina Austria Brazil Chile Czech Republic France Greece
Guatemala Hungary Italy Japan South Korea Poland Portugal
Singapore Switzerland Thailand Turkey Ukraine Vietnam

Oxford is a registered trade mark of Oxford University Press
in the UK and in certain other countries

Published in the United States
by Oxford University Press Inc., New York

© Andrew Cain 2009

The moral rights of the author have been asserted

Database right Oxford University Press (maker)

Reprinted 2010

ISBN 978-0-19-956355-5

Foreword

This book offers a fresh interpretation of Jerome's letters and uses them as the point of reference for unravelling some intriguing prob lems about the nature of their author's self-constructed spiritual and intellectual authority. My hope is that it will be of use not only to Hieronymists and scholars of the Latin epistolographic tradition but also to those who cultivate interests broadly in the literature, religion, history, culture, and law of the late antique world.

This study traces its roots back to my 2003 Cornell University doctoral dissertation, which was directed by Danuta Shanzer. Several chapters of the dissertation have since been extensively revised and published as articles. This book, parts of which naturally draw from and build on the research presented in these and other related papers, has been written entirely *de novo*.

I have benefited richly from exchanges with a number of friends and colleagues, many of whom were kind enough to read and comment on various aspects of my work: Neil Adkin, Charles Brittain, Gillian Clark, Catherine Conybeare, Florin Curta, Yves-Marie Duval, Jennifer Ebbeler, Alfons Fürst, Richard Goodrich, David Hunter, Paul Hyams, Benoît Jeanjean, Adam Kamesar, Peter Knox, Claudia Rapp, Stefan Rebenich, Philip Rousseau, Michele Salzman, David Scourfield, Cristiana Sogno, Dennis Trout, and Mark Vessey. Noel Lenski, my Classics colleague and fellow late antiquarian at the University of Colorado, was a sounding board for the seminal ideas presented in this book. His encouragement of this project from its inception, and his advice along the way, enabled this book to see the light of day sooner. My trans-oceanic collaboration with Josef Lössl on multiple fronts has been the source of much personal and professional satisfaction and has enhanced my research in many intangible ways. I wish to thank Richard Goodrich, David Hunter, and Sophie Lunn-Rockliffe for graciously providing me with the proofs of their books on John Cassian, Jovinian, and Ambrosiaster, respectively, well in advance of their appearance in print in the Oxford Early Christian Studies series. I am grateful, above all, to Danuta Shanzer and Ralph Mathisen for

their bounty of good-humoured advice over the years, without which
the dissertation and its ensuing book would never have materialized.
They alone know how much I owe them.

One of the greatest boons to my research came at the international
conference 'Jerome of Stridon: Religion, Culture, Society and Literature in Late Antiquity' (Cardiff University, 13–16 July 2006), which
I co-organized with Josef Lössl. The spirit of intellectual exploration
and camaraderie that permeated this gathering stands as a reminder
that the study of Jerome is alive and well like never before. Its proceedings, currently in press with Ashgate Publishing and entitled *Jerome of
Stridon: His Life, Writings and Legacy*, will appear at about the same
time as the present book. As will be evident from the footnotes herein,
I am greatly indebted to the many learned contributions contained in
that volume. I wish to thank my editor at Ashgate, John Smedley, for
kindly allowing me to incorporate into Chapter 3 a small portion of
my paper 'Rethinking Jerome's Portraits of Holy Women'.

Some of the codicological research that informs Chapters 1 and 3
and Appendix III was conducted at the Bibliothèque nationale de
France in Paris during the month of April in 2006. For the duration
of my month-long stay I was fortunate to have lodged with Yves-
Marie Duval and his wife Ginette at their home in Meudon. I am
enormously grateful for their invitation and generous hospitality.
Yves-Marie's passing on 12 March 2007 was a blow to the worldwide
community of Hieronymists. He was as humane as his scholarship
was impeccable. I learned much from him and shall always treasure
our friendship.

This book was read and commented on at different stages by many
scholars whom it is an immense pleasure to recognize here by name:
Charles Brittain, Gillian Clark, Yves-Marie Duval, David Hunter,
Noel Lenski, Josef Lössl, Stefan Rebenich, and Danuta Shanzer.
Gerard O'Daly, who has consented to be revealed as the external
reader at Oxford University Press, delivered a comprehensive, timely,
and helpful review. Words cannot express my gratitude to all of the
readers for their judicious criticisms and suggestions. I have tried
meticulously to address each and every point brought up by them.
It goes without saying that any remaining faults are my own.

The staff at Oxford University Press could not have guided this
book to publication any more smoothly or efficiently. For all of

their assistance I offer my heart-felt thanks, in particular to Tom
Perridge, Lizzie Robottom, Charlotte Green, Jenny Wagstaffe, and
Kartiga Ramalingam. I also wish to acknowledge Dr Paul Smith and
Dr Michael Janes for their expert copy-editing and proofreading.
Warm thanks are due to Gillian Clark and Andrew Louth, editors of
the Oxford Early Christian Studies series, for accepting this book into
their series. The cover image, which captures part of an illuminated
page from a 1470 edition of Jerome's correspondence printed by Peter
Schöffer, was graciously provided by Dr Ueli Dill, curator of medieval
manuscripts at the University of Basel library.

At the University of Colorado I thank my colleagues in the Classics
Department, as well as Deans Graham Oddie and Todd Gleeson, for
their unfailing support on many levels since my arrival in Boulder in
2003. Grants from the Council on Research and Creative Work and
from the Graduate Committee on the Arts and Humanities at the
University of Colorado facilitated my research, as did funding from
the Loeb Classical Library Foundation at Harvard University.

Finally, I must thank my parents, Susan and Cecil Cain, and my
grandparents, Lenora and James Russell, for all that they have done
for me over the years to contribute to my formation; words cannot
adequately express my profound sense of gratitude. I am most immediately thankful to my wife Anna for always keeping me grounded,
and to our two young boys, Tommy and James, for never letting me
forget that there is far more to life than long-dead church writers.

Boulder, Colorado   A.J.C.
2008

Contents

Abbreviations

AAAD	Antichità altoadriatiche
AB	Analecta Bollandiana
ABR	American Benedictine Review
AC	L'Antiquité classique
AClass	Acta Classica. Proceedings of the Classical Association of South Africa
AEHE V	Annuaire de l'École pratique des hautes études, V^e sec., sciences religieuses
AHIg	Anuario de historia de la Iglesia
ALGP	Annali del Liceo Classico G. Garibaldi di Palermo
AnnNap	Annali della facoltà di lettere e filosofia dell'Università di Napoli
AnnSE	Annali di storia dell'esegesi
AugStud	Augustinian Studies
BALAC	Bulletin d'ancienne littérature et d'archéologie chrétiennes
BHM	Bernard Lambert, Bibliotheca Hieronymiana Manuscripta. La tradition manuscrite des œuvres de Saint Jérôme (4 vols. in 6 parts, Steenbrugge, 1969–72)
BKR	Bedi kartlisa
BLE	Bulletin de littérature ecclésiastique
BN	Biblische Notizen
BSAF	Bulletin de la société nationale des antiquaires de France
CCC	Civiltà classica e cristiana
CCSL	Corpus Christianorum, Series Latina
CE	Chronique d'Égypte
ChHist	Church History
ClAnt	Classical Antiquity
COCR	Collectanea cisterciensia
CPh	Classical Philology
CQ	Classical Quarterly

CRAI	*Comptes rendus de l'Academie des inscriptions et belles-lettres*
CrSt	*Cristianesimo nella storia*
CSEL	Corpus Scriptorum Ecclesiasticorum Latinorum
EME	*Early Medieval Europe*
EphL	*Ephemerides liturgicae*
FZPhTh	*Freiburger Zeitschrift für Philosophie und Theologie*
G&H	*Gender & History*
GB	*Grazer Beiträge*
GCS	Die griechischen christlichen Schriftsteller der ersten drei Jahrhunderte
HThR	*Harvard Theological Review*
ICS	*Illinois Classical Studies*
IEJ	*Israel Exploration Journal*
JbAC	*Jahrbuch für Antike und Christentum*
JECS	*Journal of Early Christian Studies*
JEH	*Journal of Ecclesiastical History*
JMEMS	*Journal of Medieval and Early Modern Studies*
JR	*Journal of Religion*
JRS	*Journal of Roman Studies*
JSJ	*Journal for the Study of Judaism*
JSS	*Journal of Semitic Studies*
JThS	*Journal of Theological Studies*
LASBF	*Liber Annuus Studii Biblici Franciscani*
LCL	Loeb Classical Library
MEFRA	*Mélanges d'archéologie et d'histoire de l'école française de Rome, antiquité*
MGH AA	Monumenta Germaniae historica, Auctores antiquissimi
MHE	*Miscellanea historiae ecclesiasticae*
MP	*Medieval Prosopography*
NRTh	*Nouvelle revue théologique*
OCT	Oxford Classical Texts
PCBE	Charles Pietri and Luce Pietri (eds.), *Prosopographie chrétienne du bas-empire*, ii. *Prosopographie de l'Italie chrétienne (313–604)* (Rome, 1999 [pt 1], 2000 [pt 2])

PEQ	*Palestine Exploration Quarterly*
PG	Patrologia Graeca
PIBA	*Proceedings of the Irish Biblical Association*
PL	Patrologia Latina
PLRE	A. H. M. Jones, J. R. Martindale, and J. Morris (eds.), *The Prosopography of the Later Roman Empire*, i. *AD 260–395* (Cambridge, 1971); J. R. Martindale (ed.), *The Prosopography of the Later Roman Empire*, ii. *AD 395–527* (Cambridge, 1980)
POC	*Proche-orient chrétien*
RAC	*Reallexikon für Antike und Christentum*
RACr	*Rivista di archeologia cristiana*
RAM	*Revue d'ascétique et de mystique*
Rbén	*Revue bénédictine*
Rbi	*Revue biblique*
REA	*Revue des études anciennes*
REAug	*Revue des études augustiniennes*
RecAug	*Recherches augustiniennes*
RecTh	*Recherches de théologie ancienne et médiévale*
REL	*Revue des études latines*
RFHL	*Revue française d'histoire du livre*
RFIC	*Rivista di filologia e di istruzione classica*
RHE	*Revue d'histoire ecclésiastique*
RHR	*Revue de l'histoire des religions*
RicRel	*Ricerche religiose*
RicSRel	*Ricerche di storia religiosa*
RMab	*Revue Mabillon*
RPh	*Revue de philologie de littérature et d'histoire anciennes*
RPL	*Res publica litterarum*
RSLR	*Rivista di storia e letteratura religiosa*
RSR	*Revue des sciences religieuses*
RThPh	*Revue de théologie et de philosophie*
SC	Sources chrétiennes
ScC	*Scuola cattolica*

SCent	Second Century
ScrTh	Scrinium theologicum
SEJG	Sacris erudiri: jaarboek voor Godsdienstwetenschappen
SicGymn	Siculorum gymnasium
SO	Symbolae osloenses
StudMon	Studia monastica
StudPatr	Studia patristica
StudTard	Studi tardoantichi
TAPhA	Transactions of the American Philological Association
Th&Ph	Theologie und Philosophie
ThLZ	Theologische Literaturzeitung
ThS	Theological Studies
TLL	Thesaurus Linguae Latinae
TQ	Theologische Quartalschrift
TRE	Theologische Realenzyklopädie
TZ	Trierer Zeitschrift für Geschichte und Kunst des Trierer Landes und seiner Nachbargebiete
VChr	Vigiliae christianae
VetChr	Vetera christianorum
WHB	Wiener Humanistische Blätter
WS	Wiener Studien
YFS	Yale French Studies
ZAC	Zeitschrift für Antikes Christentum
ZKG	Zeitschrift für Kirchengeschichte
ZNTW	Zeitschrit für Neutestamentliche Wissenschaft
ZPalV	Zeitschrift des deutschen Palästina-Vereins
ZPE	Zeitschrift für Papyrologie und Epigraphik
ZSS	Zeitschrift der Savigny-Stiftung für Rechtsgeschichte, Romanistische Abteilung

Introduction

One day while walking down the corridors of the Vatican, Pope Sixtus V (1585–90) stopped before a painting of a penitent Jerome in the wilderness striking his breast with a stone. The pope is said to have quipped: 'You do well to carry that stone, for without it the Church would never have canonized you.'[1]

This anecdote hints at how Jerome's seemingly volatile personality, as it comes through in his writings, cast doubt in the minds of some Christians about his status as a saint more than a millennium after his death.[2] Indeed, his penchant for polemic did little to win him new supporters in his own day and strained the friendships he already had.[3] He had other public image problems besides perceived contentiousness. Born around 347, Jerome grew up in the virtually unknown town of Stridon on the northern frontier of the Roman empire.[4]

---

[1] Donald Attwater and Herbert Thurston (eds.), *Butler's Lives of the Saints* (4 vols., New York, 1956), iii. 691.

[2] This same pessimistic assessment of Jerome's character has carried over into modern scholarship. Note, for instance, the epithet Francis Murphy applied to Jerome in the title to his essay 'St. Jerome: The irascible hermit', in Francis X. Murphy (ed.), *A Monument to St Jerome: Essays on Some Aspects of His Life, Works and Influence* (New York, 1952), 3–12. More recent examples abound and are so great in number that they need not be cited here.

[3] For examples, see Andrew Cain, '*Vox clamantis in deserto*: Rhetoric, Reproach, and the Forging of Ascetic Authority in Jerome's Letters from the Syrian Desert', *JThS*, NS 57 (2006), 500–1. For studies of Jerome's polemic, see J. Brochet, *Saint Jérôme et ses ennemis: étude sur la querelle de Saint Jérôme avec Rufin d'Aquilée* (Paris, 1906); Ilona Opelt, *Hieronymus' Streitschriften* (Heidelberg, 1973).

[4] For the debate about Stridon's precise location, see Francesco Bulic, 'Stridone luogo natale di S. Girolamo', *Miscellanea Geronimiana. Scritti varii pubblicati nel XV centenario dalla morte di San Girolamo* (Rome, 1920), 253–330; I. Fodor, 'Le Lieu

His lineage was obscure and his family, although moderately prosperous, could not rival a senatorial family in economic or social prestige. Because he was not independently wealthy he had to rely on affluent patrons to fund the literary *otium* that he required in later life. His primary patrons were aristocratic Christian widows, and the socio-economic disparity between himself and them as well as his friendships with them invited suspicions that he was an opportunist with a lascivious streak. Jerome's profile was problematic for other reasons as well. He championed an extreme form of ascetic Christianity embraced by only a tiny minority, and even his partisans were put off at times by his theological and rhetorical excesses. His 'back to the sources' approach to biblical textual criticism, exegesis, and translation was widely criticized by the leading Scriptural authorities of the day. As a result, his Vulgate translation of most of the Bible into Latin, his crowning scholarly legacy, was with few exceptions rejected by contemporaries, lay and clerical alike.[5] His lavish praise of the heterodox third-century biblical exegete Origen of Alexandria raised serious questions about his theological orthodoxy, something of which he was exceedingly proud,[6] when the so-called Origenist controversy erupted in the 390s. Jerome's quest for respectability was further frustrated by the fact that his ecclesiastical status was ambiguous at best and scandalous at worst. He was not a bishop but a non-practising priest (ordained by a schismatic bishop,[7] no less) who was officially pronounced a miscreant *twice* in one decade by the churches

d'origine de s. Jérôme: reconsidération d'une vieille controverse', *RHE*, 81 (1986), 498–500. On the ancient province of Dalmatia, see John Wilkes, *Dalmatia* (London, 1969).

[5] His translation was not used widely until the ninth century, though many clerics and monks still continued up through the thirteenth century to read from and copy Old Latin versions of the Bible. See Raphael Loewe, 'The Medieval History of the Latin Vulgate', in G. W. H. Lampe (ed.), *The Cambridge History of the Bible*, ii. *The West from the Fathers to the Reformation* (Cambridge, 1975), 102–54.

[6] On many occasions he pointed out that he had been personally instructed in theology and biblical hermeneutics by Gregory Nazianzen, Didymus the Blind, and Apollinaris of Laodicea: see *Epp.* 50.1; 84.3; *Apol. c. Ruf.* 1.13. See also Pierre Jay, 'Jérôme auditeur d'Apollinaire de Laodicée à Antioche', *REAug*, 20 (1974), 36–41; Neil Adkin, 'Gregory of Nazianzus and Jerome: Some Remarks', in Michael Flower and Mark Toher (eds.), *Georgica: Greek Studies in Honour of George Cawkwell* (London, 1991), 13–24.

[7] He was ordained c.377 in Antioch by bishop Paulinus, who at the time was in schism with the local church.

at Rome (385) and Jerusalem (394). In the final tally, then, the historical Jerome was an extremely marginalized figure in his own time and therefore a far cry from the 'Saint Jerome' construct of medieval hagiography that heavily influenced most scholarly traditions down to the twentieth century and some even down to the present day.[8]

For the entirety of his career as a Christian writer, from the early 370s until his death *c*.419, Jerome's predominant ambition was to achieve pre-eminence both as an orthodox biblical scholar and as a practitioner and teacher of ascetic Christianity. He was disinclined to follow a more traditional religious career path in the ecclesiastical *cursus honorum*; a bibliophile with a strong monastic bent, he preferred to forge his own vocation as a monk–scholar.[9] By the time he released *De viris illustribus* in 393, it had become sufficiently clear that Jerome longed to be recognized for his expertise on the Bible and ascetic spirituality not only in his own time but also posthumously. He appended to this Christian literary history a detailed autobibliographical notice—the longest he gave for any living writer[10]—and in so doing he was announcing himself as the primary latter-day bearer of the patristic torch.[11] However, the thorniness of his profile forever impeded his ambitions. His personality and scandals seemed to preclude sainthood, and his innovative scholarly work and ascetic

[8] For the development of the cult of 'Saint' Jerome, see Eugene Rice, *Saint Jerome in the Renaissance* (Baltimore, Md., 1985). See also selected essays on Jerome's reception in Andrew Cain and Josef Lössl (eds.), *Jerome of Stridon: His Life, Writings and Legacy* (Aldershot, 2009).

[9] Mark Vessey, 'From *cursus* to *ductus*: Figures of Writing in Western Late Antiquity (Augustine, Jerome, Cassiodorus, Bede)', in Patrick Cheney and Frederick de Armas (eds.), *European Literary Careers. The Author from Antiquity to the Renaissance* (Toronto, 2002), 53–9.

[10] Jerome's notice on himself is also longer than any one devoted to past patristic writers except Irenaeus and Origen, both Greek Fathers. His many Latin patristic predecessors such as Tertullian, Cyprian, Lactantius, and Hilary receive less generous treatment. Contemporary Latin writers fare even worse; for example, the entry for Ambrose is dismissively curt and the biblical exegete now known as 'Ambrosiaster', one of Jerome's greatest contemporary rivals, is omitted altogether.

[11] For studies of Jerome's historiographic method in this work, see Aldo Ceresa-Gastaldo, 'La tecnica biografica del De viris illustribus di Girolamo', *Renovatio* 14 (1979), 221–36; Salvatore Pricoco, 'Motivi polemici e prospettive classicistiche nel De viris illustribus di Girolamo', *SicGymn*, 32 (1979), 69–99; Ilona Opelt, 'Hieronymus' Leistung als Literarhistoriker in der Schrift De viris illustribus', *Orpheus*, NS 1 (1980), 52–75.

propagandizing met with fierce resistance from the wider Christian community.

Two crucial interrelated questions arise. How did Jerome seek to legitimize himself in order to attract a faithful following, especially patrons to provide financial support for his labours and to facilitate the dissemination of his writings? How, furthermore, did he distinguish himself from the many rivals with whom he competed for a sympathetic readership? These questions have never before been addressed in these explicit terms, that much the less addressed in view of the complicating factor of Jerome's marginality. The present study aims to navigate these uncharted waters. I have chosen his letters as the point of departure because it is in them, I shall argue, that we see their author most deftly re-inventing himself to accommodate the ever-changing demands made upon him by ever-changing audiences.

Jerome's letters are, as one noted scholar appropriately has called them, 'the finest of Christian antiquity'.[12] Indeed, in the ancient Latin prose epistolographic tradition—broadly construed to include not only Christian letter-writers (e.g., Ambrose, Augustine, Paulinus, Sidonius) but also their non-Christian counterparts (e.g., Cicero, Seneca, Pliny, Symmachus)—Jerome is a luminary among luminaries.[13] His epistolary corpus encompasses 123 extant genuine letters.[14] Among specialists and non-specialists alike, this is probably the best-known and certainly the most widely accessible[15] portion of his vast and varied *œuvre*. Scholarly approaches to the letters traditionally have gravitated to one of two poles, which I shall call the 'literary–philological' and the 'historical–biographical'. To the first category belong fine studies on the letters' aesthetic properties

---

[12] Stefan Rebenich, *Jerome* (London and New York, 2002), 79.

[13] For a brief overview of the Latin epistolographic tradition, see Michael Trapp, *Greek and Latin Letters. An Anthology, with Translation* (Cambridge, 2003), 12–26.

[14] For a bird's-eye view of the corpus, see Appendix I.

[15] The letters have been translated into several modern languages. For a bibliography of the various editions and translations, see G. Asdrubali Pentiti and Maria Carla Spadoni Cerroni (eds.), *Epistolari cristiani (secc. I–V). Repertorio bibliografico II. Epistolari Latini (secc. IV–V)* (Rome, 1990), 31–5. Neil Adkin is currently preparing a new translation of most of the correspondence for the Paulist Press Ancient Christian Writers series.

(prose rhythm,[16] style,[17] rhetorical tropes[18]), their epistolographic features,[19] and their implementation of intertexts from the Bible[20] and classical literature.[21] There are also several excellent commentaries on individual epistles.[22] At the 'historical–biographical' end of the spectrum, the letters have been mined for the light they shed on the religious and socio-cultural milieu of a watershed period in the history of the west.[23] Biographers naturally have looked to them as the main frame of reference when mapping out the chronology and the particulars of their author's eventful life,[24] his

[16] Margaret Clare Herron, *A Study of the Clausulae in the Writings of St Jerome* (Washington, DC, 1937); Steven Oberhelman, *Rhetoric and Homiletics in Fourth-century Christian Literature* (Atlanta, Ga., 1991), 80–6 (with bibliography).

[17] Giuseppe Stoico, *L'Epistolario di san Girolamo: Studio critico-letterario di stilistica latina* (Naples, 1972); Lorenzo Viscido, *Atteggiamenti ironici nell'epistolario geronimiano* (Salerno, 1978); Francesco Trisoglio, 'Note stilistiche sull'epistolario di Girolamo', *VetChr*, 30 (1993), 267–88.

[18] John Hritzu, *The Style of the Letters of St Jerome* (Washington, DC, 1939).

[19] Barbara Conring, *Hieronymus als Briefschreiber. Ein Beitrag zur spätantiken Epistolographie* (Tübingen, 2001); Aline Canellis, 'La Lettre selon saint Jérôme: l'épistolarité de la correspondance hiéronymienne', in Léon Nadjo and Élisabeth Gavoille (eds.), *Epistulae antiquae, ii. Actes du IIᵉ colloque 'Le genre épistolaire antique et ses prolongements européens'* (Université François-Rabelais, Tours, 28–30 Sept. 2000) (2 vols., Louvain-Paris, 2002), ii. 311–32; cf. Roland Gründel, 'Des Hieronymus Briefe: Ihre literarische Bestimmung und ihre Zusammengehörigkeit', dissertation (Leipzig, 1958).

[20] Carlo Tibiletti, 'Immagini bibliche nel linguaggio figurato di S. Girolamo', in Aldo Ceresa-Gastaldo (ed.), *Gerolamo e la biografia letteraria* (Genoa, 1989), 63–79.

[21] Emil Luebeck, *Hieronymus quos noverit scriptores et ex quibus hauserit* (Leipzig, 1872); Harald Hagendahl, *Latin Fathers and the Classics: A Study on the Apologists, Jerome, and Other Christian Writers* (Göteborg, 1958), 183–214, 246–60. See also the impressive body of articles by Neil Adkin as well as Andrew Cain, '*Liber manet*: Pliny, *Ep.* 9.27.2 and Jerome, *Ep.* 130.19.5', *CQ*, NS 58 (2008), 708–10.

[22] G. J. M. Bartelink. *Hieronymus, Liber de optimo genere interpretandi (Epistula 57). Ein Kommentar* (Leiden, 1980); J. H. D. Scourfield, *Consoling Heliodorus: A Commentary on Jerome, Letter 60* (Oxford, 1993); Neil Adkin, *Jerome on Virginity. A Commentary on the Libellus de virginitate servanda (Letter 22)* (Cambridge, 2003). By the time of his death in March 2007, Yves-Marie Duval had nearly completed a commentary on *Ep.* 22, but it has not yet been published posthumously.

[23] See, e.g., the work of Peter Brown as well as the first six volumes of Adalbert de Vogüé's *Histoire littéraire du mouvement monastique dans l'antiquité* (Paris, 1991–2003).

[24] Georg Grützmacher, *Hieronymus: Eine biographische Studie zur alten Kirchengeschichte* (3 vols., Berlin, 1901–8); Ferdinand Cavallera, *Saint Jérôme: sa vie et son œuvre* (2 vols., Paris, 1922); J. N. D. Kelly, *Jerome. His Life, Writings, and Controversies* (London, 1975); Rebenich, *Hieronymus und sein Kreis. Prosopographische und sozialgeschichtliche Untersuchungen* (Stuttgart, 1992).

ascetic teaching,[25] and, in some cases, the contours of his intriguing personality.[26]

In this book I take a different but complementary approach to the letters than scholars hitherto have taken. Rather than view them exclusively as either textual artefacts or passive historical documents, I steer an interdisciplinary course and draw occasionally from both approaches while calling attention to the letters' often underappreciated but fundamentally propagandistic nature. In particular, I examine Jerome's sophisticated use of literary artistry to construct spiritual and intellectual authority for himself through idealized epistolary self-presentation. Now, it is a given that Jerome 'self-presented', and very self-consciously so, in his correspondence. What needs to be explained is why he presented himself in the way that he did in various circumstances and what the answer can tell us about the driving forces behind not only Jerome the epistolographer but also Jerome the man.[27] Previous scholarship has identified instances of autobiographical manipulation in some of the letters.[28] This book, however, is the first systematic investigation of Jerome's strategies for manufacturing authority across the whole range of his extant correspondence.

See also the impressionistic biography by Jean Steinmann, *Saint Jerome and His Times* (Notre Dame, Ind., 1959). For a study of the letters' chronology, see Nicolaus Pronberger, *Beiträge zur Chronologie der Briefe des hl. Hieronymus* (Amberg, 1913).

[25] Leopoldus Laurita, *Insegnamenti ascetici nelle lettere di s. Girolamo* (Rome, 1967).

[26] G. lo Cascio, *Girolamo da Stridone, studiato nel suo epistolario* (Catania, 1923); Pieter Steur, *Het karakter van Hieronymus van Stridon bestudeerd in zijn brieven* (Nijmegen, 1945); Massimo Marcocchi, *Motivi umani e cristiani nell'Epistolario di s. Girolamo* (Milan, 1967); Francesco Trisoglio, 'La personalità di san Girolamo attraverso l'epistolario', *ScC*, 120 (1992), 575–612. For a somewhat dated study of Jerome's personality as it comes through in the prefaces to his biblical translations and commentaries, see Charles Favez, *Saint Jérôme peint par lui-même* (Brussels, 1958).

[27] For another attempt at ascertaining the essence of Jerome the man, see Philip Rousseau, 'Jerome's Search for Self–identity', in Pauline Allen, Raymond Canning, and Lawrence Cross (eds.), *Prayer and Spirituality in the Early Church* (4 vols., Brisbane, 1998–2006), i. 125–42. Rousseau takes the biographical work of J. N. D. Kelly and Stefan Rebenich as counterpoints for his discussion.

[28] Most notably, Rebenich, *Hieronymus und sein Kreis*, 86–98 and *passim*, and Mark Vessey, 'Jerome's Origen: The Making of a Christian Literary *Persona*', *StudPatr*, 28 (1993), 135–45.

The Letters of Jerome 7

I do not attempt to provide adequately detailed coverage of every letter within Jerome's substantial epistolary corpus. I omit discussions, for instance, of his correspondence with Augustine[29] and Paulinus of Nola[30] as well as of the correspondence pertaining to his involvement in the Origenist controversy,[31] primarily because exhaustive treatments can be found elsewhere. In addition, I do not discuss at length Jerome's famous letter on 'spiritual marriage' (*Ep.* 117)[32] or his even more famous epitaph on Paula (*Ep.* 108)[33] because I have devoted separate studies to them in other publications. In general, it has been my intention to concentrate in this book on letters that have received less scholarly attention but that at the same time yield especially valuable insight into the apologetic and propagandistic features of Jerome's epistolography. I examine the letters in dossiers, some of my own arrangement (individual letters grouped together by common themes: Chapters 4, 5, 6) and others of Jerome's (letter-collections: Chapters 1, 3; and circulating epistolary couplets: Chapters 2, 6). Furthermore, four of the six chapters centre on Jerome's epistolographic activity in the years leading up to and including his second stay in Rome from 382 to 385, while the

[29] Ralph Hennings, *Der Briefwechsel zwischen Augustinus und Hieronymus und ihr Streit um den Kanon des Alten Testaments und die Auslegung von Gal. 2. 11–14* (Leiden, 1994); Alfons Fürst, *Augustins Briefwechsel mit Hieronymus* (Münster, 1999); Jennifer Ebbeler, *Disciplining Christians: Correction and Community in Augustine's Letters* (Oxford and New York, 2009). For a translation-cum-notes of the complete correspondence, see Carolinne White, *The Correspondence (394–419) between Jerome and Augustine of Hippo* (Lampeter, 1990).

[30] Pierre Courcelle, 'Paulin de Nole et Saint Jérôme', *REL*, 25 (1947), 250–80; Pierre Nautin, 'Études de chronologie hiéronymienne (393–397), iii. Les Premières Relations entre Jérôme et Paulin de Nole', *REAug*, 19 (1973), 213–39; Yves-Marie Duval, 'Les Premiers rapports de Paulin de Nole avec Jérôme: moine ou philosophe? poète ou exégète?', *StudTard*, 7 (1989), 177–216; Giuseppe Guttilla, 'Paolino di Nola e Girolamo', *Orpheus*, NS 13 (1992), 278–94. See also Aline Canellis, 'Les Rapports de Paulin de Nole avec Jérôme au-delà de 400: la Lettre 39 de Paulin et le *Commentaire sur Joël* 1, 4 de Jérôme', *Augustinianum*, 39 (1999), 311–35; Dennis Trout, *Paulinus of Nola. Life, Letters, and Poems* (Berkeley, Calif., 1999), *passim*.

[31] The literature dealing with Jerome's letters concerning the Origenist controversy is vast. A good starting-point is Elizabeth Clark, *The Origenist Controversy: The Cultural Construction of an Early Christian Debate* (Princeton, NJ, 1992).

[32] Cain, 'Jerome's *Epistula* 117 on the *subintroductae*: Satire, Apology, and Ascetic Propaganda in Gaul', *Augustinianum*, 19 (2009), forthcoming.

[33] Cain, 'Jerome's *Epitaphium Paulae*: Hagiography, Pilgrimage, and the Cult of Saint Paula', *JECS*, 18 (2010), forthcoming.

remaining two examine letters that belong to his Bethlehem years
(386–*c*.419). This selectiveness is intentional. The time Jerome spent
in Rome marked the decisive period of his career as a Christian writer.
For it is here that he made his formal debut in the west as an ascetic
essayist and biblical scholar, the two spheres of literary interest that
would continue to preoccupy him for the remainder of his life.[34] It is
also here that he forged strategic ties, some lifelong, with a reigning
pope and a circle of aristocratic Christians whose patronage made
it possible for the provincial upstart to emerge from obscurity to
become, in time, one of the most pivotal figures in the history of
western Christianity.[35]

Jerome is known to have compiled two different collections of his
personal correspondence prior to 393. The one contained letters to
miscellaneous people (*Epistularum ad diversos liber*) and the other
correspondence to his Roman patron Marcella (*Ad Marcellam epistularum liber*). This first collection has received no attention from
scholars aside from passing speculation about which of Jerome's earliest extant letters it may have contained. My aim in Chapter 1 is to
fill this gap in the scholarship by locating the *liber* in the context of
Jerome's efforts to legitimize himself as an expert on asceticism early
on in his literary career. I begin by reconstructing its plausible contents in light of the manuscript tradition and other considerations.
I then argue that this *liber* should be interpreted in the same vein
as other authorially assembled letter-collections from antiquity—
namely, as a unified artistic monument released to the public for
purposes of idealized self-presentation. A close analysis of the themes
running through its constituent letters strongly suggests that Jerome
used the compilation to provide for Latin readers a stylized narrative
of his years as a 'desert' monk in Syria. I conclude that he compiled
and began circulating the *liber* shortly after arriving in Rome in the

---

[34] Prior to coming to Rome in the autumn of 382, Jerome had produced writings such as the *Vita Pauli* (*c*.375), the *Altercatio Luciferani et Orthodoxi* (376/7),
and a commentary (now lost) on Obadiah. Nevertheless, as long as he remained in
Antioch and later in Constantinople in the late 370s and early 380s, he was a fish
out of water, a westerner living in the Greek east yet writing exclusively in Latin
and therefore for a western audience. On his literary activity in Constantinople, see
Stefan Rebenich, 'Asceticism, Orthodoxy and Patronage: Jerome in Constantinople',
StudPatr, 33 (1997), 358–77.

[35] Rebenich, *Hieronymus und sein Kreis*, 141–80.

autumn of 382 as a means to introduce himself to pious Christian patrons, and perhaps more specifically to Marcella and her coterie of monastically inclined widows and virgins, as a veteran of spiritual warfare and therefore as a competent would-be spiritual director. This letter-collection, thus interpreted, was the textual mechanism by which the unknown monk formally established for western audiences in writing, for the first time, his credentials as an authority on the ascetic life.

In Chapter 2, we turn our attention to Jerome's efforts to make his biblical scholarship seem like a necessary commodity to Christians in Rome. In the early 380s, he was still an obscure biblical scholar who championed a text-critical and hermeneutical methodology (*Hebraica veritas*) that was viewed, in the Latin-speaking Christian world at least, as a dangerous innovation. The burden thus was on him to prove why it held the key, as he claimed, to the proper understanding of the biblical text. In the chapter I make the case that Jerome circulated some of his exegetical correspondence with Pope Damasus in order to furnish proof that he was the latter's hand-picked Scriptural advisor. The apparently close relationship between this influential pope and Jerome, as it seems to unfold episodically in these exchanges, implied that his avant-garde scholarship came with a papal stamp of approval and that it therefore could be embraced with confidence by the Roman Christian community. I further argue that Jerome's additional aim in releasing his last surviving letter-exchange with Damasus was to give himself leverage against Ambrosiaster, a rival biblical authority active in Rome during the same period as Jerome.

Another segment of Jerome's richly varied epistolographic activity at Rome is the focus of Chapter 3. Here I explore the propagandistic dimensions of his other known collection of personal correspondence, the *Ad Marcellam epistularum liber*. The sixteen surviving letters that are taken to have comprised a substantial part if not all of the archetypal collection are analysed topically according to their shared themes. I suggest that Jerome released the compilation at some point before he left Italy for good in the summer of 385 in order publicly to summarize and to defend his legacy in Rome as the trusted Scriptural and spiritual mentor to a remarkable group of disciples who, to hear him tell it in this epistolary anthology, were the frontrunners of the women's ascetic movement in the fourth-century west. They were offered by Jerome as credible public faces for his controversial brand of biblical scholarship and ascetic Christianity. I argue that Jerome intended the *liber* also to serve as his personal textual presence-in-absence from faraway Palestine. It stood, on the one hand, as a sentimental reminder to Marcella, the 'star' of the collection, of the spiritual and intellectual debt she owed to him and, on the other hand, as a warning to rival spiritual directors that Marcella and her cohort were already being shepherded by an eminently qualified man of God who was willing to do whatever it took to watch out for their best spiritual interests.

During his three-year stay in Rome Jerome enjoyed many personal and professional successes but weathered even more controversies and bitter disappointments. In Chapter 4, I first take an intensive look at some of the public relations crises he faced there with an eye to emphasizing just how tenuous his standing as a Christian authority really was, even among his own followers. Much of the chapter provides a fresh reassessment of the sequence of events that precipitated Jerome's untimely expulsion from Rome in the late summer of 385. Scholars have always assumed that his demise was orchestrated by enemies he had made within the Roman clergy. However, I adduce new evidence to suggest that, while the Roman church was responsible for prosecuting him, the case against Jerome was actually instigated by members of Paula's immediate family unsympathetic with her ascetic piety and upset over her close association with Jerome, whom they saw as a meddler in their domestic affairs. I propose that when they learned of Paula's plans to go on an extended pilgrimage to the Holy Land with him, with the possibility of a permanent move there, they decided as a last resort to pursue legal action against him in the hope that Paula would come to her senses and sever ties with him. Jerome was haled before an episcopal court to face charges of clerical misconduct; there are indications that allegations of legacy-hunting and sexual impropriety were in the air. A guilty verdict evidently was handed down and he was compelled to leave Rome at once. I conclude the chapter by showing how Jerome, in an attempt to salvage his carefully crafted reputation as a pious monk, masterfully recast his shameful condemnation after the fact as the exile of a divinely ordained prophet.

The last two chapters examine how the Jerome of mature years negotiated his spiritual and intellectual authority in correspondence sent to Christians throughout the west from his monastery in Bethlehem. Chapter 5 treats selected letters of spiritual advice. I begin by setting into relief three important facets of Jerome's profile that rendered his status as an authority on the ascetic life negligible and that accordingly frustrated his attempts at making his ideological cause seem worthwhile to the wider Christian community. In the second part of the chapter I analyse letters he wrote to a priest (*Ep.* 52 to Nepotian), a monk (*Ep.* 125 to Rusticus), and a consecrated virgin (*Ep.* 130 to Demetrias), in order to determine the specific terms on which he defined his authority and why he chose the terms that he did. I argue that Jerome justified his right to advise on spiritual matters by appealing either to his tenure as a desert monk or to his fulsome bibliography of *ascetica*, both of which testified to his personal experience living as a committed Christian and to his deep insight into matters of practical spirituality that was implied by this experience. Furthermore, I suggest that his reasons for developing these specific modes of authority are best understood in the context of an antagonistic dialogue he was carrying on, at the subtextual level of each letter, with formidable authorities on the ascetic life: Ambrose (*Ep.* 52); St Martin of Tours and Sulpicius Severus (*Ep.* 125); and Pelagius (*Ep.* 130). I argue that in each instance Jerome tried ever so subtly—drawing from the full range of his impressive rhetorical repertoire—to displace the authority figure in question by trumping that person's supposed inexperience and lack of expertise with his own superabundance of both, all in an attempt to persuade prospective followers why his interpretation of Christianity was to be embraced, to the exclusion of competing interpretations.

Chapter 6 considers several biblical exegetical letters that Jerome wrote from Bethlehem. Traditionally, scholars have valued them for either their theological or prosopographical content. I observe them from a different angle and argue that they were central components of Jerome's textual campaign to justify his authority as a biblical scholar. In the first part of the chapter, I examine a dossier of correspondence to and about Fabiola, who was renowned locally in Rome for funding the construction of the first Christian-owned and -operated civilian public hospital in the nearby harbour town Portus. I argue that Jerome coupled an epistolary *epitaphium* on Fabiola, in which he glorified her as the quintessential student of Scripture, with a detailed commentary on Numbers 33 that he dedicated to her after her death. His twofold aim in doing so was to prove to a Roman Christian audience not only that his controversial Hebrew scholarship was in demand among the spiritual elite but also that to Christians who availed themselves of it, this scholarship served as a reliable road map for their pilgrimage from earthly existence to eternal life in heaven. In the second part of the chapter, I look at letters Jerome sent in 407 to the Gallic noblewomen Hedibia and Algasia answering their lists of questions about problematic New Testament passages. I argue from a close reading of their elaborate literary prefaces that he devised these replies to be circulating exegetical letter-treatises that advertised his scholarly services to a broad Gallic Christian audience. At the same time, he used these prefaces to explain to Christians in Gaul why they should take their questions about the Bible to him rather than to regional experts.

There are three appendices. In the first, I propose a new system of classifying Jerome's extant letters that is less anachronistic, and truer to the rhetorical norms of late antique epistolography, than all of the existing taxonomies devised by modern scholars. The second appendix takes inventory of letters by Jerome that are known to be lost. In the third and final appendix, I discuss the medieval manuscript tradition of the letters and conclude that Jerome did not release his complete (or even near-complete) correspondence during his lifetime, as other imperial and post-classical Latin prose epistolographers had done.

1

'The Voice of One Calling in the Desert'

In the spring of 393,[1] Jerome put the finishing touches on *De viris illustribus*, a monumental catalogue of great Christian writers past and present and their writings. After profiling others in the first 134 chapters, in the final notice he placed the spotlight on himself and his own rapidly burgeoning output. This auto-bibliography contains a near-complete listing of the works he had produced down to 393. It is of use to us here because in it Jerome lay down an editorial blueprint for how he structured some of his correspondence. Listed are seven individual letters (or epistolary treatises),[2] two letter-collections, and the innumerable daily letter-exchanges he carried on between Paula and Eustochium in Bethlehem beginning *c*.386. Of the two collections, one contained letters to Marcella (*Ad Marcellam epistularum liber unus*) and the other letters to various people (*Epistularum ad diversos liber unus*). The collection of Marcellan correspondence will be treated in Chapter 3. In the present chapter, the focus will be on this second collection of letters.

EPISTULARUM AD DIVERSOS LIBER: STRUCTURE AND CONTENTS

Which of Jerome's surviving letters might have belonged to the ensemble known as the *Epistularum ad diversos liber*? To date there

---

[1] Pierre Nautin, 'La Date du *De viris inlustribus* de Jérôme, de la mort de Cyrille de Jérusalem et de celle de Grégoire de Nazianze', *RHE*, 56 (1961), 33–5.

[2] They are listed by title: *Ad Heliodorum exhortatoria* (*Ep.* 14); *De seraphim* (*Ep.* 18A + B); *De osanna* (*Ep.* 20); *De frugi et luxurioso filiis* (*Ep.* 21); *De tribus quaestiunculis legis veteris* (*Ep.* 36); *Ad Eustochium de virginitate servanda* (*Ep.* 22); *Consolatorium de morte filiae ad Paulam* (*Ep.* 39).

has been no serious attempt to answer this question. Scholars have instead been content with the uncorroborated assumption that it included all of the seventeen surviving letters (*Epp.* 1–17) that Jerome had written prior to coming to Rome in the summer of 382.[3] A careful examination of the evidence, however, will show that this widely held view is in need of revision and that the pre-Roman letters cannot be combined indiscriminately in one and the same group. Certain clues left behind by Jerome help us to reconstruct the primitive *liber*. One relates to the internal structure of his auto-bibliography. Jerome mapped out this listing using a chronological scheme, such that works produced in and around Antioch in the 370s head the list and are followed successively by those completed in Constantinople (*c*.380), Rome (382–5), and Bethlehem (386–93).[4] Because the *liber* is the second entry in the list and is situated between the *Vita Pauli* and *Ep.* 14 to Heliodorus,[5] both of which were composed in the early to middle 370s,[6] we may conclude that whatever letters it contained were written during this period, before Jerome left for Constantinople.[7]

Evidence from the manuscript tradition enables us to pare down the contents of the *liber* with even more precision. *Ep.* 1, a *passio* of a Christian woman falsely accused of adultery dedicated to Jerome's deceased friend Innocentius,[8] most likely did not belong to the *liber*.

---

[3] e.g., Nautin, 'La Liste des œuvres de Jérôme dans le *De viris inlustribus*', *Orpheus*, NS 5 (1984), 324–5; Aldo Ceresa-Gastaldo, *Gerolamo. Gli uomini illustri (De viris illustribus)* (Florence, 1988), 341; Thomas Halton, *St Jerome: On Illustrious Men* (Washington, DC, 1999), 169 n. 6; Stefan Rebenich, *Jerome* (London and New York, 2002), 190 n. 6; Alfons Fürst, *Hieronymus: Askese und Wissenschaft in der Spätantike* (Freiburg, 2003), 223 n. 6. Cf. Jérôme Labourt, *Jérôme: Lettres* (8 vols., Paris, 1949–63), i. p. xlvii, who without stating reasons restricted the *liber* to only *Epp.* 1–13.

[4] Nautin, 'Liste', 319–34.

[5] *Vir. ill.* 135: *haec scripsi: vitam Pauli monachi, epistularum ad diversos librum unum, ad Heliodorum exhortatoriam.*

[6] Adalbert de Vogüé, 'La *Vita Pauli* de saint Jérôme et sa datation: examen d'un passage-clé (ch. 6)', in *Eulogia: mélanges offerts à Antoon A. R. Bastiaensen à l'occasion de son soixante-cinquième anniversaire* (Steenbrugge, 1991), 395–406.

[7] Thus, we can exclude from the *liber* his other extant pre-393 and post-370s letters to miscellaneous people, such as *Ep.* 18* to Praesidius (Rome, 384), *Ep.* 45 to Asella (Rome, 385), and *Ep.* 27* to Aurelius of Carthage (Bethlehem, *c*.392).

[8] André Chastagnol, 'Le Supplice inventé par Avidius Cassius: remarques sur l'histoire Auguste et la lettre 1 de Saint Jérôme', *Bonner Historia-Augusta-Colloquium* (Bonn, 1970), 95–107; J. H. D. Scourfield, 'A Literary Commentary on Jerome, Letters 1, 60, 107', dissertation (Oxford, 1983), 32–138; Filippo Capponi, 'Aspetti realistici e simbolici dell'epistolario di Gerolamo', in Aldo Ceresa-Gastaldo (ed.),

For all of its copious appearances in the medieval manuscripts of Jerome's writings, it is almost never positioned among or even anywhere near dense clusters of the pre-Roman letters.[9] *Ep.* 14, Jerome's exhortation to Heliodorus to join him in the desert monastic life in Syria, was probably not part of the archetypal *liber*, either. Jerome listed it individually in his auto-bibliography, presumably a sign that he wanted it to stand alone as an epistolary showpiece rather than have it be entrenched among his other personal letters in a collection, in which case its individual identity and rhetorical impact might be eclipsed. Pierre Nautin suggested that it belonged to the *liber* and that Jerome mentioned it separately to italicize it as a manifesto on the monastic life.[10] If Nautin is right, though, we would expect *Ep.* 14 to have been transmitted in the manuscripts among other pre-Roman letters. This is not the case at all: like *Ep.* 1, it very rarely appears in proximity to these others.

After excluding *Ep.* 1 and *Ep.* 14 from the *liber*, we are left with *Epp.* 2–13, 15–17. In a striking number of medieval manuscripts containing Jerome's correspondence, these fifteen letters regularly appear beside one another in discernible and uninterrupted clusters varying in size from six to thirteen letters.[11] One such airtight grouping,

---

Gerolamo e la biografia letteraria (Genoa, 1989), 81–103; Johannes Schwind, 'Hieronymus' Epistula ad Innocentium (epist 1)—ein Jugendwerk?', *WS*, 110 (1997), 171–86; Hildegund Müller, 'Der älteste Brief des heiligen Hieronymus. Zu einem aktuellen Datierungsvorschlag', *WS*, 111 (1998), 191–210.

[9] For an overview of its transmission, see Schwind, 'Hieronymus' Epistula ad Innocentium', 174–5. If *Ep.* 1 was not part of the *liber*, it means that Jerome did not bother to account for it at all in *Vir. ill.* 135. This, however, is not problematic inasmuch as his auto-bibliography is not exhaustive. For example, he did not list his translation of Origen's homilies on Isaiah or his now-lost commentary on Obadiah written in the 370s. See Nautin, 'Liste', 326–9; Alfons Fürst, 'Jerome Keeping Silent: Origen and his Exegesis of Isaiah', in Andrew Cain and Josef Lössl (eds.), *Jerome of Stridon: His Life, Writings and Legacy* (Aldershot, 2009), Chap. 11.

[10] 'Liste', 324: 'La lettre d'exhortation à Héliodore d'Altinum fait partie du même groupe (*epist.* 14), mais Jérôme la détache des autres pour la mettre en relief, parce qu'elle est plus longue qu'une lettre ordinaire et constitue un petit traité sur les avantages de la vie monastique.'

[11] A few representative examples out of many may be cited. Six letters: Alençon, Bibliothèque municipale 9 (13th cent.): 8 + 10 + 7 + 9 + 12 + 2; Bamberg, Staatliche Bibliothek, Class.93 (N.I.10) (15th cent.): 11 + 8 + 9 + 12 + 2 + 13. Seven letters: Brussels, Koninklijke Bibliotheek, 5478–83 (12th cent.): 6 + 8 + 10 + 7 + 9 + 12 + 2. Eight letters: Florence, Biblioteca Medicea Laurenziana, S.Croce, Plut.XV, Dext., Cod.13 (13th cent.): 12 + 11 + 13 + 10 + 7 + 2 + 17 + 8; Paris, Bibliothèque nationale,

a twelve-letter sequence, is found in the ninth-century codex Lat. 1866 housed at the Bibliothèque nationale in Paris: 9 + 12 + 11 + 13 + 10 + 7 + 15 + 2 + 16 + 17 + 8 + 6.[12] To what may we attribute this confluence of pre-Roman letters? Hardly to chance, for so many other groupings of these letters in various combinations are attested in other manuscripts. Nor can we attribute it to a compiler's fastidiousness about keeping to the timeline of Jerome's life, for medieval compilers did not concern themselves with arranging his letters chronologically.[13] Furthermore, no compiler could possibly have had the refined historical sense to bring together, with such astonishing accuracy, twelve letters all written within a three-year window. The authors of the medieval *Vitae Hieronymi* had only a very imprecise knowledge of the chronology of their subject's life, and we cannot expect anything more from scribes.[14] As a rule, when compilers sought to impose order on letters of Jerome that were available to them they would group them either by shared subject matter or by correspondent. But the twelve-letter sequence above does not bear any such organizational thumbprint; the topics of the letters and their addressees are too miscellaneous and diverse.

A further observation may be made about the twelve-letter cluster discussed above. Two letters to Pope Damasus (*Epp.* 15–16) written around 377 are embedded in it. This is striking given that medieval compilers, especially from the tenth century onward, tended

---

Lat. 573 (11th cent.): 12 + 11 + 13 + 10 + 7 + 2 + 17 + 8. Nine letters: Holkham Hall, 124 (15th cent.): 4 + 5 + 6 + 8 + 10 + 7 + 9 + 12 + 2. Two codices containing sequences of twelve and thirteen pre-Roman letters, respectively, are discussed below.

[12] This codex was produced in 887 at the abbey of Saint-Mesmin in the diocese of Orléans. It contains a medley of works by and attributed to Jerome. Included are forty-seven letters or excerpts of his genuine letters and some of Jerome's polemical treatises. For a description of the codex, see Philippe Lauer, *Bibliothèque nationale: catalogue général des manuscrits latins* (7 vols., Paris, 1940), ii. 206–7.

[13] Jerome's correspondence as a chronologically ordered collection is entirely the construct of modern editors. Domenico Vallarsi (1702–71) was the first editor to arrange the letters by chronology. He divided them into five different groups (*classes*) corresponding to major phases of Jerome's career. See *PL* 22: pp. xlvii–xlviii.

[14] Francesco Lanzoni, 'La leggenda di s. Girolamo', *Miscellanea Geronimiana. Scritti varii pubblicati nel XV centenario dalla morte di San Girolamo* (Rome, 1920), 19–42; Alberto Vaccari, 'Le Antiche vite di s. Girolamo', *Scritti di erudizione e di filologia* (2 vols., Rome, 1958), i. 31–51; Eugene Rice, *Saint Jerome in the Renaissance* (Baltimore, Md., 1985), 23–8.

to situate these two letters in correspondent-based groups among other Damasus–Jerome letters. In a fifteenth-century codex at the Biblioteca Nazionale Marciana in Venice (Patr. 27 [a.353.I.247]), which contains over 120 of Jerome's letters and fragments of letters, we come across the following thirteen-letter sequence of pre-Roman letters, the largest of its kind in any known manuscript: 5 + 4 + 7 + 2 + 10 + 9 + 6 + 17 + 8 + 12 + 11 + 13 + 3. All of the pre-Roman letters are present here except for *Epp.* 15–16, which appear earlier in the manuscript alongside other Damasus–Jerome correspondence (35 + 36 + 18A + 18B + 19 + 20 + 21 + 15 + 16). Thus, this fifteenth-century Venetian codex exhibits the scribal tendency to extract *Epp.* 15–16 from their positioning amidst other Hieronymian correspondence from the 370s and to reassign them to Damasian dossiers, while the ninth-century Bibliothèque nationale, Lat. 1866 evidently preserves the earlier tradition that pre-dates such scribal interference.

The ubiquitous clusters of pre-Roman letters in the manuscripts, moreover, are not accidental agglomerations. They also are not the handiwork of medieval compilers. Rather, they would seem to be the tangible remnants of the *liber*, which for the reasons stated above may be assumed to encompass *Epp.* 2–13, 15–17. Now that this epistolary book has been reconstituted as far as possible given the current state of the evidence, we are in a position to ask certain questions of it as a text that scholars have failed to ask, let alone answer, owing to their overwhelming tendency to read the pre-Roman letters as passive documentary sources useful mainly for plotting the chronological, prosopographical, and theological coordinates of the first stages of Jerome's career as a monk–scholar. The essential question is why Jerome would have assembled such a collection in the first place. I contend that to make sense of these letters as their author intended we must approach them from an entirely new perspective— namely, as a tightly knit bundle of interlocking propagandistic pieces.

At some point after the 370s Jerome sifted carefully through his epistolary archive and selected from it some choice specimens to go under the editorial knife and to become part of the compilation that he released under the title *Epistularum ad diversos liber*. *Epp.* 2–13, 15–17 would seem to be the felicitous outcome of this

process. Such an editorial consciousness means that this *liber*, thus
circumscribed, was anything but a random collage of letters. By its
very design, a letter-collection, as a structured literary enterprise read
as a unit, is capable of producing a many-tiered rhetorical effect
that cannot be achieved by individual letters read in isolation. In
antiquity, writers released their collected letters for any number of
reasons, the most obvious being to present an organized and flattering record of their lives to contemporaries and to posterity.[15]
The Latin prose epistolographic tradition offers many prominent
examples. Pliny the Younger comes immediately to mind. During
the first decade of the second century, he released 247 of his letters
in nine books, issuing these books in instalments.[16] After his death,
someone, possibly his protégé Suetonius, edited and released his official correspondence with Trajan on administrative matters relating
to the governing of Bithynia and then appended this collection to
the existing nine books as the tenth.[17] Pliny used the sum of his
nine-book epistolary corpus to portray himself as the consummate
friend, husband, patron, elder statesman, and well-connected man
of letters.[18] Between 395 and 397, Ambrose, consciously following in Pliny's epistolographic footsteps,[19] assembled in ten books
his selected correspondence to friends, fellow churchmen, pagan

[15] Michael Trapp, *Greek and Latin Letters. An Anthology, with Translation* (Cambridge, 2003), 12. On this 'autobiographical' aspect of the medieval letter-collection,
see Giles Constable, *Letters and Letter Collections* (Turnhout, 1976), 33. For the use of
authorially edited letter-collections for self-presentational purposes in the early modern period, see Cecil Clough, 'The Cult of Antiquity: Letters and Letter Collections', in
Clough (ed.), *Cultural Aspects of the Italian Renaissance. Essays in Honour of Paul Oskar
Kristeller* (Manchester, 1976), 33–67; Janet Altman, 'The Letter Book as a Literary
Institution, 1539–1789: Toward a Cultural History of Published Correspondences in
France', *YFS*, 71 (1986), 17–62.
[16] A. N. Sherwin-White, *Letters of Pliny. A Historical and Social Commentary*
(Oxford, 1966), 27–41, 54–6.
[17] Wynne Williams, *Pliny: Correspondence with Trajan from Bithynia (Epistles X)*
(Warminster, 1990), 4.
[18] Eleanor Leach, 'The Politics of Self-presentation: Pliny's Letters and Roman
Portrait Sculpture', *ClAnt*, 9 (1990), 14–39; Matthias Ludolph, *Epistolographie und
Selbstdarstellung. Untersuchungen zu den 'Paradebriefen' Plinius des Jüngerer* (Tübingen, 1997); Jan Radicke, 'Die Selbstdarstellung des Plinius in seinen Briefen', *Hermes*,
125 (1997), 447–69; Stanley Hoffer, *The Anxieties of Pliny the Younger* (New York,
1999).
[19] Micaela Zelzer, '*Plinius Christianus:* Ambrosius als Epistolograph', *StudPatr*,
23 (1989), 203–8; ead., 'Zur Komposition der Briefsammlung des hl. Ambrosius',

antagonists, and emperors to reinforce his political and theological authority.[20] Ambrose's contemporary, the pagan senator Symmachus, evidently intended his collected letters to serve as his political autobiography.[21] Fast-forwarding a century to the late 470s, the Gallic bishop Sidonius Apollinaris, another imitator of Pliny,[22] prepared his correspondence for its debut as an edited collection in seven books, and over the next few years he produced two more books to bring the total to nine.[23] The aim, again, was nuanced self-presentation.[24]

It is reasonable, then, to start out from the assumption that Jerome's collection of letters to 'various people', like the multiple-book, authorially assembled letter-collections of Pliny, Ambrose, and other Latin prose epistolographers, sustained its own explicit propagandistic agenda. After all, we could expect no less from someone who of all the Fathers was certainly one of the most self-conscious about his contemporary and posthumous reception. But what might Jerome's agenda have been? When and why might he have compiled and begun circulating the *Epistularum ad diversos liber*? Plausible answers to these questions will emerge from a close analysis of the letters themselves.

StudPatr, 18 (1990), 212–17; Hervé Savon, 'Saint Ambroise a-t-il imité le recueil de lettres de Pline le Jeune?', *REAug*, 41 (1995), 3–17.

   [20] J. H. W. G. Liebeschuetz, 'The Collected Letters of Ambrose of Milan: Correspondence with Contemporaries and with the Future', in Linda Ellis and Frank Kidner (eds.), *Travel, Communication and Geography in Late Antiquity: Sacred and Profane* (Aldershot, 2004), 95–107.

   [21] Cristiana Sogno, *Q. Aurelius Symmachus: A Political Biography* (Ann Arbor, Mich., 2006), 62. Symmachus was able to release only the first seven books of his correspondence by the time of his death around 401. His son Memmius edited and released books 8–10 between 403 and 408: see Jean-Pierre Callu, *Symmaque, Lettres*, i (Paris, 1972), 16–22. For Symmachus' imitation of Pliny, see Arnaldo Marcone, 'Due epistolari a confronto: Corpus pliniano e corpus simmachiano', in *Studi di storia e storiografia antiche per Emilio Gabba* (Pavia, 1988), 143–54.

   [22] See Sidonius, *Ep.* 4.22.2: *ego Plinio ut discipulus assurgo*.

   [23] Helga Köhler, *C. Sollius Apollinaris Sidonius. Briefe Buch I. Einleitung-Text-Übersetzung-Kommentar* (Heidelberg, 1995), 8–9.

   [24] Micaela Zelzer, 'Der Brief in der Spätantike: Überlegungen zu einem literarischen Genos am Beispiel der Briefsammlung des Sidonius Apollinaris', *WS*, 108 (1995), 548–9, has suggested a further motivation: Sidonius wanted to use his letters to give a commentary on contemporary events without risking criticism from writing a full-blown *historia*.

HIERONYMUS EREMITA: THE TEXTUALIZED 'SAINT'

Throughout his early letters, Jerome paints a panoramic portrait of
the desert life in broad and beautiful textual brushstrokes. In one
letter (*Ep.* 2), written around 374 from Antioch, he asks a certain
Theodosius for permission to return to his coenobitic community
in Syria on a more permanent basis.[25] This letter opens hopefully,
with Jerome expressing a keen desire to embrace their idyllic community (*admirandum consortium*). In characterizing the community's
eremitic locale, he bandies about clichés current in fourth-century
ascetic discourse. He calls the desert a metaphorical 'city lovelier than
any other' (*omni amoeniorem civitatem*). It is comparable to a new
Eden (*quasi ad quoddam paradisi instar*) whose formerly deserted
terrain is now a heavenly oasis peppered with throngs of saints
(*sanctorum coetibus*).[26] Jerome's presentation of himself in *Ep.* 2 as
an exemplary sinner, like his description of eremitic topography, is
roundly conventional. He invokes familiar biblical imagery to cast
himself as the prodigal son (*prodigus filius*)[27] and as a lost sheep
(*aberrans ovis*).[28] This sets the stage for a request for Theodosius'
intercessory prayers to free him 'from the darkness of this world'
(*ex istius saeculi tenebris*). It is telling that in seeking a remedy for
his spiritual malaise Jerome turned not to a figure of the church's

[25] Some identify this Theodosius as the one who founded a monastery at Rhôsos
(see Theodoret, *Hist. rel.* 10): e.g., Georg Grützmacher, *Hieronymus. Eine biographische Studie zur alten Kirchengeschichte* (3 vols., Berlin, 1901–8), i. 149; Ferdinand
Cavallera, *Saint Jérôme: sa vie et son œuvre* (2 vols., Paris, 1922), i. 25–6; J. N. D. Kelly,
Jerome. His Life, Writings, and Controversies (London, 1975), 37. Others, however,
remain sceptical: e.g., Adalbert de Vogüé, *Histoire littéraire du mouvement monastique
dans l'antiquité* (6 vols., Paris, 1991–2003), i. 87–8 n. 26; Stefan Rebenich, *Hieronymus
und sein Kreis: Prosopographische und sozialgeschichtliche Untersuchungen* (Stuttgart,
1992), 79 n. 346.
[26] The *locus classicus* for the desert as heaven-on-earth is the picturesque description given in the *Life of Antony* (44) of the utopian communities that sprang up around
Antony. For the idealistic conceptions of the desert in ancient monastic literature, see
Sfameni Gasparro, 'L'ermetismo nelle testimonianze dei Padri', *StudPatr*, 11 (1972),
58–64; Antoine Guillaumont, 'La Conception du désert chez les moines d'Égyptes',
RHR, 188 (1975), 3–21.
[27] Cf. *Conf.* 1.18; 3.6; 4.16; 8.3, where Augustine figures himself as the prodigal son.
[28] The biblical intertexts that saturate *Ep.* 2 are pointed out by Carlo Tibiletti,
'Immagini bibliche nel linguaggio figurato di s. Girolamo', in Aldo Ceresa-Gastaldo
(ed.), *Gerolamo e la biografia letteraria* (Genoa, 1989), 64–5.

institutional hierarchy but to a monastic authority. In doing so, he was configuring his epistolary relationship with Theodosius as that of a disciple and his *abba*.[29]

After writing to Theodosius, Jerome lingered in Antioch several months longer. In two other letters written from there (*Epp.* 3–4), we hear of his tentative plans for the near future. He was on the brink of plunging headlong into the desert ascetic life, yet he felt encumbered by an oppressive sense of his own unworthiness and by bodily sickness. Writing to Rufinus, for instance, he speaks of how 'I am unworthy' and how 'frequent illnesses have shattered my body, which is unhealthy even when it is healthy'.[30] He expresses an apparent sense of dejection again in *Ep.* 4, the cover letter for *Ep.* 3 addressed to Florentinus, whom Jerome asked to forward *Ep.* 3 to Rufinus. Florentinus was an affluent Christian living in Jerusalem and was in regular contact with Rufinus, who at the time was touring monasteries in Egypt. Jerome begs Florentinus not to judge him by Rufinus' virtues: 'In him you will see the clearest tokens of holiness; I am dust and vile dirt and ashes while I am alive. It is enough for me if the weakness of my eyes can bear the brightness of his moral excellence.'[31]

Jerome's characterization of himself as a pitiable sinner captures, in a rhetoricized manner befitting a man of his literary sensibilities, his heartfelt penitential mindset at the time. It is also designed to signal the seriousness of his monastic intentions to the immediate audience of this letter (Florentinus), as it would later to readers of the *Epistularum ad diversos liber*. According to the value system of desert Christianity, with which Jerome aligns himself in his early letters, the monk's first step toward spiritual perfection is the contrite

---

[29] For the *abba*–disciple relationship, see Graham Gould, *The Desert Fathers on Monastic Community* (Oxford, 1993), 26–87.

[30] *Ep.* 3.1: *non mereor et invalidum etiam cum sanum est corpusculum crebri fregere morbi.* Jerome's complaint about physical maladies is a recurrent theme in his letters: see Betrand Lançon, 'Maladie et médecine dans la correspondance de Jérôme', in Yves-Marie Duval (ed.), *Jérôme entre l'Occident et l'Orient, XVIᵉ centenaire du départ de saint Jérôme de Rome et de son installation à Bethléem. Actes du colloque de Chantilly, Sept. 1986* (Paris, 1988), 355–66.

[31] *Ep.* 4.2: *in illo conspicies expressa sanctitatis insignia; ego cinis et vilissimi pars luti et iam favilla, dum vegetor, satis habeo, si splendorem morum eius inbecillitas oculorum meorum ferre sustineat.*

recognition of his own sinfulness; this humility enables him to identify himself with Christ.[32] In desert spirituality, pride was the chief of
sins because it blinded the monk to his faults. Among the *Apophthegmata patrum* there are many anecdotes that warn against its dangers.
Abba John of the Thebaid put it succinctly: 'First of all the monk must
gain humility; for it is the first commandment of the Lord who said:
"Blessed are the poor in spirit, for theirs is the kingdom of heaven".'[33]
The penitential posture that Jerome assumes in *Epp.* 3–4 is therefore
of the very sort that an aspiring *monachus perfectus* in his situation
was expected to have.[34]

Jerome's plans to experience first-hand the hard life of the desert
came to fruition, albeit (as we shall see later) to a limited extent,
during his two-year stay (*c.*375–*c.*377) at Maronia, a semi-rural ham-
let about thirty miles from Antioch and near the desert around
Chalcis.[35] Representing this period are thirteen letters (*Epp.* 5–17)
in which he renders his experience in the conventional language of
contemporary eremitic culture. The locale of his monastic retreat, as
he describes it, is a desolate wasteland buried deep in the thickets
of the barbarian *Hinterland* bordering on Syria and Saracen territory.[36] Jerome's geographical displacement was aggravated by cultural
and linguistic displacement, for no Latin was spoken there. He was
overjoyed when he received a long-awaited letter from three Latin-
speaking friends in Aquileia: 'I converse with your letter, I embrace

[32] See Averil Cameron, *Christianity and the Rhetoric of Empire: The Development of
Christian Discourse* (Berkeley, Calif., 1991), 68–9.

[33] Benedicta Ward (trans.), *The Sayings of the Desert Fathers: The Alphabetical
Collection* (Kalamazoo, 1984), 106. For other anecdotes about pride, see ibid., 8–9, 15–
16, 71. See also Laura Swan, *The Forgotten Desert Mothers: Sayings, Lives, and Stories
of Early Christian Women* (New York, 2001), 26–7, and *passim*.

[34] See Brouria Bitton-Ashkelony, 'Penitence in Late Antique Monastic Literature',
in Jan Assmann and Gedaliahu Stroumsa (eds.), *Transformations of the Inner Self in
Ancient Religions* (Leiden, 1999), 179–94.

[35] For the location of this desert, see Félix-Marie Abel, *Géographie de la Palestine*
(2 vols., Paris, 1967), i. 433; Rebenich, *Hieronymus und sein Kreis*, 85–91. See also
Réne Mouterde and Antoine Poidebard, *Le Limes de Chalcis: organisation de la steppe
en Haute Syrie romaine* (2 vols., Paris, 1945).

[36] e.g., *Epp.* 5.1: *in ea mihi parte heremi commoranti, quae iuxta Syriam Sarracenis
iungitur*; 5.2: *ego arreptae solitudinis terminis arceor*; 7.1: *in ea ad me heremi parte
delatae sunt, quae inter Syros ac Sarracenos vastum limitem ducit*; 15.2: *ad eam solitudinem commigravi, quae Syriam iuncto barbariae fine determinat*; 16.2: *nunc barbaro
Syriae limite teneor*.

it, it talks to me; it alone of those here speaks Latin. For around here one must either learn a barbarous half-language or say nothing at all'.[37] Jerome's banishment to the nether regions of the empire, he is at pains to remind Pope Damasus, is voluntary (and thus not the result of exile by imperial order): 'Lest you think that I am here because another has passed sentence upon me, I myself have decided my own fate.'[38] In another letter to the same correspondent he clarifies that he has fled to this wilderness 'because of my sins' (*pro facinoribus meis*).[39] For the Oriental hermits, the desert was a redemptive *locus* where the paradise that had been lost through sin could be regained through spiritual perfection, and Jerome was consciously inscribing himself into their hallowed tradition.

The 'desert', as a foil to the 'city', was a frightening concept to many late antique urbanites on account of its otherness; in their minds, at least, it lay on the periphery of the civilized world.[40] According to the fifth-century Spanish priest Orosius, the dryness of the Egyptian desert, its sterile topsoil, and its broods of indigenous serpents made it uninhabitable for all but the monks who were brave enough to colonize it.[41] The idea that these monks could cohabit peacefully with deadly wildlife only added to their mystique as restorers of man's primal innocence.[42] Authors of fourth- and fifth-century monastic

---

[37] *Ep.* 7.2: *nunc cum vestris litteris fabulor, illas amplexor, illae mecum loquuntur, illae hic tantum Latine sciunt. hic enim aut barbarus semisermo discendus est aut tacendum est.*

[38] *Ep.* 16.2: *ne putes alterius hanc de me fuisse sententiam, quid mererer, ipse constitui.* For the desert ascetic life as a self-imposed exile, see Hans von Campenhausen, 'Die asketische Heimatlosigkeit im altkirchlichen und frühmittelalterlichen Mönchtum', in von Campenhausen, *Tradition und Leben: Kräfte der Kirchengeschichte. Aufsätze und Vorträge* (Tübingen, 1960), 290–317; Antoine Guillaumont, 'Le Dépaysement comme forme d'ascèse dans le monachisme ancien', *AEHE* V, 76 (1968–69), 31–58; Maribel Dietz, 'Itinerant Spirituality and the Late Antique Origins of Christian Pilgrimage', in Ellis and Kidner, *Travel, Communication and Geography*, 125–34.

[39] *Ep.* 15.2.

[40] Peter Brown, *The Body and Society: Men, Women, and Sexual Renunciation in Early Christianity* (New York, 1988), 214–17.

[41] *Hist. adv. pag.* 7.33.2: *vastas illas tunc Aegypti solitudines harenasque diffusas quas propter sitim ac sterilitatem periculosissimamque serpentum abundantiam conversatio humana non nosset, magna habitantium monachorum multitudo conpleverat.*

[42] Douglas Burton-Christie, *The Word in the Desert: Scripture and the Quest for Holiness in Early Christian Monasticism* (Oxford, 1993), 231–3.

vitae were aware of the potency of this animal symbolism, and they regularly made scorpions, serpents, and other beasts fixtures of their hagiographic productions.[43] To take but one example, the author of the *Life of St Antony* (15) invited readers to be impressed that Antony and his cohort crossed the Nile completely unharmed by the crocodiles that infested its waters. Desert animals could take on even more sinister connotations as visible manifestations of supernatural evil.[44] Elsewhere in the *Life* (9) demons terrorize Antony in the form of lions, bears, leopards, bulls, serpents, scorpions, and wolves. Jerome knew how to stoke the fires of the popular imagination with exotic bestiaries: he introduced into his *Vita Pauli* fairytale creatures such as the hippocentaur and the satyr.[45] When invoking animal imagery to speak of his own experience in the Chalcis letters, he was somewhat less sensational and compared himself to the basilisks and scorpions that haunt the parched regions.[46] Years later in Rome when reflecting on his time in the desert, he claimed that he had been the 'companion of scorpions and wild beasts' (*scorpionum socius et ferarum*).[47] He made calculated statements such as these presumably to convey the impression that he, like the Abba Paul and other senior desert-dwellers, was blessed with a special grace, courtesy of his having regained paradise lost, that enabled him to live peacefully among the desert's feral menagerie.

Jerome refracted his time in Chalcis through the prism of the Oriental monastic ideal in other important ways. To one correspondent he maintains that he earns his daily bread honestly, as any hard-working desert monk worth his salt is expected to do: 'I have not taken anything from anyone, I receive nothing idly, but every day I earn my sustenance with my own sweat and hand, knowing that it has

[43] Lucien Regnault, *La Vie quotidienne des pères du désert en Égypte au IV*ᵉ *siècle* (Paris, 1990), 209–22.

[44] David Brakke, *Demons and the Making of the Monk: Spiritual Combat in Early Christianity* (Cambridge, Mass., 2006), 31–2, 107–10, 117–18.

[45] Paul Harvey, 'Saints and Satyrs: Jerome the Scholar at Work', *Athenaeum*, 86 (1998), 35–56; Robert Wisniewski, '*Bestiae Christum loquuntur*: ou des habitants du désert et de la ville dans la *Vita Pauli* de saint Jérôme', *Augustinianum*, 40 (2000), 105–44. For Jerome's hagiographic agenda in the *Vita*, see now Stefan Rebenich, 'Inventing an Ascetic Hero: Jerome's *Life of Paul the First Hermit*', in Cain and Lössl, *Jerome of Stridon*, Chap. 1.

[46] *Ep.* 7.3: *quasi reguli et scorpiones arentia quaeque sectamur.*   [47] *Ep.* 22.7.

been written by the apostle: "He who does not work should not eat" (2 Thess. 3: 10)'.[48] Equally formulaic but somewhat more eccentric in flavour is Jerome's description of his physical appearance. He speaks of rolling 'in sackcloth and ash' (*in sacco et cinere*) and having a 'chain, squalor, and long hair' (*catena, sordes et comae*),[49] all of which are outward symbols of his penitential rigor and mortification of the flesh.[50] The visual image is poignant. As he poses for the reader on his two-dimensional textual canvas, Jerome very much looks the part of the stereotypical wild and woolly Syrian holy man immortalized by Theodoret of Cyrrhus in the pages of his *History of the Monks of Syria*.[51] Theodosius of Rhôsos, for instance, is said to have worn some of the same idiosyncratic badges of sanctity as Jerome: a bristly hair shirt, iron chains around his neck, waist, and hands, and unkempt hair stretching down to his feet.[52] What Theodoret later did for Theodosius and other fourth- and fifth-century Syrian monks, Jerome did for himself in encapsulating himself as a model of eremitic holiness.

RHETORIC AND REPROACH

Bearing in mind how this anchoritic voice dominates the narrative landscape of the *Epistularum ad diversos liber*, we turn now

[48] *Ep.* 17.2: *nihil alicui praeripui, nihil otiosus accipio. manu cotidie et proprio sudore quaerimus cibum scientes ab apostolo scriptum esse: qui autem non operatur, nec manducet.* Cf. *V. Ant.* 3: εἰργάζετο γοῦν ταῖς χερσίν, ἀκούσας· ὁ δὲ ἀργὸς μηδὲ ἐσθιέτω. On the work ethic of self-sufficiency in desert Christianity, see Daniel Caner, *Wandering, Begging Monks. Spiritual Authority and the Promotion of Monasticism in Late Antiquity* (Berkeley, Calif., 2002), 200–3.

[49] *Ep.* 17.2.

[50] Cf. Jerome's comment to the monk Rusticus that 'filthy clothing should be a sign of a pure mind' (*Ep.* 125.7). On ascetic physiognomy, see Georgia Frank, *The Memory of the Eyes: Pilgrims to Living Saints in Christian Late Antiquity* (Berkeley, Calif., 2000), 134–70.

[51] See Theresa Urbainczyk, *Theodoret of Cyrrhus: The Bishop and the Holy Man* (Ann Arbor, Mich., 2002).

[52] *Hist. rel.* 10.2: προσετίθει δὲ τούτοις τὸ ἐκ σιδήρου φορτίον αὐχένι καὶ ὀσφύι καὶ ἀμφοῖν τοῖν χεροῖν· καὶ κόμην δὲ ἔφερεν αὐχμηρὰν καὶ μέχρις αὐτῶν διήκουσαν τῶν ποδῶν καὶ περαιτέρω προβαίνουσαν καὶ τούτου χάριν τῇ ἰξύι προσδεδεμένην. For other examples of chain-clad monks in the same work, see 3.19; 6.6, 12; 10.2; 11.3; 21.8; 23.1; 24.6, 10; 29.4. Derwas Chitty, *The Desert a City* (Crestwood, Il., 1966), 17 n. 36, points out that chain-wearing was primarily a phenomenon of Syrian monasticism.

to a dossier of eight remarkable letters (*Epp.* 6–9, 11–13, 16) that Jerome wrote from Chalcis/Maronia to a diverse pool of clerical and lay friends throughout Italy and one blood relative in his native Dalmatia.[53] These letters share the common theme of frustration over these friends' failure to reciprocate correspondence. Jerome appears possessive of their time and unable to grasp why they refuse to return his messages even as he continues to barrage them with letter after letter. He is racked with the suspicion that their silence implies dissolution of friendship and consequent abandonment of him. This, at any rate, is the brooding curmudgeon we encounter in the pages of J. N. D. Kelly's influential biography on Jerome. Noting the apparent pathos of these eight letters, Kelly psychoanalysed them and pronounced moralizing judgements on Jerome's motivations as a writer. One of the letters reveals 'a deep sense of injury' and another, to the monk Antony, 'is even more bitter, [for] although Jesus was uniformly compassionate in his dealings with sinners, Antony is so stuck up that he has not deigned to answer his injured friend's ten letters with so much as a grunt'. 'There are letters to other friends regretting their silence, pathetically begging them to write to him'. Kelly offered some summary remarks about the desert letters as an ensemble and the light they allegedly shed on the tenor of Jerome's interpersonal relationships: 'The warmth of his affections, his passionate desire to be loved, his prickly readiness to take offence, his rapid switches from bitter self-reproach to self-righteous indignation, his intense dislike of being alone—all these traits come to light in them.'[54] This view of the 'Jerome' of these letters as a borderline neurotic has been rather fashionable in the past three decades.[55] The eight letters in question undoubtedly are the products of a man who, at the time of writing, felt agitated that his friends were not as assiduous as he was about staying in touch. Nevertheless, to reduce them to being diary-like

---

[53] His maternal aunt Castorina (*Ep.* 13); the monks Chrysocomas (*Ep.* 9) and Antony (*Ep.* 12); some unnamed virgins at Aemona (*Ep.* 11); the subdeacon Niceas (*Ep.* 8); the deacons Eusebius (*Ep.* 7) and Julian (*Ep.* 6); the archdeacon Jovinus (*Ep.* 7); the priest Chromatius (*Ep.* 7); Pope Damasus (*Ep.* 16).

[54] All quotations come from Kelly, *Jerome*, 51.

[55] e.g., Vogüé, *Histoire littéraire*, i. 116; Rebenich, *Hieronymus und sein Kreis*, 46 n. 161; Carolinne White, *Christian Friendship in the Fourth Century* (Cambridge, 1992), 131; Steven Driver, 'The Development of Jerome's Views on the Ascetic Life', *RecTh*, 62 (1995), 53.

cris de cœur oversimplifies the impressive literary artistry at work in them as well as their collective rhetorical import as edited components of a released letter-collection. Let us begin, then, by noting their literary artistry, which has gone underappreciated by scholars.

I submit that these eight letters are expertly executed specimens of the epistolary genre of reproach (ὀνειδιστικός). In antiquity, there was an unspoken understanding among friends that whoever received the 'gift' of a letter incurred a debt of gratitude to the sender, a debt that could be paid only by reciprocation with a reply.[56] Correspondents in any given epistolary relationship had to follow this same give-and-take protocol if the equilibrium in the friendship was to be maintained. But, when one party shirked the duty of writing, this equilibrium was momentarily upset and the sender would complain of neglect. This mild form of censure was itself an expression of friendly affection insofar as it provoked the other party to write back and to reaffirm the pact of friendship. Cicero and Pliny invoked the reproach *topos* on occasion,[57] as did many Christian letter-writers after them.[58]

More so than any other classical or patristic writer, Jerome deployed the reproach *topos* both as a component of a generic letter of friendship and as a full-blown epistolary type. In fact, his early letters are the most exquisite surviving pieces of their kind in all of ancient Latin literature with regard to their rhetorical sophistication and stylish *variatio* on the otherwise one-sided theme of reproach. An analysis of a few representative examples will suffice to show that these letters are polished showpieces of considerable aesthetic quality in which Jerome manifested the strength and versatility of his compositional technique by juxtaposing delightful pastiches of classical and biblical intertexts for increased effect.[59]

---

[56] Philippe Bruggisser, *Symmaque ou le rituel épistolaire de l'amitié littéraire: recherches sur le premier livre de la correspondance* (Freiburg, 1993), 4–16; Catherine Conybeare, *Paulinus Noster: Self and Symbols in the Letters of Paulinus of Nola* (Oxford, 2000), 24–6.

[57] For examples and further discussion, see Cain, 'Vox clamantis in deserto: Rhetoric, Reproach, and the Forging of Ascetic Authority in Jerome's Letters from the Syrian Desert', *JThS*, NS 57 (2006), 505–6.

[58] e.g., Synesius of Cyrene: *Epp.* 8, 10, 23, 46, 138; Basil of Caesarea: *Epp.* 4, 12, 13, 21, 209; Gregory Nazianzen: *Ep.* 150; John Chrysostom: *Epp.* 186, 202.

[59] For an inventory of Jerome's quotations from classical literature in these early letters, see Harald Hagendahl, *Latin Fathers and the Classics: A Study on the Apologists, Jerome, and Other Christian Writers* (Göteborg, 1958), 100–5.

Ep. 8 to Niceas is a prime example. It begins with a quotation from the now-fragmentary comic playwright Turpilius that theorizes letter-exchange as a *sermo absentium*: 'The exchange of letters is the only thing that makes present those who are absent'.[60] Jerome then drops an obscure detail from archaic Roman history and applies it brilliantly as a reproach device. He mentions that the boorish (*rudes*) Casci, prior to the invention of parchment, communicated with one another using only crude wooden tablets. Ennius and Cicero are gratuitously cited as sources for this information.[61] Jerome's argument is that if the Casci, who lived in such a state of uncouthness (*apud quos erat cruda rusticitas*), had a sense of epistolary courtesy, then how much more should we cultivate it who live in polite society! This pre-historical *exemplum* functions as a touchstone for the reprimand of Niceas about tearing apart their newly forged friendship (*recentem amicitiam*) by his failure to write. To add another layer of classical erudition to his writing Jerome weighs in with the authority of Cicero, who expressly forbids unfriendly behaviour of this kind in his treatise on friendship (*quod prudenter Laelius vetat*).[62] In closing, he puts his own personalized touch on the conventional injunction to write back no matter what: 'If you think well of me, then write back; even if you are angry with me, write back anyway.'[63]

The letter (*Ep.* 12) to the monk Antony illustrates how Jerome 'biblicized' the reproach theme. In the first half, he presents a collage of biblical passages and allusions demonstrating the evils of pride, to make a subtle insinuation about the reason for his correspondent's

---

[60] *Ep.* 8.1: *Turpilius comicus tractans de vicissitudine litterarum*: 'sola', inquit, 'res est, quae homines absentes praesentes faciat'. Cf. *Ep.* 29.1: *epistolare officium est de re familiari aut de cotidiana conversatione aliquid scribere et quodammodo absentes inter se praesentes fieri, dum mutuo, quid aut velint aut gestum sit, nuntiant, licet interdum confabulationis tale convivium doctrinae quoque sale condiatur.* On the *sermo absentium*, see Klaus Thraede, *Grundzüge griechisch-römischer Brieftopik* (Munich, 1970), 162–4.

[61] Cicero, *Tusc.* 1.27: *priscis illis, quos cascos appellat Ennius*; Cicero, *Inv.* 1.2: *fuit quoddam tempus, cum in agris homines passim bestiarum modo vagabantur et sibi victu fero vitam propagabant.*

[62] The passage in question is *Amic.* 76: *tales igitur amicitiae sunt remissione usus eluendae et ut Catonem dicere audivi, dissuendae magis quam discindendae.*

[63] *Ep.* 8.3: *si amas, rescribe; si irasceris, iratus licet scribe.*

refusal to reply.[64] One allusion in particular pointedly inculcates the reproach: 'Although the Lord spoke with his servants, you, a brother, do not speak with your brother.'[65] Jerome brings everything to a close with a request that weaves together themes developed throughout the letter: 'I beg you again that you love one who loves you and that you, a fellow servant, grant conversation to another fellow servant.'[66] This concluding plea to reciprocate friendship is a Hieronymian variation on the basic formula '*cura ut valeas nosque ames*' that is ubiquitous in Cicero's extant correspondence.[67]

In other letters Jerome constructs mosaics out of biblical inter-texts to serve as instruments of reproach. In *Ep.* 13 he reprimands his maternal aunt Castorina for her long silence that resulted from an old quarrel (*vetus rancor*) between them. He accordingly strings together a *corolla* of biblical passages that warn against being angry with one's neighbour.[68] When rebuking Pope Damasus in *Ep.* 16 for not replying to his previous letter (*Ep.* 15), Jerome treads more lightly—not unexpectedly given the identity of his correspondent—and quotes passages that are not so much accusatory of Damasus and his *negligentia* as they are self-effacing and apologetic for himself.[69] Likening himself to the nagging mother who after much begging con-vinced Jesus to heal her demon-possessed daughter, Jerome defends his persistence in demanding a timely reply, thereby implying that he, and not Damasus, is the object of reproach.

Of the fifteen surviving letters that presumably belonged to the *liber*, almost half are of the reproach genre. I suggest that Jerome pre-served such a dense collocation of this type of letter in order to project a number of images of himself to readers of the *liber*. The letters' deep saturation in the Latin classics and the Bible introduces him as a first-rate *littérateur* able to appeal comfortably to an educated Christian aristocracy. Perhaps as an invitation to future correspondents he also

---

[64] Isa. 14: 12–15; 40: 15; Matt. 18: 3; 26: 48–50; Mark 16: 9; Luke 10: 39; 11: 43; 18: 10–14; John 13: 5; 1 Pet. 5: 5.

[65] *Ep.* 12.3: *domino loquente cum servis frater cum fratre non loqueris.*

[66] *Ep.* 12.4: *rursus precor, ut et diligentem te diligas et conservo sermonem conservus inpertias.*

[67] E.g., *Att.* 1.4; 1.5; *Fam.* 13.47; 15.20.

[68] Ps. 4: 5; Matt. 5: 23–4; Eph. 4: 26; 1 John 3: 15.

[69] Matt. 15: 21–8; Luke 11: 5–8; 19: 8–9.

presents himself as an assiduous correspondent who dutifully answers letters even when others do not, and he accordingly offers a 'Jerome' who is eager not only to maintain existing friendships but also to cultivate new ones. Above all, by including a preponderance of unanswered letters Jerome was able tangibly to document his solitude and to reinforce the appearance that he had lived heroically as a hermit cut off from human society and most notably from the friends he held dear.

AN ASCETIC CONVERSION STORY IN LETTERS

The foregoing analysis suggests that Jerome's primary aim with the *Epistularum ad diversos liber* was to transform himself textually into a living desert 'saint'. Along these lines, the *liber* may be said to detail the origins and evolution of his ascetic vocation proper. In it he documents the three distinct stages of his monastic *cursus*: expressing a profound desire to embrace the ascetic lifestyle (*Ep.* 2); eagerly pining for it but none the less remaining in limbo (*Epp.* 3–4); and finally realizing his ideal (*Epp.* 5–13, 15–17). This diachronic reading grid assumes that Jerome arranged the letters in the *liber* in more or less chronological order so that he could provide readers with a timeline of his early ascetic experience, just as he would later arrange his works chronologically in his auto-bibliography in order to give readers a temporal sense of his evolution as a Christian writer. If indeed he did arrange the letters chronologically, the internal ordering found in a grouping of pre-Roman letters from the tenth-century Vatican codex Lat. 5762 may reflect to some extent the one he imposed on his archetype: $2 + 5 + 6 + 7 + 8 + 9 + 10 + 12 + 17$. It is impossible to date most of these letters relative to one another with absolute certainty. We are unable to know, for instance, whether *Ep.* 8 was written before *Ep.* 9. What we can know is that of these nine letters *Ep.* 2 was the first written and *Ep.* 17 the last, and that *Ep.* 5 probably pre-dates every letter in this sequence except *Ep.* 2.

The letter to Theodosius (*Ep.* 2) is a fitting introductory epistle to headline the *liber* because it foreshadows the Chalcis/Maronia letters in which Jerome is seen achieving the monastic goals announced to

Theodosius. What come next chronologically are two letters (*Epp.* 3–4), also written from Antioch, in which he is observed making a concerted effort to realize these goals. He appears human—all too human—and is still held back by bodily illness and a somewhat weak resolve. The majority of the letters (*Epp.* 5–13, 15–17) belong to the Chalcis period when Jerome finally entered in earnest on the road to monastic perfection. *Ep.* 17 at first glance seems to be an uncomfortable fit in the *liber* because it reveals his time in the desert not as the stylized spiritual *otium* portrayed in other letters but as being in flux and riddled with theological and personal controversies. This letter, written only a few months prior to his departure from Chalcis, was addressed to a certain Mark who was a leader of the coenobitic community with which Jerome was affiliated. Jerome complains bitterly about a band of local monks badgering him for holding supposedly unorthodox Trinitarian views.[70] 'I cannot have so much as a corner of the desert. Every day I am asked for my confession of faith ... I subscribe to their formulas, but they do not believe me. They are content with one thing only: that I leave from here'.[71] He appealed to Mark for safe haven and submitted a signed statement of faith (originally appended to *Ep.* 17 but now lost[72]) that certified his loyalty to Nicene orthodoxy. But it was too late. He sensed that his days there were numbered and he asked permission only to remain in the vicinity for another month or two longer until the advent of spring.

Why did Jerome include in the *liber* such an anti-climactic and potentially embarrassing snapshot of his monastic venture as teetering on collapse? What, moreover, does *Ep.* 17 contribute to the *liber* from a narrative standpoint? Fundamentally, it serves to make clear how and why the high-flying ascetic ambitions so grandiosely enunciated throughout his early letters plummeted so hard and quickly back to the ground. If Jerome did arrange the letters in the *liber* by chronology, then *Ep.* 2 and *Ep.* 17 functioned as bookends to represent both

---

[70] See Kelly, *Jerome*, 54–6.

[71] *Ep.* 17.3: *non mihi conceditur unus angulus heremi. cotidie exposcor fidem ... subscribo: non credunt. unum tantum placet, ut hinc recedam.*

[72] Both the letter and this signed *confessio* would originally have been composed in Latin but presumably translated into Syriac by one of Jerome's bilingual fellow monks, possibly the 'reverend Cyril' mentioned in *Ep.* 17.4.

ends of the continuum of his early monastic experience. *Ep.* 2 reveals him as an aspiring initiate into eastern eremitic spirituality, while *Ep.* 17 clarifies exactly why this spiritual odyssey, decisive stages of which are documented in the remainder of the *liber*, abruptly spun out of control: not because of his own moral failure but because of the crusading of witch-hunting monks. He may also have placed *Ep.* 17 there as a pre-emptive strike against critics who might call into question the authenticity of his desert experience and therefore his unique claims to ascetic authority.[73]

While the letter to Mark focuses on how theological controversy disrupted Jerome's day-to-day life in the Syrian desert, the two letters to Damasus (*Epp.* 15–16), written a few months before he left Chalcis, detail the technical content of the controversy itself.[74] *Ep.* 15 opens with a finely tuned *captatio benevolentiae* that takes the form of a series of *encomia* of the papal see and of Damasus as its worthy occupant. Jerome notes that, although the eastern church is ravaged by senseless schisms, the church at Rome stands strong as the last bastion of orthodoxy on earth. It is therefore to this church, the one into which he had been baptized a decade or so earlier, that Jerome turns for answers to his pressing theological concerns.[75] His first question is which of the rival claimants to the episcopate at Antioch is the true bishop and thus the one with whom he must communicate? He goes on to complain that the followers of one of these claimants, Meletius, have been pressuring him to adopt their Trinitarian formula of the three hypostases. This, he thinks, is a dangerous novelty. For, if God is thought of as three distinct persons or essences, then the eternal unity of the Godhead is compromised and Arianism will be waiting at the door.[76] Jerome asks the pope to settle the matter once and for all by enacting a new decree that will uphold the Nicene creed.

[73] See Nautin, 'Hieronymus', *TRE*, 15 (1986), 304.

[74] For the theological background of *Ep.* 15, see Thomas Lawler, 'Jerome's First Letter to Damasus', in Patrick Granfield and Josef Jungmann (eds.), *Kyriakon. Festschrift Johannes Quasten* (2 vols., Münster, 1970), ii. 548–52; Barbara Conring, *Hieronymus als Briefschreiber. Ein Beitrag zur spätantiken Epistolographie* (Tübingen, 2001), 198–215; Rebenich, *Jerome*, 70–4.

[75] *Ep.* 15.2: *nunc meae animae postulans cibum, unde olim Christi vestimenta suscepi.*

[76] Jerome's preoccupation with Arianism from 374 to 382 is discussed by Benoît Jeanjean, *Saint Jérôme et l'hérésie* (Paris, 1999), 16–21, 149–68.

Jerome seems to be aware of how presumptuous his request sounds. To increase the likelihood that he will receive a positive response he asks Damasus to address the reply to Evagrius of Antioch, his own literary and monastic patron and the pope's longtime political supporter.

Epp. 15–16, read in conjunction with *Ep.* 17, serve to reaffirm Jerome's unwavering allegiance to Nicene orthodoxy. This would have ingratiated him, in theory at least, to theologically conservative circles at Rome and would have defined him in contradistinction to Manichaeans, Sabellians, Novatianists, Montanists, Valentinians, and other heterodox sectarians who were vying for power in the City's doctrinal melting pot.[77] In addition, by presumably including the two Damasian letters in the *liber* Jerome might have hoped to impress Roman readers with his ties to their reigning pope, for he could point to these two letters as documentation of an association with Damasus that reached back several years.[78] The embarrassing fact that both letters went unanswered, while it seems striking to modern readers, may have been beside the point as far as Jerome was concerned. After all, these letters were apparently the only correspondence that he had sent to Damasus before coming to Rome, and if he was eager to document a longstanding connection to him, however tenuous it actually had been prior to 382, he would have had no choice but to make do with whatever written material he had at his disposal.

INTRODUCING ... JEROME

When he returned to Rome in the late summer of 382, for the first time since his student days in the 360s, Jerome was a virtually unknown *novus homo* from a rural backwater in Illyria, with literary ambitions and an iron-willed determination to make his mark on the competitive Christian 'publishing market' there. However, breaking into this market was no easy feat, especially for a provincial outsider like Jerome. Like all aspiring writers in his position, he needed

---

[77] Harold Maier, 'The Topography of Heresy and Dissent in Late Fourth-century Rome', *Historia*, 44 (1995), 232–49.

[78] For Jerome's readiness to identify himself publicly with Damasus, see Chapter 2.

strategic social connections to facilitate his upward mobility as well as the patronage these connections afforded to fund his scholarly enterprises. For, even though Jerome had some inherited wealth, it was not enough to afford him the luxury of financial self-sufficiency.[79] Competition among prospective Christian *clientes* could be cut-throat.[80] In order to procure patronage he had to find some way to stand out unforgettably from a crowd of well-qualified rivals in Rome—a crowd that included the likes of the prolific biblical exegete Ambrosiaster[81] and probably a young Pelagius.[82] Jerome required some way to explain who he was, where he came from, and to what profitable uses he could be expected to put his wide-ranging talents.

I propose that Jerome, shortly after arriving in Rome, compiled and released the *Epistularum ad diversos liber* in order to introduce himself to an educated Christian audience there via a carefully constructed autobiographical anthology. He used this collection to provide for Roman readers an abridged but romanticized version of his life as a monk in the Syrian desert through snapshots in the first-person narrative. He did not present himself, however, as some dime-a-dozen anchorite stamped in a generic eastern mould; his profile was more nuanced. He was a zealous advocate of Petrine primacy and Nicene orthodoxy. He was an expert prose stylist who crafted rhetorically sophisticated letters to meet any occasion, and he peppered them with quotations from the Latin classics and the Bible. Furthermore, he announced himself as a writer of hagiographic short stories.[83] He was the quintessential hero of *askesis* who had lived as an

---

[79] Elizabeth Clark, 'Patrons, not Priests: Gender and Power in Late Ancient Christianity', *G&H*, 2 (1990), 258–9.

[80] John Curran, 'Jerome and the Sham Christians of Rome', *JEH*, 48 (1997), 213–29.

[81] See below, pp. 51–52, 59–66.

[82] The chronology of Pelagius' early career is murky. Most scholars agree that he was in Rome in the early 380s: e.g., Georges de Plinval, *Pélage: ses écrits, sa vie et sa réforme* (Lausanne, 1943), 64 n. 5; Bryn Rees, *Pelagius: A Reluctant Heretic* (Suffolk, 1988), pp. xii–xiv, 140; cf. Duval, 'Pélage en son temps: données chronologiques nouvelles pour une présentation nouvelle', *StudPatr*, 38 (2001), 95. In his *In Hier.* 4.1.6 (*c*.414) Jerome speaks of a '*vetus necessitudo*' with Pelagius, perhaps a reference to the two having been acquainted at Rome in the 380s. See also Augustine, *Ep.* 177.2 and *Grat. Chr.* 2.24 on Pelagius' residency in Rome.

[83] e.g., see the publicity notice about his *Vita Pauli* in *Ep.* 10.3: *misimus interim tibi, id est Paulo seni, Paulum seniorem, in quo propter simpliciores quosque multum in deiciendo sermone laboravimus.*

anchorite, and yet, being the refined Latin gentleman he also was, he never abandoned the social institution of *amicitia*. Unlike some of the unapproachable hermits of Syria and Egypt, who made it a point to shun human contact whenever possible, he was gregarious and eager to reach out to the world around him.

While Jerome would presumably have envisaged for the *liber* a generally upper-class Christian audience with ascetic and Nicene theological sympathies, it is possible that he principally had in mind the wealthy widow Marcella and her coterie of female ascetics whom he met soon after his arrival in Rome.[84] Marcella was born in Rome in the 330s into an extraordinarily well-off household.[85] Her ancestral pedigree was prestigious, to say the least: consuls and praetorian prefects numbered among her forefathers,[86] and her mother Albina[87] came from the Ceionii, one of the most distinguished families in the late Roman west.[88] Marcella wed at a young age but she lost her husband after only seven months of childless marriage. Albina tried to contract a marriage between her daughter and the elderly ex-consul Naeratius Cerealis[89] in order to secure her daughter's financial future. Marcella stubbornly refused to go along with the arrangement and allegedly said: 'If I wanted to get married and had no desire to dedicate myself to perpetual chastity, I would look for a husband, not an inheritance.'[90] Determined to live the rest of her days as a chaste widow, she converted her mansion in an upscale neighbourhood on the Aventine, the southernmost of Rome's seven hills, into a makeshift domestic nunnery. Jerome made the (greatly exaggerated) claim that she had been the first '*nobilis femina*' in Rome to make a profession

[84] Christa Krumeich, *Hieronymus und die christlichen feminae clarissimae* (Bonn, 1993); Barbara Feichtinger, *Apostolae apostolorum. Frauenaskese als Befreiung und Zwang bei Hieronymus* (Frankfurt, 1995).

[85] *PCBE*, ii. 1357–62 ('Marcella 1'); Karin Sugano, 'Marcella von Rom. Ein Lebensbild', in Michael Wissemann (ed.), *Roma renascens. Beiträge zur Spätantike und Rezeptionsgeschichte. Festschrift Ilona Opelt* (Frankfurt, 1988), 355–70; Sylvia Letsch-Brunner, *Marcella—Discipula et Magistra. Auf den Spuren einer römischen Christin des 4. Jahrhunderts* (Berlin, 1998).

[86] *Ep.* 127.1.   [87] *PCBE*, ii. 74–5 ('Albina 1').

[88] M. T. W. Arnheim, *The Senatorial Aristocracy in the Later Roman Empire* (Oxford, 1972), 104.

[89] *PLRE*, i. 197–9 ('Naeratius Cerealis 2').

[90] *Ep.* 127.2: *si vellem nubere et non aeternae me cuperem pudicitiae dedicare, utique maritum quaererem, non hereditatem.*

of the monastic life.[91] According to him, the inspiration for the oriental-style ascetic lifestyle that she adopted came from meeting the Alexandrian bishops Athanasius and later Peter, both of whom regaled her with tales about the austerities of St Antony and other Egyptian monks.[92] By the 370s, Marcella had gathered around herself a group of aristocratic Christian widows and virgins (the so-called 'Aventine circle') who shared her dedication to the monastic life and study of the Bible.[93]

One of Marcella's monastic compatriots was the widow Paula. Paula too boasted an impressive lineage. Her mother Blesilla was descended from the Scipiones and the Gracchi and her father Rogatus came from a noble family in Greece that improbably traced its roots back to Agamemnon.[94] Paula was born in 347. She grew up in Rome and in the early 360s she married Iulius Toxotius, who allegedly had the blood of Aeneas running through his veins.[95] The couple had five children: four daughters (Blesilla, Paulina, Rufina, Eustochium) and one son named after his father.[96] When the elder Toxotius died in 381[97] Paula vowed herself to perpetual widowhood, evidently

[91] *Ep.* 127.5: *nulla eo tempore nobilium feminarum noverat Romae propositum monachorum.*

[92] Both bishops passed time in Rome in exile, Athanasius from 339 to *c*.343 and Peter from 373 to 378. Kelly, *Jerome*, 92 n. 9, and Patrick Laurence, *Jérôme et le nouveau modèle féminin: la conversion à la vie parfaite* (Paris, 1997), 20, point out the improbability of a meeting with Athanasius on the basis of her young age (she would have been around ten years old).

[93] Kelly, *Jerome*, 91–103; Krumeich, *Hieronymus*, 70–9; Maurice Testard, 'Les Dames de l'Aventin, disciples de saint Jérôme', *BSAF* (1996), 39–63; E. Glenn Hinson, 'Women Biblical Scholars in the Late Fourth Century: The Aventine Circle', *StudPatr*, 23 (1997), 319–24. On their domestic monasticism, see Gian Domenico Gordini, 'Origine e sviluppo del monachesimo a Roma', *Gregorianum*, 37 (1956), 238–40, 244–5, 256–7.

[94] *Ep.* 108.3. For the doubts raised by scholars about her lineage as it is reported by Jerome, see Anne Ewing Hickey, *Women of the Roman Aristocracy as Christian Monastics* (Ann Arbor, Mich., 1987), 21–3.

[95] *Ep.* 108.4.

[96] *PCBE*, ii. 1617–26 ('Paula 1'); Elmore Paoli, 'Autour de Paula (347–404). Subsidia prosopographica', *ZPE*, 103 (1994), 241–9; Christa Krumeich, *Paula von Rom: christliche Mittlerin zwischen Okzident und Orient. Eine Biographie* (Bonn, 2002); Andrew Cain, 'Jerome's *Epitaphium Paulae*: Hagiography, Pilgrimage, and the Cult of Saint Paula', *JECS*, 18 (2010), forthcoming.

[97] Pierre Nautin, 'Études de chronologie hiéronymienne (393–397), i. Le Livre de Jérôme contre Jean de Jérusalem', *REAug*, 18 (1972), 217–18.

learning the ropes of this vocation from Marcella.[98] Like Marcella, she was a connoisseur of eremitic lore. When the bishops Paulinus and Epiphanius visited Rome in 382 she spent time with them and even hosted Epiphanius at her house (this was probably how Jerome first met her). She was so inspired by their virtues (*accensa virtutibus*) that she very nearly abandoned her family and substantial estate holdings on the spot to venture alone out into the desert where Pauls and Antonies resided (*incomitata ad heremum Antoniorum atque Paulorum*).[99]

Even though Marcella and some of her friends had been practising their own informal brand of urban monasticism for some years before Jerome made their acquaintance, the group lacked a crucial cohesive element that female Christian associations such as theirs ultimately needed: a male authority figure, either a cleric or monk, to provide spiritual guidance.[100] Jerome had just the right profile. He was an ordained priest, though his priestly status was probably not what initially piqued their interest, that much the less because he apparently was not a practising priest at the time. In the recent past, he had tried his hand at biblical exegesis[101] and so he could furnish proof of Scriptural expertise and a working knowledge of Hebrew, both of which were bound to be attractive to these intellectually inclined women.[102] As devout ascetics, they would also have been intrigued by Jerome's seemingly extensive experience with the Syrian desert ascetic life. Here was a relatively young but by all appearances seasoned monk who claimed to have first-hand knowledge of the legendary monastic culture of the east. What is more, he could authenticate his claim with a batch of letters written during the period in question. The Christian monastic movement had arrived on Syrian

---

[98] In Jer.*Ep.* 46.1, Paula praises Marcella as Eustochium's and her '*magistra*', the one who first inspired them to embrace the ascetic life (*prima scintillam nostro fomiti subiecisti*). Cf. *Ep.* 127.5: *in huic* [sc. *Marcellae*] *nutrita cubiculo Eustochium.*

[99] *Ep.* 108.6. Cf. ibid., 14, on Paula's enthusiasm when visiting the cells of famous hermits during her brief tour of the Egyptian desert in early 386.

[100] See Brown, *Body and Society*, 265–6. See also Jan Willem Drijvers, 'Virginity and Asceticism in Late Roman Western Elites', in Josine Blok and Peter Mason (eds.), *Sexual Asymmetry: Studies in Ancient Society* (Amsterdam, 1987), 246–8.

[101] i.e., a now-lost commentary on Obadiah as well as a commentary on the vision of Isa. 6.

[102] Jerome later would claim (*Ep.* 127.7) that Marcella eagerly tracked him down upon his arrival in Rome because of his reputation for Scriptural expertise.

soil before the middle of the fourth century, and perhaps much ear-lier. By the 380s, its tradition there was viable and noteworthy in its own right.[103] Nevertheless, owing to the popularity of the *Life of St Antony*,[104] which by the early 370s was available to Latin readers in two translations,[105] Egypt was thought of as the glorious cradle of monasticism by many western Christians. Even though an Egyptian monastic pedigree may have sounded more familiar and therefore perhaps more credible to his target audience in Rome, Jerome was forced to work within the confines of his own experience and to make the most of it. He did so by connecting with contemporary stereotypes about Syrian monasticism and by glamorizing himself as a rugged, chain-wearing hermit. Syrian monks, with their notoriously outrageous austerities, were the 'stars of the ascetic movement',[106] and Jerome brilliantly appropriated their exotic 'star power' for himself.

Jerome presumably suspected that his monastic training in the far-off Syrian desert—if presented seductively—would certify him in the eyes of ascetic Christians in Rome as a veteran of spiritual warfare and therefore as an exceptionally well-qualified doctor of souls (pro-vided, of course, that the quality of his spiritual advice lived up to the expectations created by his supposed monastic pedigree). A key

---

[103] Arthur Vööbus, *History of Asceticism in the Syrian Orient* (2 vols., Leuven, 1958); J. H. W. G. Liebeschuetz, *Antioch. City and Imperial Administration in the Later Roman Empire* (Oxford, 1972), 234–7; Joseph Patrich, *Sabas, Leader of Palestinian Monasticism. A Comparative Study in Eastern Monasticism, Fourth to Seventh Centuries* (Washington, DC, 1995), 22–8; Andrea Sterk, *Renouncing the World Yet Leading the Church: The Monk–Bishop in Late Antiquity* (Cambridge, Mass., 2004), 20–5. See also Burton-Christie, *Word in the Desert*, 39–43, on the connections between incipient monasticism in Syria and Egypt. See also William Harmless, *Desert Christians: An Introduction to the Literature of Early Monasticism* (Oxford, 2004), 417–48, for a discussion of the points of contact between the various early monastic traditions.

[104] Philip Rousseau, *Ascetics, Authority, and the Church in the Age of Jerome and Cassian* (Oxford, 1978), 92–5; James Goehring, *Ascetics, Society, and the Desert: Studies in Early Egyptian Monasticism* (Harrisburg, Pa., 1999), 18–20; Harmless, *Desert Christians*, 97–100.

[105] One of the translations was done by Jerome's patron Evagrius of Antioch before 373. The other translation, released anonymously, appeared some time before Evagrius'. For an overview of the chronology, see G. J. M. Bartelink, *Vie d'Antoine— Athanase d'Alexandrie. Introduction, texte critique, et traduction* (Paris, 1994), 95–8. Bartelink's critical text of the anonymous one, accompanied by a facing-page Italian translation by Pietro Citati and Salvatore Lilla, is printed in Christine Mohrmann (ed.), *Vita di Antonio, Vite dei Santi*, i (Milan, 1974).

[106] Peter Brown, *World of Late Antiquity* (London, 1971), 98.

passage from his *Libellus de virginitate servanda* (*Ep.* 22), written in 384 to Paula's daughter Eustochium, illustrates how in another, later context Jerome parlayed his past experience in the desert into spiritual authority in the present:

How often, when I was living in the desert—in that open wilderness, scorched by the heat of the sun, which gives monks a savage dwelling place— how often did I imagine that I was among the forbidden pleasures of Rome! I used to sit all alone because I was filled with bitterness. Sackcloth disfigured my unshapely limbs and my dirty skin had become like an Ethiopian's from long neglect. Each day I poured forth tears, each day I let out groans, and if ever the onset of sleep overcame me, my bare bones, which barely held together, would clash against the ground. I say nothing about my food and drink, for even when they are sick [the solitaries] do not take anything but cold water, and to eat one's food cooked is looked upon as self-indulgence ... In my fear of hell I consigned myself to this prison, where I had no companions except scorpions and wild beasts ... Wherever I saw hollow valleys, craggy mountains, steep cliffs, there I made my place of prayer, the house of correction for my unhappy flesh. There, also—the Lord is my witness—when I shed copious tears and strained my eyes towards heaven, I sometimes felt that I was among angelic hosts.[107]

Jerome inserted this stretch of purple prose at a strategic point (7) to show that his own life experience embodied the ascetic precepts he had just dispensed in the foregoing sections. In the section that immediately follows this quotation, he produces another round of precepts, beginning with a prohibition against wine-drinking. He appeals to his first-hand monastic *experientia* as a justifiable basis for speaking authoritatively on this and all matters of practical Christian living: 'If there can be any good sense in me, if one who has experience may be trusted, I advise the bride of Christ to avoid wine as if it were

---

[107] *Ep.* 22.7: *o quotiens in heremo constitutus et in illa vasta solitudine, quae exusta solis ardoribus horridum monachis praestat habitaculum, putavi me Romanis interesse deliciis! sedebam solus, quia amaritudine repletus eram. horrebam sacco membra deformis, squalida cutis situm Aethiopicae carnis adduxerat. cotidie lacrimae, cotidie gemitus et, si quando repugnantem somnus inminens oppressisset, nuda humo vix ossa haerentia conlidebam. de cibis vero et potu taceo, cum etiam languentes aqua frigida utantur et coctum aliquid accepisse luxuriae sit...ob gehennae metum tali me carcere ipse damnaveram, scorpionum tantum socius et ferarum...sicubi concava vallium, aspera montium, rupium praerupta cernebam, ibi meae orationi locus, illud miserrimae carnis ergastulum; et, ut mihi ipse testis est dominus, post multas lacrimas, post caelo oculos inhaerentes nonnumquam videbar mihi interesse agminibus angelorum.*

poison.'[108] Later in the letter (29) Jerome proposes the following to
Eustochium: 'If there is anything of which you are ignorant, if you
have any concern about Scripture, ask one whose life commends
him, whose age puts him above suspicion, whose reputation does
not belie him.'[109] Needless to say, the thirty-something Jerome has
himself in mind when he speaks of one 'whose age puts him above
suspicion, whose reputation does not belie him'. He therefore cleverly
intertwines his identities as an ascetic virtuoso and biblical exegete,
making the one indispensable to the other.[110]

Jerome's compelling self-portraiture as a solitary anchorite captured the imaginations of Italian Renaissance artists.[111] The rich
iconographic legacy that it inspired is a resounding tribute to his
enduring genius as a storyteller. Until relatively recently, scholars
accepted at face value most aspects of Jerome's depiction of his way
of life during these years. A decade and a half ago, Stefan Rebenich
broke important new ground when he pointed out that Jerome had
grossly exaggerated the facts about his 'exile' in an attempt to bring his
life-story in line with contemporary oriental monastic stereotypes.[112]
Jerome stayed not in a cave or in a barren, sun-scorched wilderness, as
he leads us to believe,[113] but on an expansive semi-rural estate owned

[108] *Ep.* 22.8: *si quid itaque in me potest esse consilii, si experto creditur, hoc primum moneo, hoc obtestor, ut sponsa Christi vinum fugiat pro veneno.*

[109] *Si quid ignoras, si quid de Scripturis dubitas, interroga eum, quem vita commendat, excusat aetas, fama non reprobat.*

[110] Elsewhere in *Ep.* 22 (e.g., at 17: *crebrius lege et disce quam plurima. tenenti codicem somnus obrepat et cadentem faciem pagina sancta suscipiat*), and also in other letters, Jerome prescribes for his disciples a twin-tiered regimen of Scripture reading (*lectio divina*) and ascetic practice. See Leopoldus Laurita, *Insegnamenti ascetici nelle lettere di s. Girolamo* (Rome, 1967), 4–21; Luciana Mirri, 'Girolamo e la lectio divina', in Enzo Bianchi and Benedetto Calati (eds.), *La lectio divina nella vita religiosa* (Magnano, 1994), 107–24; Laurence, *Jérôme et le nouveau modèle féminin*, 396–413.

[111] Renate Jungblut, *Hieronymus: Darstellung und Verehrung eines Kirchenvaters* (Tübingen, 1967); Herbert Friedmann, *A Bestiary for Saint Jerome: Animal Symbolism in European Religious Art* (Washington, DC, 1980), 48–100; Bernhard Ridderbos, *Saint and Symbol: Images of Saint Jerome in Early Italian Art* (Groningen, 1984), 63–88; Daniel Russo, *Saint Jérôme en Italie. Étude d'iconographie et de spiritualité (XIIIᵉ–XVᵉ siècle)* (Paris, 1987), 201–51.

[112] See Rebenich, *Hieronymus und sein Kreis*, 86–98.

[113] Cf. Fergus Millar, *The Roman Near East, 31 BC–AD 337* (Cambridge, 1993), 239, on how 'outposts on the margins of the steppe' such as Chalcis constituted 'a mixed zone; by no means a true, empty desert, but crossed by tracks and dotted by small settlements'. Cf. also Peter Brown, 'The Rise and Function of the Holy Man

by his wealthy patron Evagrius. He did not live in complete solitude, either. He had at his disposal a team of copyists ready to transcribe texts that he borrowed from contacts such as the bibliophiles Florentinus in Jerusalem and the centenarian Paul in Concordia.[114] In addition, he was visited frequently by Evagrius[115] and kept in constant contact with friends in Antioch and Aquileia, as his representative correspondence (*Epp.* 5–17) from this period attests.

If modern readers of the letters have so easily been swayed by Jerome's embellished rendition of his experience, one can only imagine how taken in an ancient audience might have been. Indeed, Marcella, Paula, and their friends apparently were so impressed by Jerome that they retained him as their spiritual advisor; Paula would even go on to become his lifelong monastic companion in Bethlehem. These women admired the eastern hermits from a distance and were not immediately inclined to imitate them in a radical renunciation of house and home. Some of them (e.g., Paula) secretly longed to experience the desert life for themselves. What stood in their way, however, were lingering family ties and cumbersome property holdings, the liquidation of which was an enormously complicated and impracticable affair for well-bred Romans.[116] When Jerome first met these women, they had been content simply to withdraw to suburban retreats where they would spend their aristocratic *otium* on asceticism, Scriptural studies, and works of charity.[117] They may not have been willing or able to venture out into the desert, but Jerome could bring the desert to them, so to speak. Many of these women had been

in Late Antiquity', *JRS*, 61 (1971), 83 on the mild climate and occasional rainfall in the steppelands of Chalcis—not exactly the parched frontier of Jerome's literary imagination!

[114] *Ep.* 5.2: *habeo alumnos, qui antiquariae arti serviant.* From Florentinus he requested Hilary of Poitiers' commentary on the Psalms (*Ep.* 5.2). He asked Paul for Fortunatian's commentaries, Novatian's letters, and some of Aurelius Victor's historical works (*Ep.* 10.3). On Paul, see Paolo Zovatto, 'Paolo da Concordia', *AAAD*, 5 (1974), 165–80.

[115] *Ep.* 7.1. Evagrius has a recurring role in Jerome's pre-Roman letters: see *Epp.* 3.3; 4.2; 5.3; 15.5.

[116] Dennis Trout, *Paulinus of Nola. Life, Letters, and Poems* (Berkeley, Calif., 1999), 145; John Curran, *Pagan City and Christian Capital. Rome in the Fourth Century* (Oxford, 2000), 311–15.

[117] Anne Yarbrough, 'Christianization in the Fourth Century: The Example of Roman Women', *ChHist*, 45 (1976), 157–8.

practising some kind of informal monasticism for at least a decade before ever encountering him. But Jerome (gave the impression that he) institutionalized, as it were, whatever regimen they already had in place by codifying some ethical guidelines and adapting them to the women's urban context. In so doing, he was essentially leveraging himself to take credit for their monasticism as if he had been its grand architect all along.[118]

Practical spiritual advice for everyday living, though, was not the only useful service that Jerome was able to offer his band of urban ascetics. He was a scholar conversant in the biblical languages and the Greek and Latin exegetical traditions. Hence, he had the credentials and competence necessary to mentor them in their Scriptural studies. Study of the Bible seems to have been integral to their Christian experience even before his arrival, but he nevertheless reinforced their Bible-centred piety and, playing to his exegetical strengths, advocated for them a life regulated by a knowledge of the Scriptures.[119] Jerome may not have been the only one to enjoy some form of monetary support from these women during his time in Rome,[120] but he certainly went to unprecedented lengths to insure that he would be their most visible and vocal client. What he required, both for his own personal satisfaction and for the sake of making his cause seem reputable to upper-class western Christians, was a core of well-reputed followers. To believe Jerome, he found just such a following in Marcella, Paula, and their friends. And, if the hypothesis advanced in this chapter is accepted, it provides exciting new insight into the (literary) mechanism by which Jerome set all of this into motion by formally establishing himself as a figure of spiritual authority in Rome.

---

[118] See further Cain, 'Rethinking Jerome's Portraits of Holy Women', in Cain and Lössl, *Jerome of Stridon*, Chap. 4.

[119] Cf. *Ep.* 30.7: *quae enim alia potest esse vita sine scientia Scripturarum?*

[120] For this intriguing suggestion, see Rebenich, *Jerome*, 40. See also Mercedes Serrato Garrido, *Ascetismo Femenino en Roma. Estudios sobre San Jerónimo y San Agustín* (Cadiz, 1993), 79.

2

A Pope and His Scholar

The surviving Roman correspondence between Pope Damasus and Jerome ranks among the most famous letter-exchanges to come down from Christian antiquity. This body of correspondence encompasses three letters from the former (*Epp.* 20, 21, 36) and three from the latter (numbered *Ep.* 19 and *Ep.* 35 in Jerome's epistolary corpus; the third of Damasus' letters is preserved as an embedded letter in Jerome's response, *Ep.* 21). Modern scholars have valued these letters principally for the insight they seem to provide into the interpersonal relationship between a legendary pope and his monkish protégé. Consequently, the one aspect of this correspondence that perhaps mattered the most to Jerome in his contemporary context has remained concealed. It is this aspect that I wish to explore in the present chapter.

JEROME ON DAMASUS ON JEROME: REVISIONIST REMINISCENCES

Pope Damasus I was the longest-reigning pope of the fourth century, ruling the Roman see from 1 October 366 until his death on 11 December 384.[1] He was arguably the most resourceful one as well. Among the highlights of his rich pontifical legacy are

---

[1] M. A. Norton, 'Prosopography of Pope Damasus', *Folia*, 4 (1950), 13–31; 5 (1951), 30–55; 6 (1952), 16–39.

unprecedented liturgical reforms[2] and architectural ventures,[3] an increasing centralization of papal power based on the notion of Petrine primacy,[4] and promotion of the cult of the martyrs[5] through his poems in Vergilian hexameters.[6] Jerome first met this charismatic cleric, who was then in his late seventies, when he arrived in Rome in the late summer of 382 as an interpreter for the ecclesiastical delegation of the bishops Paulinus of Antioch and Epiphanius of Salamis. Years earlier, it will be recalled, he had made at least two abortive attempts to establish epistolary contact with Damasus.[7] Now, however, he was no longer an unknown monk writing as an outsider from the Syrian outback but a dignified man of letters keeping close company with bishops. This time Damasus did not ignore Jerome. Quite to the contrary, he must have been impressed with his educational

[2] Massey Shepherd, 'The Liturgical Reform of Damasus I', in Patrick Granfield and Josef A. Jungmann (eds.), *Kyriakon. Festschrift Johannes Quasten* (2 vols., Münster, 1970), ii. 847–63; Maura Lafferty, 'Translating Faith from Greek to Latin: *Romanitas* and *Christianitas* in Late Fourth-century Rome and Milan', *JECS*, 11 (2003), 21–62.

[3] John Curran, *Pagan City and Christian Capital. Rome in the Fourth Century* (Oxford, 2000), 142–7.

[4] Louise André-Delastre, *Saint Damase 1ᵉʳ : défenseur de la doctrine de la primauté de Pierre, des saintes écritures et patron des archéologues* (Paris, 1965); Charles Pietri, *Roma christiana: recherches sur l'Église de Rome, son organisation, sa politique, son idéologie de Miltiade à Sixte III (311–440)* (2 vols., Paris, 1976), ii. 1618–22; J. N. D. Kelly, *The Oxford Dictionary of Popes* (Oxford, 1986), 33.

[5] Pietri, 'Concordia apostolorum et renovatio urbis (Cult des martyrs et propagande pontificale)', *MEFRA*, 73 (1961), 275–322; Tomas Lehmann, 'Eine spätantike Inschriftensammlung und der Besuch des Papstes Damasus an der Pligerstätte des Hl. Felix in Cimitile/Nola', *ZPE*, 91 (1992), 243–82; Jean Guyon, 'Damase et l'illustration des martyrs', in Mathijs Lamberigts and Peter van Deun (eds.), *Martyrium in Multidisciplinary Perspective: Memorial Louis Reekmans* (Leuven, 1995), 157–77; Marianne Sághy, '*Scinditur in partes populus*: Pope Damasus and the Martyrs of Rome', *EME*, 9 (2000), 273–87; Dennis Trout, 'Damasus and the Invention of Early Christian Rome', *JMEMS*, 33 (2003), 517–36.

[6] See Antonio Ferrua, *Epigrammata Damasiana* (Rome, 1942), 81–259 for a critical text and commentary on Damasus' surviving epigrams. See also Jacques Fontaine, *Naissance de la poésie dans l'occident chrétien* (Paris, 1981), 111–25; id., 'Damase poète théodosien: l'imaginaire poétique des *Epigrammata*', *Saecularia Damasiana. Atti del convegno internazionale per il XVI centenario della morte di Papa Damaso* (Vatican City, 1986), 113–45.

[7] Some time in 384, after the two were on familiar terms, Damasus made a point of saying (*Ep.* 35.1) that he recently had read with great interest (*tota aviditate legi*) the letters that Jerome had written from the desert (*quas in heremo aliquando dictaveras*). It is perhaps telling that he used '*legi*' ('I have read') instead of '*relegi*' ('I have reread'). This may be a tacit admission that, for whatever reason, he had not read the two letters back when Jerome first sent them.

pedigree,[8] linguistic competence, and modicum of imperial administrative experience,[9] because he appointed him a part-time secretary of the papal chancery who would 'assist' him in drafting official correspondence to churches in the east and west.[10] If we are to believe Jerome, this position gave him rare, behind-the-scenes access to the papal court.[11] Take, for instance, an intriguing passage in his letter of *c*.392 to bishop Aurelius of Carthage in which he awkwardly recalls a virtual encounter with Aurelius, then an archdeacon, years earlier in Rome:

You remind me and I recall that you had been sent to Rome as a legate with the holy bishop of Carthage, Cyrus, of blessed memory. When one day I asked my holy and venerable bishop Damasus who you were—for your silent expression was a guarantee of the greatness of your spirit—he replied that you were the archdeacon of the church at Carthage, an office that your conduct and his praise of you merited. It was because of my own bashfulness that I did not get to know you or initiate a friendship by striking up a conversation. It would allow me neither to appear as if I were rashly pursuing someone I did not know nor to force myself on the company of a man who had not granted me any occasion to speak with him.[12]

[8] e.g., in Rome during the 360s he had studied Latin grammar and literature under Aelius Donatus, the renowned grammarian and commentator on Terence and Vergil.

[9] In the late 360s, after completing his rhetorical training in Rome, Jerome (along with his boyhood friend from Stridon, Bonosus) headed to the Gallic city of Trier to pursue employment opportunities in the imperial bureaucracy. For an unspecified amount of time they held posts as official couriers (*agentes in rebus*). On *agentes in rebus* in late antiquity, see A. H. M. Jones, *The Later Roman Empire, 284–602: A Social, Economic, and Administrative Survey* (2 vols., Oxford, 1964), ii. 578–82. See A. D. Booth, 'The Chronology of Jerome's Early Years', *Phoenix*, 35 (1981), 258 n. 64, for the suggestion that Jerome had a legal career in mind and 'wanted to be called to the bar of the praetorian prefect'. For a discussion of Jerome's time in Trier, see J. Steinhausen, 'Hieronymus und Laktanz in Trier', *TZ*, 20 (1951), 126–54.

[10] *Ep.* 123.9: *ante annos plurimos, cum in chartis ecclesiasticis iuvarem Damasum, Romanae urbis episcopum, et orientis atque occidentis synodicis consultationibus responderem*. The imperfect tense for both verbs indicates continuity in the past but does not specify frequency, i.e., how often Jerome served in this secretarial capacity. See Yves-Marie Duval, *La Décrétale Ad Gallos Episcopos: son texte et son auteur. texte critique, traduction française et commentaire* (Leiden, 2005) for a papal decretal addressed to bishops in Gaul in the 380s that Jerome may have drafted.

[11] See J. N. D. Kelly, *Jerome. His Life, Writings, and Controversies* (London, 1975), 80–90; Stefan Rebenich, *Hieronymus und sein Kreis: Prosopographische und sozialgeschichtliche Untersuchungen* (Stuttgart, 1992), 141–53.

[12] *Ep.* 27*.2: *admones et recordor te cum sancto episcopo ac beatae memoriae Cyro, Carthaginiensis ecclesiae [nunciavit] sacerdotem Romam legatum fuisse directum; cumque quadam die <a> sancto mihi atque venerabili Damaso episcopo sciscitarer*

In his recreation of the original scene that day Jerome subtly leaves the impression that he was on close speaking terms with Damasus. Was he, as one scholar has alleged, Damasus' 'confidante',[13] or, as another has put it, did there exist 'a close, indeed affectionate relationship'[14] between them? The tone of their last surviving mutual correspondence (to which we shall turn later in this chapter) certainly does suggest that a certain familiarity existed between them. Nevertheless, it is not my intention here to speculate about the precise degree of intimacy the two may have shared. What is of more immediate interest is how Jerome represented their relationship in his writings— and why he represented it in the way he did. In one particular case it can be shown that his reminiscences of his purportedly close ties to Damasus served above all else an apologetic end: to rehabilitate his embattled public image in Rome during his controversy with Jovinian in the early 390s. Immediately following its release Jerome's *Adversus Iovinianum* was criticized throughout Rome, even by his own friends, for its acerbic tone and inordinate praise of virginity.[15] The Christian senator Pammachius asked him to write a follow-up treatise to clarify some of the more questionable statements he had made in the writing. Jerome replied with *Ep.* 49, which he dedicated to Pammachius. Late in this epistolary *apologia* he makes a point of reminding his Roman audience of the profound respect that their own recent pope had for him:

While Damasus of holy memory was still alive, I wrote a book against Helvidius on the perpetual virginity of the blessed Mary in which I found it necessary to say many things about the troubles of marriage so as to point out

quisnam esses—nam acumen ingenii tui silens quoque vultus pollicebatur—respondit archidiaconum Carthaginiensis ecclesiae, talem virum qualem et tua vita et illius de te testimonium merebatur. ut autem pleniorem familiaritatem tecum non inirem, pudor nobis prohibuit ne ignotum viderer imprudenter appetere et me ingerere necessitudini hominis qui nullam mihi secum loquendi tribuerat occasionem. For the dating and circumstances of this letter, see the notes by Yves-Marie Duval in Johannes Divjak and Franz Römer, *Œuvres de saint Augustin 46B: Lettres 1*–29** (Paris, 1987), 560–8. For assorted text-critical notes on this letter, see Ilona Opelt, 'Aug.*Epist.*, 27* Divjak: ein Schreiben des Hieronymus an Bischof Aurelius von Karthago', *Augustiniana*, 40 (1990), 19–25. See more recently Duval, 'Sur trois lettres méconnues de Jérôme concernant son séjour à Rome (382–385)', in Andrew Cain and Josef Lössl (eds.), *Jerome of Stridon: His Life, Writings and Legacy* (Aldershot, 2009), Chap. 2.

[13] Thomas Halton, *St Jerome: On Illustrious Men* (Washington, DC, 1999), 137 n. 1.
[14] Kelly, *Jerome*, 83.   [15] See below, pp. 135–40.

the blessedness of virginity. Did that eminent man versed in the Scriptures—a virgin doctor of the virgin church—reprimand anything in that writing?[16]

Jerome argues that his theological credentials should not be called into question for the simple reason that Damasus found nothing objectionable about his teachings. The pope was, after all, a 'virgin doctor of the virgin church'—an epithet meant to evoke his reputation as an essayist and poet on virginity.[17] Furthermore, Damasus was an 'eminent man versed in the Scriptures' and therefore he was perfectly qualified to sit in judgement on Jerome's interpretations of the Bible. One cannot help but appreciate the irony of Jerome invoking, as a buffer against criticism, the name of someone who was a lightning rod for scandal in his own right.[18] Damasus' political wrangling with his papal rival Ursinus in 366, which resulted in riots and even bloodshed, cast a dark shadow of intrigue over much of his nearly twenty-year episcopate.[19] As if this were not enough, the pope was dogged by rumors that he was a panderer to Rome's affluent Christian widows, an 'ear-tickler of matrons' (*matronarum auriscalpius*).[20] Damasus also had a reputation for living in obscene luxury. The pagan senator and prefect of Rome Vettius Agorius Praetextatus, no

[16] *Ep.* 49.18: *dum adviveret sanctae memoriae Damasus, librum contra Helvidium de beatae Mariae virginitate perpetua scripsimus, in quo necesse nobis fuit ad virginitatis beatitudinem praedicandam multa de molestiis dicere nuptiarum. num vir egregius et eruditus in Scripturis et virgo ecclesiae virginis doctor aliquid in illo sermone reprehendit?*

[17] Jerome celebrated Damasus' verse and prose *opuscula* on virginity elsewhere in his writings. See *Ep.* 22.22: *super hac re versu prosaque conposita...scripsit opuscula*; *Vir. ill.* 103: *elegans in versibus componendis ingenium habuit multaque et brevia opuscula heroico metro edidit.*

[18] For an inventory of contemporary *testimonia* relating to Damasus' scandal-ridden episcopate, see Ferrua, *Epigrammata*, 59–77. See also Erich Caspar, *Geschichte des Papstums von den Anfängen bis zur Höhe der Weltherrschaft* (2 vols., Tübingen, 1930–3), i. 196–256; Pietri, 'Damase, évêque de Rome', *Saecularia Damasiana. Atti del convegno internazionale per il XVI centenario della morte di Papa Damaso* (Vatican City, 1986), 31–58.

[19] Ammianus Marcellinus, *Rer. gest. lib.* 27.3.12–13. See Adolf Lippold, 'Ursinus und Damasus', *Historia*, 14 (1965), 105–28; André Chastagnol, *La Préfecture urbaine à Rome sous le bas-empire* (Paris, 1960), 152–6; Pietri, *Roma christiana*, i. 408–23.

[20] Jacques Fontaine, 'Un sobriquet perfide de Damase, matronarum auriscalpius', in Danielle Porte and Jean-Pierre Néraudau (eds.), *Hommages à Henri le Bonniec: res sacrae* (Brussels, 1988), 177–92. Damasus was given this pejorative nickname in the contemporary pro-Ursinian document *Libellus precum ad imperatores*, which has been preserved through the *Collectio Avellana* (CSEL, 35/1).

poor man himself, eyed the extravagance of the papal court with
envy and is said to have joked often with Damasus that he gladly
would become a Christian right away if only he were elected pope.[21]
Additionally, Ammianus Marcellinus may have had Damasus in mind
when he drew a seering contrast between the upscale lifestyles of
Roman bishops and the modest living of provincial bishops.[22] Damasus' infamy must have put Jerome, an outspoken critic of aristocratic
and clerical *luxuria*,[23] in a difficult place. For obvious reasons in
the passage above he turns a blind eye to the allegations about his
former patron's exorbitance. For his overriding concern during the
Jovinianist controversy was to paint a sanitized portrait of Damasus
as a sound judge of character and theology in order to show that his
ascetic crusading had enjoyed the institutional backing of the Roman
church at the highest levels.[24]

THE GREAT COMMISSION

Patronage from a pope, even one as controversial as Damasus, not
only guaranteed a scholar sufficient income and leisure to work, but
it also made it more likely that his labours would be met with a
favourable reception—or at least in influential pro-Damasian circles.
The numerous practical benefits of such patronage, needless to say,
would have appeared attractive to the aspiring biblical scholar from
Stridon. Jerome made the most of his proximity to Damasus by pushing various items on his scholarly agenda. One of his ambitions was
to make the theological wisdom of the Greek east available to western
readers in Latin translation. In Rome he began a translation of *On
the Holy Spirit* by Didymus the Blind. Three years later in Bethlehem
(387), when he finally finished the project, he claimed in its preface

---

[21] *C. Ioh. Hier.* 8. On Damasus' relations with Praetextatus, see Maijastina Kahlos,
'Vettius Agorius Praetextatus and the Rivalry between the Bishops in Rome in 366–
367', *Arctos*, 31 (1997), 41–54.

[22] *Rer. gest. lib.* 27.3.14–15.   [23] e.g., *Ep.* 22.28.

[24] None of this is of course to doubt that Damasus really *did* support Jerome to
the extent that Jerome claimed in the letter to Pammachius. To be sure, as I discuss
below, Damasus certainly does seem to have accommodated Jerome, and even doted
over him, in a way that his successor Siricius never did.

that 'Damasus was the one who first had put me to this work'.[25] This seems to contradict his remark in a letter of 384 to Damasus that, 'I have in my hands Didymus' book *On the Holy Spirit*, which I hope to dedicate to you once it has been translated'.[26] The wording in this second passage suggests that the initiative for the project lay with Jerome and not Damasus. In the preface to the translation, however, Jerome presents a different version of the facts, presumably to give his translation a retroactive papal stamp of approval.[27]

It was specifically Origen's body of exegetical work that Jerome was most intent upon bringing to the attention of his fellow Latins. A few years earlier, when he was staying in Constantinople, he had first felt drawn to Origen.[28] In 380/1, he translated Origen's thirty-seven homilies on Isaiah, Jeremiah, and Ezekiel and dedicated them to his priest friend Vincentius.[29] When he came to Rome, he had every intention of continuing his Latinization of Origen. However, for such a labour-intensive project he needed substantial material support. He also needed a patron whose reputation for orthodoxy might make the venture seem more attractive to a Nicene Christian audience in Rome—the very city in which a century and a half earlier Origen had been condemned for heterodoxy by a local synod.[30] For help Jerome turned to none other than Damasus, who cultivated a reputation

---

[25] *Didym. spir. sanct.*, prologue: *Damasus, qui me ad hoc opus primus impulerat.*

[26] *Ep.* 36.1: *Didymi de spiritu sancto librum in manibus habeo, quem translatum tibi cupio dedicare.*

[27] In his entry on Didymus in *Vir. ill* 109, Jerome's wording is more neutral. He says only that he translated *On the Holy Spirit* and he does not mention Damasus' alleged commission of the work.

[28] Kelly, *Jerome*, 70–1 suggests that Gregory Nazianzen may have been responsible for introducing him to Origen's writings.

[29] *Orig. Hiez.*, prologue. See Pierre Nautin, 'La Lettre *Magnum est* de Jérôme à Vincent et la traduction des homélies d'Origène sur les prophètes', in Duval (ed.), *Jérôme entre l'Occident et l'Orient, XVIe centenaire du départ de saint Jérôme de Rome et de son installation à Bethléem. Actes du colloque de Chantilly*, Sept. 1986 (Paris, 1988), 27–39; Pierre Jay, 'Combien Jérôme a-t-il traduit d'homélies d'Origène?', *StudPatr*, 23 (1989), 133–7; Theodore Bergren, 'Jerome's Translation of Origen's Homily on Jeremiah 2. 21–22', *RBén*, 104 (1994), 260–83; Alfons Fürst, 'Jerome Keeping Silent: Origen and his Exegesis of Isaiah', in Cain and Lössl, *Jerome of Stridon*, Chap. 11.

[30] Jerome's *Ep.* 33.5 is our earliest source for this detail: *Roma ipsa contra hunc cogit senatum.* Jerome most likely gleaned it from Pamphilus' *Apology for Origen*. See Cain, 'Origen, Jerome, and the *senatus Pharisaeorum*', *Latomus*, 65 (2006), 728–9.

for orthodoxy.[31] In 383/4 he translated two of Origen's homilies on the Song of Songs and presented the *opusculum* to the pope. In the brief dedicatory epistle he praises Origen's massive commentary on the Song of Songs as his *chef-d'œuvre* ('although he has outdone everyone in the rest of his books, in the Song of Songs he has outdone himself'[32]). He goes on to remark that translating such a voluminous work requires 'almost boundless leisure and labour and money'. In the meantime, he has translated two of the homilies on this biblical book so that Damasus can see from these representative samples 'how great a value the larger work possesses, when the small gives you such satisfaction'.[33] Damasus, however, apparently expressed no interest in sponsoring this project.

Damasus did not initiate the translation of Didymus' treatise and he declined to underwrite the costly and time-consuming translation of Origen's works, but he did keep Jerome occupied on another scholarly front: he charged him with revising the many existing versions of the Old Latin Gospels according to their Greek original.[34] It goes without saying that he must have had supreme confidence in Jerome's expertise to hand him the commission of normalizing the biblical

---

[31] Chastagnol, *Préfecture*, 168–9; Pietri, *Rome christiana*, i. 733–6, 741–5, 832–40.

[32] *Orig. Cant.*, prologue: *cum in caeteris libris omnes vicerit, in Cantico Canticorum ipse se vicit.* For a recent study of this work, see J. Christopher King, *Origen on the Song of Songs as the Spirit of Scripture: The Bridegroom's Perfect Marriage-Song* (Oxford, 2005).

[33] *Orig. Cant.*, prologue: *itaque illo opere praetermisso, quia ingentis est otii, laboris et sumptuum, tantas res, tamque dignum opus in Latinum transferre sermonem, hos duos tractatus...interpretatus sum: gustum tibi sensuum eius, non cibum offerens; ut animadvertas quanti sint illa aestimanda, quae magna sunt, cum sic possint placere, quae parva sunt.* Rufinus was under the impression that Damasus had asked Jerome to translate these two homilies (see Jerome, *Ep.* 80.1), an impression that Jerome was probably responsible for creating. See, e.g., his letter to Aurelius (*Ep.* 27*.2): *duabus homeliis cantici canticorum quas ammonitu beati Damasi Romae transtuli*; cf. *Ep.* 84.2: *praefatiuncula ad Damasum in omeliis cantici canticorum.*

[34] On the Old Latin Gospels, see Bruce Metzger, *The Early Versions of the New Testament* (New York, 1977), 285–374; Jean Gribomont, 'Les Plus anciennes traductions latines', in Jacques Fontaine and Charles Pietri (eds.), *La Bible de tous les temps*, ii. *Le Monde latin antique et la Bible* (Paris, 1985), 43–65; James Elliott, 'The Translations of the New Testament into Latin: The Old Latin and the Vulgate', in Wolfgang Haase (ed.), *Aufstieg und Niedergang der römischen Welt*, II.26.1 (Berlin and New York, 1992), 198–245; Philip Burton, *The Old Latin Gospels: A Study of their Texts and Language* (Oxford, 2000).

text of the Latin-speaking world (beginning with the Gospels)—and a very risky commission at that, inasmuch as his own name would be forever linked with it, for better or worse.[35]

Jerome completed his path-breaking revision in 384. It did not receive a warm welcome among many Christians in Rome. In a letter to Marcella written shortly after its release he complains bitterly about critics who accused him of tampering with the Lord's words when he emended passages in the Gospels 'against the authority of the ancients and the opinion of the entire world'.[36] He defends himself by pointing out that, 'I wanted to restore the corruption of the Latin manuscripts, which is evident from the variations present in them all, to their Greek original, from which my critics do not deny they were translated'.[37] Most scholars agree that a biblical exegete active in Rome during the second half of Damasus' pontificate, known only to us by the appellation 'Ambrosiaster' given to him in later centuries,[38] was most probably one of the anonymous critics, if not the chief one, whom Jerome targets in his letter to Marcella.[39] As we learn from a revealing passage in his commentary on Romans, which post-dates the appearance of the Gospels revision, Ambrosiaster objected to Jerome's brand of textual criticism (without actually naming him) on the grounds that an editor can too easily adulterate the accepted biblical text and adopt readings that further his own special interests:

---

[35] I therefore disagree with Megan Hale Williams, *The Monk and the Book: Jerome and the Making of Christian Scholarship* (Chicago, 2006), 52, who asserts that Damasus 'needed little from one such as Jerome' and that in terms of his reputation 'it cost him little to dispense his patronage'. To the contrary, Damasus was making a calculated gamble of immense proportions on his young protégé.

[36] *Ep.* 27.1: *adversus auctoritatem veterum et totius mundi opinionem.* For a study of the language and style of the Vulgate, see G. Q. A. Meershoek, *Le Latin biblique d'après saint Jérôme: aspects linguistiques de la rencontre entre la Bible et le monde classique* (Nijmegen, 1966); Catherine Brown Tkacz, '*Labor tam utilis*: The Creation of the Vulgate', *VChr*, 50 (1996), 42–72.

[37] *Ep.* 27.1: *Latinorum codicum vitiositatem, quae ex diversitate librorum omnium conprobatur, ad Graecam originem, unde et ipsi translata non denegant, voluisse revocare.*

[38] For the debate about his identity, see Sophie Lunn-Rockliffe, *Ambrosiaster's Political Theology* (Oxford, 2007), 33–44.

[39] So Heinrich Vogels, 'Ambrosiaster und Hieronymus', *RBén*, 66 (1956), 14–19; Kelly, *Jerome*, 89–90; Lunn-Rockliffe, *Ambrosiaster's Political Theology*, 22–3.

People want to pontificate to us from the Greek manuscripts, as if these did not differ from one another. This makes for a controversial issue. When someone is not able to score a victory by relying on his own authority, he tampers with the words of Scripture to impose his own meaning on them, with the end result that (his own) authority, and not sound judgement, seems to decide the matter. It is well known, moreover, that there are some (Old) Latin manuscripts, translated a while ago from Greek ones, which the innocence of the times has preserved and validates as incorrupt...Today things that are condemned in the (Old) Latin manuscripts are found to have been regarded as true by the writers of old Tertullian, Victorinus, and Cyprian.[40]

Jerome must have had a sense of the controversial nature of his revision and even took measures in the preface to the work to insulate himself pre-emptively from criticism. He opens this preface by emphasizing Damasus' ultimate accountability for the project: 'You force me to make a new work out of an old one' (*novum opus facere me cogis ex veteri*).[41] He strategically places '*novum*' as the first word in order to cast the edition as a masterful innovation while at the same time affirming, with the forceful '*cogis*', that it was not undertaken presumptuously at his own initiative but rather at Damasus' prodding. Later in the preface he uses another strong verb of compulsion (*iubes*) to underscore yet again the point that Damasus was the impetus behind the work: 'You who are the supreme bishop order that it be done' (*tu qui summus sacerdos es fieri iubes*).[42]

---

[40] *In Rom.* 5.14: *sic praescribere nobis volunt de Graecis codicibus, quasi non ipsi ab invicem discrepent. quod facit studium contentionis. quia enim propria quis auctoritate uti non potest ad victoriam, verba legis adulterat, ut sensum suum quasi verbis legis adserat, ut non ratio, sed auctoritas praescribere videatur. constat autem quosdam Latinos porro olim de veteribus Graecis translatos codicibus, quos incorruptos simplicitas temporum servavit et probat. postquam autem a concordia animis dissidentibus et hereticis perturbantibus torqueri quaestiones coeperunt, multa inmutata sunt ad sensum humanum, ut hoc contineretur in litteris, quod homini videretur. unde etiam ipsi Graeci diversos codices habent. hoc autem verum arbitror, quando et ratio et historia et auctoritas conservatur. nam hodie quae in Latinis reprehenduntur codicibus, sic inveniuntur a veteribus posita, Tertulliano et Victorino et Cypriano.*

[41] Robert Weber (ed.), *Biblia Sacra iuxta Vulgatam Versionem* (Stuttgart, 1983), 1515–16.

[42] Tore Janson, *Latin Prose Prefaces: Studies in Literary Conventions* (Stockholm, 1964), 120, notes that verbs such as '*iubere*' are used to 'indicate that the person demanding was so influential that the author had no choice'.

THE CORRESPONDENCE: 'HEBREW VERITY' AND AMBROSIASTER

From time to time Damasus and Jerome would engage in a dialogue about Scripture through correspondence. Damasus sent Jerome questions about various passages or topics in the Bible that puzzled him, and Jerome provided learned responses. This facet of their relationship is represented by six items of extant correspondence, two from Damasus and four from Jerome, that date to the years 383 and 384. Damasus' letters request answers to his questions about the Hebrew word 'hosanna' (*Ep.* 19) and about five passages in Genesis (*Ep.* 35). Two of Jerome's letters (*Ep.* 20 and *Ep.* 36) are responses to these. In another (*Ep.* 21), Jerome expounds the parable of the prodigal son. There is also a fourth composition (*Ep.* 18A + B), an epistolary commentary on the vision in Isaiah 6 that has come down to us in the manuscript tradition under the heading '*Ad Damasum*'. Jerome originally composed this piece of exegesis around 380 in Constantinople but revised it and dedicated it to Damasus when he was in Rome.[43] At first glance, *Ep.* 21 is the only one of Jerome's three replies not paired with a separate letter from Damasus. However, at the beginning of *Ep.* 21, Jerome preserves at least a portion (if not all) of Damasus' letter by directly quoting his question at length.[44] Therefore, all three of Damasus' requests, in their original wording, can be said to survive along with Jerome's corresponding replies, two as self-standing letters and one as an embedded letter.

In his exegetical replies to Damasus Jerome demonstrates that he can comfortably straddle the Old and New Testaments as well as access biblical texts in their original languages, Greek and especially Hebrew, when called upon to elucidate difficult points of text-critical

[43] Nautin, 'Le *De Seraphim* de Jérôme et son appendice *ad Damasum*', in Michael Wissemann (ed.), *Roma renascens. Beiträge zur Spätantike und Rezeptionsgeschichte. Festschrift Ilona Opelt* (Frankfurt, 1988), 257–93.

[44] He begins the response: *Beatitudinis tuae interrogatio disputatio fuit et sic quaesisse quaerenda viam est dedisse quaesiti. sapienter quippe interroganti sapientia reputabitur. ais: 'quis est iste in evangelio pater ...'* Seven lines in Hilberg's edition follow from here until we encounter another seven-line block of text introduced by Jerome's editorializing connector '*addis insuper*'. A third seven-line block, introduced by a second '*ais*', follows this section.

and exegetical interest.[45] Three of these letters in particular (*Epp.* 18A + B, 20, 36) exemplify his application of *Hebraica veritas*, or 'Hebrew verity', a hermeneutical methodology that privileges the Hebrew text as the holder of 'truth' in all matters of Old Testament exegesis.[46] Thus, for instance, their first surviving correspondence (*Epp.* 19–20). In his letter to Jerome (*Ep.* 19) Damasus inquires about the meaning of the biblical exclamation 'hosanna to the son of David'.[47] He states that he has searched high and low for an answer to his question in the commentaries of orthodox Greek and Latin patristic writers, but in vain, for they offer mutually conflicting opinions. He invites Jerome to settle the matter once and for all and to explain to him, just as he has done for many other topics (*sicut et de multis*), precisely what this phrase means for the Jews (*quid se habeat apud Hebraeos*).[48] Jerome willingly accepts the role of expert Hebraist prescribed for him by his epistolary interlocutor. He opens his reply

[45] For the debate about Jerome's actual knowledge of Hebrew, see Rebenich, 'Jerome: The *vir trilinguis* and the *Hebraica veritas*', *VChr*, 47 (1993), 56–62; Hillel Newman, 'How Should We Measure Jerome's Hebrew Competence?', in Cain and Lössl, *Jerome of Stridon*, Chap. 10.

[46] Caroline Hammond Bammel, 'Die Hexapla des Origenes: Die *Hebraica veritas* im Streit der Meinungen', *Augustinianum*, 28 (1988), 125–49; Adam Kamesar, *Jerome, Greek Scholarship, and the Hebrew Bible: A Study of the Quaestiones Hebraicae in Genesim* (Oxford, 1993); Gianfranco Miletto, 'Die *Hebraica veritas* in s. Hieronymus', in Helmut Merklein, Karlheinz Müller, and Günter Stemberger (eds.), *Bibel in jüdischer und Christlicher Tradition. Festschrift Johann Maier* (Frankfurt, 1993), 56–65; Rebenich, '*vir trilinguis*'; Christoph Markschies, 'Hieronymus und die *Hebraica Veritas*: ein Beitrag zur Archäologie des protestantischen Schriftverständnisses', in Martin Hengel and Anna Maria Schwemer (eds.), *Die Septuaginta zwischen Judentum und Christentum* (Tübingen, 1994), 131–81; Pierre Jay, *L'exégèse de saint Jérôme d'après son Commentaire sur Isaïe* (Paris, 1985), 89–102; Emanuela Prinzivalli, '*Sicubi dubitas, Hebraeos interroga*: Girolamo tra difesa dell'*Hebraica veritas* e polemica antigiudaica', *AnnSE*, 14 (1997), 179–206; and most recently, Michael Graves, *Jerome's Hebrew Philology: A Study Based on His Commentary on Jeremiah* (Leiden, 2007).

[47] Damasus' interests in liturgical reform probably prompted his question about this phrase from the Palm Sunday liturgy. The subject matter may tentatively allow us to date *Ep.* 19 to the spring (383), around Holy Week, when the phrase was perhaps more likely to have been at the forefront of his mind than at any other time.

[48] *Ep.* 19: *commentaria cum legerem Graeco Latinoque sermone in evangeliorum interpretatione a nostris, id est orthodoxis, viris olim ac nuper scripta de eo, quod legitur: osanna filio David, non solum diversa, sed etiam contraria sibimet proferunt. dilectionis tuae ardenti illo strenuitatis ingenio abscisis opinionibus ambiguitatibusque subplosis, quid se habeat apud Hebraeos, vivo sensu scribas, ut de hoc, sicut et de multis, tibi curae nostrae in Christo Iesu gratias referant.*

by seconding Damasus' frustration about the 'varying ideas' (*diversa*)
among patristic writers. After going on to summarize the erroneous
interpretations proposed by Hilary of Poitiers (*noster Hilarius*)[49] and
some unnamed writers, Jerome leads into his own explanation with a
programmatic statement about his methodology:

We therefore must pass over the little streams of opinion and rush back to
the very source from which the Gospel writers drew... The Hebrew words
themselves must be presented and the opinion of all the commentators must
be weighed, so that the reader, after considering all of these, may more readily
discover for himself the proper way of thinking about the issue in question.[50]

At the end of the letter, Jerome remarks that he can easily do what
these other writers have done and fabricate some unfounded explanation (*ficta sententia*) that does not address the problem at hand.[51]
However, his passion for truth (*ob veritatem*) leaves him no choice
but to revert directly to the Hebrew text as the final arbiter in solving
otherwise unsolvable conundra.[52] Thus, Jerome defines a working
knowledge of Hebrew as the prerequisite for excellence in Old Testament exegesis.

'Hebrew verity' looms large also in the second and last surviving
letter-exchange between the two men (*Epp.* 35–6). This exchange,
which was initiated by Damasus asking for clarification about five

---

[49] Cf. *Ep.* 34.3, where Jerome, writing to Marcella about Psalm 127, criticizes
Hilary's ignorance of Hebrew (*Hebraei sermonis ignarus fuit*). On Hilary's exegetical
methodology, see Jean Doignon, 'Les Premiers commentateurs latins de l'écriture et
l'œuvre exégétique d'Hilaire de Poitiers', in Fontaine and Pietri, *La Bible de tous les
temps*, ii. 509–20; Marcello Marin, 'Ilario di Poitiers e Gerolamo', in Claudio Moreschini and Giovanni Menestrina (eds.), *Motivi letterari ed esegetici in Gerolamo. Atti del
convegno tenuto a Trento il 5–7 dicembre 1995* (Brescia, 1997), 137–57.

[50] *Ep.* 20.2: *restat ergo, ut omissis opinionum rivulis ad ipsum fontem, unde ab evan-
gelistis sumptum est, recurramus... ipsa Hebraea verba ponenda sunt et omnium interpretum opinio digerenda, quo facilius, quid super hoc sentiendum sit, ex retractatione
cunctorum ipse sibi lector inveniat.* Cf. *Epp.* 28.5: *haec nos de intimo Hebraeorum fonte
libavimus non opinionum rivulos persequentes neque errorum, quibus totus mundus
expletus est, varietate perterriti, sed cupientes et scire et docere, quae vera sunt*; 34.4:
restat, igitur, ut rursum ad fontem sermonis recurramus Hebraei.

[51] Cf. *Ep.* 78.11: *miror quosdam eruditos et ecclesiasticos viros ea voluisse transferre,
quae in Hebraico non habentur, et de male interpretatis fictas explanationes quaerere.*

[52] *Ep.* 20.4: *facile et nos potuimus aliquid ementiri, quod ex una voce solveret quaestionem, sicuti et ceteros fecisse monstravimus. sed magis condecet ob veritatem laborare
paulisper et peregrino aurem adcommodare sermoni, quam de aliena lingua fictam ferre
sententiam.*

cruces in Genesis, has been mired in controversy during the past two and a half decades. Its genuineness had always been taken for granted by scholars until the early 1980s, when Pierre Nautin argued, mainly on stylistic grounds, that Jerome authored *both* letters in 387, almost three years after Damasus' death, as part of a veiled revenge plot against bishop Ambrose of Milan for allegedly conspiring with others to have him expelled from Rome in the late summer of 385.[53] A close reading of the two letters in the Latin, however, shows that Nautin's conclusions about the Hieronymian authorship of the letter attributed to Damasus are untenable because they follow from a series of unwarranted assumptions on both the textual and extra-textual levels.[54] In addition, as I shall suggest below, the subtext of the correspondence was not Jerome's supposed hostility toward Ambrose but a professional rivalry Jerome was carrying on at the time with another contemporary biblical exegete.

The warm and jocular tone of this second letter-exchange stands in stark contrast to the somewhat formal and businesslike one we encounter in the first exchange (*Epp.* 19–20). This noticeable change in tone probably reflects the increasing familiarity that presumably developed between Damasus and Jerome over the course of about a year. Another fundamental difference between the two surviving correspondences is the sophistication of the rhetorical performance put on by each writer. In his letter (*Ep.* 35), Damasus steps forward as a consummate Christian *vir litteratus*. He stylishly invokes epistolary *topoi*[55] and adorns his prose with quotations from the Latin classics and the Bible.[56] As in *Ep.* 19, he appears widely read in patristic literature and even dismisses Lactantius for being verbose, tedious,

---

[53] Nautin, 'Le Premier [*sic*] échange épistolaire entre Jérôme et Damase: lettres réelles ou fictives?', *FZPhTh*, 30 (1983), 331–44. For the circumstances surrounding Jerome's expulsion from Rome, see Chapter 4.

[54] Cain, 'In Ambrosiaster's Shadow: A Critical Re–evaluation of the Last Surviving Letter-exchange between Pope Damasus and Jerome', *REAug*, 51 (2005), 257–77.

[55] e.g., the *brevitas* convention at *Ep.* 35.2: *servans utrobique moderamen, ut nec proposita solutionem desiderent, nec epistulae brevitatem.* Also, epistolary discourse as a *sermo absentium* at 35.1: *neque vero ullam puto digniorem disputationis nostrae confabulationem fore, quam si de Scripturis inter nos sermocinemur.*

[56] e.g., at *Ep.* 35.1, Jerome artfully juxtaposes quotations from Ps. 118: 103 (*quam dulcia, inquit propheta, gutturi meo eloquia tua, super mel ori meo*) and Cicero, *De orat.* 1.32–3 (*nam cum idcirco, ut ait praecipuus orator, homines bestiis differamus, quod loqui possumus*).

and insufficiently orthodox for his tastes.[57] As in the case of *Epp.* 19–20, so here, both correspondents script explicitly defined roles for themselves and for each other, with Damasus playing the inquisitive seeker to Jerome's biblical sage. Damasus fixes the terms of their interaction in this exchange as follows: 'I do not think that there is any topic more worthy of our letter-exchange than if we converse with each other about the Scriptures, that is, if I ask the questions and you provide the answers.'[58]

At the beginning of the letter Damasus announces that he is forwarding Jerome some questions because he has not heard from him in a while and suspects that he has been 'sleeping' (*dormientem*)—that is, engaged in reading and study rather than in writing.[59] This round of questions is supposed to rouse Jerome from his scholarly slumber. The day before, Damasus had sent a messenger to see if Jerome had any letters for him. Because he had none Damasus writes now to remind him to make good on his promise to dictate something—and that 'something' happens to be answers to questions about Genesis.[60] Nautin was bothered by this. He reasoned that by pestering Jerome for a letter Damasus was grovelling in a manner unbefitting a pope: how could the figurehead of western Christendom condescend to play the 'disciple' to Jerome's 'maître'?[61] Nautin's misgivings about Damasus' tone arise, I believe, from a fundamental misunderstanding of the dynamics of ancient epistolary role play. The so-called inappropriate self-deprecation is actually conventional late Roman *politesse.* In epistolary situations, this amounts to the writer's exaltation of

[57] *Ep.* 35.2: *fateor quippe tibi, eos, quos mihi iam pridem Lactantii dederas libros, ideo non libenter lego, quia et plurimae epistulae eius usque ad mille versuum spatia tenduntur et raro de nostro dogmate disputant.*

[58] *Ep.* 35.1: *neque vero ullam puto digniorem disputationis nostrae confabulationem fore, quam si de Scripturis inter nos sermocinemur, id est, ut ego interrogem, tu respondeas.*

[59] *Ep.* 35.1: *dormientem te et longo iam tempore legentem potius quam scribentem quaestiunculis ad te missis excitare disposui.* In classical and patristic Latin, the verb '*dormire*' could be used metaphorically to denote idleness: see TLL, s.v. '*dormire*', V.i.2032–3.

[60] *Ep.* 35.1: *heri tabellario ad me remisso nullas te iam epistulas habere dixisti . . . ultro pollicitus es te furtivis noctium operis aliqua, si vellem, posse dictare.*

[61] 'Échange', 334–5: 'Il est surprenant de voir Damase solliciter, fût-ce une seule fois, une lettre de Jérôme; et il est encore plus incroyable qu'après avoir essuyé un premier refus il se soit abaissé jusqu'à insister . . . Le pape, tel un disciple, posera les questions et Jérôme, tel un maître, répondra.'

the addressee at the expense of himself.[62] Such decorum was central to the friendship discourse of Christian antiquity; and it often transposed into the humility *topos*.[63] Likewise, when Damasus' seemingly inordinate flattery of Jerome couched in the letter's *exordium*—'how praiseworthy is he who outdoes all others in this very thing [eloquence] in which men surpass beasts?'[64]—is considered from the perspective of ancient rhetorical standards, it reads as a *captatio benevolentiae* designed to make Jerome more amenable to the request for answers to the appended questions.[65]

Jerome accepted Damasus' invitation to engage in a literary give-and-take and he produced a reply that is equally if not more impressive from a rhetorical standpoint. He plays the expert to Damasus' seeker but he does so in a cleverly roundabout way that emphasizes his status as a scholar of the 'Hebrew verity'. He says that, as soon as he received Damasus' letter, he summoned his secretary and prepared to dictate a reply. Then, all of a sudden, he was interrupted by a Jew (*Hebraeus*) who had arrived from the synagogue with some Hebrew books that Jerome wanted to borrow. He insisted that Jerome put aside all else for the time being and focus only on copying these texts. Jerome buckled under the pressure and did as he was told.[66] This

---

[62] Philippe Bruggisser, *Symmaque ou le rituel épistolaire de l'amitié littéraire: recherches sur le premier livre de la correspondance* (Freiburg, 1993), 20: 'Les relations épistolaires sont empreintes de discrétion par rapport à soi et d'éloge d'autrui. La bienséance commande, en particulier dans le domaine littéraire, le dénigrement de soi-même (dépréciation de soi) et l'exaltation de l'autre'. Cf. Antonio Garzya, *Il mandarino e il quotidiano. Saggi sulla letteratura tardoantica e bizantina* (Naples, 1983), 126–7.

[63] David Konstan, 'Problems in the History of Christian Friendship', *JECS*, 4 (1996), 87–113, esp. 97–106.

[64] *Ep.* 35.1: *qua laude dignus est, qui in ea re ceteros superat, in qua homines bestias antecellunt?*

[65] *Ep.* 35.2: *accingere igitur et mihi, quae subiecta sunt, dissere.* On *captatio* in oratory, on which the epistolary *captatio* was modelled, see Cicero, *Inv.* 1.20–2 and Anon., *Rhet. Herenn.* 1.7–8. On epistolary *captatio*, see Gustav Karlsson, *Idéologie et cérémonial dans l'épistolographie byzantine* (Uppsala, 1962), 79–83.

[66] *Ep.* 36.1: *postquam epistulam tuae sanctitatis accepi, confestim accito notario, ut exciperet, imperavi; quo ad officium praeparato, quod eram voce prompturus, ante mihi cogitatione pingebam. interim iam et ego linguam et ille articulum movebamus, cum subito Hebraeus intervenit deferens non pauca volumina, quae de synagoga quasi lecturus acceperat. et ilico 'habes,' inquit, 'quod postulaveras' meque dubium et, quid facerem, nescientem ita festinus exterruit, ut omnibus praetermissis ad scribendum transvolarem; quod quidem usque ad praesens facio.*

book-borrowing scene sounds too circumstantial to be invented. But, regardless of whether or not it is contrived, there are good reasons why Jerome might have chosen to report it. Creatively harnessing the power of anecdote, he assures his patron that he has not been squandering his time in useless pursuits but has been engaging in an activity that furthers his scholarship.[67] The nature of this activity implies that Jerome is a connoisseur of Judaica and that he maintains close ties to contemporary Jews[68] and the rabbinic tradition.[69]

Damasus' questions 1–5 correspond exactly to five questions (6, 9, 10, 12, 11, respectively) posed and then answered by Ambrosiaster in his *127 Quaestiones veteris et novi testamenti*. This work belongs to the late fourth century; individual *quaestiones* within the larger compilation that are datable have been assigned to the early 380s.[70] If we are to judge by the relatively low frequency of occurrence of the above five questions in extant fourth- and fifth-century theological literature, their virtual duplication in *Ep.* 35 seems to be something more than a coincidence. The repetition of one or two questions might be attributed to chance but not the repetition of all five,

[67] In this sense Jerome was voicing the timeless anxiety of the *cliens*. Cf. Horace, *Epod.* 14, where the poet, stricken with a '*mollis inertia*' evidently brought on by a recent love affair, responds to Maecenas' frequent inquiries about the snail-paced progress of his verse output.

[68] Gustave Bardy, 'St Jérôme et ses maîtres hébreux', *RBén*, 46 (1934), 145–64; Ilona Opelt, 'S. Girolamo ed i suoi maestri ebrei', *Augustinianum*, 28 (1988), 327–38; Günter Stemberger, 'Hieronymus und die Juden seiner Zeit', in Dietrich-Alex Koch and Hermann Lichtenberger (eds.), *Begegnungen zwischen Christentum und Judentum in Antike und Mittelalter. Festschrift für Heinz Schreckenberg* (Göttingen, 1993), 347–64.

[69] C. T. R. Hayward, 'Jewish Traditions in Jerome's Commentary on Jeremiah and the Targum of Jeremiah', *PIBA*, 9 (1985), 100–20; id., 'Saint Jerome and the Aramaic Targumim', *JSS*, 32 (1987), 105–23; id., 'Some Observations on St Jerome's "Hebrew Questions on Genesis" and the Rabbinic Tradition', *PIBA*, 13 (1990), 58–76; Ralph Hennings, 'Rabbinisches und Antijüdisches bei Hieronymus Ep. 121.10', in Johannes van Oort and Ulrich Wickert (eds.), *Christliche Exegese zwischen Nicaea und Chalcedon, 325–451* (Kampen, 1992), 49–71; Kamesar, *Jerome, Greek Scholarship, and the Hebrew Bible*, 176–91; Sandro Leanza, 'Gerolamo e la tradizione ebraica', in Moreschini and Menestrina (eds.), *Motivi letterari*, 17–38; John Cameron, 'The Rabbinic Vulgate?', in Cain and Lössl, *Jerome of Stridon*, Chap. 9.

[70] The *Quaestiones* evidently circulated in two different authorial recensions in the late fourth century. See Caelestinus Martini, 'De ordinatione duarum Collectionum quibus Ambrosiastri "Quaestiones" traduntur', *Antonianum*, 21 (1947), 23–48; id., 'Le recensioni delle "Quaestiones Veteris et Novi Testamenti" dell'Ambrosiaster', *RicSRel*, 1 (1954), 40–62.

especially when phraseological echoes suggest a genetic relationship between the two texts.[71] Thus, there does seem to be a connection between Damasus' questions and Ambrosiaster's *Quaestiones*. But, what is the connection? Scholars have long suspected that Damasus lifted the questions from Ambrosiaster's work and then sent them to Jerome, presumably to ask for a second opinion.[72] This scenario seems plausible enough. If Damasus did indeed have access to the five *quaestiones*, it would imply that they were in circulation in Rome in the early 380s. This raises an interesting question: did Jerome have prior exposure to Ambrosiaster's work, such that he would have been aware, upon receipt of Damasus' letter, that he already had answered these five questions?

Ambrosiaster was not a writer of little or no consequence who was likely to escape the notice of a fellow Latin who aspired to be a professional biblical scholar. Far from it, in fact: his *Quaestiones* and commentaries on the Pauline epistles influenced major exegetes such as Augustine[73] and Pelagius.[74] Characteristically anonymous criticisms of Ambrosiaster's interpretations in Jerome's post-Roman writings are evidence of his knowledge of, and bitter clashes with, his elder contemporary later in his career.[75] Even when he was in Rome he is bound to have been familiar, perhaps even intimately so, with the *œuvre* of a rival biblical exegete who was active there at the same time he was and with whom he competed for an audience. Furthermore, I suggest not only that Jerome was aware of the Ambrosiastrian subtext

---

[71] e.g., Ambrosiaster, *Quaest.* XII (*quare Abraham fidei suae signum circumcisionem accepit?*) and Damasus, *Quaest.* IV (*cur Abraham fidei suae signum in circumcisione suscepit?*).

[72] Alexander Souter, *The Earliest Latin Commentaries on the Epistles of St Paul* (Oxford, 1927), 42–3; Vogels, 'Ambrosiaster', 15; Kelly, *Jerome*, 89–90.

[73] N. Cipriani, 'Un'altra traccia dell'Ambrosiaster in Agostino (De pecc. mer. remiss. II, 36, 58–9)', *Augustinianum*, 24 (1984), 515–25; Antoon A. R. Bastiaensen, 'Augustin commentateur de saint Paul et l'Ambrosiaster', *SEJG*, 36 (1996), 37–65; Eric Plumer, *Augustine's Commentary on Galatians. Introduction, Text, Translation, and Notes* (Oxford, 2003), 53–6.

[74] Alfred Smith, 'The Latin Sources of the Commentary of Pelagius in the Epistle of St Paul to the Romans', *JThS*, 19 (1918), 162–230; Souter, *Pelagius' Expositions of Thirteen Epistles of St Paul* (3 vols., Cambridge, 1922–31), i. 176–83; Ernesto Buonaiuti, 'Pelagio e l'Ambrosiastre', *RicRel*, 4 (1928), 1–17.

[75] Souter, *A Study of Ambrosiaster* (Cambridge, 1905), 169–71; Vogels, 'Ambrosiaster'; Lunn-Rockliffe, *Ambrosiaster's Political Theology*, 19–26.

of Damasus' letter but also that he used the occasion of his reply to make a critique of Ambrosiaster's hermeneutical technique.

Jerome's criticism of Ambrosiaster's method manifests itself indirectly. Jerome answers only three of the five questions put to him by Damasus on the grounds that the other two have already been addressed satisfactorily by Tertullian and Novatian in Latin and by Origen in Greek.[76] His deferring to these writers is, on one level, an obvious nod to two of his patristic heroes, Tertullian and Origen.[77] In addition, by directing Damasus to past Christian writers rather than to able *recentiores* such as Ambrosiaster—whose answers to these very questions were apparently already available to Damasus—Jerome essentially was dismissing Ambrosiaster's work as being superfluous, and certainly not of sufficient quality to be mentioned in the same breath as, much less to supplant, the time-tested research of the *antiquiores*.

In his replies to the remaining three questions, Jerome's demonstration of his mastery of the Greek and Latin patristic traditions[78] and his facility in accessing the Old Testament in its various Greek translations as well as in the original Hebrew,[79] may also be said to serve in one respect as a silent indictment of Ambrosiaster. For Ambrosiaster was no philologist or textual critic of the order of Jerome. Because he was ignorant of Hebrew, the Old Testament was completely inaccessible to him in its original language. If he knew Greek (it has been suggested implausibly that this was his native language[80]), he showed no interest in his *Quaestiones* in consulting

[76] *Ep.* 36.1: *duabus tantum quaestiunculis praetermissis, non quo non potuerim et ad illas aliquid respondere, sed quod ab eloquentissimis viris, Tertulliano nostro scilicet et Novatiano, Latino sermone sint editae et, si nova voluerimus adferre, sit latius disputandum ... nam et Origenes in quarto Pauli ad Romanos ἐξηγητικῶν tomo de circumcisione magnifice disputavit et de mundis atque inmundis animalibus in Levitico plura disseruit, ut, si ipse invenire nihil possem, de eius tamen fontibus mutuarem.*

[77] Duval, 'Gerolamo tra Tertulliano e Origene', in Moreschini and Menestrina (eds.), *Motivi letterari*, 107–35.

[78] Hippolytus (16); Origen (9); Victorinus (16).

[79] e.g., 2: *antequam de quaestione dicamus, rectum videtur, ut editiones interpretum singulorum cum ipso Hebraico digeramus, quo facilius sensus Scripturae possit intellegi*; 4: *sicuti in quodam Hebraeo volumine scribitur*; 12: *dicam in Hebraeo non esse diversum*; 13: *volumen Hebraeum replico* and *quae lingua Hebraea 'dor' dicitur.*

[80] Micaela Zelzer, 'Zur Sprache des Ambrosiaster', *WS*, 4 (1970), 196–213. For Hellenistic aspects of his style, see Souter, *Earliest Latin Commentaries*, 84–95.

variant readings in the biblical text as a means to settle disputed interpretations. For Jerome, however, the *scientia Scripturarum* entailed
fluency in the biblical languages, a solid grasp of the principles of
philology and textual criticism, and an encyclopedic knowledge of
the Greek and Latin exegetical traditions.

In his reply to Damasus, moreover, Jerome attempts to outclass
Ambrosiaster simply by displaying the superiority of his own exegetical method.[81] But, if Jerome composed his responses with Ambrosiaster in mind, why did he go about criticizing him in such an
indirect manner? There are at least two possible reasons. If Jerome
knew or suspected that Damasus was partial to Ambrosiaster's work
or to the man himself, he may have wished to avoid offending
his patron by engaging in open polemical mudslinging.[82] It is also
plausible that Jerome simply wished to suppress even the remotest
mention of his rival to avoid legitimizing him any more than was
absolutely necessary. This, at any rate, seems to be why he did not
devote an entry to Ambrosiaster in his *De viris illustribus*—a conscious omission Heinrich Vogels aptly called 'eine Art von *damnatio
memoriae*'.[83]

Jerome refers to his four surviving exegetical letter-treatises dedicated to Damasus throughout his writings and most notably in his
auto-bibliography, where he lists them by title: *De seraphim* (*Ep.*
18A + B); *De osanna* (*Ep.* 20); *De frugi et luxurioso filiis* (*Ep.* 21); *De*

---

[81] For a comparison of their exegetical methods, Jerome in *Ep.* 36 (*Quaest.* 3) and
Ambrosiaster in *Quaest.* 10, see Annelie Volgers, 'Ambrosiaster: Persuasive powers
in progress', in Volgers and Claudio Zamagni (eds.), *Erotapokriseis. Early Christian
Question-and-Answer Literature in Context. Proceedings of the Utrecht Colloquium, 13–
14 October 2003* (Leuven, 2004), 104–8. On Ambrosiaster's technique, see Giacomo
Raspanti, 'Aspetti formali dell'esegesi paolina dell'Ambrosiaster', *AnnSE*, 16 (1999),
507–36. For discussions of Jerome's exegetical method, see Angelo Penna, *Principi e
carattere dell'esegesi di s. Gerolamo* (Rome, 1950); Jay, *L'exégèse de saint Jérôme, passim*;
Dennis Brown, *Vir Trilinguis. A Study in the Biblical Exegesis of Saint Jerome* (Kampen,
1992).

[82] The kind of polemical naughtiness, for instance, that made another one of his
Roman patrons, Marcella, wince. The following passage (*Ep.* 27.2), in which Jerome
anticipates Marcella's reaction to the tongue-lashing he gave critics of his revision of
the Gospels in the same letter, gives some interesting insight into the dynamics of their
relationship: *scio te, cum ista legeris, rugare frontem et libertatem rursum seminarium
timere rixarum ac meum, si potest, os digito velle conprimere, ne audeam dicere, quae
alii facere non erubescunt.*

[83] 'Ambrosiaster', 15.

tribus quaestiunculis legis veteris (Ep. 36).[84] This eagerness to bring
them to the attention of later readers tells us that he regarded them
not as 'private' exchanges for his and Damasus' eyes alone but rather
as writings available to an indefinitely large Christian readership.
Jerome, then, released his letters to Damasus at some point prior to
393, the date of his auto-bibliographical notice. Additionally, there is
reason to think that he also preserved Damasus' letters to him and
released them with their respective replies.[85] Two interesting features
of this correspondence, one codicological and the other cosmetic,
would seem to point in this direction. First of all, *Epp.* 19–20 are
always paired in the medieval manuscripts of Jerome's works, as are
Epp. 35–6.[86] This may well reflect their circulation pattern in the
late fourth and early fifth centuries. Secondly, both of Damasus'
letters and one of Jerome's replies have authentic-looking opening
salutations-cum-honorifics.[87] The one for *Ep.* 19 is a full salutation
of the sort that could plausibly have appeared in Damasus' original letter: *Dilectissimo filio Hieronymo Damasus episcopus in domino
salutem.* This form contains all three of the necessary ingredients of
an opening salutation: the *intitulatio* (sender's name = *Damasus episcopus*); the *inscriptio* (recipient's name = *dilectissimo filio Hieronymo*);
and the *salutatio* proper (greeting = *in domino salutem*). The opening salutations in *Ep.* 35 (*Dilectissimo filio Hieronymo Damasus*) and
Ep. 36 (*Beatissimo papae Damaso Hieronymus*) also conform to this

---

[84] *Vir. ill.* 135. *Ep.* 20 is mentioned in *In Math.* 3: *porro quod sequitur: osanna
filio David, quid significet et ante annos plurimos in brevi epistula ad Damasum tunc
Romanae urbis episcopum dixisse me memini; Ep.* 21 in *Adv. Iov.* 2.31: *super qua
parabola libellum quemdam Damaso episcopo, dum adhuc viveret, dedicavi; Ep.* 36 in
Quaest. hebr. 9: *pro septem vindictis aquila septempliciter interpretatus est, Symmachus
septimum, Theodotion per hebdomadem: super quo capitulo extat epistula nostra ad
episcopum Damasum.*

[85] *Ep.* 20 with *Ep.* 19; *Ep.* 36 with *Ep.* 35; *Ep.* 21 contains Damasus' embedded
letter; *Ep.* 18A + B, it will be recalled, has no accompanying letter because it was only
later dedicated to Damasus.

[86] See *BHM* 1(B), 406–17, 423–49, 513–25.

[87] On salutation formulae, see Carol Lanham, *Salutatio Formulas in Latin Letters to
1200: Syntax, Style, and Theory* (Munich, 1975). For studies of honorifics in late Latin
letters, see August Engelbrecht, *Das Titelwesen bei den spätlateinischen Epistolographen*
(Vienna, 1893); Mary O'Brien, *Titles of Address in Christian Latin Epistolography to 543
AD* (Washington, DC, 1930); Ernst Jerg, *Vir Venerabilis. Untersuchungen zur Titulatur
der Bischöfe in den Ausserkirchlichen Texten der Spätantike als Beitrag zur Deutung ihrer
öffentlichen Stellung* (Vienna, 1970).

standard, except that they lack a formal greeting. Such a greeting could have been edited out by a scribe early on in the textual transmission (scribal tampering could also explain why opening salutation formulae have not survived for *Epp.* 20–1). By retaining the original salutations Jerome might have hoped to accomplish two things simultaneously. First, their presence adds a touch of realism, enhancing ancient readers' impressions that they were observing freeze-frames of a dynamic relationship between a patron and his client, or rather between a student of the Bible (Damasus) and his learned teacher (Jerome). There is also the issue of authenticity. Without Damasus' letters in hand critics could claim that Jerome simply addressed exegetical treatises to him and crafted his rhetoric in such a way as to make it sound as if Damasus had requested them, even if he had not. By circulating the pope's letters alongside his replies to them, Jerome would have aimed to forestall such (not wholly unfounded) cynicism.

Furthermore, I suggest that Jerome released both sides of his epistolary exchanges with Damasus initially in Rome in order to announce to Christians there that he was the personal Scriptural advisor to a renowned pope. These letters provided 'proof' not only that his exegetical expertise was in great demand in high places within the church, but also that his controversial Hebrew scholarship came with a papal seal of approval. Papal approbation was exactly what this fledgling scholar needed at this critical juncture in his career, for his work (e.g., the revision of the Gospels) had received little if any applause outside his relatively small circle of Roman friends. Origen was the great pioneer of the 'Hebrew verity' among early Christian biblical scholars.[88] Jerome, who looked to Origen for scholarly inspiration,[89] was a pioneer in his own right in that he was the first *Latin* biblical scholar to apply this methodology systematically to his translation and exegesis of the Old Testament.

Modern scholars of the Bible take for granted a reading knowledge of Hebrew as being essential to their discipline. In the late fourth

---

[88] Nautin, *Origène: sa vie et son œuvre* (Paris, 1977); Bernhard Neuschäfer, *Origenes als Philologe* (2 vols., Basle, 1987).

[89] Nautin, 'Hieronymus', *TRE*, 15 (1986), 310–11; Peter Brown, *The Body and Society: Men, Women, and Sexual Renunciation in Early Christianity* (New York, 1988), 367, 379–80; Mark Vessey, 'Jerome's Origen: The Making of a Christian Literary Persona', *StudPatr*, 28 (1993), 135–45.

century, however, the climate could not have been more different. The leading Latin biblical scholars of the day looked askance at 'Hebrew verity' as a working hermeneutical concept. By advocating the supremacy of the Hebrew text Jerome was challenging the assumption, widely held among Greek and Latin contemporaries, that the Septuagint was divinely inspired.[90] Even Christians such as Augustine who had the utmost reverence for the Septuagint but did not necessarily believe in its infallibility[91] were jolted by what they saw as Jerome's iconoclasm. A story related by Augustine in a letter of 403 to Jerome, told in the context of his criticism of the latter's Hebrew scholarship, illustrates the kind of controversy that Jerome's translation of the Old Testament *iuxta Hebraeos* generated. The bishop of Oea (modern-day Tripoli in Libya) adopted Jerome's translation for use in his diocese. During one service, when a passage was read from Jonah (4: 6) describing a plant that provided Jonah with shade, a near-riot broke out in the congregation. The people were upset because they heard the unfamiliar word '*hedera*' ('ivy') instead of the traditional '*cucurbita*' ('gourd') found in the Old Latin Bible.[92] Local Jewish rabbis were consulted on the matter and sided against Jerome, maintaining that the Hebrew manuscripts supported the Old Latin reading. As a result, the bishop ordered that the wording in Jerome's version be changed.

Lay Christians in provincial North Africa were not the only ones to question the legitimacy of Jerome's translation of the Old Testament

---

[90] Pierre Benoît, 'L'inspiration des Septante d'après les Pères', in *Homme devant Dieu. Mélanges P. G. de Lubac* (Paris, 1964), i. 169–87; Giuseppe Veltri, 'L'ispirazione della LXX tra leggenda e teologia. Dal racconto di Aristea alla *veritas hebraica* di Gerolamo', *Laurentianum*, 27 (1986), 3–71. For Rufinus' harsh estimate of Jerome's demotion of the Septuagint and his translation *iuxta Hebraeos*, see *Apol. c. Ruf.* 2.24–35.

[91] For Augustine's view of the Septuagint, see *Civ. dei* 18.43; A. D. R. Polman, *The Word of God According to Augustine* (London, 1961), 183–90. Throughout his career, Augustine remained loyal to the Old Latin version of the Old Testament translated from the Septuagint: see Anne-Marie la Bonnardière, 'Augustin a-t-il utilisé la Vulgate de Jérôme?', Bonnardière (ed.), *Saint Augustin et la Bible* (Paris, 1986), 303–12; Peter Walsh (ed. and trans.), *Augustine: De bono coniugali; De sancta virginitate* (Oxford, 2001), pp. xxx–xxxi, 152–7.

[92] Pierre Hamblenne, 'Relectures de philologue sur le scandale du lierre/ricin (Hier. In Ion. 4.6)', *Euphrosyne*, 16 (1988), 183–223; Alfons Fürst, 'Kürbis oder Efeu? Zur Übersetzung von Jona 4,6 in der Septuaginta und bei Hieronymus', *BN*, 72 (1994), 12–19.

from the Hebrew. Dissenting voices were heard also in Christian aristocratic circles in Rome in the early to middle 390s. A certain 'Canterius',[93] who hailed from the *gens Cornelia* and who reputedly was a descendant of the Roman republican historian and consul Gaius Asinius Pollio, accused Jerome of sacrilege for translating 'ivy' instead of 'gourd' in Jonah 4: 6.[94] The charge of *sacrilegium* indicates that he was criticized not on philological grounds but on theological ones: his translation contradicted the divinely inspired Septuagint.[95]

Jerome faced an uphill battle every step of the way as he tried to convince western Christians, beginning with those in Rome, of the relevance and legitimacy of the innovative work on which he had staked much of his identity as a biblical scholar and more specifically as an Old Testament specialist. An endorsement from a reigning pope, especially one known for his progressive policies, increased the likelihood, at least in principle, that this novel work would receive instant visibility and credibility among an audience otherwise predisposed to being sceptical about it. Read in this light, the last surviving correspondence between Damasus and Jerome (*Epp.* 35–6) takes on additional significance. I argued above that Jerome formulated his answers to the questions put to him by Damasus being fully aware that answers to the same questions by Ambrosiaster were already circulating in Rome. By the early 380s, Ambrosiaster was, in terms of the volume of his literary output, far more accomplished than Jerome. For this reason, and also because he publicly called into question the legitimacy of Jerome's *ad fontes* approach to biblical textual criticism, Ambrosiaster posed a serious threat to Jerome's efforts to establish himself as an authoritative biblical scholar in Rome. By circulating *Ep.* 36 along with its cover letter from Damasus Jerome could provide the Roman Christian community with an alternative approach to biblical studies to the one championed by Ambrosiaster, an approach that by all appearances was sanctioned by the bishop of bishops.

---

[93] 'Cant<h>erius', which in Latin means a castrated male horse, would not have been his real name but rather a derogatory nickname applied to him by Jerome.

[94] *In Ion.* 4.6: *in hoc loco quidam Canterius, de antiquissimo genere Corneliorum, sive, ut ipse iactat, de stirpe Asinii Pollionis, dudum Romae dicitur me accusasse sacrilegii quod pro cucurbita hederam transtulerim.* Cf. *Apol. c. Ruf.* 1.30; *Ep.* 112.22.

[95] Rebenich, '*Vir trilinguis*', 59.

Posterity has been intensely fascinated by the supposedly close relationship between Pope Damasus and Jerome. The name recognition of both men—two of the celebrities of late antique Christianity—insured their genuine correspondence immense popularity in later generations. Their fame also contributed to an explosive demand in the Middle Ages for apocryphal correspondence between them.[96] The earliest and perhaps best-known spurious exchange is the two-part preface to the *Liber Pontificalis* (*LP*) contained in most of the *LP*'s earliest manuscripts.[97] 'Jerome' writes to 'Damasus' to ask for supplementary biographical records for all of the popes who served prior to his accession. 'Damasus' compliments him on having written a satisfactory history of the popes already, but he nevertheless promises to send 'Jerome' any additional material that he may find. A sixth-century compiler prefixed the *LP* with this exchange in order to lend credibility to his work by asserting authoritative ancient authorship of all entries prior to Damasus.[98] Thus, within a century of his death, forgers already were making creative use of Jerome's relationship with Damasus in order to construct authority for themselves and their works, just as Jerome had done with such finesse during his own lifetime.

[96] Giovanni Mercati, 'Il carme Damasiano *de Davide* e la falsa corrispondenza di Damaso e Girolamo riguardo al Salterio', *Note di letteratura biblica e cristiana antica* (Rome, 1901), 113–26; P. Blanchard, 'La Correspondance apocryphe du pape s. Damase et de s. Jérôme', *EphL*, 63 (1949), 376–88; Jeanne Bignami-Odier, 'Une lettre apocryphe de saint Damase à saint Jérôme sur la question de Melchisédech', *MEFRA*, 63 (1951), 183–90; Adalbert de Vogüé, 'La Règle du Maître et la lettre apocryphe de saint Jérôme sur le chant des Psaumes', *StudMon*, 7 (1965), 357–67; R. E. Reynolds, 'An Early Medieval Mass Fantasy: The Correspondence of Pope Damasus and St Jerome on a Nicene Canon', in Peter Linehan (ed.), *Proceedings of the Seventh International Congress of Medieval Canon Law* (Rome, 1988), 73–89. For a general survey of ancient Christian apocryphal correspondence, see Gustave Bardy, 'Faux et fraudes littéraires dans l'antiquité chrétienne', *RHE*, 32 (1936), 5–23, 275–302.

[97] For the text of the two letters, see Louis Duchesne, *Le Liber pontificalis: texte, introduction et commentaire* (2 vols., Paris, 1886–92), i. 117.

[98] On the dating and authorship of the *LP*, see Raymond Davis, *The Book of Pontiffs (Liber Pontificalis): The Ancient Biographies of the First Ninety Roman Bishops to AD 715* (Liverpool, 2000), pp. xii–xvi, xlvi–xlviii.

3

Claiming Marcella

In Chapter 1, Jerome's collection of his selected pre-Roman letters (*Epistularum ad diversos liber*) was placed in context as the ingenious means by which the obscure provincial formally introduced himself to aristocratic Christians in Rome as a titan of ascetic spirituality. In the present chapter, I investigate his other known collection of personal correspondence, the *Ad Marcellam epistularum liber* (hereafter *liber*), and suggest why and in what ways it, too, is a vital piece of the puzzle of Jerome's campaign to manufacture personal authority for himself early on in his career.

AD MARCELLAM EPISTULARUM LIBER: STRUCTURE AND CONTENTS

Of the countless letters Jerome and Marcella must have traded during a friendship that spanned three decades, all that survive are nineteen from him to her. Sixteen were written in Rome, between 384 and 385,[1] and three others over the course of almost two decades in Bethlehem—an invitation to the Holy Land written in the names of Paula and Eustochium but drafted by him[2] (*Ep.* 46); an exegetical letter that answers her questions about five biblical passages (*Ep.* 59); and one letter addressed jointly to Pammachius and Marcella on the subject of Origenism (*Ep.* 97). Which of the nineteen letters might have belonged to the *liber*? It was compiled no later than 393 and so

---

[1] *Epp.* 23–9, 32, 34, 37, 38, 40–4.
[2] Neil Adkin, 'The Letter of Paula and Eustochium to Marcella: Some Notes', *Maia*, 51 (1999), 97–110.

we may safely exclude *Ep.* 59 and *Ep.* 97 because they were composed in 395 and 402, respectively. Furthermore, in his auto-bibliography, Jerome situates the Marcellan *liber* between two Roman writings— *Ep.* 22 to Eustochium on virginity and *Ep.* 39 to Paula on Blesilla's death[3]—and so we can be assured that whatever letters belonged to it were written at Rome. By this reckoning, *Ep.* 46, which was written in the spring of 386 after Jerome had settled into Bethlehem,[4] would not have been part of it. The same goes for the now-lost voluminous correspondence that he claimed to have maintained with Marcella after leaving Rome.[5] Therefore, of his nineteen surviving letters to Marcella, only the sixteen he wrote in Rome qualify as plausible candidates for the *liber*.

Several cross-references among these sixteen letters demonstrate internal cohesion that argues in favour of many of them being the descendants of the fourth-century collection compiled by Jerome. At the beginning of his epistolary *vita Asellae* (*Ep.* 24) he mentions the *vita Leae* (*Ep.* 23), which had been written two days earlier (*nudius tertius de beatae memoriae Lea aliqua dixeramus*). In *Ep.* 26.5 he announces his intention to explain the meaning of various Hebrew words in the Psalms (*vellem tibi aliquid et de diapsalmate scribere*), a promise he kept by writing *Ep.* 28 shortly thereafter. Finally, in *Ep.* 27.1, he refers back to *Ep.* 26 (*post priorem epistulam, in qua de Hebraeis verbis pauca perstrinxeram*).

Codicological evidence supports the hypothesis that the sixteen Roman letters to Marcella belonged to the *liber* (this is to say nothing of lost letters that may have belonged to it). Dense clusters of ten or more of them are a frequent occurrence in the medieval manuscripts of Jerome's correspondence. The most substantial grouping is found in a twelfth-century codex from Signy (Charleville-Mézières, Bibliothèque municipale, 196.d). All sixteen Roman letters to Marcella

---

[3] *Vir. ill.* 135: *ad Eustochium de virginitate servanda, ad Marcellam epistularum liber unum, consolatorium de morte filiae ad Paulam.*

[4] Pierre Nautin, 'La Lettre de Paule et Eustochium à Marcelle (Jérôme, Ep. 46)', *Augustinianum*, 24 (1984), 441–8.

[5] *Ep.* 127.8: *interim absentiam nostri mutuis solabamur adloquiis et, quod carne non poteramus, spiritu reddebamus. semper se obviare epistulae, superare officiis, salutationibus praevenire. non multum perdebat, quae iugibus sibi litteris iungebatur.* With the apparent exception of *Epp.* 46, 59, 97, all of these letters are lost.

(bracketed) are represented: [37] + 59 + [40 + 26 + 25 + 27 + 41 + 42 + 44 + 43 + 38 + 29 + 34 + 32 + 28 + 23 + 24]. This sequence of Roman correspondence is uninterrupted except for the presence of *Ep.* 59, which presumably was introduced by a compiler. Of course, because Jerome's letters were often grouped by correspondent in medieval manuscripts as per scribal convention, it is impossible to say with certainty whether the grouping of sixteen Roman letters above and similar groupings found in other manuscripts descend from the archetypal *liber* or are the products of scribal compilation. Nevertheless, because we do know that the *liber* contained Roman correspondence, and because we happen to have a generous smattering of letters written to Marcella in Rome, it seems reasonable to work from the tentative assumption that these sixteen letters comprised the bulk if not the whole of the original *Ad Marcellam epistularum liber.*

The letters to Marcella are remarkably diverse. Five are technical explanations of some words or phrases from the Hebrew Bible (*Epp.* 25, 26, 28, 29, 34). One criticizes the deceased Gallic episcopal writer Reticius of Autun (*Ep.* 37). One is a defence of Jerome's Gospels revision (*Ep.* 27). Another reports his progress in revising various Old Testament books (*Ep.* 32). Three are miniature *vitae* of aristocratic women in Jerome's Roman network (*Epp.* 23, 24, 38). One exhorts Marcella to forsake city life in Rome for monastic solitude in the countryside (*Ep.* 43). Another letter thanks her on behalf of Paula and Eustochium for some miscellaneous gifts she sent to them (*Ep.* 44). One is an attack on the Roman priest 'Onasus' (*Ep.* 40), while two others are refutations of Montanist (*Ep.* 41) and Novatianist (*Ep.* 42) theology.

Scholars have tended to value these sixteen letters for the glimpses they purport to give into Jerome's daily round at Rome, not as interconnected pieces of an authorially assembled collection which, being the sum total of its parts, would have aimed to achieve specific propagandistic goals.[6] Mark Vessey, however, has proposed that Jerome used the Marcellan collection to portray himself to the Latin-speaking

[6] For instance, Sylvia Letsch-Brunner's monograph *Marcella–Discipula et Magistra. Auf den Spuren einer römischen Christin des 4. Jahrhunderts* (Berlin, 1998) consists almost entirely of close (mostly biographical) readings of Jerome's Roman letters to Marcella, but no attempt is made to interpret them as a unified compilation.

west as the next Origen.[7] Vessey noted three main areas in which
Jerome presents his activities in these letters as closely mirroring
Origen's. First, Jerome is a tireless scholar whose labours are made
possible only by the financial support of a generous but demanding
patron (cf. Origen's support from his patron Ambrose). Secondly,
like Origen, but unlike other contemporary exegetes, Jerome has a
firm command of Hebrew and is able to access the Old Testament in
its original language. Thirdly, Origen's prodigious scholarly achievements remain unsurpassed; Jerome, as the next Origen, will one day
be the standard by which biblical scholars in the Latin world are to
be measured. Vessey's analysis calls attention to what is certainly one
of the thematic undercurrents of many of the Marcellan letters. Nevertheless, in this chapter I shall argue that in terms of its immediate
pragmatic function there was more to this colourful epistolary mosaic
than Jerome's 'Origenizing' of himself.

HAGIOGRAPHY, HERMENEUTICS, HEBREW, AND HERETICS

Hagiography

Three of the letters, all written in 384, are quasi-hagiographic tributes to religious women—a lifelong virgin (Asella) and two chaste
widows (Lea and Blesilla)—with whom Marcella and Jerome were
acquainted.[8] These epistolary *vitae*-in-brief are referenced by scholars
customarily as sources for Jerome's social network during a crucial
period in his career, and more generally for women's ascetic spirituality in the late fourth-century west. But, as I hope to show, these letters
have an even more compelling story to tell us about their author's
determination to leave a lasting mark on Roman Christianity.

By the time Jerome penned the letter about Asella she was a virgin in her fifties.[9] In the first part of his narrative, Jerome gives an

---

[7] Vessey, 'Jerome's Origen: The Making of a Christian Literary *Persona*', StudPatr,
28 (1993), 135–45.

[8] *Ep.* 24.1: *Asella nostra; Ep.* 23.2: *Lea nostra; Ep.* 38.2, 5: *Blesilla nostra* (cf. 38.4:
vidua nostra).

[9] *PCBE*, ii. 199–200 ('Asella 1'). The date of her death is unknown. She may
have been the same wealthy cloistered virgin Asella whom Palladius (*Hist. laus.* 41.4)

account of how she came to embrace this lifestyle. In the second part, he describes Asella's virtues in such a way as to present her as the consummate embodiment of his precepts for ascetic living, as we find them articulated most notably in his *Libellus de servanda virginitate* to Eustochium (*Ep.* 22)—which he released in Rome in the spring of 384, not long before writing *Ep.* 24. In fact, many echoes, phraseological and otherwise, from *Ep.* 22 are woven into the textual fabric of *Ep.* 24 (these are documented below in the footnotes).[10]

Asella lives an angelic life shut up in a small room in the family mansion; this *cellula* was her 'paradise'.[11] She works with her hands, mindful of the apostle's decree that anyone who does not work should not eat.[12] She cares nothing for the refinements of fashion or for gaudy dress.[13] In prayer and psalmody, she constantly speaks to Christ, her Bridegroom.[14] She restricts herself to an anchorite's meagre diet of bread, salt, and cold water.[15] Throughout the year, she continually carries out two- or three-day fasts, but during Lent she fasts for a week at a time, all the while keeping a cheerful

---

mentioned seeing during a visit to Rome around 404: εἶδον δὲ καὶ ἐν ῾Ρώμῃ τὴν καλὴν ᾿Ασέλλαν τὴν παρθένον γεγηρακυῖαν ἐν τῷ μοναστηρίῳ, σφόδρα πραυτάτην γυναῖκα καὶ ἀνεχομένην συνοδίας.

[10] For evocations of *Ep.* 22 in Jerome's later correspondence, see Andrew Cain, 'Liber manet: Pliny, *Ep.* 9.27.2 and Jerome, *Ep.* 130.19.5', *CQ*, NS 58 (2008), 708–10.

[11] *Ep.* 24.3: *unius cellulae clausa angustiis latitudine **paradisi** fruebatur.* Cf. *Ep.* 22.41: *ad **paradisum** mente transgredere.*

[12] *Ep.* 24.4: *operabatur manibus suis sciens scriptum esse: qui non operatur, nec manducet.* Cf. *Ep.* 17.2: *nihil alicui praeripui, nihil otiosus accipio. manu cotidie et proprio sudore quaerimus cibum scientes ab apostolo scriptum esse: qui autem non operatur, nec manducet.* On the work ethic of self-sufficiency in desert Christianity, see Daniel Caner, *Wandering, Begging Monks. Spiritual Authority and the Promotion of Monasticism in Late Antiquity* (Berkeley, Calif., 2002), 200–3.

[13] *Ep.* 24.5: *idem semper habitus, **neglecta mundities** et inculta **veste** cultus ipse sine cultu.* Cf. *Ep.* 22.27: ***vestis** nec satis **munda** nec sordida.*

[14] *Ep.* 24.4: *intra **cubiculi sui secreta custodiit**, ut numquam pedem proferret in publicum ... **sponso** aut orans **loquebatur** aut psallens.* Cf. *Ep.* 22.25: *semper te **cubiculi tui secreta custodiant,** semper tecum sponsus ludat intrinsecus. oras: **loqueris ad sponsum.***

[15] *Ep.* 24.3: *pane et sale et **aqua frigida** concitabat magis esuriem, quam restinguebat.* Cf. *Ep.* 22.7: *de cibis vero et potu taceo, cum etiam languentes **aqua frigida** utantur et coctum aliquid accepisse luxuriae sit.* Cf. also *V. Ant.* 7.6: καὶ ἦν αὐτῷ ἡ τροφὴ ἄρτος καὶ ἅλας, καὶ τὸ ποτὸν μόνον ὕδωρ.

countenance.[16] Her face is pale, but not in an ostentatious way.[17] She rarely steps into public, and when she does it is to visit the shrines of the martyrs.[18] This incorrigible lover of solitude has become an urban anchorite, finding the desert amidst the bustle of Rome.[19] Her reputation for sanctity is unassailable; the good praise her, and the wicked do not dare to slander her.[20]

Even though Asella had been living as a consecrated virgin for over forty years before coming into contact with him, Jerome, by running her virtues through the subtextual filter of *Ep.* 22, was in effect assuming responsibility for her monastic successes and giving the impression that her accomplishments were directly attributable to her adherence to his counsel. At the outset of *Ep.* 24, he instructs Marcella, the ostensible addressee, to read the letter to young women so that they may take Asella as the model of the perfect life.[21] This point is reiterated and expanded upon at the end of the letter: 'Let widows and virgins imitate her, let wedded wives make much of her, let sinful women fear her, and let bishops look up to her.'[22] The *imitatio* that Jerome advocates has far-reaching ramifications not only for Asella but also for himself. Christian widows and virgins, in patterning themselves after her, will be partaking in an expression of the spiritual life recommended by Jerome. As for bishops and other ecclesiastical figures, in showing Asella reverence they will

[16] *Ep.* 24.4: *cumque per omnem annum iugi* **ieiunio** *pasceretur, biduo triduoque sic permanens, tum vero in quadragesima navigii sui vela tendebat omnes paene ebdomadas* **vultu laetante** *coniungens.* Cf. *Ep.* 22.27: *cum ieiunas, laeta sit facies tua.*

[17] *Ep.* 24.5: *ita* **pallor in facie est**, *ut, cum continentiam indicet, non redoleat ostentationem.* Cf. *Ep.* 22.17: *sint tibi sociae, quas videris quod ieiunia tenuant, quibus* **pallor in facie est.**

[18] *Ep.* 24.4: *ad* **martyrum** *limina paena invisa properabat.* Cf. *Ep.* 22.17: **martyres** *tibi quaerantur in cubiculo tuo.*

[19] *Ep.* 24.4: *solitudinem putaret esse delicias et in urbe turbida inveniret heremum monachorum.*

[20] *Ep.* 24.5: *sola vitae suae qualitate promeruit, ut in urbe pompae, lasciviae, deliciarum, in qua humilem esse miseria est, et boni eam praedicent et mali detrahere non audeant.*

[21] *Ep.* 24.1: *his potius, quae adulescentulae sunt, legere dignare, ut ad exemplum eius se instituentes conversationem illius perfectae vitae normam arbitrentur.*

[22] *Ep.* 24.5: *viduae imitentur et virgines, maritae colant, noxiae timeant, suspiciant sacerdotes.*

be acknowledging that Jerome's spiritual teachings are salutary. The
vita, then, serves to affirm Jerome's interpretation of ascetic Christianity to his circle of female disciples and to prospective (female)
followers by furnishing them with a Hieronymized model of piety
(*exemplum pudicitiae et virginitatis insigne*[23]) around which they can
rally. It has an apologetic dimension as well. By pinning his controversial teachings on a woman evidently already distinguished for
her holiness—and made more distinguished by his praise of her—
Jerome could vindicate these teachings in the face of mounting criticism from the wider Roman Christian community and especially its
clergy.[24]

While Asella was a lifelong virgin untainted by the sins of a dis-
solute youth, the subject of another epistolary *vita*, Paula's daughter
and Eustochium's older sister, Blesilla, became an ascetic enthusiast
only after having been a *bon vivante* for much of her young life. When
Jerome first met her, possibly in early 383, she was in her late teens
and engaged to be married.[25] Seven months into the marriage, her
husband died and left her a childless widow.[26] Around the middle
of the summer of 384, she succumbed to a month-long illness that
nearly ended her life. Shaken to the core by this near-death experience, she had a religious conversion and vowed herself thenceforth
to chaste widowhood. Jerome took her under his wing and would
later say that he had been her 'father in spirit' (*patrem spiritu*) and
'foster-father in affection' (*nutricium caritate*).[27] After her conversion, she took an interest in biblical exegesis and asked him to write
for her a commentary on Ecclesiastes[28] and to translate Origen's
twenty-five homilies on Matthew, his five on Luke, and thirty-five on
John.[29]

It was Blesilla's chronic high fever that taught her to renounce the
pleasures of the body that would one day be devoured by worms.[30]
In order to situate Blesilla's trial by fever in a biblical matrix, Jerome
opens the *vita Blesillae* (*Ep.* 38) with five examples of Old and New

---

[23] *Ep.* 45.7.   [24] See below, pp. 99–102.   [25] *PCBE*, ii. 310–11 ('Blesilla').
[26] *Ep.* 22.15: *soror tua Blesilla aetate maior, sed proposito minor, post acceptum
maritum septimo mense viduata est.*
[27] *Ep.* 39.2.   [28] *In Eccl.*, prologue.   [29] *Orig. Luc.*, prologue.
[30] *Ep.* 38.2: *Blesillam nostram vidimus ardore febrium per triginta ferme dies iugiter
aestuasse, ut sciret reiciendas delicias corporis, quod paulo post vermibus exarandum sit.*

Testament figures whose faith in God was strengthened by adversity.[31]
His concise narration of her conversion follows along the same lines:

The Lord Jesus has come to her and has touched her hand and, behold,
she arises and ministers to him (Mark 1: 30–1). Her life used to smell of
carelessness, and she used to lie in the tomb of the world, bound as she was
by the bands of riches. But, Jesus groaned, and, troubled in spirit, cried out to
her: 'Blaesilla, come forth' (John 9: 38–44). She rose up at his beckoning and
came forth, and now eats with the Lord (John 12: 2). Let the Jews threaten
her and be haughty, let them try to kill this one who has been raised from the
dead (John 12: 10).[32]

Jerome stitches together a series of biblical intertexts to create a firm
typological link between Blesilla's life and the life of Christ, and also,
more subtly, between himself as *auctor* and the Gospel writers.[33] He
is not as interested in her conversion experience per se as he is in
the profound impact it had on her day-to-day morality. He goes
on to contrast the 'before-and-after' Blesilla and produces a long
list of creature comforts she renounced in favour of an abstemious
lifestyle.[34] She also vowed herself to perpetual widowhood. Christian friends and family who disapproved of her religious fervour
were outraged by her refusal to remarry and bear children.[35] Jerome
responded by formulating a stern reproof of them that occupies about
half of *Ep.* 38.[36] His approach is confrontational: by opposing her

---

[31] Abraham tempted to kill his son (Gen. 22); Joseph sold into slavery (Gen. 37);
Hezekiah's fear of imminent death (2 Kgs 20); Peter's denial of Christ (Luke 22: 54–
62); and St Paul's conversion (Acts 9: 3–18).

[32] *Ep.* 38.2: *venit et ad hanc dominus Iesus tetigitque manum eius et ecce surgens
ministrat ei. redolebat aliquid neglegentiae et divitiarum fasciis conligata in saeculi iace-
bat sepulchro, sed confremuit Iesus et conturbatus in spiritu clamavit dicens: Blesilla, exi
foras. quae vocata surrexit et egressa cum domino vescitur. Iudaei minentur et tumeant,
quaerant occidere suscitatam.*

[33] On Christ as the supreme hagiographic model, see Lynda Coon, *Sacred Fictions:
Holy Women and Hagiography in Late Antiquity* (Philadelphia, 1997), 13–15. For the
uses of biblical typology in hagiographic writings, see Derek Krueger, 'Typological
Figuration in Theodoret of Cyrrhus's Religious History and the Art of Postbiblical
Narrative', *JECS*, 5 (1997), 393–419; id., *Writing and Holiness: The Practice of Author-
ship in the Early Christian East* (Philadelphia, 2004), 15–32; Claudia Rapp, 'Holy Texts,
Holy Men and Holy Scribes: Aspects of Scriptural Holiness in Late Antiquity', in
William Klingshirn and Linda Safran (eds.), *The Early Christian Book* (Washington,
DC, 2007), 194–222.

[34] *Ep.* 38.4.   [35] *Ep.* 38.2.   [36] *Ep.* 38.3, 5.

holy resolve, they show that they are not true Christians at all.[37]
Nothing they say matters anyway, for Blesilla will have the last laugh:
'Our Blesilla will laugh and will not lower herself to listen to the
taunts of such croaking frogs.'[38] Not long after he had written these
words Blesilla died unexpectedly from malnutrition brought on by
excessive fasting.[39] In his epitaph on her Jerome promises her literary immortality: 'As long as breath animates my body...I vow, I
promise, I pledge that my tongue will always utter Blesilla's name,
that my labours will be dedicated to her honour, that my talents
will be devoted to her praise...In my writings she will never die,'[40]
By presumably including *Ep.* 38 in the Marcellan *liber* Jerome could
begin to make good on this promise.

Jerome used his *vita Leae* (*Ep.* 23), as he did his *vita Blesillae*,
simultaneously to memorialize a dearly departed friend and to level
a criticism, in this case against pagan high culture at Rome. Like
Blesilla, Lea was a widow who went against the grain and opted for
chaste widowhood rather than remarriage.[41] By the time of her death
in 384, she was overseeing a community of virgins at Rome.[42] Jerome
captures the essence of Lea's sanctity in a series of compact, stylized
phrases that evoke *Ep.* 22 as well as *Ep.* 24 on Asella. She wore coarse
sackcloth, passed sleepless nights in prayer, and taught her monastic
daughters by deed more than by word.[43] Walled up in her cell,[44] she
had a sparse diet and did not fret over how she dressed or whether
her hair was styled.[45] After briefly cataloguing Lea's many virtues,

[37] *Ep.* 38.2: *qui Christianus est, gaudeat; qui irascitur, non esse se indicat Christianum.*

[38] *Ep.* 38.5: *Blesilla nostra ridebit nec dignabitur loquacium ranarum audire convicia.*

[39] See below, pp. 102–5.

[40] *Ep.* 39.8: *dum spiritus hos artus regit...spondeo, promitto, polliceor: illam mea
lingua resonabit, illi mei dedicabuntur labores, illi sudabit ingenium. nulla erit pagina,
quae non Blesillam sonet...numquam in meis moritura est libris.*

[41] *Ep.* 24.1: *de beatae memoriae Lea aliqua dixeramus...de secundo ordine castitatis
locuti sumus.* See *PCBE*, ii. 1268 ('Lea 2').

[42] *Ep.* 23.2: *ita eam totam ad dominum fuisse conversam, ut monasterii princeps,
mater virginum fieret.*

[43] *Ep.* 23.2: *sacco membra trivisse; orationibus duxisse noctes et comites suas plus
exemplo docuisse quam verbis.* Cf. *Ep.* 22.17: *ad orationem tibi nocte surgenti.*

[44] *Ep.* 23.3: *quam unius cubiculi secreta vallabant.* Cf. *Ep.* 22.25: *semper te cubiculi
tui secreta custodiant; Ep.* 24.4: *intra cubiculi sui secreta custodiit.*

[45] *Ep.* 23.2: *inculta vestis, vilis cibus, neglectum caput.* Cf. *Ep.* 22.27: *vestis nec satis
munda nec sordida; Ep.* 24.5: *neglecta mundities et inculta veste cultus ipse sine cultu.*

Jerome gives a creative rereading of a familiar biblical parable. Just as the poor man Lazarus resting comfortably in Abraham's bosom had seen the rich man in Tartarus begging him for a drop of water to ease his torment, so also did Lea now see the 'consul', not decked out in his triumphal robe but wrapped in a robe of mourning, begging her for a drink. The 'consul' alluded to here is none other than Vettius Agorius Praetextatus, the former prefect of Rome (from summer 367 to autumn 368) who died within days of Lea (between 9 September and 31 December) while he was serving as the praetorian prefect.[46]

Jerome aimed to teach a moral lesson by portraying Lea as a modern-day beggar—a very awkward fit for an aristocratic lady, needless to say—and Praetextatus as the unrighteous rich man roasting in an underworld furnace. The lesson, put simply, is that 'we should not want to possess both Christ and the world, but let eternal things take the place of things that are short-lived and transitory... In order that we may live for ever, let us recognize that we shall die'.[47] By Jerome's reckoning Praetextatus epitomized worldly ambition at its most unblushing. Up until the very day of his death, he would enter the Capitol like a general returning victorious from battle, flanked by dignitaries and cheered by all who saw him. When he died all of Rome was moved to tears.[48] Now in death this imperial celebrity is alone, naked, and held prisoner in the foulest darkness.[49] Jerome's Lea, by contrast, enjoys everlasting happiness and is welcomed by choirs of angels as she is comforted in Abraham's bosom.[50] Although from the upper echelon of late Roman society, she did not flaunt her

---

[46] *Ep.* 23.3: *ille, quem ante paucos dies dignitatum omnium culmina praecedebant.* See Johanna Nistler, 'Vettius Agorius Praetextatus', *Klio*, 10 (1910), 462–75; André Chastagnol, *Les fastes de la préfecture de Rome au Bas-Empire* (Paris, 1962), 171–8; Maijastina Kahlos, *Vettius Agorius Praetextatus. A Senatorial Life in Between* (Rome, 2002).

[47] *Ep.* 23.4: *non pariter et Christum habere velimus et saeculum, sed pro brevibus et caducis aeterna succedant ... non nos perpetuos aestimemus, ut possimus esse perpetui.* Cf. *Epp.* 53.11: *facile contemnit omnia, qui se semper cogitat esse moriturum;* 54.18: *cogita te cotidie esse morituram, et numquam de secundis nuptiis cogitabis.*

[48] *Ep.* 23.3. For the reaction of the Roman *plebs* to hearing the news of his death, see Symmachus, *Rel.* 10.2.

[49] *Ep.* 23.3: *desolatus est, nudus ... in sordentibus tenebris continetur.* In section 2 Jerome states that one of the reasons he decided to write the *vita Leae* was to show that the 'consul' was 'in tartaro'.

[50] *Ep.* 23.3: *aeterna beatitudine fruitur: excipitur angelorum choris, Abrahae sinibus confovetur.*

privileged socio-economic status[51] but lived as if she had never had it in the first place—trading riches and rank in this world for infinitely greater glory in the next. The message of the *vita Leae* is loud, clear, and uncompromising: follow the ascetic interpretation of the Gospel as preached by Jerome and as personified by Lea or face grave eternal consequences.

In the epistolary drama that unfolds in the *liber*, Marcella has an obvious starring role, but other women step in as supporting actresses (Asella, Blesilla, Lea) and a few others make 'cameo appearances' (Albina, Paula, Eustochium[52]). We may infer from this preponderant female presence that one of Jerome's central concerns in the *liber* is to show that he is at the centre of a vibrant network of holy women— and not just any holy women, but scions of some of Rome's noblest families. Each woman's personal identity is summarily reduced, in typical hagiographic fashion, to pastiches of biblical commonplaces and ascetic clichés. However, these *vitae* are not dispassionate sketches of women whom Jerome happened to know and to admire; he transformed his subjects, each in her own way, into idealized personifications of his ascetic ideology. By taking charge, first as (presumably) their actual spiritual mentor and then as their publicist, Jerome was able to praise these women as his precocious disciples whose spiritual successes were the direct result of his mentoring.[53]

Hermeneutics and Hebrew

When Jerome textualized the lives of three of his female friends, he put his own distinct stamp on their spirituality. His aim was not only to make literary tributes to women he obviously admired deeply but also to present them as reputable public faces for his controversial

[51] Cf. *Ep.* 22.27, where he commends Eustochium for not boasting about her rank: *neque vero moneo, ne de divitiis glorieris, ne de generis nobilitate te iactes, ne te ceteris praeferas: scio humilitatem tuam.*

[52] Marcella's mother Albina is mentioned in *Ep.* 32.2 and Paula and Eustochium in *Ep.* 32.1.

[53] See further Cain, 'Rethinking Jerome's Portraits of Holy Women', in Andrew Cain and Josef Lössl (eds.), *Jerome of Stridon: His Life, Writings and Legacy* (Aldershot, 2009), Chap. 4.

brand of piety. In a similar but far more complex way, he portrayed Marcella as his star pupil with whom he enjoyed a close-knit and intellectually stimulating relationship. The two were on such familiar terms, in fact, that Jerome was a permanent fixture in her household and was even able affectionately to call her mother his own.[54] This at any rate is the impression relayed to readers of the *Ad Marcellam epistularum liber*. In one letter, he recounts the circumstances under which he and Marcella first heard the unsettling news about Lea's death. He vividly recaptures the scene, when he had been giving her a private Scripture lesson, in such a way as to place himself at the centre of the action, first as her biblical tutor and then as her comforter in a time of emotional distress:

Today at about the third hour when we had begun to read the seventy-second Psalm, that is, the beginning of the third book...suddenly word came to us that the most holy Lea had died. Right then and there I saw you turn so pale that assuredly there is little or no soul that does not escape in sadness on the shattering of the earthen vessel. You indeed wept, not because you were uncertain of what would happen to her in the afterlife, but because you had not had a chance to pay your last respects at the funeral. Finally, as we were still talking, we learned that her remains had already been taken to Ostia.[55]

The principal role that 'Marcella' plays in the *liber*, hinted at in the passage above, is that of the inquisitive student of Scripture who turns to Jerome whenever she has any questions that require expertise in the biblical languages.[56] In his replies, it is Jerome's linguistic and

---

[54] See *Ep.* 32.2: *Albinam, communem matrem, valere cupio ... eamque per te salutari obsecro et duplici pietatis officio focilari, quo in una atque eadem Christiana simul diligatur et mater.*

[55] *Ep.* 23.1: *cum hora ferme tertia hodiernae diei septuagesimum secundum psalmum, id est tertii libri principium, legere coepissemus ... repente nobis nuntiatum est sanctissimam Leam exisse de corpore. ibique ita te palluisse conspexi, ut vere aut pauca aut nulla sit anima, quae fracto vase testaceo non tristis erumpat. et tu quidem, non quod futuri incerta esses, dolebas, sed quo triste funeri obsequium non dedisses. denique in mediis fabulis rursum didicimus reliquias eius iam Ostia fuisse delatas.* On the difficult phrase '*ibique ... erumpat*', see Neil Adkin 'A Further Misunderstood Passage in Jerome's Eulogy of Lea (*Epist.*, 23.1.2)', *Eranos*, 101 (2003), 1–5.

[56] *Epp.* 25.1: *studiosissime postulasti, ut tibi universa nomina cum sua interpretatione dirigerem;* 26.1: *nuper, cum pariter essemus, non per epistulam ... sed praesens ipsa quaesisti;* 28.1: *nostram sententiam flagitaras;* 29.1: *postulasti, ut, quid sentirem, statim rescriberem;* 34.3: *illud quoque de eodem psalmo interrogare dignata es.* Cf. *Ep.* 59.1 to

text-critical know-how that always saves the day. In one letter, he playfully chides Marcella for making him earn his scholarly keep:

You are engaged in reading and you write nothing to me except what befuddles me and forces me to read the Bible. After posing a most challenging question yesterday, you now have asked me to write back immediately with my opinion. As if I occupied the Pharisees' seat of authority, such that whenever there is a quarrel about Hebrew words I am called upon as the judge and jury![57]

Almost one-third of the surviving Marcellan *liber*, as it is circumscribed in this chapter, consists of Jerome's highly technical explanations of various words or phrases from the Hebrew Old Testament (*Ep.* 25 on the ten names of God; *Ep.* 26 on the meaning of certain Hebrew words (e.g., 'alleluia' and 'amen') left untranslated in the Greek and Latin renderings of the Old Testament; *Ep.* 28 on the meaning of the word '*selah*'; *Ep.* 29 on the meaning of the words '*ephod bad*' and '*teraphim*'; *Ep.* 34 on two phrases in Psalm 127). The convergence of so many letters of this type would seem to suggest that one of Jerome's objectives with the *liber* was to use it, as he did his released exegetical letters to Damasus, as a platform for promoting *Hebraica veritas*. Indeed, in these letters he carefully cultivates an image as a scholar who lives and breathes Hebrew. In one letter, for instance, he makes the affected remark that, 'as you know, I have spent so much time reading the Hebrew language that I have become rusty in Latin'.[58]

In several other letters Jerome inculcates how essential it is to revert to the Hebrew text of the Bible to separate truth from the opinions offered by sincere but misguided interpreters. He says in the letter explaining the meaning of the word '*selah*':

Marcella: *magnis nos provocas quaestionibus et torpens otio ingenium, dum interrogas, doces; In Gal.* 1, prologue: *certe, cum Romae essem, numquam tam festina me vidit ut non de Scripturis aliquid interrogaret.*

[57] *Ep.* 29.1: *in tractatibus occuparis, nihil mihi scribis, nisi quod me torqueat et Scripturas legere conpellat. denique heri famosissima quaestione proposita postulasti, ut, quid sentirem, statim rescriberem; quasi vero pharisaeorum teneam cathedram, ut, quotienscumque de verbis Hebraicis iurgium est, ego arbiter et litis sequester exposcar.*

[58] *Ep.* 29.7: *Hebraici sermonis lectione detenti in Latina lingua rubiginem obduximus.*

I have drawn these meanings out of the deepest spring of the Hebrews. I have neither followed the rivulets of opinions nor been deterred by the multiplicity of false interpretations with which the entire world is filled, but rather I am eager to know and to teach things that are true.[59]

As we saw in the previous chapter, Jerome's methodology put him at loggerheads with great Latin exegetes of the past, such as Hilary, whose interpretations he thought fell short of the mark because they were not grounded in the Hebrew.[60] In one letter to Marcella he criticizes another prominent fourth-century Gallic exegete, Reticius of Autun, for being ignorant of Hebrew and for producing botched interpretations of certain Hebrew terms.[61] When Marcella asked to borrow his personal copy of Reticius' commentary on the Song of Songs Jerome refused to lend it to her because, while he praised his predecessor's eloquence,[62] he found more in the commentary to censure than to praise.[63]

The five letters to Marcella on Hebrew matters, along with his four letters to Damasus and one to Paula on the so-called alphabetical Psalms (*Ep.* 30), represent Jerome's earliest surviving experimentations with the epistolary medium as a vehicle for exegesis. He opens one of the Marcellan letters with the following programmatic statement:

The purpose of letter-writing is to communicate about one's personal affairs or everyday life and to bring it about that friends not together in person somehow become physically present with each other, while they relay

---

[59] *Ep.* 28.5: *haec nos de intimo Hebraeorum fonte libavimus non opinionum rivulos persequentes neque errorum, quibus totus mundus expletus est, varietate perterriti, sed cupientes et scire et docere, quae vera sunt.* Cf. *Epp.* 34.2: *ad Hebraeum recurrens*; 34.4: *restat, igitur, ut rursum ad fontem sermonis recurramus Hebraei.*

[60] See above, p. 55.

[61] For Reticius' episcopate and literary career, see Louis Duchesne, *Fastes épiscopaux de l'ancienne Gaule* (2 vols., Paris, 1894), ii. 174–7; Jean Berthollet, *L'évêché d'Autun* (Autun, 1947), 17–23. Jerome was aware only of his commentary on the Song of Songs and a 'great volume' against the Novatianists (*Vir. ill.* 82).

[62] *Ep.* 37.3: *est sermo quidem conpositus et Gallicano coturno fluens.* A decade earlier Jerome (*Ep.* 5.2) had praised Reticius' eloquence in this commentary: *Canticum Canticorum sublimi ore disseruit.*

[63] *Ep.* 37.3–4: *innumerabilia sunt, quae in illius mihi commentariis sordere visa sunt … frustra igitur a me eiusdem viri commentarios postulas, cum mihi in illis multo displiceant plura, quam placeant.*

requests or news. It is good for such a conversational feast to be seasoned from time to time with the salt of teaching (*doctrinae sale*) as well.[64]

Jerome begins by stating commonplaces of Latin epistolary theory since at least Cicero—namely, that epistolary communication is a *sermo absentium* and that the letter enables friends to keep up to date concerning the everyday happenings of each other's lives.[65] So far, so conventional—but then in the final clause he applies to an epistolary context the Pauline injunction that Christians' conversation be 'seasoned with salt',[66] reminding Marcella that they need not confine themselves to the mundane and trivial when they write to each other but that they should communicate about matters of the faith. Since St Paul, Christians had used the *epistula* for moral exhortation and theological exposition, among many other things.[67] Jerome evidently saw himself as making his own personalized modification to this longstanding epistolographic tradition. For, when he speaks of '*doctrina*' in the context of this letter to Marcella, he does not mean 'Christian teaching' in the general sense; he instead has in mind a specialized kind of Hebrew knowledge that no Latin biblical commentator before him possessed.

In effect, Jerome initially created a new species of the Latin exegetical *epistula* in order to accommodate his own interests in Hebrew philology. However, with this innovation came potential drawbacks. Because in Jerome's hands this kind of letter tended to dwell on extremely technical and often obscure text-critical *minutiae*, he was self-conscious about even the interested reader finding the subject matter dull or tedious, and the Ciceronian in him worried that the unadorned style would be instantly off-putting. In the midst of explaining three different problematic passages in the Old Testament

---

[64] *Ep.* 29.1: *epistolare officium est de re familiari aut de cotidiana conversatione aliquid scribere et quodammodo absentes inter se praesentes fieri, dum mutuo, quid aut velint aut gestum sit, nuntiant, licet interdum confabulationis tale convivium doctrinae quoque sale condiatur.*

[65] Klaus Thraede, *Grundzüge griechisch-römischer Brieftopik* (Munich, 1970), 27–47; Gustav Karlsson, *Idéologie et cérémonial dans l'épistolographie byzantine* (Uppsala, 1962), 40–5.

[66] Col. 4: 6 (Vulg.): *sermo vester semper sit in gratia, sale conditus.*

[67] Stanley Stowers, *Letter Writing in Greco–Roman Antiquity* (Philadelphia, 1986), 41–7; Thraede, *Grundzüge*, 187–91.

to Pope Damasus, Jerome gave an apology for his use of the 'plain style' in exegetical discourse:

I know that these things are burdensome for the reader, but when discussing Hebrew literature it is not fitting to look for the arguments of Aristotle. Likewise, one's stylistic stream should not be drawn from the river of Cicero's eloquence, nor should the ears be soothed by the declamation of the schools or by the rhetorical refinements of Quintilian. What is needed is a plain and somewhat informal style that does not give the impression of being the product of a long night's work, but that explicates the passage at hand, analyzes its meaning, makes obscure things clear and is not flowery in its word-arrangement. Let others be grandiloquent, let them receive praise as they wish, and let them balance their frothy words in swollen cheeks. As for me, it suffices to speak so that I may be understood and so that when I discuss the Scriptures I may imitate their simplicity.[68]

In addition to stylistic considerations there also was the ever-present anxiety, which Jerome voiced in more than one of his exegetical letters, about writing too much and thus violating one of the cardinal rules of letter-writing that a letter be brief and to the point.[69] These reservations notwithstanding, the 'letter' provided Jerome with a convenient literary venue, distinct from but complementary to his biblical commentaries, for communicating *in absentia* his expert knowledge of the Bible.[70]

In his various exegetical replies to Marcella Jerome sculpts her into his *alter ego*. So much so, in fact, that upon reading these letters one comes away with the feeling that Marcella was single-mindedly

[68] *Ep.* 36.14: *scio haec molesta esse lectori, sed de Hebraeis litteris disputantem non decet Aristotelis argumenta conquirere nec ex flumine Tulliano eloquentiae ducendus est rivulus nec aures Quintiliani flosculis et scolari declamatione mulcendae. pedestris et cotidianae similis et nullam lucubrationem redolens oratio necessaria est, quae rem explicet, sensum edisserat, obscura manifestet, non quae verborum conpositione frondescat. sint alii diserti, laudentur, ut volunt, et inflatis buccis spumantia verba trutinentur: mihi sufficit sic loqui, ut intellegar et ut de Scripturis disputans Scripturarum imiter simplicitatem.* See also *Epp.* 21.42; 29.1; *In Eph.* 1, prologue.

[69] e.g., *Epp.* 26.5: *vellem tibi aliquid et de diapsalmate scribere ... nisi et modum epistolici characteris excederem;* 55.1: *brevis epistula longas explanare non valet quaestiones;* 64.21: *ego iam mensuram epistulae excedere me intellego.* For epistolary *brevitas*, see Thraede, *Grundzüge*, 162–4; G. J. M. Bartelink, 'Een gemeenplaats uit de briefliteratuur bij een Christelijk auteur: Brevitas epistolaris bij Hieronymus', *Lampas*, 10 (1977), 61–5.

[70] See Chapter 6.

fascinated by the very same kinds of arcane textual issues that tickled his scholarly senses. We can only assume that she was genuinely interested in such things and that she eagerly availed herself of Jerome's expertise for as long as she had ready access to it. But was she interested only in the Old Testament, as the subject matter of Jerome's extant Roman replies to her implies? Probably not. In 395/6 she sent him a list of five exegetical questions, all of which dealt with problem passages from the *New* Testament.[71] Presumably, her interests were similarly well rounded a decade earlier. Why, then, might Jerome have included in the *Ad Marcellam epistularum liber* only replies to questions about the Old Testament? Perhaps he felt that they were his most polished exegetical letters to her. Perhaps he had another incentive. As I pointed out in the previous chapter, *Hebraica veritas* as a hermeneutical concept was far from being in vogue among westerners at this time.[72] By championing it, Jerome risked criticism and the appearance of being an ivory-tower pedant doing work that seemed out of touch with the practical spiritual needs of the wider Christian community. However, by putting forth Marcella, a respected figure in Roman ascetic circles, as a staunch Hebraist and patron of his Scriptural programme, Jerome could demonstrate that his expertise was not only relevant but also in demand among influential Christians in Rome.

If the five exegetical letters in the Marcellan collection stand as specimens of Jerome's microtextual biblical exegesis, then two other letters represent another major facet of his biblical scholarship: his work as a translator and textual critic. The first letter (*Ep.* 27) is a spirited defence of his revision of the Old Latin Gospels according to the Greek against 'weakly men' (*homunculos*) and 'two-legged asses' (*bipedes asellos*) who accused him of blasphemously altering the words of Scripture.[73] He probably wrote this letter in part as an exercise in catharsis, to vent his bitter disappointment at the ridicule to which his hard work had been subjected. However, perhaps the most immediate aim of the letter was to assure Marcella, one of the sponsors of the Roman phase of his scholarly career, that his edition was legitimate because it was built upon only the soundest of text-critical principles. Those who found fault with it did so because they

---

[71] See Jerome's reply, *Ep.* 59.   [72] See above, pp. 64–6.   [73] *Ep.* 27.1, 3.

were wilfully ignorant.[74] In other words, they had no right to criticize in the first place because they were incompetent. His revision of the Gospels, for all of the controversy it stirred up, was the jewel in the crown of Jerome's scholarly achievements during his Roman years. Because it was so integral to his reputation as a biblical authority, it seems natural that he would have inserted into the Marcellan collection a written defence of it.

Elsewhere in the *liber* Jerome spotlights his activities as a biblical translator and textual critic, but this time he sheds the *persona* of the choleric polemicist and idealizes himself as an indefatigable scholar toiling away in quiet seclusion in his library, like the subject of Albrecht Dürer's famous copperplate engraving 'St Jerome in His Study'.[75] He dashed off the following terse note to an impatient Marcella who had not heard from him lately and had dispatched a messenger to retrieve any letters that he might have had for her:

The reason for my writing such a short letter is twofold: the messenger was in a hurry and I am busy with another task and did not want to occupy myself with this side project, as it were. What business, you may ask, is so important and so urgent that the duty of chatting by letter is put on hold? ... Having now already carefully revised the Prophets, Solomon, the Psalter, and the books of Kings, I am presently working on Exodus, which the Hebrews call '*ele smoth*', and I am about to move on to Leviticus. You see, then, that no business must come before this task.[76]

The 'Marcella' who peeks at the reader from behind the curtain of Jerome's reply is a doting patron who waits with bated breath to receive a letter from her perpetually busy client. Twice in this passage,

---

[74] *Ep.* 27.1: *illi [rusticitatem] solam pro sanctitate habent piscatorum se discipulos adserentes, quasi idcirco iusti sint, si nihil scierint.*

[75] The image of a lone Jerome studiously working in his library was popular among Renaissance artists. See Herbert Friedmann, *A Bestiary for Saint Jerome: Animal Symbolism in European Religious Art* (Washington, DC, 1980), 29–47; Bernhard Ridderbos, *Saint and Symbol: Images of Saint Jerome in Early Italian Art* (Groningen, 1984), 15–62.

[76] *Ep.* 32.1: *ut tam parvam epistulam scriberem, causae duplicis fuit: quod et tabellarius festinabat et ego alio opere detentus hoc quasi parergio me occupare nolui. quaeras, quidnam illud sit tam grande, tam necessarium, quo epistolicae confabulationis munus exclusum sit ... nunc iam Prophetis, Salomone, Psalterio, Regnorumque libris examussim recensetis Exodum teneo, quem illi 'ele smoth' vocant, ad Leviticum transiturus. vides igitur, quod nullum officium huic operi praeponendum est.*

Jerome makes a show of ducking her invitation to engage in an epistolary conversation, thus emphasizing the exigency of his time-consuming revision of the Old Testament. In the course of snubbing Marcella's overtures, he makes himself out to be a superhumanly productive scholar. Holed away in his study, he refuses to be side-tracked from his project for any reason, even to trade letters with his distinguished friend. This is not the only place in his Roman correspondence in which he portrays himself as temporarily putting off a patron in favour of completing some Hebrew-related task. We saw in the last chapter how he postponed sending a reply to a few of Damasus' questions until he had finished copying some Jewish books.[77] The subliminal message conveyed in both cases is that Marcella and Damasus are the ones seeking him out, and not the other way around.

Heretics

In two other letters, Jerome offers Marcella guidance of a somewhat different kind. On one occasion she was discussing theology with a 'certain follower of Montanus' who, eager to win her as a convert to his sect, confronted her with Montanist proof-texts culled from the Gospel of John concerning Christ's promise to send the Paraclete following his ascension.[78] She seems to have been swayed by what she heard and she wrote to Jerome for his thoughts. He responded with a dismissively brief letter (*Ep.* 41) refuting the main tenets of Montanism.[79] According to him, it was an easy victory:

---

[77] See above, pp. 58–9.

[78] *Ep.* 41.1: *testimonia, quae de Iohannis evangelio congregata tibi quidam Montani sectator ingessit* ... For Montanist appropriations of this Gospel, see Ronald Heine, 'The Role of the Gospel of John in the Montanist Controversy', *SCent*, 6 (1987), 1–18; id., 'The Gospel of John and the Montanist Debate at Rome', *StudPatr*, 21 (1989), 95–100. The Montanist proselytizing of the Roman wealthy in this period is discussed by Harold Maier, 'The Topography of Heresy and Dissent in Late Fourth-century Rome', *Historia*, 44 (1995), 232–49; id., 'Religious Dissent, Heresy and Households in Late Antiquity', *VChr*, 49 (1995), 49–63.

[79] For Jerome's disapproval of Montanist theology, see Benoît Jeanjean, *Saint Jérôme et l'hérésie* (Paris, 1999), 224–33.

To expose the infidelity of the Montanists is to triumph over it. The compact style befitting a letter is not needed to knock down the absurdities they bring forward. You are well acquainted with the Scriptures, and, as I take it, you have written, not because you have been disturbed by their cavils, but only to learn my opinion about them.[80]

Jerome undoubtedly suspected Marcella of flirting with Montanist ideas[81]—in his view, women were particularly vulnerable to heresy[82]—but in his letter he refuses to give life to his suspicions by openly acknowledging her apparent leanings. He broaches this touchy subject in such a way as both to angle himself as a trustee of orthodox teaching and to preserve the doctrinal integrity of a student he claimed as his own. Marcella wrote not because she was at all persuaded by what she had heard (she knew the Bible too well to be deceived) but because she simply wanted to find out her teacher's opinion on the matter.

Marcella gave consideration to other sectarian teachings besides Montanist ones. She wanted to know Jerome's thoughts about Novatian's teaching that the unpardonable sin against the Holy Spirit (Matt. 12: 31–2) consisted in a Christian renouncing his faith under pain of torture. In his reply (*Ep.* 42), Jerome exposes the absurdity of this interpretation and dismisses the Novatianists with the same confidence with which he brushed aside the Montanists.[83] His opening statement sets a self-assured tone for the entire letter: 'The question which you have sent is brief and its answer clear.'[84] After presenting

[80] *Ep.* 41.4: *perfidiam eorum exposuisse superasse est. nec necesse est, ut singula deliramenta, quae proferunt, brevior epistulae sermo subvertat, cum et tu ipse Scripturas adprime tenens non tam ad eorum mota sis quaestiones, quam, quid sentirem, a me volueris sciscitari.*

[81] So Philip Rousseau, ' "Learned Women" and the Development of a Christian Culture in Late Antiquity', *SO*, 70 (1995), 140; Stefan Rebenich, *Jerome* (London and New York, 2002), 40.

[82] Patrick Laurence, 'L'implication des femmes dans l'hérésie: le jugement de saint Jérôme', *REAug*, 44 (1998), 241–67.

[83] For Jerome's criticism of Novatianist ideology, see Jeanjean, *Jérôme et l'hérésie*, 233–8.

[84] *Ep.* 42.1: *brevis quaestiuncula, quam misisti, et aperta responsio est.* Later in the letter (2) Jerome emphasizes that the biblical passage in question is sufficiently clear if only one reads it properly (the Novatianists do not, in his opinion): *tibi ipsa Scriptura atque contextus adtentius lecta poterunt demonstrare.*

his counter-argument to the Novatianist reading, Jerome brings an abrupt close to the letter:

> I ought to have discussed the matter more fully, but because I could not be inhospitable to friends who had stopped by and because by the same token it seemed supercilious not to answer you at once, I have compressed a wide-reaching subject into a few words and have sent you not so much a letter (*epistulam*) as an explanatory note (*commentariolum*).[85]

Jerome clearly is insinuating that the Novatianists are not worth his effort; he has more profitable ways to spend his time than dealing with them, such as entertaining houseguests. To add insult to injury, he even downgrades his *epistula* to a '*commentariolum*'.[86] This letter is not simply some passing attack on a long-dead third-century schismatic. Novatian's latter-day followers, like those of Montanus, maintained an active presence in Rome in the 380s.[87] Marcella's question about one of their central teachings may have been prompted by a personal encounter with a Novatianist and/or through a contemporary Novatianist tract, perhaps the same one to which Ambrose responded at length in his *De paenitentia* (2.20–8) some time between 384 and 394.

In *Ep.* 41 and *Ep.* 42, Jerome attacks two fringe theological factions that in late fourth-century Rome were canvassing the Christian aristocracy for converts. In another letter (*Ep.* 40), he takes aim at a different type of opponent: legacy-hunters within the Roman clerical establishment. This letter is a biting satire about the priest 'Onasus of Segesta'. 'Onasus' almost certainly was not his real name.[88] Jean-Georges Préaux was probably right to suggest that this nickname evokes the '*homo nobilissimus*' Onasus of Segesta mentioned in

---

[85] *Ep.* 42.3: *fuerat quidem prolixius disserendum, sed quoniam et amicis, qui ad nostrum hospitiolum convenerunt, praesentiam nostram negare non possumus et tibi non statim respondere admodum visum est adrogantis, latam disputationem brevi sermone conprehendimus, ut non tam epistulam quam commentariolum dictaremus.*

[86] On '*commentariolum*' for '*epistula*', see Barbara Conring, *Hieronymus als Briefschreiber. Ein Beitrag zur spätantiken Epistolographie* (Tübingen, 2001), 101, 103–4.

[87] Antonio Ferrua, *Epigrammata Damasiana* (Rome, 1942), 171–2; Maier, 'Topography', 234 n. 10.

[88] *Pace* Giuseppe Nenci, 'Onasus Segestanus in Girolamo, *Ep.* 40', *RFIC*, 123 (1995), 90–4.

Cicero's Verrine orations.[89] If this is correct, then Jerome presumably was making an ironic allusion to the privileged position enjoyed by his own ignoble Onasus.[90] Onasus criticized *Ep.* 22,[91] notably the part in which Jerome warns Eustochium to be on guard against those 'who seek the priesthood and the diaconate in order to see women more freely'[92] and who 'have devoted the whole of their energies and life to the single object of knowing the names, houses, and habits of matrons'.[93] In this same section of *Ep.* 22, Jerome draws an arresting caricature of these priests as men-about-town decked out in expensive jewellery. Onasus took exception to this characterization, according to Jerome, because he saw himself in the mirror: 'On whatever vice my sharp-pointed pen is brandished, you whine that you are the one meant.'[94]

SEALING A SPIRITUAL AND SCHOLARLY LEGACY

Jerome's sixteen Roman letters to Marcella were written over the course of two years: ten in 384 (*Epp.* 23–9, 32, 38, 40); one in 384/5 (*Ep.* 34); and the remaining five in the winter and spring of 385

[89] *Verr.* 5.45.120: *Onasum Segestanum, hominem nobilem... vir primarius, homo nobilissimus.*

[90] Préaux, 'Procédés d'invention d'un sobriquet par saint Jérôme', *Latomus*, 17 (1958), 659–64. The pseudonym 'Onasus' was convenient for another reason. Because it bears a striking resemblance to the word '*nasus*' ('nose'), it afforded Jerome an opportunity to make a satiric pun about the priest's nose (*Ep.* 40.2: *nasum fetentem; truncos nares*). See Jérôme Labourt, *Jérôme: Lettres* (8 vols., Paris, 1949–63), ii. 196; David Wiesen, *Saint Jerome as a Satirist* (Ithaca, NY, 1964), 204; Rebenich, *Jerome*, 82; but cf. Neil Adkin, 'Whose Nose and Whose Knees? Two Notes on St Jerome', *Orpheus*, NS 24 (2003), 1–3.

[91] Cf. the phraseological echoes at *Ep.* 22.27 (*noctuas et bubones*) and at *Ep.* 40.2 (*de noctua, de bubone*).

[92] *Ep.* 22.28: *qui ideo ad presbyterium et diaconatum ambiunt, ut mulieres licentius videant.*

[93] *Ep.* 22.28: *in hoc omne studium vitamque posuerunt, ut matronarum nomina, domos moresque cognoscant.* Cf. *Ep.* 22.16, for Jerome's criticism of priests taking money for visiting the homes of well-to-do women.

[94] *Ep.* 40.2: *in quodcumque vitium stili mei mucro contorquetur, te clamitas designari.* This was Jerome's classic defence of his satiric technique: see Cain, 'Jerome's *Epistula* 117 on the *Subintroductae*: Satire, Apology, and Ascetic Propaganda in Gaul', *Augustinianum*, 49 (2009), forthcoming.

(*Epp.* 37, 41–4).[95] If, indeed, they all belonged to the *liber*, then we are able to establish the spring of 385 as the *terminus post quem* for its date of compilation (and 393—the dating of Jerome's auto-bibliography, as the *terminus ante quem*). Let us adopt the working hypothesis that in the spring or early summer of 385, when it had become abundantly clear to him that his days in Rome were numbered, or perhaps soon after permanently settling in Bethlehem in the spring of 386, Jerome sorted through what must have been a considerable number of letters he had written to Marcella at Rome.[96] Out of this stockpile he selected some representative correspondence that would come to constitute, in probably edited form,[97] the *Ad Marcellam epistularum liber*. I submit that he released this compilation in either of two scenarios mentioned above as a creative means to summarize and to defend the legacy of ascetic teaching and biblical scholarship he had forged for himself in Rome. We have seen the great lengths to which Jerome goes in these collected letters to stake his proprietary claim 'in print' on a remarkable group of aristocratic Christian women who, to hear him tell it, were the most recognizable faces of the female monastic movement in the late fourth-century west. By emphasizing their spiritual and intellectual dependence upon him, he presumably hoped to bring a sense of legitimacy to his ascetic and Scriptural programmes. Here was plain evidence that, despite whatever criticism he faced—and the criticism was deafening—he had a nucleus of faithful followers who had unwavering confidence in him.

There is another likely reason why Jerome felt compelled to brand the women of the 'Aventine circle' as *his* disciples exclusively. He knew well that as soon as he left Rome rival spiritual directors and perhaps also aspiring biblical scholars—or, worse still, heretical sectarians— would try to ingratiate themselves with these women. As their (presumed) mentor he must have cringed at the thought of someone else taking his place. Economic considerations undoubtedly factored

---

[95] I follow the chronology adopted by Pierre Lardet, *L'Apologie de Jérôme contre Rufin: un commentaire* (Leiden, 1993), 491.

[96] The hypothesis presented here necessarily anticipates the discussion in Chapter 4 of Jerome's abrupt departure from Rome in August of 385.

[97] As with the surviving letters of the *Epistularum ad diversos liber*, there is no way ultimately of knowing to what extent Jerome may have touched up his archival copies as he prepared them for publication.

into the equation as well. Jerome had depended on them for material support in the previous two years and he would continue to
depend on them after leaving for the east to be his literary agents
in Rome.[98] New clients posed an obvious threat to this continued
patronage. It is apparent from a letter he wrote from Bethlehem
to his Roman friend Domnio in the middle 390s that Jerome was
uneasily alert to the possibility of competitors compromising his
relationship with these women. In it he attacks a certain unnamed
monk, who some scholars suspect was none other than Pelagius,[99] for
giving private Scripture tutorials to widows and virgins in Rome.[100]
Of all the women with whom he associated in Rome, Marcella was
a particularly attractive prospective patron owing to her extraordinary wealth and wide-reaching social connections. During Jerome's
time with her, she was wooed by everyone from fringe theological
sectarians to legacy-hunting priests. There is every indication that
this trend continued after his departure. We know, for instance, that
at some point his arch-rival Pelagius tried to recruit Marcella as
a theological partisan by sending her a flattering letter of spiritual
exhortation.[101]

While Jerome was still in Rome he was at least around to fend
off rivals and promptly to recall his *discipulae* to their senses with
oral or written admonitions. However, it would be a different story

---

[98] Pierre Nautin, 'L'activité littéraire de Jérôme de 387 à 392', *RThPh*, 115
(1983), 249–51; Stefan Rebenich, *Hieronymus und sein Kreis: Prosopographische und
sozialgeschichtliche Untersuchungen* (Stuttgart, 1992), 197.

[99] e.g., Georges de Plinval, *Pélage: ses écrits, sa vie et sa réforme* (Lausanne, 1943),
50–4; John Ferguson, *Pelagius: A Historical and Theological Study* (Cambridge, 1956),
44–5, 77–8; Otto Wermelinger, *Röm und Pelagius: die theologische Position der römischen Bischöfe im pelagianischen Streit in den Jahren 411–432* (Stuttgart, 1975), 46–
50; Bryn Rees, *Pelagius: A Reluctant Heretic* (Suffolk, 1988), 4–5. But cf. Yves-Marie
Duval, 'Pélage est-il le censeur inconnu de l'*Adversus Iovinianum* à Rome en 393?
ou: du "portrait–robot" de l'hérétique chez s. Jérôme', *RHE*, 75 (1980), 525–57, for
the argument that Jerome was drawing not a true-to-life portrait of Pelagius but an
identikit sketch of the stereotypical heretic.

[100] *Ep.* 50.3: *audio praeterea eum libenter virginum et viduarum cellulas circumire et
adducto supercilio de sacris inter eas litteris philosophari.*

[101] *Ep. ad Marc.* has sometimes been attributed to either Jerome or Paulinus of
Nola, hence its appearance in the CSEL volume of Paulinus' letters (29: 429–36). However, the attribution to Pelagius is now generally accepted. See Plinval, 'Recherches sur
l'œuvre littéraire de Pélage', *RPh*, 8 (1934), 33, 41; id., *Pélage*, 172; Ferguson, *Pelagius*,
186; Letsch-Brunner, *Marcella*, 225–6.

altogether once he was in faraway Bethlehem, geographically cut off
by hundreds of miles of open sea from his former base of operations.
Of course, he would still be able to maintain contact with Marcella
and other Roman contacts through correspondence.[102] However,
these letters would have to be few and far between, for seasonal
winds and inclement weather conditions restricted sea travel and
therefore inhibited the carriage of correspondence between Italy and
Palestine except during the late spring and the summer months.[103]
Thus, once Jerome left he would, for all intents and purposes, be out
of the picture. Nevertheless, through the *Ad Marcellam epistularum
liber* he could maintain an abiding textualized presence in Rome,
one that was not contingent upon the caprice of the maritime postal
system. This collection would be his constant, unchanging 'voice'
in absentia, and could stand in his place just as assuredly as the
epistula, in the view of the ancients, projected the virtual presence
of its physically absent author.[104] It was Jerome's stern warning to
would-be poachers that Marcella and her circle were already spoken
for by an eminently qualified ascetic and Scriptural expert. Jerome
was amply prepared to pull out all the polemical stops to watch out
for the best spiritual interests of his flock, even if that meant agitat-
ing opponents by publicly reducing them to humiliating caricatures.
And, lest Marcella should forget where her true loyalties lay, here she
would have a collection of correspondence proudly bearing her name
to serve as a tangible reminder of her shared personal history with her
teacher.

Marcella was a self-confident, strong-willed, and fiercely indepen-
dent woman who defied the norms of contemporary aristocratic
society, first by going against her mother's wishes that she remarry
and later by taking the initiative as the leader of a group of devout
women ascetics. She was highly intelligent, widely read in Christian

[102] i.e., the 'Aventine circle', that is, minus Paula and Eustochium, who as far as we
know were the only members of this entourage to follow Jerome to Palestine.
[103] See Lionel Casson, *Ships and Seamanship in the Ancient World* (Princeton, NJ,
1971), 270–3; Jean-Marie André and Marie-Françoise Baslez, *Voyager dans l'antiquité*
(Paris, 1993), 483–8. See also Jean Rougé, 'La Navigation hivernale sous l'empire
romain', *REA*, 54 (1952), 316–25.
[104] Giles Constable, *Letters and Letter Collections* (Turnhout, 1976), 13–14; Antonio
Garzya, *Il mandarino e il quotidiano. Saggi sulla letteratura tardoantica e bizantina*
(Naples, 1983), 132–3.

literature, and theologically open-minded, so much so in fact that
she evidently entertained heterodox ideas, much to Jerome's chagrin.
Jerome's literary compartmentalization of her in the *Ad Marcellam
epistularum liber* was a bold move to assert his intellectual and spiritual proprietorship over a woman who in real life had her own mind
and was anything but a meek and submissive devotee. And this was
while she was alive. When Marcella died, Jerome made sure that
posterity would remember her for all time—but wholly on his own
terms, as his devoted protégée. We see him doing this in the epitaph
he wrote on her (*Ep.* 127) in 412. Jerome dedicated this epistolary
vita to Marcella's close friend and fellow Roman ascetic, Principia,
but there are indications that he fully intended it eventually to reach
an audience that extended well beyond his inner circle in Rome.[105]
The Hieronymized 'Marcella' sketched here predictably reprises her
role, so often rehearsed in the *liber*, as his beloved Scriptural student.
In Rome

she never came to me without asking some question about Scripture...whatever in me had been attained by long study and had become
second nature by constant meditation, this she tasted, this she learned and
made her own, with the result that, after my departure, if a dispute arose
about some passage of Scripture, people would go to her to settle it.[106]

Like any good apprentice, Marcella learned the craft from her teacher
so thoroughly that she was able to become his surrogate. Nevertheless,
Jerome does not allow her to appear *too* emancipated, and insists
on her complete indebtedness to him: 'Whenever she was asked a
question, she would respond in such a way as to give her opinion
not as being her own but as being mine or someone else's so that
she could admit that she was still a student in respect to what she
taught.'[107] Jerome continues:

[105] See, e.g., *Ep.* 127.10, where Jerome pre-empts objections by hostile readers: *ne
legenti fastidium faciat odiosa replicatio et videar apud malivolos sub occasione laudis
alterius stomachum meum digerere.*

[106] *Ep.* 127.7: *numquam convenit, quin de Scripturis aliquid interrogaret... quicquid
in nobis longo fuit studio congregatum et meditatione diuturna quasi in naturam versum,
hoc illa libavit, hoc didicit atque possedit, ita ut post profectionem nostram, si aliquo
testimonio Scripturarum esset oborta contentio, ad illam iudicem pergeretur.*

[107] *Ep.* 127.7: *sic interrogata respondebat, ut etiam sua non sua diceret, sed vel mea
vel cuiuslibet alterius, ut et in ipso, quod docebat, se discipulam fateretur.*

I heard that you immediately took my place and attached yourself to her as a companion and that you never strayed from her side by more than a finger's breadth (as the saying goes). You both occupied the same house, the same room, and one bed, with the result that it became known to all in the famous city that you had found a mother in her and she a daughter in you. An estate outside the city limits, a farm chosen for its isolation, served as your monastery. You lived together for such a long time that, thanks to your example and the upright conduct of many women, I rejoiced that Rome had turned into Jerusalem. Monasteries for virgins were so numerous and the crowd of monks was so great that, with all those servants of God there, what beforehand had been something to be ashamed of later became a badge of honour.[108]

The reader is left to infer that during Jerome's time in Rome he was never separated from Marcella 'by more than a finger's breadth' and that his departure left an aching void in her life that she was forced to fill by taking Principia as her new companion. Jerome goes on to credit Marcella with almost single-handedly transforming Rome from a pagan into a Christian monastic capital. He claims elsewhere in the epitaph that the sun of Roman female monasticism rose and set with her.[109] It is, of course, patently untrue that she was the first woman of rank in Rome to adopt the monastic life. We know, for instance, that a community of virgins dedicated to the teenage martyr St Agnes was present there already in the early decades of the fourth century.[110] Because he had his finger on the pulse of Roman Christian

---

[108] *Ep.* 127.8: *in nostrum locum statim audivimus te illius adhaesisse consortio et numquam ab illa ne transversum quidem unguis, ut dicitur, recessisse eadem domo, eodem cubiculo, uno usam cubili, ut omnibus in urbe clarissima notum fieret et te matrem et illam filiam repperisse. suburbanus ager vobis pro monasterio fuit et rus electum propter solitudinem. multoque ita vixistis tempore, ut imitatione vestri et conversatione multarum gauderemus Romam factam Hierosolymam. crebra virginum monasteria, monachorum innumerabilis multitudo, ut pro frequentia servientium deo, quod prius ignominiae fuerat, esset postea gloriae.*

[109] *Ep.* 127.5: *nulla eo tempore nobilium feminarum noverat Romae propositum monachorum.*

[110] This was certainly not the only community of its kind. See P. Schmitz, 'La Première communauté de vierges à Rome', *RBén*, 38 (1926), 189–95; René Metz, *La Consécration des vierges dans l'église romaine* (Paris, 1954), 77–8; Gian Domenico Gordini, 'Forme di vita ascetica a Roma nel IV secolo', *ScrTh*, 1 (1953), 9–54; id., 'Origine e sviluppo del monachesimo a Roma', *Gregorianum*, 37 (1956), 220–60; Rudolf Lorenz, 'Die Anfänge des abendländischen Mönchtums im 4. Jahrhundert', *ZKG*, 77 (1966), 1–61.

spirituality, Jerome must have been aware of this and similar communities; furthermore, he certainly would have known that in the middle 350s, a few years before Marcella made her profession, Marcellina, the older sister of his rival Ambrose, had taken the virgin's veil in a ceremony at St Peter's Basilica presided over by Pope Liberius.[111] Even though Jerome knew that Marcella was not the first of her kind, he gave pride of place to her, ignoring earlier and contemporaneous examples of Roman religious women, so as to tout *his* disciple as the one who spearheaded the paradigm-shifting 'asceticization' of the aristocracy in Rome. He cast her in a leading role, and in doing so he was in turn setting up himself, her spiritual guide and the official documenter of her *acta*, as the producer, director, and choreographer of this unfolding drama.[112]

Jerome had another possible motive for dwelling on Marcella's monastic leadership role. In the early spring of 386, soon after he and Paula had settled in at Bethlehem, he sent Marcella a prolix letter (*Ep.* 46) in the names of Paula and Eustochium inviting her to leave Rome and to join them in their blossoming monastic enterprise. Marcella declined the invitation, Nautin argued, due to some falling out that supposedly had occurred between her and Jerome.[113] As indirect evidence for this rift, he cited the dearth of surviving correspondence between them between 385 and 394. However, aside from *Ep.* 46, only one letter by Jerome has survived from his first seven years in Bethlehem (*Ep.* 27* to Aurelius of Carthage). By Nautin's

---

[111] Ambrose, *Virg.* 3.1; Paulinus of Milan, *V. Ambr.* 4. Jerome would presumably have known this fact about Marcellina from word of mouth, not to mention also from Ambrose's *De virginibus*, which he had read in Rome and accessed when composing *Ep.* 22; for his knowledge of this treatise, see Yves-Marie Duval, 'L'originalité du *De virginibus* dans le mouvement ascétique occidental: Ambroise, Cyprien, Athanase', in id. (ed.), *Ambroise de Milan: XVIᵉ centeniare de son élection épiscopale* (Paris, 1974), 64–6.

[112] This is not the only time Jerome situated himself and his friends at the centre of the action. For instance, he made Eustochium the '*prima virgo nobilis*' at Rome (*Ep.* 22.15) and Pammachius the first senator to become a monk (*Ep.* 66.13). This is true also of the heroes of his hagiographic romances: in the *Vita Pauli*, Paul bests Antony to become the true though intentionally secret founder of the eremitical life, while in the *Vita Hilarionis* Hilarion is celebrated as the first monk of Palestine. On Paul and Antony, see now Stefan Rebenich, 'Inventing an Ascetic Hero: Jerome's *Life of Paul the First Hermit*', in Cain and Lössl, *Jerome of Stridon*, Chap. 1.

[113] Pierre Nautin, 'La Liste des œuvres de Jérôme dans le *De viris inlustribus*', *Orpheus*, NS 5 (1984), 330–2.

logic, we could infer from this silence that Jerome was not writing
letters to anyone! Nautin was struck also by the fact that during his
first decade in Palestine Jerome did not dedicate any of his biblical
commentaries to Marcella; the vast majority were addressed jointly
to Paula and Eustochium. This observation, however, is less evidence
of an estrangement between Marcella and Jerome than it is a positive
acknowledgement of Paula's role as the primary patron of his work
during this period.[114] As was noted above, in 395/6 Marcella asked
Jerome to explain five New Testament passages.[115] But what about the
intervening years? There is evidence to suggest that she remained in
regular contact with Jerome and continued to support his scholarship
immediately after he left Rome. In the prologue to the second book of
his commentary on Ephesians (386) Jerome speaks of Marcella making requests '*per epistulas*' for his exegesis on this Pauline book,[116]
and in the prologue to the third book he acknowledges her prayerful
(and probably financial) support.[117] Moreover, there are no plausible
grounds on which to think that Marcella's failure to relocate to the
Holy Land had anything to do with an alleged falling out with Jerome.

The real reason why Marcella balked at coming to the Holy Land
probably had to do with her not sharing Jerome's view that there
was anything intrinsically special about living there as opposed to
her native Italy. It is telling that he spends a substantial portion
of *Ep.* 46 (4–8) debunking certain contemporary stereotypes that
the Holy Land, despite having been the hallowed territory of God's
people in ages past, has been under a divine curse ever since the
crucifixion of Christ. He directly addresses Marcella several times[118]
and pre-emptively answers each of her anticipated objections to his
arguments—something he would not have bothered to do if he did

---

[114] It should be noted as an aside that Jerome dedicated his commentary on Daniel
(407) to Pammachius and Marcella: see *In Dan.*, prologue.

[115] See above, p. 84.

[116] *In Eph.* 2, prologue: *secundum orationibus vestris, o Paula et Eustochium, ad
Ephesios aggredimur librum: nova quoque Romam munuscula transmissuri. non quod
haec dignetur legere doctorum senatus, et bibliothecis veterum ascribere: sed quod sancta
Marcella idipsum fieri per epistulas flagitet.*

[117] *In Eph.* 3, prologue: *nunc ergo quoniam orationum vestrarum et sanctae Marcellae fultus auxilio . . . in eandem epistulam dicto librum.*

[118] e.g., 4: *te cupientem in verba prorumpere ipsi litterarum apices sentiunt et venientem contra charta intellegit quaestionem*; 6: *sed dicis*; 7: *ne putares.*

not think that she needed convincing.[119] The idea of picking up and moving to distant Palestine rather than simply going there on pilgrimage for a few weeks or months was not something that the vast majority of late fourth-century Christian aristocrats found appealing; the Melanias and the Paulas were definitely exceptions to the rule. It is additionally possible that Marcella's decision to stay in Italy was influenced by a desire to keep a safe distance from Jerome, at least for the time being, due to the bad publicity that had attended his ejection from Rome.[120] Marcella's failure to come to dwell in the Holy Land, or even to visit on pilgrimage, was nevertheless an embarrassing problem that confronted Jerome as he set out to pen her *vita*. For in the back of readers' minds there might always be that nagging question about why his most precocious Roman disciple had not accompanied her teacher on this potentially path-breaking monastic mission. Did she think that it was a lost cause, a pointless endeavour? Jerome presumably wanted to forestall any suspicions on the part of his readers, and so he danced around the problem and made it sound as if Marcella had stayed intentionally so that she could continue the urban ascetic campaigning that he had begun.[121]

As soon as the historical Marcella was refracted by the lens of Jerome's epistolary narrative, whether in *Ep.* 127 or in the *Ad Marcellam epistularum liber*, she became an iconic symbol for his

[119] For Jerome's attitude toward the practice of Holy Land pilgrimage, see Pierre Maraval, 'Saint Jérôme et le pèlerinage aux lieux saints de Palestine', in Yves-Marie Duval (ed.), *Jérôme entre l'Occident et l'Orient, XVIe centenaire du départ de saint Jérôme de Rome et de son installation à Bethléem. Actes du colloque de Chantilly, Sept. 1986* (Paris, 1988), 346–8; id., 'L'attitude des Pères du IVe siècle devant les lieux saints et les pèlerinages', *Irénikon*, 65 (1992), 15–21; Hillel Newman, 'Between Jerusalem and Bethlehem: Jerome and the Holy Places of Palestine', in Alberdina Houtman, Marcel Poorthuis, and Joshua Schwartz (eds.), *Sanctity of Time and Space in Tradition and Modernity* (Leiden, 1998), 215–27; Brouria Bitton-Ashkelony, *Encountering the Sacred: The Debate on Christian Pilgrimage in Late Antiquity* (Berkeley, Calif., 2005), 65–105.

[120] See Chapter 4.

[121] Later in the epitaph (9–11) he emphasizes how she was his theological ambassador in Rome as well. It was she, he claims (10), who was solely responsible for securing Pope Anastasius' condemnation of Rufinus and his Origenism (*huius tam gloriosae victoriae origo Marcella est*). See Kelly, *Jerome*, 246–9; Elizabeth Clark, *The Origenist Controversy: The Cultural Construction of an Early Christian Debate* (Princeton, NJ, 1992), 29; Patrick Laurence, 'Marcella, Jérôme et Origène', *REAug*, 42 (1996), 267–93.

ascetic, Scriptural, and theological special interests.[122] Consequently, Jerome insured that her legacy would be noteworthy only at the points where it intersected with the arc of his own legacy.[123] It is precisely the help of this 'Marcella' that he would so desperately need as he stared down the infamy of his final days in Rome, to which we now turn.

---

[122] Jerome did much the same thing for Paula and Fabiola in his epitaphs on them. On Paula, see Cain, 'Jerome's *Epitaphium Paulae*: Hagiography, Pilgrimage, and the Cult of Saint Paula', *JECS*, 18 (2010), forthcoming. On Fabiola, see below, pp. 171–8.

[123] This point becomes that much the more significant when we consider that Marcella is not attested outside Jerome's writings.

4

Expulsion from Rome

The years Jerome spent in Rome from 382 to 385 were marked by great personal and professional successes as well as by equally great disappointments and frustrated ambitions. On the one hand, he continued to advance in his two-pronged vocation as a teacher of asceticism and as a biblical scholar and in the process he forged strategic connections with a pope and very distinguished Christian women. On the other hand, his labours and accomplishments, with whatever degree of approbation they were met by those within his immediate circle, were regarded with suspicion and even outrage by the greater Christian community in Rome. As we have seen, he aroused opposition on the scholarly front by producing a revision of the Gospels that many thought undermined the authority of the universally accepted Old Latin Bible.[1] What is more, his determination to promote Origen's work in Latin translation raised eyebrows in a city where the Alexandrian was still blacklisted in some quarters for heterodoxy.[2] Jerome's extreme ascetic teaching, not to mention the aggressive rhetoric in which he framed it, further alienated mainstream Christians from his cause. In particular, Ambrosiaster and other clerical moderates, who were in the clear majority during this period in Rome,[3] and also their ideological counterparts among the

---

[1] See above, pp. 50–2.

[2] For Origen's hostile reception in late fourth-century Rome, see J. N. D. Kelly, *Jerome. His Life, Writings, and Controversies* (London, 1975), 229; Hervé Inglebert, *Les Romains chrétiens face à l'histoire de Rome* (Paris, 1996), 206; Patrick Laurence, 'Marcella, Jérôme et Origène', *REAug*, 42 (1996), 278–9.

[3] Charles Pietri, *Roma christiana: recherches sur l'Église de Rome, son organisation, sa politique, son idéologie de Miltiade à Sixte III (311–440)* (2 vols., Paris, 1976), i. 684–721; id., 'Le Mariage chrétien à Rome', in Jean Delumeau (ed.), *Histoire vécue du peuple chrétien* (Toulouse, 1979), 105–31.

laity who happened to be *au courant* on doctrinal debates, were put off by his debasement of marriage and excessive praise of virginity, as sounded out in his two principal Roman ascetic writings, *De Mariae virginitate perpetua adversus Helvidium* and the *Libellus de virginitate servanda* to Eustochium (*Ep.* 22).[4]

THEOLOGICAL CONTROVERSY

In early 383, the Roman priest(?) Helvidius took up his pen against a certain Carterius who had written a tract advocating the superiority of the virginal life to the married state and had cited Mary's perpetual virginity as proof thereof.[5] Helvidius, representing the moderate wing of Roman Christianity, countered that virginity and marriage were on equal footing in the eyes of God and that Mary, though she had been a virgin prior to giving birth to Jesus, afterwards lived a normal married life and gave birth to more children.[6] Hence, she was a role model for married Christians, not just celibate ones. Later in 383, Jerome wrote *De Mariae virginitate perpetua adversus Helvidium* in which he refuted each of Helvidius' points and argued that Mary had been ever-virgin and exemplified the way of life that was most pleasing to God.[7] At the beginning of the tract he invokes the Father, Son, and Holy Spirit[8] and claims that he initially did not plan to

[4] Ambrosiaster was, by contrast with Jerome, a more balanced Christian voice when it came to questions of marital and sexual ethics. He seems to have taken issue with Jerome's denigration of marriage and in fact his *quaestio* on original sin may have been a response to the proliferation of Jerome's ascetic ideas in Rome in the 380s. See David Hunter, 'On the Sin of Adam and Eve: A Little-known Defence of Marriage and Childbearing by Ambrosiaster', *HThR*, 82 (1989), 283–99. See also id., *Marriage, Celibacy, and Heresy in Ancient Christianity: The Jovinianist Controversy* (Oxford, 2007), Chapter 5.

[5] On Mary's place in the fourth-century debate about the relative merits of marriage and virginity, see Hunter, 'Helvidius, Jovinian, and the Virginity of Mary in Late fourth–century Rome', *JECS*, 1 (1993), 47–71.

[6] Helvidius' tract is lost, but his views have been reconstructed from Jerome's counter-arguments: see G. Joussard, 'La Personnalité d'Helvidius', in *Mélanges J. Saunier* (Lyons, 1944), 139–56.

[7] Giancarlo Rocca, *L'Adversus Helvidium di san Girolamo nel contesto della letteratura ascetico-mariana del secolo IV* (Berne, 1998).

[8] *Adv. Helv.* 2: *sanctus mihi invocandus est Spiritus…invocandus est Dominus Iesus…ipse quoque Deus pater est imprecandus.*

write at all, lest by the act of writing he should admit that Helvidius, whom incidentally he had never met in person,[9] was actually worth the effort to refute. But Jerome finally gave in 'because of the scandal caused to the brothers who were disturbed by his madness'.[10] Thus, he presents himself as being the appointed spokesman for what he implies (by the numerically ambiguous term *fratres*) to be a silent majority.

In the spring of the following year (384) Jerome released his *Libellus de virginitate servanda* (*Ep.* 22), and with this writing he endeavoured once more to establish himself as an authoritative voice in the theatre of late fourth-century ascetic debate.[11] Of all the writings on spirituality he would produce throughout his long career this was the one of which he was proudest—if we are to judge, that is, by how often he mentioned it in his later writings and recommended it to chaste widows and virgins as essential reading.[12] He wrote this *épître-traité* ostensibly as a guide for Paula's teenage daughter Eustochium (who had been consecrated a virgin a year or two before meeting Jerome) on how to preserve her virginity. But Eustochium was only the incidental addressee;[13] *Ep.* 22 was an open letter of instruction to all Christian virgins from aristocratic families. Nevertheless, the fact remains that Eustochium was the disciple on whom Jerome chose publicly to pin his controversial ascetic teachings. She was living proof, as was her sister Blesilla (for a while, anyway), whom he singled out by name in *Ep.* 22.15 for her chaste widowhood, that there were well-bred Roman Christians who were willing to stake their eternal salvation on his counsel.

---

[9] *Dial. adv. Pelag.*, prologue 2: *quem omnino in carne non vidi.*

[10] *Adv. Helv.* 1: *ob scandalum fratrum, qui ad eius rabiem movebantur.*

[11] For a thoroughgoing commentary of this remarkable letter, see Neil Adkin, *Jerome on Virginity. A Commentary on the Libellus de virginitate servanda (Letter 22)* (Cambridge, 2003).

[12] E.g., *Epp.* 31.2; 49.18; 52.17; 123.17; 130.19; *Vir. ill.* 135; *Adv. Iov.* 1.13; *Apol. c. Ruf.* 1.30. Within a decade of its release Jerome's friend Sophronius translated it into Greek (*Vir. ill.* 134), though the precise extent of its influence in the east is not known. In its Latin version it circulated widely in the west and had a profound impact on the development of female monasticism: see Adalbert de Vogüé, *Histoire littéraire du mouvement monastique dans l'antiquité* (6 vols., Paris, 1991–2003), i. 325.

[13] Her name is dropped only twice in the body of this very lengthy tract (*Ep.* 22.2, 26).

Almost immediately following its release, *Ep.* 22 became something of a sensation in Christian circles at Rome, though not quite in the way Jerome had hoped. His insinuation that marriage was a necessary evil reserved for second-class spiritual citizens (e.g., at 2, 15, 19) incensed Christians who did not subscribe to his ideology. Equally offensive were elitist comments such as his advice to Eustochium that she learn a 'holy arrogance' and realize that she was 'better' than other Christians.[14] In later years, Jerome acknowledged that a great many lay and clerical Christians had been repulsed by his satirizing of their 'worldly' lifestyles.[15] Around 400, Rufinus scolded him for the inflammatory tone of *Ep.* 22 and reported the fascinating detail that pagans had applauded Jerome for airing the dirty laundry of Roman Christianity for all to see—and that they had made a cottage industry out of copying the treatise.[16]

THE GATHERING STORM: BLESILLA'S DEATH

Plagued as it was by constant personal and professional squabbles, Jerome's life in Rome began finally to unravel in the autumn of 384, when he experienced the most perilous public relations crisis of his career to date. Some time between the middle of September and late October, within four months of her conversion to a life of self-renunciation, Paula's oldest daughter Blesilla died unexpectedly, at the age of twenty,[17] apparently from carrying her fasting regimen to an unhealthy extreme.[18] At the funeral, the distraught mother

[14] *Ep.* 22.16: *disce in hac parte superbiam sanctam, scito te illis esse meliorem.*

[15] *Epp.* 52.17; 117.1; 130.19. See Patrick Laurence, 'L'épître 22 de Jérôme et son temps', in Léon Nadjo and Élisabeth Gavoille (eds.), *Epistulae antiquae*, i. *Actes du Ier colloque 'Le genre épistolaire antique et ses prolongements'* (Université François-Rabelais, Tours, 18–19 Sept. 1998) (Louvain–Paris, 2000), 63–83; Andrew Cain, 'Jerome's *Epistula* 117 on the *Subintroductae*: Satire, Apology, and Ascetic Propaganda in Gaul', *Augustinianum*, 49 (2009), forthcoming.

[16] *Apol. c. Hier.* 2.5, 43.

[17] Pierre Nautin, 'L'activité littéraire de Jérôme de 387 à 392', *RThPh*, 115 (1983), 251 n. 20.

[18] On the fine line between anorexia and fasting among (medieval) Christian ascetics, see Caroline Walker Bynum, *Holy Feast and Holy Fast: The Religious Significance of Food to Medieval Women* (Berkeley, Calif., 1987).

wept uncontrollably and even fainted. Her fellow aristocrats watched in outrage and whispered among themselves that 'those detestable monks' were to blame for seducing this naive young woman into being a party to their fanaticism. There was talk of stoning them and driving them out of Rome.[19] Jerome must have sensed that he, as Blesilla's spiritual advisor, was the foremost target. He promptly composed a consolation letter for Paula (*Ep.* 39) that is as much a traditional *consolatio* as it is a passionate defence of his spiritual authority.[20]

While Blesilla was alive, Jerome championed her as an *exemplum virtutis*.[21] However, he was now put in the awkward position of explaining how her sudden death could have followed from the very lifestyle he had recommended to her.[22] In *Ep.* 39, he argues that her premature death is not a mournful occasion by any means, for it crowns a life that was, in its final months at least, thoroughly pleasing to God. Implicit in this emphasis on her death as the entrance into eternal blessedness is the suggestion that his teachings were responsible for her salvation.[23] Furthermore, Jerome must have been keen to divert Paula's attention from an encroaching sense of physical loss[24] and to quash whatever feelings of resentment she may have harboured towards him. It has been hypothesized that Paula had

---

[19] *Ep.* 39.6. On anti-monastic sentiment in late fourth-century Rome, see Gian Domenico Gordini, 'Origine e sviluppo del monachesimo a Roma', *Gregorianum*, 37 (1956), 251–4; id., 'L'opposizione al monachesimo a Roma nel IV secolo', in Mario Fois, Vincenzo Monachino, and F. Litva (eds.), *Dalla Chiesa antica alla Chiesa moderna* (Rome, 1983), 19–35. This sentiment was felt more broadly throughout the west: see Louis Gougaud, 'Les Critiques formulées contre les premiers moines d'occident', *RMab*, 24 (1934), 145–63; Yves-Marie Duval, 'Bellepheron et les ascètes chrétiens: melancholia ou otium?', *Caesarodunum*, 3 (1968), 183–90.

[20] Cf. Barbara Feichtinger, 'Konsolationstopik und Sitz im Leben: Hieronymus' ep. 39 ad Paulam de obitu Blesillae im Spannungsfeld zwischen Christlicher Genusadaption und Lesermanipulation', *JbAC*, 38 (1995), 75–90.

[21] See above, pp. 74–6.

[22] For the centrality of fasting to Jerome's ascetic programme, see Patrick Laurence, *Jérôme et le nouveau modèle féminin: la conversion à la vie parfaite* (Paris, 1997), 103–39; Veronika Grimm, *From Feasting to Fasting: The Evolution of a Sin* (London, 1996), 157–79; Teresa Shaw, *The Burden of the Flesh: Fasting and Sexuality in Early Christianity* (Minneapolis, 1998), 96–112.

[23] Cf. *Ep.* 39.3: *faveamus Blesillae nostrae, quae de tenebris migravit ad lucem et inter fidei incipientis ardorem consummati operis percepit coronam.*

[24] e.g., *Ep.* 39.5: *redit tibi in memoriam confabulatio eius, blanditiae, sermo, consortium et, cur his careas, pati non potes.*

originally been opposed to Blesilla's decision to remain a widow because she was counting on her for grandchildren (her youngest daughter, Eustochium, was already a consecrated virgin).[25] If this were the case then Blesilla's untimely death would further have complicated Paula's grieving process.

The stakes could not have been higher for Jerome. As long as Paula was languishing in personal turmoil, her continued trust in him as a friend and mentor hung precariously in the balance. Intent upon remaining closely associated with her bloodline, he warned her that even though Blesilla was now safely out of danger Eustochium urgently needed a guardian to keep her alert to the Devil's machinations.[26] Practically speaking, however, the Devil was perhaps not as immediate a threat as rival spiritual directors ready and waiting to offer their services to Paula and her family. The ever-present threat that these men posed to him kept Jerome nervously aware of the actual insecurity of his position. A year earlier, he had warned Paula that the safety of her '*domestica ecclesia*' was jeopardized as long as such men were poised for a siege like an enemy army at the gates (*hostili exercitu obsidente*).[27] Around this same time, he had told Eustochium to beware of worldly monks, possibly of Syrian extraction,[28] who put on pietistic airs and a penitential façade in order to gain the confidence of Christian noblewomen. These men were loaded down with chains, had long hair like women and shaggy beards like goats, they wore black cloaks, and they braved the cold in bare feet. These things, Jerome warned, are 'tokens of the Devil.'[29] During his stay in the 'desert', Jerome had portrayed himself as having a 'chain, squalor, and long hair' (*catena, sordes et comae*).[30] But now the ex-anchorite momentarily distanced himself from these

---

[25] Anne Yarbrough, 'Christianization in the Fourth Century: The Example of Roman Women', *ChHist*, 45 (1976), 155.

[26] *Ep.* 39.6; cf. *Ep.* 22.3, 4, 29.   [27] *Ep.* 30.14.

[28] For the presence of foreign (e.g., Syrian) monks in Rome around this time, see Gustave Bardy, 'Pèlerinages à Rome vers la fin du IVᵉ siècle', *AB*, 67 (1949), 229–33.

[29] *Ep.* 22.28: *viros quoque fuge, quos videris catenatos, quibus feminei contra apostolum crines, hircorum barba, nigrum pallium et nudi in patientiam frigoris pedes. haec omnia argumenta sunt diaboli.*

[30] *Ep.* 17.2. See above, p. 25.

external accoutrements of holiness because impostors could use them to beguile the unsuspecting.[31]

THE BEGINNING OF THE END

Before the dust had settled from Blesilla's death, Jerome's fortunes took another major turn for the worse. On 11 December 384, Pope Damasus died at the age of seventy-nine. Jerome was now all of a sudden left without his most powerful political ally, indeed the one person who probably had been instrumental in keeping his critics among the Roman clergy at bay. The man speedily chosen as Damasus' successor, the Roman deacon Siricius, was decidedly lukewarm toward western ascetics.[32] Jerome could not have been at all pleased with the new regime's unwillingness to accommodate his special interests. He went from being a satellite member of Damasus' entourage to being an outcast from the papal court.

Jerome saw the writing on the wall. As the next few months wore on, he grew increasingly restless and disenchanted with his life in Rome. In a letter to Marcella written in the spring of 385, he expressed a yearning for the idyllic *otium* of the countryside, far removed from the bustle of an urban metropolis.[33] By the late spring or early summer, he was setting in stone plans to leave Rome for the Holy Land, possibly for a prolonged pilgrimage but more probably to settle there permanently, if the surroundings ended up suiting his tastes. This news must have been welcomed by Christians in Rome who had had enough of this divisive troublemaker. All indeed would have been

---

[31] See also Augustine, *Serm. dom. mon.* 2.12.41, who criticizes monks who dress shabbily only to deceive others with a crafty semblance of holiness (*dolosa imagine sanctitatis*).

[32] For his ambivalence and even hostility toward western ascetics, see David Hunter, 'Rereading the Jovinianist Controversy: Asceticism and Clerical Authority in Late Ancient Christianity', *JMEMS*, 33 (2003), 454–7. See also Dennis Trout, *Paulinus of Nola. Life, Letters, and Poems* (Berkeley, Calif., 1999), 113–15, on how Siricius gave the cold shoulder to Paulinus of Nola during the latter's visit to Rome in the summer of 395.

[33] *Ep.* 43. See Yves-Marie Duval, 'Sur trois lettres méconnues de Jérôme concernant son séjour à Rome (382–385)', in Andrew Cain and Josef Lössl (eds.), *Jerome of Stridon: His Life, Writings and Legacy* (Aldershot, 2009), Chap. 2.

well had it simply been a matter of *him* leaving. But word spread that Paula was going to accompany him on this trans-Mediterranean voyage. These rumours precipitated a final dramatic showdown between Jerome and the hostile forces that had been brewing against him in Rome for the duration of his stay. The ugly, brutal end for him was about to begin. Little could he have anticipated at the time just *how* ugly that end would in fact be.

THE 'DISGRACE OF A FALSE CHARGE'

At some point that summer, perhaps in July or early August, Jerome was haled before an episcopal court to participate in formal proceedings that had been brought against him. Here before his clerical colleagues he would stand to face the 'disgrace of a false charge' (*infamia falsi criminis*),[34] the details of which will be discussed below. The verdict was not in Jerome's favour and in August he left Rome as disgruntled as could be. Just prior to boarding an eastbound ship out of the Roman harbour Portus he penned an epistolary *apologia pro vita sua* (*Ep.* 45) and addressed it ostensibly to Asella, though it was intended more broadly for all the friends and supporters whom he was leaving behind in Rome.[35] This was his last chance while on Italian soil to clear his name so that his friends and financial backers there would not sever ties with him; for their abandonment of him would severely have crippled his social network in the west.

Ep. 45 is presented to readers as a letter composed in extreme haste and with tears and groans (*raptim flens dolensque conscripsi*).[36] Here, as elsewhere in his correspondence, Jerome's disavowal of slow and thoughtful dictation is rhetorical smoke-and-mirrors to impress readers with his seeming ability to manufacture elegant prose

---

[34] *Ep.* 45.6. For the various shades of meaning of '*infamia*' in the Roman world, see Max Kaser, '*Infamia* und *ignominia* in den römischen Rechtsquellen', *ZSS*, 73 (1956), 220–78.

[35] In *Ep.* 45.7, Jerome greeted some of them by name: Paula, Eustochium, Albina, Marcella, Marcellina, Felicitas.

[36] *Ep.* 45.6.

effortlessly and at a moment's notice.[37] In this instance, the pretence of spontaneity enhances the sense of urgency and melodrama that saturates the letter at every turn. This letter is in fact one of the most carefully conceived masterpieces of apology to survive from his pen.[38]

Jerome spoke defiantly, like a prophet scorned: 'To speak evil things about the righteous is a sin not easily pardoned. The day will come, it surely will come, when you along with me will weep that many burn in flames.'[39] In whatever grandiose terms Jerome saw himself, his detractors sensed a different, more sinister reality. 'Some call me a mischief-maker'[40] and say that 'I am infamous, that I am chameleon-like and too slippery to get a handle on, and that I am a liar and someone who deceives others with the cunning of Satan'.[41] It can be inferred from a key passage in *Ep.* 45 that the victims of this alleged smooth-talker were aristocratic Christian women:

A great crowd of virgins frequently surrounded me. To some of them I often explained the divine Scriptures as best I could. Study had brought about constant companionship, companionship comfortableness, and comfortableness a sense of mutual trust. Let them speak up: what have they ever detected in me that was not befitting a Christian? Whose money have I taken? Have I not refused all gifts whether small or great? Has the chink of anyone's coin been heard in my hand? Has my speech ever been laced with innuendo or has my eye ever leered lustfully?[42]

Jerome does not deny associating with women on a more than casual level, but he is adamant that their '*familiaritas*' is based solely on a

---

[37] Examples abound. A striking one is found in the preface to his polished letter to the Dalmatian nobleman Julian (*Ep.* 118.1): *extemporalis est epistula absque ordine sensuum, sine lenocinio et compositione sermonum, ut totum in illa amicum, nihil de oratore repperias.* For more references, see below, pp. 174–5.

[38] See Steven Oberhelman, *Rhetoric and Homiletics in Fourth-century Christian Literature* (Atlanta, Ga., 1991), 85, for the use of prose rhythm in this letter.

[39] *Ep.* 45.1: *non facilis venia prava dixisse de rectis. veniet, veniet illa dies, et mecum dolebis ardere non paucos.*

[40] *Ep.* 45.6: *maleficum me quidam garriunt.*

[41] *Ep.* 45.2: *ego probrosus, ego versipellis et lubricus, ego mendax et satanae arte decipiens!*

[42] *Ep.* 45.2: *multa me virginum crebro turba circumdedit; divinos libros, ut potui, nonnullis saepe disserui; lectio adsiduitatem, adsiduitas familiaritatem, familiaritas fiduciam fecerant. dicant, quid umquam in me aliter senserint, quam Christianum decebat? pecuniam cuius accepi? munera vel parva vel magna non sprevi? in manu mea aes alicuius insonuit? obliquus sermo, oculus petulans fuit?*

shared passion for Scriptural study. He words his prose delicately, making '*virginum turba*' the subject and '*me*' the direct object of '*cir-cumdedit*', to make it clear that the women sought him out—and not the other way around. He also mentions that 'a sense of mutual trust' (*fiducia*) is the glue that cements their relationship; hence the women do not perceive him as a threat of any kind. But why would they any-way? Jerome indirectly answers this by next posing a series of rhetori-cal questions that seem almost certainly to respond to allegations that were levelled against him (otherwise, why unnecessarily make issues out of things that are not issues to begin with?). Three of the questions deflect criticism that he is a gold-digger: 'Whose money have I taken? Have I not refused all gifts whether small or great? Has the chink of anyone's coin been heard in my hand?' His personal integrity and chastity were assailed as well: 'Has my speech ever been laced with innuendo (*obliquus sermo*) or has my eye ever leered lustfully (*oculus petulans*)?' The phrase '*obliquus sermo*' may refer to speaking deceptively in general or it may have an added sexual connotation, such as speaking in ribald double entendres.[43] '*Oculus petulans*' has more obvious lascivious overtones.[44] This phrase, proverbial among the ancient Latins, is perhaps best translated into English idiom as 'the wandering eye'.[45] Jerome was pegged not only as an opportunist but as a dirty-minded one at that.[46] He posed all of these rhetorical questions to make it clear that he had been completely honest and straightforward in his dealings with his female disciples and that no ulterior motives of a financial or sexual nature had ever once clouded his judgement.

It is easy to see how external observers, especially those not recep-tive Jerome's teachings or his combative personality, might have been

[43] TLL, s.v. '*obliquus*', IX.ii.102.

[44] On the lexical range of '*petulans*', esp. as it relates to lustfulness, see TLL, s.v. '*petulans*', X.xiii.1984–6.

[45] It is first attested by Petronius (*Sat.* 138.6), who used it to describe Paris' lustful stare at Circe. This phrase does not appear anywhere else in Jerome's extant writings, though other Latin Fathers employed it with more frequency: see, e.g., Ambrose, *Ieiun.* 18.66; *Ios.* 5.22; *Psal.* 118.30; *Ep.* 7.36.20. John Cassian used it in his discussion of fornication in *Instit. coen.* 6.12: *petulantes oculos notans non tam eos arguit quam illum interiorem sensum, qui officio eorum male utitur ad videndum.*

[46] Legacy-hunting in the ancient world sometimes had a sexual component. See Edward Champlin, *Final Judgments: Duty and Emotion in Roman Wills, 200 BC–AD 250* (Berkeley, Calif., 1991), 89–90.

predisposed to read between the lines and to suspect him of seedy conduct. The appearance of things certainly did not work in his favour. For one thing, he was a man in a position of power holding clandestine meetings with virgins and widows: who knew what really was going on behind closed doors? It mattered little in the court of public opinion that he professed to be a celibate monk. After all, some monks used their religious profession as a cover for worming their way into the purses, and even the beds, of rich Christian women.[47] Jerome had made a name for himself exposing monastic pretenders and legacy-hunting clerics in Rome. If these men had pulled the wool over others' eyes, could not he have been doing the same? Perhaps the only difference is that he was cleverer than they were at concealing his true motives, for by incessantly pointing out others' vices he could draw the attention away from his own. Jerome was well aware of the scandal potentially created when religious men visited unmarried women's homes.[48] Thus he spoke of two pseudo-monks, Antimus and Sofronius, who were making the rounds in Rome in the early 380s: 'After they infiltrate the homes of the high-born, they put on a sad face and drag out long, pretended fasts while they secretly feast at night. Modesty forbids me from saying anything more lest I seem like I am writing invective rather than admonition.'[49] This passage tapers off with an insinuating paraleipsis leading readers to infer that these monks proceeded to engage in wild orgies with their female hosts.

The inescapable fact of Jerome's socio-economic status only worsened his predicament. He had an obscure, non-senatorial background and came from a backwater of the Roman empire. This in itself would not have been that problematic were it not for the fact that he depended heavily if not entirely on others' financial support

[47] See, for instance, the condemnation of such monks in the late fourth-century *Cons. Zacc. Apoll.* 3.3.

[48] Cf. the warning by Ambrose (*Off.* 1.87) that young clergymen should never enter the homes of widows or virgins alone lest they be tempted or give any grounds for suspicion. See also Jerome's similar advice to Nepotian in *Ep.* 52.5. See further *Ep.* 117, with Cain, 'Jerome's *Epistula* 117 on the *Subintroductae*'.

[49] *Ep.* 22.28: *qui postquam nobilium introierint domos ... tristitiam simulant et quasi longa ieiunia furtivis noctium cibis protrahunt; pudet reliqua dicere, ne videar invehi potius quam monere.* The identity of these two arch-impostors is not known, but for some suggestions see Adkin, *Commentary*, 257.

for his scholarship and general well-being.[50] Nobody could reasonably deny that wealthy widows provided his main source of income in Rome,[51] although Jerome does try in the passage quoted above to make himself sound self-sufficient. As far as his critics were concerned, he was a hypocrite. On the one hand, he preached voluntary poverty and, on the other hand, he hobnobbed with a pope infamous for his excesses and enjoyed close ties to some of Rome's wealthiest Christian women. This looked like a blatant case of opportunism if ever there was one. Jerome knew it, and so did his enemies.

PAULA'S SEDUCER?

In the end, it was his relationship with Paula, or rather people's misperception of it, that Jerome blamed for his public relations problems. He made the preposterous claim that prior to his last-minute reversal of fortunes the entire city of Rome had showered goodwill on him[52] and that everyone had deemed him worthy of the papal throne.[53] But everything changed, according to Jerome, when it was discovered that Paula was planning to leave with him to distant Palestine: 'No charge is laid against me except my sex, and this is never an issue except when there is talk of Paula going to Jerusalem.'[54] Jerome, of course, was oversimplifying the situation in that his gender would not have been the *only* reason why this news sparked a scandal. For, as we saw above, there are hints in *Ep.* 45 that he had been suspected of bilking Christian heiresses out of their millions. His and Paula's

---

[50] Barbara Feichtinger, *Apostolae apostolorum. Frauenaskese als Befreiung und Zwang bei Hieronymus* (Frankfurt, 1995), 283–90.

[51] e.g., in *Ep.* 31 he thanks Eustochium for sending him several gifts in celebration of St Peter's feast. Cf. *Ep.* 52.5, 16, for Jerome's prohibitions against clerics accepting gifts.

[52] *Ep.* 45.3: *totius in me urbis studia consonabant.*

[53] *Ep.* 45.3: *omnium paene iudicio dignus summo sacerdotio decernebar.* Some have taken Jerome at his word that he was being groomed as Damasus' successor: e.g., Ferdinand Cavallera, *Saint Jérôme: sa vie et son œuvre* (2 vols., Paris, 1922), i. 116; Kelly, *Jerome*, 111; Pierre Nautin, 'Hieronymus', *TRE*, 15 (1986), 305; Neil Adkin, 'Pope Siricius' "Simplicity" (Jerome, *Epist.*, 127.9.3)', *VetChr*, 33 (1996), 25.

[54] *Ep.* 45.2: *nihil mihi aliud obicitur nisi sexus meus, et hoc numquam obicitur, nisi cum Hierosolyma Paula proficiscitur.*

rumoured trip to Palestine was not simply a matter of two Christians going on pilgrimage. It was really about an extremely wealthy widow leaving her life and family behind in Rome to follow a perceived legacy-hunter and drifter to (for all intents and purposes) the other side of the world. In response to these rumours, official action was taken. It has always been assumed that the first move was made by Roman church authorities. But, while the local church did end up handling the affair in its own judicial system, I shall argue that the principal instigators of the case against Jerome were members of Paula's own family, for it is they who had the most to lose—financially and otherwise—if Paula left for good. Scholars have not yet explored Jerome's expulsion from this perspective, but I believe that doing so will provide some fresh insight into a perennially perplexing problem.

In the late fourth century aristocratic Christians and especially women frequently faced considerable resistance from members of their own families if they chose to espouse a radical ascetic lifestyle.[55] According to the ascetic world view, the fundamental duty a woman owed to her family—getting married and procreating in order to produce heirs—was secondary to the devotion she owed to her heavenly Bridegroom. This devotion meant in practical terms that a virgin would remain unmarried and that a widow, whether childless or not, would not remarry. This mentality clearly threatened the societal status quo because in worst-case scenarios it jeopardized the survival of centuries-old bloodlines.[56] Furthermore, financial worries usually lay at the heart of opposition to ascetic conversion within upper-class families.[57] Relatives feared that the otherworldly among their kin would fritter away their inheritances on 'frivolous' things such as charity to the poor.

There are indications that interrelated anxieties about heir production and fiscal responsibility were bones of contention in Paula's family. We hear from Jerome about an incident in which Eustochium's paternal uncle, the pagan Hymetius—a former proconsul of Africa

---

[55] Gillian Clark, *Women in Late Antiquity. Pagan and Christian Life–styles* (Oxford, 1993), 50–6; John Curran, *Pagan City and Christian Capital. Rome in the Fourth Century* (Oxford, 2000), 269–80.

[56] Cf. *Ep.* 54.4: *an vereris, ne proles Furiana deficiat et ex te parens tuus non habeat pusionem?*

[57] Antti Arjava, *Women and Law in Late Antiquity* (Oxford, 1996), 159.

(366–8)[58]—and his wife Praetextata, tried in vain to thwart Paula's plans to dedicate her as a virgin in the early 380s. At Hymetius' instigation Praetextata gave Eustochium a cosmetic makeover, fitting her in fancy clothes and arranging her dishevelled hair into a flowing wave to make her look like a respectable aristocrat instead of a beggar.[59] Paula evidently was an only child,[60] and, because her husband and both of her parents were dead, her brother-in-law Hymetius was the nearest adult male relative of her children and so he was probably Eustochium's legal ward (*tutor*).[61] Hence his assertion of a virtual *patria potestas* to insure that she one day would become a matriarch of the *gens Iulia*, something she would forfeit by remaining a virgin.[62] Paula's family also scolded her for what they thought was egregious mismanagement of her fortune: she spent so much on the poor and sick in Rome that she 'robbed' her children. To disapproving relatives she replied that she was leaving them a greater inheritance in the mercy of Christ.[63]

Once Jerome entered the picture, Paula's kin had even more reason to be concerned. Ascetic teachers were often regarded by more secularized Christian families as pernicious influences on their impressionable loved ones. As it was perceived, they meddled in others' financial affairs and coaxed their unwitting disciples into unloading their wealth in mass quantities, all in the name of 'charity'.[64] Jerome

[58] *PLRE*, i. 447 ('Iulius Festus Hymetius').

[59] *Ep.* 107.5: *Praetextata ... iubente viro Hymetio, qui patruus Eustochiae virginis fuit, habitum eius cultumque mutavit et neglectum crinem undanti gradu texuit vincere cupiens et virginis propositum et matris desiderium.*

[60] See *PLRE*, i. 1143 (stemma 23).

[61] Wards for underage children customarily were chosen from among relatives on either the mother's or father's side and designated as such in the father's will (*tutor testamentarius*). Who was chosen as the *tutor* was dictated by the family's circumstances. See Jane Gardner, *Family and Familia in Roman Law and Life* (Oxford, 1998), 241–7.

[62] Curran, *Pagan City*, 276–7. On *patria potestas* during this period of the empire, see Antti Arjava, 'Paternal Power in Late Antiquity', *JRS*, 88 (1988), 147–65.

[63] *Ep.* 108.5: *expoliabat filios et inter obiurgantes propinquos maiorem se eis hereditatem Christi misericordiam dimittere loquebatur.* Jerome praises Paula's generosity throughout his epitaph on her (*Ep.* 108): see Cain, 'Jerome's *Epitaphium Paulae*: Hagiography, Pilgrimage, and the Cult of Saint Paula', *JECS*, 18 (2010), forthcoming.

[64] For the theological underpinnings of Jerome's notion of almsgiving, with some discussion of the suspicions about him being a *captator*, see Danuta Shanzer, 'Jerome, Tobit, alms, and the *Vita aeterna*', in Cain and Lössl, *Jerome of Stridon*, Chap. 7.

had the smell of trouble: he was a middling provincial from a virtually unknown town who recently had appeared on the Roman Christian scene and in the space of three short years worked his way into prominent circles. From a purely economic standpoint, Jerome had everything to gain from befriending Paula, while she had absolutely nothing to gain and in fact much potentially to lose by associating with him.

Just how much Paula would lose became tragically apparent in the autumn of 384 when Blesilla died unexpectedly. Blesilla's surviving relatives must have felt deeply saddened by this terrible loss and enraged at the monk who seemingly had her blood on his hands. However much they may have tried to convince the grieving mother to come to her senses and to break ties with Jerome, it was all in vain. Blesilla's death evidently had the unexpected effect of drawing the two even closer together, for by the coming summer Paula was already booking her Jerusalem-bound trip out of Rome with him. This would have been distressing news to her relatives for a number of reasons,[65] though concerns about the fate of Paula's inheritance were bound to have loomed large in their minds. From their perspective it may have seemed as if a suspect character was about to whisk her away hundreds of miles from Italy and out from under their watchful monitoring, where he could gain virtually unlimited access to her fortune. Not that Paula was necessarily naive enough to allow this to happen willingly. It was not a question so much of her naivety as it was of Jerome's alleged craftiness—after all, according to critics, he was 'someone who deceives others with the cunning of Satan'. He must have cast a spell on her, one from which she could not escape. How else could one explain why she stayed by his side through good times and bad, ignoring the warnings and protestations of her friends and family, in the wake of Blesilla's death? And, how else to account for why Paula was willing to drop everything—her friends, her way of life in Rome, and even two of her three remaining children—to follow Jerome to a land that was so unfamiliar from anything she had ever known?

---

[65] Cf. the resistance with which Jerome's aristocratic Roman friend Fabiola met from friends and family when she decided to pick up and leave for Palestine: see *Ep.* 77.7.

Paula's family would not have been the only ones ever to suspect Jerome of having a controlling hand on her. Around 420, Palladius, no friend of Jerome's, praised Paula as having been 'a woman of great distinction in the spiritual life'; her awe-inspiring virtues notwithstanding, Jerome held her back from realizing her true potential by his own jealousy, and he manipulated her to serve his own purposes.[66] In Palladius' estimation, Paula clearly was too good to keep company with such a scoundrel.

THE CASE AGAINST JEROME: TRIAL AND CONVICTION

Paula's concerned friends and relatives knew one thing for certain: things had gone far enough. Seeing that they had failed to persuade her to break with Jerome, a more drastic measure—a legal course of action—was now called for as a last resort. Valentinian's law criminalizing legacy-hunting seems at first glance as if it might have been an attractive judicial option. On 30 July 370, the emperor ordered an edict to be read in the churches at Rome (*lecta in ecclesiis Romae*) forbidding clergymen, ex-clergymen, and monks from entering the households of rich widows and orphans for the purpose of exploiting them and being written into their wills. Anyone related by blood or marriage to alleged victims had the right to report suspected offenders to civil authorities. Convicted legacy-hunters were to be banished by the public courts (*publicis iudiciis*) and prohibited from obtaining a single cent from their victims either through an act of generosity or through a last will and testament.[67] This legislation appears not to have had quite the impact Valentinian had anticipated. Despite

---

[66] *Hist. laus.* 41.2: ἧς ἐμπόδιον γέγονεν Ἱερώνυμός τις ἀπὸ Δαλματίας· δυναμένην γὰρ αὐτὴν ὑπερπτῆναι πασῶν, εὐφυεστάτην οὖσαν, προσενεπόδισε τῇ ἑαυτοῦ βασκανίᾳ ἑλκύσας αὐτὴν πρὸς τὸν ἴδιον αὐτοῦ σκοπόν.

[67] *C. Th.* 16.2.20: *ecclesiastici aut ex ecclesiastici vel qui continentium se volunt nomine nuncupari, viduarum ac pupillarum domos non adeant, sed publicis exterminentur iudiciis, si posthac eos adfines earum vel propinqui putaverint deferendos. censemus etiam, ut memorati nihil de eius mulieris, cui se privatim sub praetextu religionis adiunxerint, liberalitate quacumque vel extremo iudicio possint adipisci.*

the complaints of Christians such as Ambrose (*Ep.* 73 [18].13–14) and Jerome (*Ep.* 52.6) about the restrictions it placed on clerics' rights to inherit money and property, there is every indication that *captatio* continued more or less unchecked.[68] Valentinian's legislation fell flat for two reasons. First, legacy-hunting was difficult to prove in a court of law.[69] More problematic, though, was the loophole in the law by which *captatores* could evade prosecution. It was easy to set up trusts (*fideicommissa*) by which a testator could request his or her heir to hand over money or property to a third-party *captator*.[70]

If Jerome's case seemed in some ways to be an open-and-shut case of legacy-hunting, then perhaps the two considerations above can explain why he was not charged under Valentinian's law and why he instead landed in an episcopal court. Because *captatio* as defined by that emperor was a criminal offence, suspects had to be tried in a secular court. This meant that no clergyman could be tried in an ecclesiastical context for this or any other offence classed as a crime in the late Roman legal system. All criminal action, even if committed by churchmen, had to be dealt with by secular authorities. An imperial edict issued on 17 May 376 gave episcopal courts jurisdiction over 'slight offences pertaining to religious observance', but it required that every '*actio criminalis*' be heard by ordinary and extraordinary judges in the secular sphere.[71] Less than a decade later, on 4 February 384, the emperor Theodosius I reaffirmed the supreme jurisdiction of episcopal courts in non-criminal and non-civil cases involving clerics,[72] adding that cases pertaining to moral conduct (*Christiana sanctitas*) fell under their jurisdiction as well:

---

[68] Ivor Davidson, '*Captatio* in the Fourth–century West', *StudPatr*, 34 (2001), 39.

[69] Champlin, *Final Judgments*, 96.

[70] Jerome (*Ep.* 52.6) alerts us to the possibility: *per fideicommissa legibus ludimus.* On the arrangement of *fideicommissa*, see David Johnston, *The Roman Law of Trusts* (Oxford, 1988), 76–107.

[71] *C. Th.* 16.2.23: *qui mos est causarum civilium, idem in negotiis ecclesiasticis obtinendus est: ut, si qua sunt ex quibusdam dissensionibus levibusque delictis ad religionis observantiam pertinentia, locis suis et a suae dioceseos synodis audiantur: exceptis, quae actio criminalis ab ordinariis extraordinariisque iudicibus aut inlustribus potestatibus audienda constituit.*

[72] See Tony Honoré, *Law in the Crisis of Empire, 379–455 AD: The Theodosian Dynasty and its Quaestors* (Oxford, 1998), 34–5.

By this perpetual law We sanction that the name of bishop or of those persons who serve the needs of the Church shall not be haled before secular courts, whether the courts of the judges ordinary or those of extraordinary judges. For such clerics shall have their own judges and shall not have anything in common with the public laws, in so far, however, as the matter pertains to ecclesiastical cases which are properly decided by the episcopal authority. Therefore, if a suit that pertains to Christian sanctity (*Christianam sancti-tatem*) should be instituted against any persons, they shall properly litigate under that judge in order that he may be the superior of all of the priests in his own district.[73]

This law perhaps holds the key to understanding the legal justification behind Jerome's prosecution by Roman church authorities. First of all, the fact that he was tried in an ecclesiastical court proves that the charge on which he was indicted was not technically a crime in the eyes of the imperial government. I argued earlier in this chapter that this charge concerned opportunistic and lascivious conduct; Jerome was accused of being a dangerous financial *and* sexual predator. It stands to reason, after all, that the formal charge stemmed directly from the very suspicion that he went out of his way to defuse post trial. Indictment on legacy-hunting was out of the question for the reasons stated above, but indictment on sexual impropriety was a viable option, for the Theodosian law of 384 specified that cases involving issues of non-criminal clerical immorality, especially one as grave as Jerome's, fell within the purview of ecclesiastical authori-ties.[74] Because Jerome almost certainly did not practise his priesthood while in Rome he would not have belonged officially to the ranks of the local clergy during his stay there, but this did not exempt him from judicial action. He was still an ordained priest, and as long as he lived in Rome, the 'scene of the crime', so to speak, he had to answer

---

[73] *Sirm. Const.* 3; translation taken from Clyde Pharr, *The Theodosian Code and Novels and the Sirmondian Constitutions* (Princeton, NJ, 1952), 478.

[74] For more recent studies on the jurisdictional rights of bishops and secular magistrates in late antiquity, see Maria Rosa Cimma, *L'episcopalis audientia nelle costituzioni imperiali da Costantino a Giustiniano* (Turin, 1989); Giulio Vismara, *L'audientia episcopalis* (Milan, 1995); Jill Harries, *Law and Empire in Late Antiquity* (Cambridge, 1999), 191–211; Noel Lenski, 'Evidence for the *audientia episcopalis* in the New Letters of Augustine', in Ralph Mathisen (ed.), *Law, Society, and Authority in Late Antiquity* (Oxford, 2001), 83–97; Claudia Rapp, *Holy Bishops in Late Antiquity: The Nature of Christian Leadership in an Age of Transition* (Berkeley, Calif., 2005), 242–52.

to the church in Rome. As per the Theodosian legislation, allegations of grave unethical conduct would clearly have been a matter of *Christiana sanctitas.*

Like most episcopal courts in late antiquity, the one that heard Jerome's case was probably convened at the residence of the local bishop,[75] the *episcopeion* of Pope Siricius. Whether Siricius himself oversaw the proceedings or appointed a clerical judge to stand in for him[76] he would probably have had to approve the decision reached about Jerome.[77] Jerome remained curiously silent about the details surrounding the outcome of his trial, evidently because the verdict did not go in his favour. One piece of evidence that points in the direction of a guilty verdict is an allusion in *Ep.* 45 to a witness who testified against him:

They believed him when he lied, so why do they not believe him when he recants? He is the very same man now that he was. He who previously said that I was guilty now confesses that I am innocent. And surely torture squeezes out the truth better than laughter, unless it is the case that what is gladly listened to, whether it is made up or not, is fabricated under compulsion (*ut fingatur, inpellitur*).[78]

This accuser was most likely a slave, for *honestiores* were ordinarily exempt from torture in legal proceedings, while slaves were routinely subjected to corporal torture.[79] He may even have been one of Paula's

[75] John Lamoreaux, 'Episcopal Courts in Late Antiquity', *JECS*, 3 (1995), 156–7. See also Luke Lavan, 'The Political Topography of the Late Antique City: Activity Spaces in Practice', in Luke Lavan and William Bowden (eds.), *Theory and Practice in Late Antique Archaeology* (Leiden, 2003), 325.

[76] Bishops sometimes delegated the adjudication of cases: see Humfress, *Orthodoxy and the Courts*, 170–1.

[77] This would help to explain why Jerome had nothing nice to say about the pope. See Adkin, 'Pope Siricius' "simplicity" '. According to one legend, a version of which is preserved in an eighth-century manuscript containing the Whitby *Life of Pope Gregory the Great*, Siricius, driven by utter contempt for Jerome's virtues, expelled him from Rome. See Mark Vessey, 'Jerome and the "Jeromanesque" ', in Cain and Lössl, *Jerome of Stridon*, Chap. 17.

[78] *Ep.* 45.2: *crediderunt mentienti; cur non credunt neganti? idem est homo ipse, qui fuerat: fatetur insontem, qui dudum noxium loquebatur; et certe veritatem magis exprimunt tormenta quam risus, nisi quod facilius creditur, quod aut fictum libenter auditur aut non fictum, ut fingatur, inpellitur.*

[79] Harries, *Law and Empire*, 122–3. On the use of torture in ecclesiastical courts, see Timothy Barnes, 'The Crimes of Basil of Ancyra', *JThS*, NS 47 (1996), 550–4; Leslie

domestic servants—someone with ready access to the behind-the-scenes happenings of her household and therefore someone in a position to give 'credible' testimony about her travel plans for the near future. Furthermore, the phrase '*ut fingatur, inpellitur*' indicates that the slave, at least according to Jerome's understanding of what had transpired, was not acting on his own behalf but was put up to fabricating a story by someone else. At any rate, whoever this informant was, it is significant that Jerome mentions only *his* testimony. As a rule, in the secular and ecclesiastical trials of late antiquity at least *two* witnesses were required to prosecute any given case.[80]

Unless Jerome's case somehow deviated from the norm—and there is no reason for thinking that it did—this 'lying' witness would not have been the only one to testify. But what about the other witnesses? Why did Jerome not mention them? It is possible that they reported the same or similar allegations as the accuser in question, yet, unlike him, they did not buckle under torture and recant their sworn testimony. This could explain Jerome's intriguing comment that those sitting on the ecclesiastical tribunal 'do not believe him when he recants'. If he did indeed recant, then his testimony would have been nullified; and Jerome could not have been convicted on the basis of falsified testimony. The unwillingness of the court to side with him despite this tainted testimony implies conviction. The word of the other witnesses would seem to have outweighed the word of the one who had changed his mind in the midst of the proceedings. Jerome bothered to mention only one explicit detail about his trial—namely, the 'lie' of the one accusing witness, for this may have been the one aspect of the proceedings that did go in his favour. If he had legitimately been acquitted of the charge brought against him, one imagines that he would have said so plainly instead of grasping at straws about the falsified testimony of a single witness, while presumably concealing the damning testimony of the other witness or witnesses.

This is not the only time that Jerome was evasive when discussing the outcome of his trial. In the preface to his translation of

Dossey, 'Judicial Violence and the Ecclesiastical Courts in Late Antique North Africa', in Mathisen, *Law, Society, and Authority*, 98–114.

[80] Harries, *Law and Empire*, 109.

Didymus' *On the Holy Spirit*, completed and sent to Rome in 387,[81] he recalls how 'the senate of the Pharisees made their outcry, and not just one false scribe but the whole faction of ignorance conspired (*coniuravit*) against me as if a war over doctrine had been declared'.[82] He brands the Roman church hierarchy collectively the 'senate of the Pharisees',[83] the implication being that he is a divinely inspired prophet persecuted by the modern-day successors to the Jews who plotted against Christ. This 'faction of ignorance' conspired against him under the pretext of a theological dispute (*quasi indicto sibi praelio doctrinarum*). The vague allusion to a supposed theological controversy as the reason for his departure from Rome is a red herring meant to conceal the *real*, far more embarrassing reason. The allegations against him, as reconstructed from *Ep.* 45, centre on his connection to Paula and not on any doctrinal dispute. Had the issue been even partly about theology, we would expect Jerome to have said as much in order to sidestep the suspicions of ethical shadiness that he was forced to confront in the letter to Asella.

Jerome spoke explicitly about his trial on only one other occasion in his surviving post-Roman writings, around 400 in the context of his pamphlet war with Rufinus. In a letter that is now lost, Rufinus brought up this touchy subject and threatened to reveal the details about what *really* had happened:

Am I not able to recount how you left the City, what verdict was handed down about you at the time, what was written afterward, what you swore, where you boarded the ship, how sanctimoniously you avoided perjury? I could have elaborated, but I decided to keep back more than I relate.[84]

---

[81] Nautin, 'L'activité littéraire', 257–8.

[82] *Didym. spir. sanct.*, prologue: *Pharisaeorum conclamavit senatus; et nullus scriba vel fictus sed omnis, quasi indicto sibi praelio doctrinarum, adversum me imperitiae factio coniuravit.*

[83] Cain, 'Origen, Jerome, and the *senatus Pharisaeorum*', *Latomus*, 65 (2006), 727–34. For Jerome's use of Judaizing epithets for his enemies, see Hillel Newman, 'Jerome's Judaizers', *JECS*, 9 (2001), 421–52. Other church writers such as Augustine and Optatus caricatured schismatics and heretics as Pharisees: see Ilona Opelt, *Die Polemik in der Christlichen lateinischen Literatur von Tertullian bis Augustin* (Heidelberg, 1980), 140.

[84] Jerome quotes Rufinus' provoking words *verbatim* in *Ep. adv. Ruf.* 21: *numquid et ego non possum enarrare tu quomodo de urbe discesseris, quid de te in praesenti iudicatum sit, quid postea scriptum, quid iuraveris, ubi navim conscenderis, quam sancte periurium vitaveris? poteram pandere, sed plura reservare statui quam proferre.*

This veiled threat probably caught Jerome by surprise. He had gone
out of his way for at least a decade to bury this part of his past from
public memory,[85] but now it had come back to haunt him. Someone
who knew him very well personally—someone to whom he undoubtedly had given, in his own words, a detailed account of the trial shortly
after the fact[86]—was putting him on the metaphorical witness stand
to explain his condemnation all over again. Latin Christendom had
been watching this conflict between Rufinus and Jerome unfold,[87]
and with so many eyes fixed on his next tactical move Jerome did not
have the luxury of retreating. This is his carefully formulated response
to Rufinus:

I do not want you to be silent about what was decided about me at Rome
and what was written down afterward, especially seeing that you have the
proof of written documents and seeing that I am to be tried by the writings
of the church and not by your words, which you are able to fake and blurt
out with unpunished mendacity. See how much I fear you: if you produce
even a scant record of the bishop of Rome or of any other church against
me I shall own up to all the crimes that have been ascribed to you, as being
my own. Could I not bring up your departure, how old you were, where and
at what time you travelled by ship, where you lived, and with what people
you kept company? But, far be it from me to do what I criticize you for
doing and bring the nonsense of old women's quarrels into an ecclesiastical
dispute. Let this response alone satisfy Your Prudence: be careful not to
say anything against another when that very charge can be turned back
on you.[88]

---

[85] See below, pp. 130–4.

[86] i.e., in the autumn of 385 when he was staying with Rufinus at the latter's
monastery on the outskirts of Jerusalem. The two were still on friendly terms and
so Jerome probably felt comfortable discussing the recent turn of events.

[87] See Augustine, *Ep.* 73.6.

[88] *Ep. adv. Ruf.* 22: *quid autem de me Romae iudicatum sit et quid postea scriptum,
nolo taceas, praesertim cum habeas testimonium scripturarum, et ego non verbis tuis,
quae simulare potes et impunito iactare mendacio, sed scriptis ecclesiasticis arguendus
sim. vide quantum te timeam: si vel parvam schedulam contra me romani episcopi
aut ulterius ecclesiae protuleris, omnia quae in te scripta sunt mea crimina confitebor.
numquid et ego non possem profectionem tuam discutere, cuius aetatis fueris, unde, quo
tempore navigaris, ubi vixeris, quibus interfueris? sed absit ut quod in te reprehendo
faciam et in ecclesiastica disputatione anilium iurgiorum deliramenta conpingam. hoc
solum prudentiae tuae dixisse sufficiat, ut caveas in alterum dicere quicquid in te statim
retorqueri potest.*

Jerome does not deny that a guilty verdict was handed down ('record of the bishop of Rome...*against* me') nor does he deny that there existed official documentation outlining the decision.[89] He seems to assume that Rufinus is not bluffing and that he either has a copy of this court report or could obtain one without much difficulty. Jerome also does not attempt to plead his innocence to the charge originally brought against him at Rome, and in fact he fails to volunteer a single detail about this charge. He is content to leave well enough alone. If he takes Rufinus' bait and frankly confesses what Rufinus already knew, but what perhaps few others in his general reading audience knew, he would have to rehash the whole sordid affair all over again, and this could have the effect of planting seeds of doubt about his spiritual authority in the minds of Christians unaware of his chequered past. Additionally, he cannot fabricate any reasons for his condemnation, as he tried to do in the preface to the translation of Didymus, for Rufinus surely would confront him about such a blatant manipulation of the facts, just as he so relentlessly held Jerome accountable for breaking his solemn vow in the Ciceronian dream never again to read the pagan classics.[90] Jerome found himself backed into a corner. He had no substantive defence, so he went on an aggressive counter-attack and warned Rufinus that if he tried to expose any more of his past he should brace himself for an unprecedented smear campaign. Jerome was fully prepared to drag his former friend down into the mire with him and to accuse him of the very things of which he stood accused.[91]

The main points of the argument may be summarized. In the late spring or early summer of 385 Jerome and Paula began planning for a pilgrimage to the Holy Land. Paula's family, already incensed over her continuing association with the *novus homo* from Stridon, intervened to keep her from leaving and taking her vast fortune with

[89] Some scholars—e.g., Cavallera, *Jérôme*, 2.87–8, and Jérôme Labourt, *Jérôme: Lettres* (8 vols., Paris, 1949–63), ii. 198—have not taken Jerome literally and deny that such documentation even existed.

[90] Rufinus, *Apol. c. Hier.* 2.6–7; Jerome, *Apol. c. Ruf.* 1.30–1; *Ep. adv. Ruf.* 32. See Neil Adkin, 'Jerome's Vow "Never to Reread the Classics": Some Observations', *REA*, 101 (1999), 161–7.

[91] We do not know what (if any) incriminating information Jerome may actually have had about Rufinus, other than that Rufinus, too, had a lady friend in Christ (Melania) with whom he was living abroad in close proximity in a monastic context.

her, where Jerome could have far freer access to it than in Rome. They presumably reasoned that if they could prove to her that he was the manipulator they believed him to be, then she might cut ties with him once and for all. Or, if she did not finally come to her senses, they would look for a way forcibly to keep him from her. Paula's family found a sympathetic ear for their grievance in Roman church authorities, many of whom had had enough of Jerome anyway and would have welcomed any pretext on which to banish him from their midst. Jerome was charged with behaviour that violated the code of ethics to which the universal church held its clergy. At least two witnesses testified under oath against him, one of whom recanted his testimony under torture. But this evidently was not enough to persuade the episcopal court to absolve Jerome from all suspicion of wrongdoing.

As to what sentence Jerome faced after having been found guilty of clerical misconduct, we can only speculate. One component of the punishment would have been an official censure by the Roman church, perhaps short of actual excommunication. Given the gravity and sensitive nature of the offence as well as the perceived threat he posed to Christians at Rome, especially those who were upper class and female, Jerome may have been ordered to leave Rome at once. This may not have been all, either. Let us take a closer look at Rufinus' challenge to Jerome: 'Am I not able to recount how you left the City, what verdict was handed down about you at the time, what was written afterward, what you swore, where you boarded the ship, how sanctimoniously you avoided perjury?' The phrase 'what was written afterward' refers to the standard post-trial document that recorded details such as the names of the plaintiff(s), defendant(s), witnesses, the charge, the date of the trial, the verdict, the punishment (if any) meted out, and any conditions attached to the sentence.[92] As for the cryptic phrases 'what you swore' and 'how sanctimoniously you avoided perjury', they would seem to refer to the oath normally sworn by plaintiffs and defendants of a case heard in an episcopal court that they would abide by the bishop's ruling and whatever stipulations

---

[92] On the recording of such information by *notarii*, see Caroline Humfress, *Orthodoxy and the Courts in Late Antiquity* (Oxford, 2007), 169–70.

it entailed.[93] A tantalizing possibility is that Jerome was ordered to leave Rome at once and was prohibited from taking Paula with him, a condition of the sentence that would have been very appealing to her family. Paula did depart from Rome and a few weeks later joined him, and by leaving separately and at a later date she could show that she was leaving of her own volition and not under compulsion by Jerome. Hence, on this technicality Jerome could avoid breaking the oath he had sworn.

Pierre Nautin suggested in passing that Roman church authorities expelled Jerome under Canon 16 of the Council of Nicea, which stipulated that a clergyman who abandoned his home diocese had to return immediately—and if he refused he would be subject to immediate excommunication.[94] This, according to Nautin, explains why Jerome, after sailing out of Rome, made a stop at Antioch for several weeks to spend time with Paulinus, the bishop who had ordained him to the priesthood a little under a decade earlier. But there are problems with this hypothesis. In his brief discussion Nautin ignored the evidence volunteered by Jerome himself about his trial and the nature of the charges brought against him. Had he been expelled on some technicality of canon law,[95] he would have said so rather than dwell exclusively on the far more humiliating charge of immoral behaviour. Furthermore, there is a perfectly logical explanation for Jerome's extended stay at Antioch. Antioch was a major Mediterranean port city where floods of Christian pilgrims arrived by ship from the west and thence undertook their journey by land to the Holy Land.[96] Not coincidentally, this was the rendezvous point for Paula and Jerome, and once reunited they commenced their own pilgrimage by heading first to Jerusalem.

No matter how severe a punishment the Roman church could have meted out to Jerome, it paled in comparison with the psychological

[93] Lamoreaux, 'Episcopal Courts', 158.

[94] Nautin, 'L'excommunication de saint Jérôme', *AEHE V*, 80–1 (1972–3), 8.

[95] It may be noted that this eighty-year-old canon was still being enforced by the early 400s, for Augustine referred to it in a letter (*Ep.* 64.3) to a priest at Carthage named Quintianus.

[96] Jean Rougé, *Recherches sur l'organisation du commerce maritime en Méditerranée* (Paris, 1966), 126–9; E. D. Hunt, *Holy Land Pilgrimage in the Later Roman Empire, AD 312–460* (Oxford, 1982), 72.

damage he must have sustained from his conviction. He had now been pronounced a religious charlatan by an ecclesiastical court. This pulpiteer on sexual ethics who had satirized the double-dealing of his corrupt clerical *confrères* was, according to his accusers, caught red-handed in a stupendous hypocrisy of his own. His reputation lay in shambles. 'They have laid on me the disgrace of a false charge,' he lamented to Asella, 'but I know that one enters the kingdom of heaven through both a good and bad reputation.'[97] Enduring the kind of *infamia* he did, Jerome understandably chose Asella as the ostensible recipient of his epistolary farewell to Rome. Because she was a lifelong virgin, with a solid reputation for moral purity,[98] he could lay claim to innocence-by-association by fostering the appearance that she was his trusted friend and confidante. Furthermore, she seems to have wielded some influence among Jerome's Roman circle of friends and so she would have been in a position to help mobilize from within his support base now that he would no longer be there to do so himself.[99]

EXILE OF A 'PROPHET'

Once his fate had been sealed by ecclesiastical sanctions in the summer of 385, Jerome made preparations for a swift exit by ship from the Roman harbour Portus. Years later, when responding to Rufinus'

---

[97] *Ep.* 45.6: *infamiam falsi criminis inportarunt, sed scio per bonam et malam famam perveniri ad regna caelorum.*

[98] At *Ep.* 45.7, Jerome calls her an '*exemplum pudicitiae et virginitatis insigne*'. See *Ep.* 24.5 on how Asella stood out for her virtuousness in a city (Rome) so full of moral corruption, so much so that the good praised her and the wicked did not dare to slander her (*boni eam praedicent et mali detrahere non audeant*). For the ancient Roman concept of *pudor*-by-association, see Robert Kaster, *Emotion, Restraint, and Community in Ancient Rome* (Oxford, 2005), 38–42.

[99] He continued to cultivate his relationship with Asella after leaving Rome. For instance, in the early 390s he dedicated his *Vita Hilarionis* to her: see Paul Harvey, 'Jerome Dedicates his *Vita Hilarionis*', *VChr*, 59 (2005), 286–97. For the dating of this work, see Pierre Leclerc and Edgardo Morales (eds. and trans.), *Jérôme: trois vies de moines (Paul, Malchus, Hilarion)* (Paris, 2007), 20.

threat to expose him, he painted this gripping picture of the scene of his departure:

Do you wish to hear how my departure from the City proceeded? I shall tell the story in brief. It was the month of August and the etesian winds were blowing. At peace with myself, I boarded the ship at the port of Rome accompanied by the holy priest Vincentius, my younger brother, and other monks who are now living at Jerusalem. An incredibly large crowd of saints followed me [to the ship].[100]

This is a heavily doctored retelling of past events. Jerome neglects to mention his sentence and that his departure had anything to do with it. He asserts that he boarded the ship without a care in the world (*securus*),[101] though we know from the emotionally charged tone of *Ep.* 45, which he wrote at that very time, that nothing could be further from the truth. Jerome also claims that he was escorted to the ship in a grand procession by 'an incredibly large crowd of saints' and then was accompanied on the actual journey by a holy priest and monks.[102] Jerome declines to elaborate on the identities of those who comprised this 'crowd'. We may not know who was present, but we do know who was conspicuously absent. At the end of *Ep.* 45, Jerome asks Asella to convey his greetings to Paula, Eustochium, Marcella, her mother Albina, and the otherwise unknown women named Marcellina[103] and Felicitas.[104] Had any of them been by his side there would have been no need for such a request. The same logic applies to Asella. Had she accompanied him to the dock, there

---

[100] *Ep. adv. Ruf.* 22: *vis nosse profectionis meae de urbe ordinem? narrabo breviter. mense autem augusto, flantibus etesiis, cum sancto Vincentio presbytero et adulescente fratre et aliis monachis qui nunc Hierosolymae commorantur, navim in romano portu securus ascendi, maxima me sanctorum frequentia prosequente.*

[101] Commenting on Jerome's word-choice, Pierre Lardet, *L'Apologie de Jérôme contre Rufin: un commentaire* (Leiden, 1993), 305, notes: 'J[érôme] donne le change sur son départ, présenté ... comme complètement "serein".'

[102] Vincentius ended up settling with him at Bethlehem: see Jerome, *Ep.* 51.1.

[103] Some have taken her to be Ambrose's sister, but she almost certainly was not. See Neil Adkin, 'Is the Marcellina of Jerome, *Epist.*, 45.7 Ambrose's Sister?', *Phoenix*, 49 (1995), 68–70.

[104] *Ep.* 45.7: *saluta Paulam et Eustochium—velit nolit mundus, in Christo meae sunt—saluta matrem Albinam sororesque Marcellam, Marcellinam quoque et sanctam Felicitatem.*

would have been no reason to address a letter to her in the first place, seeing that the fundamental purpose of the 'letter' in antiquity was to unite friends who were not together in person. Moreover, what in reality was probably a rather modest gathering—minus (surprisingly) some of Jerome's key Roman patrons—is amplified into a farewell party befitting a king.[105] By shaping the account in the way that he does Jerome is essentially posing a rhetorical question to readers: if so many of the Christian faithful at Rome believed so staunchly in my innocence, how could I possibly have been guilty in the first place?

Back in 385, Jerome had viewed his departure as anything *but* the tranquil event portrayed fifteen years later. He had regarded it as a forced exile but one that nevertheless was following a predetermined divine script. He wrote to Asella:

Pray that I may leave Babylon behind and again enter Jerusalem, and that Joshua, the son of Josedech, may have control over me, and not Nebuchadnezzar. Pray that Ezra, whose name in Hebrew means 'helper', may come and lead me back to my homeland. I was foolish for wanting to sing the Lord's song in a strange land and for seeking the aid of Egypt after deserting Mount Sinai. I did not remember that Gospel passage which says that he who leaves Jerusalem immediately falls among robbers, is robbed, beaten, and killed.[106]

Jerome dramatizes his expulsion as an event of epic biblical proportions. Superimposing an Old Testament template on his personal experience, he places his flight to Jerusalem on a par with the Jews' return there from their Babylonian captivity. He makes a symbolic connection between the two events by evoking two Jewish figures (Ezra and Joshua) who played leading roles in negotiating the return of their people to their homeland. The comparison of Rome to

---

[105] In Greco–Roman antiquity parties often would accompany important persons to a ship prior to voyage. See Denys Gorce, *Les Voyages, l'hospitalité et le port des lettres dans le monde chrétien des IVe et Ve siècles* (Paris, 1925), 106–7.

[106] *Ep.* 45.6: *ora autem, ut de Babylone Hierosolyma regrediar nec mihi dominetur Nabuchodonosor, sed Iesus, filius Iosedech; veniat Hesdras, qui interpretatur 'adiutor', et reducat me in patriam meam. stultus ego, qui volebam cantare canticum domini in terra aliena et deserto monte Sion Aegypti auxilium flagitabam. non recordabar evangelii, quod, qui Hierusalem egreditur, statim incidit in latrones, spoliatur, vulneratur, occiditur.*

Babylon is lifted directly from the pages of the New Testament,[107] and, in the years following his condemnation, this became Jerome's metaphor of choice for Rome.[108] The Italian capital is now the godless centre of tyranny that Babylon was for the ancient Jews, and both cities stand in stark contrast to Jerusalem. After years of wandering in exile, he prays that Ezra, the 'helper',[109] may at last 'come and lead me back to my homeland'. The pull he felt towards the Holy Land dated back at least as far as the early 370s when he and a group of friends from northern Italy had set out on a pilgrimage there. But, owing to health problems and weariness from the taxing journey, he had made it only as far as Antioch. There he lodged with Evagrius and postponed his travel plans to Palestine indefinitely to pursue literary and monastic prospects in the eastern capital before moving on to various locales and eventually landing in Rome. This temporary derailment of his plans, he says now in retrospect, was a colossal mistake, and he regrets ever 'wanting to sing the Lord's song in a strange land'.[110]

Rome was, indisputably, the cradle of Jerome's first major successes as a biblical scholar and teacher of asceticism, not to mention the site of his baptism in the 360s—something of which he was quite proud.[111] Nevertheless, the exiled Jerome played down its pivotal significance for his personal and professional development and dismissed it as a temporary stopover *en route* to his final destination, the Holy Land.[112] Two years after his expulsion he wrote

[107] 1 Pet. 5: 13; Rev. 17–18.
[108] *Epp.* 45.6; 46.12; 64.8; *Did. spir. sanct.*, prologue; *Adv. Iov.* 2.31, 38.
[109] The incorrigible Hebrew philologist could not resist, even in a time of great personal distress, inserting this etymological sidebar.
[110] From Ps. 136: 4: *quomodo cantabimus canticum Domini in terra aliena?* Jerome's quotation is apt. This psalm is about a temple singer who refused to sing the Psalms while the Jews were still in captivity in Babylon. In the preface to *Didym. spir. sanct.* he recycles the same verse in a virtually identical context: *canticum quod cantare non potui in terra aliena, hic a vobis in Iudaea provocatus immurmuro.*
[111] *Epp.* 15.1; 16.2.
[112] On his changing opinion of Rome, see Patrick Laurence, 'Rome et Jérôme: des amours contrariées', *RBén*, 107 (1997), 227–49. See also Karin Sugano, *Das Rombild des Hieronymus* (Bern, 1983).

that Rome, hopelessly entrenched in pagan culture as it was,[113] had stifled his creative energies. But now that he was in Judea and was surrounded on all sides by the inspirational sights and sounds of salvation history, his work finally would thrive as in no other place on earth.[114]

---

[113] Rufinus (*Apol. c. Hier.* 2.23) later chastized him for speaking of Christian Rome in condescending terms as if it were still a pagan capital.

[114] There is evidence that Jerome remained steadfast in this conviction after establishing himself in Bethlehem. In the preface to his translation of the Septuagint Chronicles (*PL* 29: 423), written about three years after he had left Rome, he stated: 'He who has studied Judea with his own eyes will have a far clearer comprehension of Holy Scripture' (*sanctam Scripturam lucidius intuebitur, qui Iudaeam oculis contemplatus est*).

5

The Embattled Ascetic Sage

The landscape of Christian Latin literature in late antiquity was densely populated by theologians—Ambrose, Jovinian, Jerome, Augustine, and Pelagius, to name but a few—who were driven by a sense of responsibility to educate fellow Christians about how they could best live their faith. In the course of propagating their ideas in writing, all of them constantly engaged to one degree or another in self-justification in order to explain on what authority they taught.[1] Because none of them was writing in a vacuum for himself alone, each inevitably had to clarify to readers in his own (polemical or non-polemical) way why his approach was to be embraced to the exclusion of other approaches.[2] Jerome was no different. In fact, he went to greater lengths than most to make the case for why his teachings were intrinsically more beneficial than the ones promulgated by writers with whom he competed for a sympathetic audience.

In the foregoing chapters I argued that in taking such care to present himself via the epistolary text as an ascetic virtuoso during the pre-Roman and Roman phases of his career Jerome was motivated by, among other things, the unsettling realization that he was but one of many spiritual authorities attempting to make his voice distinctly audible, and attractive-sounding, in an already noisy room. In this

---

[1] For the case of a Greek Father, see Neil McLynn, 'A Self-made Holy Man: The Case of Gregory Nazianzen', *JECS*, 6 (1998), 463–83.

[2] See Elizabeth Clark, *Reading Renunciation: Asceticism and Scripture in Early Christianity* (Princeton, NJ, 1999), who shows that these ideological clashes usually devolved from disagreements about how to interpret Scripture. Recently Richard Goodrich, *Contextualizing Cassian: Aristocrats, Asceticism, and Reformation in Fifth-century Gaul* (Oxford, 2007), has examined how John Cassian tried to outmatch Basil, Jerome, Sulpicius Severus, and other authorities in an effort to win a hearing for his teachings in Gaul.

chapter, I examine a cross-section of his epistolography from the Bethlehem years (386–*c*.419) and show that this same fundamental concern continued to preoccupy Jerome well into the twilight of his career. We begin by looking in detail at certain problematic aspects of his personal, theological, and ecclesiastical profiles that persistently threatened to undermine his credibility in the eyes of prospective followers. Then we take an intensive look at a selection of letters of spiritual advice Jerome wrote to a priest, a monk, and a consecrated virgin. My aim is not to elucidate the content of his ascetic teaching as it can be distilled from these writings.[3] Rather, my focus will be the specific terms on which Jerome defined his authority— and why he chose the terms that he did—in three separate epistolary situations.

JEROME'S PERSONAL, THEOLOGICAL, AND ECCLESIASTICAL PROFILES

The immoral moralist?

One of Jerome's best-known literary identities, the subject of a classic study by David Wiesen,[4] is that of the world-weary satirist of contemporary *mores*. In his own lifetime, Jerome was criticized as a cantankerous moralist who revelled in pointing out others' faults.[5] He seems never to have taken any of these criticisms to heart but always maintained that those who complained about his satire did so because they were irritated that he had exposed their vices to the light of day.[6] To be a moralist in the Christian sense presupposes complete disentanglement from the world's corruption, and so whenever Jerome assumed this identity he was in effect making a claim to possess an extraordinary personal sanctity. For instance, at the end of

[3] For which, see, e.g., Patrick Laurence, *Jérôme et le nouveau modèle féminin. La conversion à la vie parfaite* (Paris, 1997).

[4] Wiesen, *Saint Jerome as a Satirist* (Ithaca, NY, 1964). On the satiric *persona* in some classical Latin literary traditions, see Susanna Morton Braund, *The Roman Satirists and their Masks* (London, 1996); Ellen Oliensis, *Horace and the Rhetoric of Authority* (Cambridge, 1998), 17–63.

[5] See *Epp.* 27.1; 52.17; 117.1; 125.5; 130.19.

[6] See above, pp. 88–9, and below, p. 161.

his letter to Nepotian on clerical morals, he suggests that he is able to be a critic only because he has reached the pinnacle of moral purity: 'I have been a harsh judge not only of them but also of myself, and when I wished to remove the splinter from another's eye I first yanked the plank out of my own eye.'[7]

Legacy-hunting clerics rank among the favourite targets of Jerome's satire.[8] This is ironic, to say the least, considering that he was driven out of Rome amidst suspicions that he had taken advantage of affluent Christian women. As personally humiliating as that whole ordeal had been for him, far more devastating was what it implied— namely, that his allegedly seedy conduct in private belied the moral high ground on which he had built his public identity as a monk and teacher of holiness. There was the very real possibility that with this kind of reputation preceding him, no upper-class Christian woman with her wits about her would dare to entrust her soul to him. In the approximately two years following his ejection from Rome, Jerome defended himself vigorously against the charges in carefully worded statements.[9] Thereafter he seems to have dropped the issue, perhaps in the hope that it eventually would fade from public memory. When Rufinus rehashed the affair almost fifteen years after the fact, Jerome put the most positive spin on what little he did have to say in his own defence, possibly because he did not wish to risk volunteering further self-incriminating information.

Jerome took other steps to expunge this disgrace from his legacy. In his epitaph on Marcella (412) he says that as soon as he had left Rome Principia took his place with Marcella; he does not, however, so much as hint at *why* he left.[10] We detect revisionist tendencies at work in the epitaph on Paula he composed in 404.[11] Jerome makes Paula's departure from Rome (autumn of 385) coincide with the departure of bishops Paulinus and Epiphanius from there (autumn

---

[7] *Ep.* 52.17: *neque in illos tantum, sed et in nos ipsos severi iudices fuimus volentesque festucam de oculo alterius tollere nostram prius trabem eiecimus.*

[8] e.g., *Epp.* 22.28; 40; 52.5–6; 130.19. See Wiesen, *Saint Jerome as a Satirist*, 65–112.

[9] See above, pp. 124–8.

[10] *Ep.* 127.7–8. See further Andrew Cain, 'Rethinking Jerome's Portraits of Holy Women', in Andrew Cain and Josef Lössl (eds.), *Jerome of Stridon: His Life, Writings and Legacy* (Aldershot, 2009), Chap. 4.

[11] For a thematic analysis of this famous letter, see Cain, 'Jerome's *Epitaphium Paulae*: Hagiography, Pilgrimage, and the Cult of Saint Paula', *JECS*, 18 (2010), forth-coming.

of 382).[12] Furthermore, he attributes her decision to leave Rome to her desire to live the hermit's life in the eastern desert, a desire he says was prompted by her intense admiration for the bishops' virtues.[13] Jerome omits himself completely from the narrative and thus leaves the misleading impression that Paula's departure had nothing to do with him, even though it in fact had *everything* to do with him. Elsewhere in the epitaph, he may be attempting to brush aside lingering suspicions among some readers about his relationship with Paula when he emphasizes how she never dined with a man after the death of her husband[14] and how she died destitute and consequently was unable to leave behind an inheritance even for Eustochium.[15]

However much Jerome tried to extinguish the public relations fire surrounding his expulsion, some smouldering embers still crackled in Rome at least a decade later. This made his efforts to enlist new recruits to his cause from among the Roman aristocracy that much more difficult. In the spring of 395, he sent a letter (*Ep.* 54) to Paula's cousin Furia, a member of the *gens Furia* who the previous year had lost her husband, a son of the praetorian prefect Sextus Claudius Petronius Probus.[16] Because the marriage had produced no children to continue the family line, her father, possibly the future prefect of Rome (398/9) Quintilius Laetus,[17] pressured her to remarry. Furia, who was exploring the option of chaste widowhood, sent a letter to Bethlehem requesting counsel about what to do next. Jerome exhorted her to remain a widow and to spend her vast inheritance on charitable activities such as feeding the poor—advice he knew would not resonate with her family or his critics.[18] 'The leaders will rise together', he predicts, 'and the crowd of the patricians will thunder against my letter, crying out that I am a sorcerer and seducer who should be exiled to the ends of the earth'.[19] Evidently anticipating

---

[12] *Ep.* 108.6.   [13] Ibid.   [14] *Ep.* 108.15.   [15] *Ep.* 108.2, 26.

[16] See *PCBE*, ii. 878–9 ('Furia') and *PLRE*, i. 736–40 ('Sex. Claudius Petronius Probus 5').

[17] See *PLRE*, i. 492–3 ('Quintilius Laetus 2'). Cf. *Ep.* 54.6, where Jerome may be punning on Laetus' name: *pater tuus... inpleat nomen suum et laetetur filiam Christo se genuisse, non saeculo.*

[18] *Ep.* 54.4, 12, 14–15. On family opposition to ascetic decisions, see Anne Yarbrough, 'Christianization in the Fourth Century: The Example of Roman Women', *ChHist*, 45 (1976), 154–7; Clark, *Reading Renunciation*, 242–3.

[19] *Ep.* 54.2: *consurgent proceres et adversum epistulam meam turba patricia detonabit me magum, me seductorem clamitans et in terras ultimas asportandum.*

that critics (and perhaps Furia herself) would question his motives, he added the following disclaimer: 'Except by letter we do not know each other, and where there is no knowledge according to the flesh, the only motive there can be is a religious one.'[20] Jerome, ironically, was compelled to rely on the letter-as-text to be his surrogate, yet at the same time he played down this virtual *praesentia* so that the text might become an impassable barrier for insincere motives on his part.

Well into the 390s, Jerome's critics kept the memory of his Roman disgrace alive by making insinuations about his continuing close relationships with aristocratic Christian women. In particular, they pointed out that virtually all of his biblical commentaries were dedicated to (and therefore funded by) women. In the preface to his commentary on Zephaniah (392), dedicated to Paula and Eustochium, he strikes out at those who hold him up for ridicule (*irridendum*) for not writing to or for men.[21] Five years later, he sent Principia a commentary on Psalm 45 dressed as a letter (*Ep.* 65). To the commentary proper he affixed a preface explaining why he gave preferential treatment to his female Scriptural students. He acknowledges first of all that, 'I know that I am criticized by many for occasionally(!) writing to women and for preferring the weaker sex to men'. Without missing a beat, he retorts: 'I would not speak to women if men were asking the questions about Scripture.'[22] Jerome then adduces numerous examples of women in the Bible who took the initiative in the things of God when men refused to do so. The subtle suggestion here is that his female disciples are exemplary modern-day counterparts to these illustrious women of old and that his detractors are like the scoffers in the Bible whose blessings God took away and gave to these believing women. In the body of the letter, Jerome interprets the bridal song in Psalm 45 as an allegorical call to arms to the Christian virgin.[23] But not just any virgin: the letter is offered up as a personalized

[20] *Ep.* 54.3: *exceptis epistulis ignoramus alterutrum, solaque causa pietatis est, ubi carnis nulla notitia est.*
[21] *In Soph.*, prologue: *respondendum videtur his qui me irridendum aestimant, quod omissis viris, ad vos scribam potissimum, o Paula et Eustochium.*
[22] *Ep.* 65.1: *scio me...a plerisque reprehendi, quod interdum scribam ad mulieres et fragiliorem sexum maribus praeferam...si viri de Scripturis quaererent, mulieribus non loquerer.*
[23] David Hunter, 'The Virgin, the Bride, and the Church: Reading Psalm 45 in Ambrose, Jerome, and Augustine', *ChHist*, 69 (2000), 290–5.

exhortation to Principia. He looks forward to the glorious day when she will be brought before the heavenly King to receive her just reward for a life lived righteously—a life that Jerome assumes responsibility for prescribing to her. Lest Principia should ever be tempted to listen to the naysayers who impugn her teacher's credibility, he reminds her of how indebted she is to his wise counsel: 'Remember me, who with the Lord's help explained this psalm to you.'[24]

Jerome's middling provincial background made him especially susceptible to the charges that had been brought against him in Rome. It continued to be an issue during his Bethlehem years whenever he would approach highborn Christian women, unannounced, through correspondence. One such woman was Salvina, the daughter of Count Gildo, the former governor of Africa.[25] In 392, she married the empress Flaccilla's nephew Nebridius[26] and the couple had two children. When Nebridius died around 399 Jerome used the occasion as a pretext for initiating contact with his widow, with whom he had never corresponded or met in person.[27] In the first half of his letter (*Ep.* 79) he consoles her and eulogizes Nebridius and in the second half he takes it upon himself to lay down some principles by which she should live in order to preserve her widowhood. By offering Salvina unsolicited spiritual advice he was attempting to fix the terms of what he undoubtedly hoped would become a fruitful relationship between them. Nevertheless, as a *novus homo* with no distinguished socio-economic pedigree to speak of, and also as someone who could not readily be recognized by a bishopric, he apparently suspected that writing to her out of the blue was a presumptuous move because of how it might be perceived by others and perhaps by Salvina herself. Hence, twice in the letter he makes a point of denying that he is out to flatter her and to insinuate himself into the imperial court under the appearance of offering consolation.[28]

---

[24] *Ep.* 65.22: *recordare et mei, qui huius psalmi tibi domino revelante intellegentiam tribui.*

[25] *PLRE,* i. 395–6 ('Gildo').   [26] *PLRE,* i. 620 ('Nebridius 3').

[27] *Ep.* 79.1: *loquimur ad eam, cuius faciem ignoramus.*

[28] *Ep.* 79.1, 4. Jerome's overtures to Salvina almost certainly fell on deaf ears. According to Palladius (*Dial.* 10), in 404 she was a deaconess in the inner circle of Jerome's avowed enemy, John Chrysostom. In 399, when she received Jerome's letter, she may already have been John's disciple, as many other women of the eastern imperial court were at that time. At any rate, it seems improbable that Salvina would

The rejected saviour of Roman Christianity

Jerome championed a radical form of asceticism that appealed to only a tiny minority of contemporary Christians. This fact alone pushed him to the periphery of 'mainstream' Christian piety, but at times his theological and rhetorical excesses catapulted him even to the fringes of the ascetic movement in the west. A prime example is the self-ascribed role he played in the early 390s in the controversy about Jovinian's teachings.[29] Jovinian registers on the historical radar for the first time in late-380s Rome when, Jerome tells us, he 'threw the faith of Rome into disarray in my absence'.[30] He composed a treatise, now lost, in which he advanced four theses, the gist of which was that all baptized and morally conscientious Christians are equal before God.[31] Although a monk himself, Jovinian did not believe that ascetic Christians are any better, or will receive a greater eternal reward, than their non-ascetic brothers and sisters in the faith. In the process, he indirectly attacked Jerome's *Ep.* 22 as an example of how *not* to do applied ascetic theology.[32]

Jovinian's movement took Rome by storm, attracting enthusiastic recruits from both the lay and clerical ranks.[33] Jerome was none too pleased to hear of this, especially (one imagines) in view of the fact that his own teachings had never enjoyed anything approximating this degree of popularity. In the early spring of 393 he composed *Adversus Iovinianum* in two books in which he rigorously subjected Jovinian's arguments to his own counter-arguments from Scripture

ever have become a follower of Jerome's, at least as long as she was associated in any capacity with John. For Salvina's association with John, see Wendy Mayer, 'Constantinopolitan Women in Chrysostom's circle', *VChr*, 53 (1999), 270–2.

[29] For a concise chronology of the Jovinianist controversy, see Pierre Nautin, 'Études de chronologie hiéronymienne (393–397), iv. Autres lettres de la période 393–396', *REAug*, 20 (1974), 253–5. For exhaustive treatments of the controversy from theological and social-historical standpoints, see Yves-Marie Duval, *L'affaire Jovinien: d'une crise de la société romaine à une crise de la pensée chrétienne à la fin du IVe et au début du Ve siècle* (Rome, 2003); David Hunter, *Marriage, Celibacy, and Heresy in Ancient Christianity: The Jovinianist Controversy* (Oxford, 2007).

[30] *Dial. adv. Pelag.*, prologue 2: *Iovinianus ... Romanam fidem me absente turbavit.*

[31] Jerome preserves this list in *Adv. Iov.* 1.3.

[32] Hunter, 'Helvidius, Jovinian, and the Virginity of Mary in Late fourth–century Rome', *JECS*, 1 (1993), 52–4.

[33] Hunter, *Marriage*, 17–18.

and the Fathers. The impetus for writing came, he says, from friends in Rome: 'Very few days have elapsed since the holy brethren in Rome sent to me the treatises of a certain Jovinian with the request that I reply to the follies contained in them and crush with evangelical and apostolic vigour the Epicurus of the Christians.'[34] To show that he was not some unwanted guest who arrived at the party uninvited, Jerome portrayed himself, as he had done during his pamphlet war with Helvidius, as the appointed spokesperson of an organized brigade of ascetics.[35] His triumphalist rhetoric about squashing Jovinian 'with evangelical and apostolic vigour',[36] his claim about writing such a long treatise in 'very few days', and his numerous remarks about Jovinian's alleged theological and stylistic incompetence, are tactics meant to dismiss him as a third-rate opponent.[37] Yet such he was not; and Jerome knew it. In fact, in many respects Jovinian was an *alter Hieronymus*. He was a monk,[38] he was highly educated,[39] he wrote with seductive eloquence,[40] and he had a deft command of the classical canon[41] as well as an extensive working knowledge of Scripture.[42] The monk of Bethlehem had finally met his match.

As Jerome was busily working on *Adversus Iovinianum*, Pope Siricius convoked a synod at Rome that condemned Jovinian (*conscriptio temeraria*).[43] Shortly thereafter Jovinian fled to Milan, only to

[34] *Adv. Iov.* 1.1: *pauci admodum dies sunt, quod sancti ex urbe Roma fratres cuiusdam mihi Ioviniani commentariolos transmiserunt, rogantes, ut eorum ineptiis responderem, et Epicurum Christianiorum, evangelico atque apostolico vigore contererem.*

[35] See above, p. 101. Cf. *Dial. adv. Pelag.*, prologue: *crebra fratrum expostulatio fuit, cur promissum opus ultra differrem.*

[36] Benoît Jeanjean, *Saint Jérôme et l'hérésie* (Paris, 1999), 33, sensibly suggests that Jerome compactly cites his credentials as a translator and interpreter of the Bible by alluding here to his revision of the Gospels (384) and commentaries on four of St Paul's epistles (386).

[37] See Ilona Opelt, *Hieronymus' Streitschriften* (Heidelberg, 1973), 37–63.

[38] *Adv. Iov.* 1.40: *cum monachum esse se iactitet.*

[39] *Ep.* 48.3: *norunt litteras, videntur sibi scioli.* Cf. *Ep.* 49.13: *legimus, o eruditissimi viri, in scolis pariter et Aristotelia illa vel de Gorgiae fontibus manantia simul didicimus.*

[40] Cf. *Adv. Iov.* 1.3: *illo venustissimus eloquentiae suae flore.*

[41] See *Adv. Iov.* 1.41.

[42] Jerome refers to the 'endless proof-texts from Scripture [Jovinian] had piled together' (*Adv. Iov.* 2.35: *infinita de Scripturis exempla congesserat*) and calls his writings '*commentarii*' and '*commentarioli*' because they consisted mostly of Scriptural passages cited followed by running commentaries on them (*Adv. Iov.* 1.1, 41). See also Vincent of Lérins, *Comm.* 35, on Jovinian's command of the Bible.

[43] Siricius, *Ep.* 7.

be censured by a council convened there by bishop Ambrose that upheld the decision of the Roman church (*conscriptio horrifica*).[44] Jerome was not aware that Jovinian's fate was already being decided by two separate ecclesiastical bodies. Put another way, he had no idea that two of his own sworn enemies (Siricius[45] and Ambrose[46]) were pre-empting him and that his efforts would not at all contribute to Jovinian's discomfiture. Jerome imagined that he was the lone *deus ex machina*. In the closing paragraph of *Adversus Iovinianum* he describes himself as a new Jonah preaching repentance to the latter-day Nineveh (Rome) and exhorting her to turn back to her pristine faith (i.e., *his* faith) before it is too late.[47] Implicit in this grandiose call to repentance is the suggestion that Jerome was the divinely appointed custodian of Roman Christianity: he and he alone had the prophetic wherewithal to show a backsliding Rome the error of her ways.

In refuting Jovinian Jerome earnestly believed that he was placing Rome's Christian community forever in his debt. The overwhelming majority of Christians there, however, did not agree with him. His incendiary tract ignited a firestorm when it arrived on Italian soil. Jerome had heaped unqualified praise on virginity and seemed to condemn marriage as something intrinsically evil.[48] Critics were quick to charge him with Manichaean dualism.[49] To be accused of Manichaeism was a matter of grave consequence in the late Roman empire,[50] especially for Catholics such as Jerome who prided

---

[44] Ambrose, *Ep. ex. coll.* 15.   [45] See above, pp. 105, 117.

[46] See below, pp. 149–51.

[47] *Adv. Iov.* 2.38: *potes effugere per poenitentiam, habens exemplum Ninivitarum.*

[48] *Ep.* 49.2: *reprehendunt in me quidam, quod...nimius fuerim vel in laude virginum vel in suggillatione nuptiarum.* Cf. *Adv. Iov.* 1.26, where he says that the filth of marriage (*sordes nuptiarum*) is not able to be erased from one's soul even by dying a martyr's death.

[49] *Ep.* 49.2: *dum contra Iovinianum presso gradu pugno, a Manicheo mea terga confossa sunt.* Rufinus (*Apol. c. Hier.* 2.39, 43) later accused Jerome of teaching the 'dogma of the Manichaeans' in *Adversus Iovinianum.* Cf. *Adv. Iov.* 1.3, 5, where Jerome responds to allegations Jovinian makes in his writing that teachers such as Jerome are crypto-Manicheans. On Manichaean monasticism, see Arthur Vööbus, *History of Asceticism in the Syrian Orient* (2 vols., Leuven, 1958), ii. 109–37.

[50] Raymond van Dam, *Leadership and Community in Late Antique Gaul* (Berkeley, Calif., 1985), 78–87.

themselves on their orthodoxy.[51] The emperors in the west became increasingly intolerant of its practice.[52] For example, in 385/6, the Spanish bishop and ascetic Priscillian was executed by the imperial authorities on charges relating to sorcery and Manichaeism.[53] In an interesting twist of fate, Jerome had set out to expose Jovinian as a heretic[54] but in the end he emerged looking like one himself.

Even Jerome's own Christian friends who did agree with him that virginity was superior to marriage thought he had pushed the envelope too far in his (at times) scathing appraisal of marriage. The Roman priest Domnio sent him a letter with an attached list of controversial statements made in the work that he wanted Jerome either to clarify or to correct.[55] The senator Pammachius, Paula's son-in-law and Jerome's long-time acquaintance from his student days in Rome, also was put off by the writing and demanded that his old *condiscipulus* explain or retract portions of it. He was troubled by its tone, too, for Jerome seemed more interested in waxing polemical than in recalling Jovinian from his error in a calm and civil fashion.[56] The satirizing of Jovinian and his followers as morally lax 'Epicureans'[57] was bound to have touched a raw nerve with Pammachius, for some of these very people were his senatorial friends and colleagues.[58] As an

---

[51] Thus Augustine, after his Catholic 'conversion' and especially once he entered into an ecclesiastical career, went out of his way to distance himself from his Manichaean past. See Leo Ferrari, 'Young Augustine: Both Catholic and Manichee', *AugStud*, 26 (1995), 109–28; Hunter, *Marriage*, 270–3. See also Caroline Bammel Hammond, 'Pauline Exegesis, Manichaeism and Philosophy in the Early Augustine', in Lionel Wickham and Caroline Hammond Bammel (eds.), *Christian Faith and Greek Philosophy in Late Antiquity: Essays in Tribute to George Christopher Stead* (Leiden, 1993), 1–25.

[52] Peter Brown, 'The Diffusion of Manichaeism in the Roman Empire', *JRS*, 59 (1969), 92–103; Samuel Lieu, *Manichaeism in the Later Roman Empire and Medieval China: A Historical Survey* (Manchester, 1985), 161–4.

[53] Henry Chadwick, *Priscillian of Avila: The Occult and the Charismatic in the Early Church* (Oxford, 1976), 20–56, 111–48; Virginia Burrus, *The Making of a Heretic: Gender, Authority, and the Priscillianist Controversy* (Berkeley, Calif., 1995), 47–78.

[54] Jeanjean, *Jérôme et l'hérésie*, 31–7.

[55] *Ep.* 50.3: *excerpta de volumine per ordinem digessisti poscens, ut vel emendarem vel exponerem.*

[56] *Ep.* 49.14: *indignamini mihi, quod Iovinianum non docuerim, sed vicerim.*

[57] *Adv. Iov.* 1.1; 2.21, 36, 38.

[58] See John Curran, *Pagan City and Christian Capital. Rome in the Fourth Century* (Oxford, 2000), 296.

indication of how taken aback he was by Jerome's treatise, he removed as many copies as he could from circulation right away.[59]

In a frantic attempt to mend his severely fractured support base at Rome, Jerome composed a lengthy epistolary apology (*Ep.* 49) in which he pleaded his case again from the authority of Scripture and the Fathers.[60] He addressed this work to Pammachius, whom he had hoped to enlist as his publicist *pro tempore*. In the cover letter to the apology, also addressed to Pammachius, Jerome states: 'I have dedicated to you a defence of the work in question and once you read it you will (I feel sure) satisfy others on my behalf'.[61] Two decades later Jerome remarked that 'Rome joyfully received' this letter to Pammachius.[62] However, if we take into account the universally hostile reception of *Adversus Iovinianum*, it is hard to imagine that Jerome's follow-up defence of it could have fared much better. His greatly exaggerated report about its popularity must be understood in the context of his personal and theological feud with Pelagius. In the 410s, the latter had tried to revive public criticism of *Adversus Iovinianum* and Jerome responded by pointing to the success his teaching had enjoyed at Rome.

Rival contemporary Christian writers were no more sanguine about *Adversus Iovinianum* than were Jerome's own friends. Take, for instance, the anonymous Christian author of the *Conversations of Zacchaeus and Apollonius* (*Consultationes Zacchaei et Apollonii*), an apologetic dialogue in three books between two fictitious characters—the Christian Zacchaeus and the pagan philosopher Apollonius. Martin Allen Claussen argues persuasively that this dialogue was composed around 394 in part to counter the hyperascetic teaching of *Adversus Iovinianum*.[63] Although the author

---

[59] Jerome, *Ep.* 48.2; Rufinus, *Apol. c. Hier.* 2.42.

[60] M. T. Messina, 'Hier. *Epist.*, 49.19: Il numero dispari e gli scrittori cristiani', *Sileno*, 28–9 (2002), 61–80.

[61] *Ep.* 48.2: ἀπολογητικόν ipsius operis tibi προσεφώνησα, quem cum legeris... ipse pro nobis ceteris satisfacies.

[62] *In Hier.*, prologue: legat eiusdem operis apologian, quam ante annos plurimos adversum magistrum eius gaudens Roma suscepit.

[63] Claussen, 'Pagan Rebellion and Christian Apologetics in Fourth-century Rome: The Consultationes Zacchaei et Apollonii', *JEH*, 46 (1995), 589–614. Jean-Louis Feiertag, *Les Consultationes Zacchaei et Apollonii: étude d'histoire et de sotériologie* (Freiburg, 1990), 106, suggests that the anonymous author of the *Consultationes*

himself preferred the ascetic way of life, he remained open-minded about other, less austere expressions of the Christian experience and thought that one could be a pious householder and still please God just as much as the desert hermit waging heroic battles with demons.

The most famous contemporary rejoinder to Jerome's *Adversus Iovinianum* came from the pen of Augustine, who in 401 wrote *De bono coniugali*, and then *De sancta virginitate* as its companion piece, in order to silence the boasting that Jovinian could not be refuted by praising marriage but only by disparaging it.[64] Robert Markus calls Augustine's attempt at rehabilitating the married state in these two works 'his covert work *Against Jerome*'.[65] While Augustine did grant that virginity is superior to marriage, he collapsed the distinction between the two and argued that all Christians, whether married or celibate, belong to the Lord's flock and consequently share a common calling to love and serve God to the best of their abilities.[66]

As far as most of his contemporaries were concerned, Jerome had stepped over the line in *Adversus Iovinianum*, and they accordingly set out to correct some of the more outlandish assertions he had made in it. Notwithstanding the criticism levelled against his treatise, Jerome publicly put on a confident face (what else could he do?) and proudly promoted it as an ascetic classic.[67] Nevertheless, the damage had already been done and he had succeeded against his best intentions at marginalizing himself further within the western Christian community.[68]

intended 'corriger la position de Jérôme'. David Hunter, *Marriage, Celibacy, and Heresy*, 250–6, seconds Feiertag's suggestion and expands upon Claussen's argument.

[64] Augustine, *Retract.* 2.22: *iactabatur Ioviniano responderi non potuisse cum laude sed cum vituperatione nuptiarum.*

[65] Markus, *The End of Ancient Christianity* (Cambridge, 1990), 45.

[66] Willemien Otten, 'Augustine on Marriage, Monasticism, and the Community of the Church', *ThS*, 59 (1998), 385–405; Mathijs Lamberigts, 'A Critical Evaluation of Critiques of Augustine's View of Sexuality,' in Robert Dodaro and George Lawless (eds.), *Augustine and His Critics: Essays in Honour of Gerald Bonner* (London, 2000), 176–97; Carol Harrison, *Augustine: Christian Truth and Fractured Humanity* (Oxford, 2000), 158–93. For translations of the relevant writings by Augustine, see Elizabeth Clark, *St Augustine on Marriage and Sexuality* (Washington, DC, 1996), 42–70; Peter Walsh (ed. and trans.), *Augustine: De bono coniugali; De sancta virginitate* (Oxford, 2001).

[67] See *Epp.* 54.18; 58.6; 59.2; 123.8; 133.3; *In Ion.*, prologue.

[68] In this respect the remark by Hans van Campenhausen, *Lateinische Kirchenväter* (Stuttgart, 1960), 126, that 'Jerome is the most assiduous but also the most inadequate

The rogue priest

Reservations by some fellow Christians about his character and theological competence aside, Jerome's overall failure at gaining substantial respectability as a churchman frustrated any attempt by him to
ground his ascetic authority primarily or even partially in an ecclesiastical context—as, for instance, Ambrose did. Jerome's ecclesiastical status was ambiguous. He was a priest but in name only, as he
evidently never practised his vocation with any degree of regular-
ity.[69] Furthermore, the validity of his ordination in the late 370s was
questionable inasmuch as his ordaining bishop, Paulinus, had been
in schism with the church at Antioch at the time.[70] But what rendered Jerome's official standing in the institutional church even more
problematic was that within a decade he was officially pronounced a
miscreant *twice* by high-profile sees—first by the Roman church in
385 and then again in the late spring or early summer of 394 by the
Jerusalem church, as part of the opening act of the Origenist controversy.[71] Jerome's anti-Origenist ally bishop Epiphanius of Salamis
ordained Jerome's younger brother Paulinian and several others in
his monastery, without the permission of bishop John of Jerusalem,
who had jurisdiction over the Church of the Nativity at Bethlehem,
with which Jerome's monastic community was closely affiliated. John
responded to the affront by excommunicating Jerome and all those
who belonged to his community. This sentence ended up lasting three
long years.[72] Its effects were far reaching: Jerome and his cohorts
were barred from entering the Cave and the Church of the Nativity

theologian of asceticism the ancient Church produced' ('Hieronymus ist der eifrigste,
aber auch der dürftigste Theologe der Askese, den die alte Kirche hervorgebracht hat')
seems justified.

[69] e.g., in Bethlehem he refused to perform the sacramental duties of his priesthood
when called upon to do so: see *Ep.* 51.1; Philip Rousseau, *Ascetics, Authority, and the
Church in the Age of Jerome and Cassian* (Oxford, 1978), 130–1.

[70] J. N. D. Kelly, *Jerome. His Life, Writings, and Controversies* (London, 1975), 57–8,
66–7.

[71] Nautin, 'L'excommunication de saint Jérôme', *AEHE* V, 80–1 (1972–3), 7–37.
For a narrative of the Origenist controversy, see Clark, *The Origenist Controversy: The
Cultural Construction of an Early Christian Debate* (Princeton, NJ, 1992). For a concise
summary of Jerome's role in it, see Rebenich, *Jerome* (London and New York, 2002),
41–51.

[72] It was lifted by John on Holy Thursday (2 Apr.) of 397.

as well as other churches in the diocese of Jerusalem;[73] the priests in his monastery were not allowed to administer the sacraments;[74] indeed, it seems that nobody in the community was permitted even to receive the Eucharist.[75] Things went from bad to worse in the early autumn of 395. John obtained from Flavius Rufinus, the powerful praetorian prefect of the east, an official order banishing Jerome and his monks permanently from Palestine.[76] Rufinus was assassinated on 27 November 395, before the order could be carried out. The matter was abruptly dropped and Jerome managed to dodge one of the most fatal bullets of his entire war-torn career.

There was nothing dishonourable about being a priest, provided that one lived an unblemished life. To be sure, for some Christians in the late Roman empire the attainment of the priesthood was a mark of some distinction; it was proof that one had 'arrived'. Nevertheless, in terms of the real and perceived authority that they wielded in both the visible church and in the unseen spiritual realm by virtue of their respective offices, there was a qualitative difference between priests and bishops.[77] Because Jerome was not a bishop his writings, like those of fellow freelancing monks Pelagius and Rufinus, did not

---

[73] *C. Ioh. Hier.* 42.   [74] Ibid.   [75] Nautin, 'L'excommunication', 16–17.

[76] *C. Ioh. Hier.* 43; *Ep.* 82.10. See *PLRE*, i. 778–81 ('Flavius Rufinus'). Melania, by now no longer a friend of Jerome's, undoubtedly had used her connections with the eastern imperial court (on which, see E. D. Hunt, *Holy Land Pilgrimage in the Later Roman Empire, AD 312–460* (Oxford, 1982), 170–1, 174–7) to expedite the process. If Jerome knew about Melania's activities on this front, it certainly would explain in large part why he nursed such a nasty grudge against her from the middle 390s until at least 415. In a letter to Paula (*Ep.* 39.5), written during the autumn of 384, Jerome had idealized Melania as an *exemplum peregrinationis* and encouraged Paula to follow in her footsteps. By the middle 390s, however, he was of a different mindset. Rufinus (*Apol. c. Hier.* 2.26) alleged that Jerome even tried to strike her name from the historical record by removing his flattering notice on her from personal copies of his *Chronicon* (entry for 374 AD). See also *Ep.* 133.3 (*c.*415), in which Jerome mockingly puns on the Greek etymology of Melania's name: *ad eam, cuius nomen nigredinis testatur perfidiae tenebras.*

[77] For an overview of the bishop's many functions in the early Christian centuries, see Henry Chadwick, 'The Role of the Christian Bishop in Ancient Society', in *Center for Hermeneutical Studies, Protocol of the Thirty-fifth Colloquy (Feb. 1979)* (Berkeley, Calif., 1980), 1–14; see also the essays in *Vescovi e pastori in epoca teodosiana. In occasione del XVI centenario della consacrazione episcopale di s. Agostino, 396–1996* (Rome, 1997). Augustine (*Ep.* 82.33) comments on how according to the parlance of ecclesiastical hierarchy (*honorum vocabula*), the *episcopatus* is greater than the *presbyterium.*

come with the sanction of episcopal authority, as did those of other contemporary writers such as Ambrose and Augustine. This is not to say of course that a bishop's writings came with an automatic *imprimatur* simply because their author held high ecclesiastical office. Indeed, there are numerous late antique examples (Priscillian being one) for whom this clearly was not the case. All things being equal, though, the episcopate did invest one's writings with a certain dignity that the writings of somebody who was not a bishop did not intrinsically possess. In principle, then, Jerome's word could never carry as much weight as that of a bishop—something of which he was all too conscious. When called upon to rebuke an unnamed mother and daughter in Gaul for cohabiting with clerical paramours, he initially declined on the grounds that this kind of counselling was the prerogative of the bishop: 'As if I held an episcopal chair instead of being shut up in a monastic cell where, far removed from the world's turmoil, I lament the sins of the past and try to avoid present temptations!'[78]

An illustration of how Jerome's ambiguous ecclesiastical status affected his reception as an authority figure is the way in which Augustine appropriated his name in a pamphlet war with Julian, the Pelagian bishop of Eclanum.[79] Around 421, a couple of years after Jerome's death, Augustine composed his massive *Contra Iulianum* in which he defended his positions on original sin, infant baptism, and marriage. He rested his case on the infallible authority of Scripture and the consensus of the Fathers, from Irenaeus to John Chrysostom in the east and from Cyprian to Ambrose in the west.[80] He made a point of citing orthodox writers who were also bishops, and he reminded the reader of their official status by inserting the title '*episcopus*' at every opportunity. The only non-episcopal writer to make

---

[78] *Ep.* 117, prologue: *quasi vero episcopalem cathedram teneam et non clausus cellula ac procul a turbis remotus vel praeterita plangam vitia vel vitare nitar praesentia.* For a study of this fascinating letter, see Cain, 'Jerome's *Epistula* 117 on the *Subintroductae*: Satire, Apology, and Ascetic Propaganda in Gaul', *Augustinianum*, 49 (2009), forthcoming.

[79] On Julian's life and works, see Josef Lössl, *Julian von Aeclanum. Studien zu seinem Leben, seinem Werk, seiner Lehre und ihrer Überlieferung* (Leiden, 2001).

[80] Fernando Perago, 'Il valore della tradizione nella polemica tra s. Agostino e Giuliano d'Eclano', *AnnNap*, 10 (1962), 143–60. See also Éric Rebillard, 'A New Style of Argument in Christian Polemic: Augustine and the Use of Patristic Citations', *JECS*, 8 (2000), 559–78.

Augustine's list is Jerome. In the first book, after running through a roll-call of patristic authorities, he arrives at Jerome. As if anticipating Julian's prejudice against Jerome's priestly status, Augustine cautions his episcopal colleague: 'Do not think that holy Jerome should be looked down upon because he was a priest.'[81] He then tries to compensate for Jerome's lack of episcopal rank by replacing it with intellectual authority, praising his trilingualism (*qui Graeco et Latino, insuper et Hebraeo, eruditus eloquio*) and encyclopaedic knowledge of all Christian theological literature (*omnesque vel pene omnes qui ante illum aliquid ex utraque parte orbis de doctrina ecclesiastica scripserant legit*). Later in the same writing, Augustine again shows a palpable unease when invoking Jerome as a doctrinal authority.[82] He produces a shortlist of episcopal writers who he claims have espoused his notion of original sin. He tacks Jerome on at the end almost as an afterthought: 'I add to these Jerome the priest, whether you like it or not' (*quibus addo presbyterum, velis nolis, Hieronymum*).[83] The phrase '*velis nolis*' has a snappish ring to it here. Augustine goes on the defensive and makes excuses for Jerome because, being a bishop himself, he is fully aware of how Julian and any other elitist-minded bishop for that matter may object to this 'mere' priest being named in the same distinguished company as episcopal writers.[84]

JEROME'S SPIRITUAL ADVICE

We have just examined key facets of Jerome's profile that seriously impaired his efforts to establish himself in the eyes of contemporary Christians as a credible figure of spiritual authority. In light of this

[81] *C. Iul.* 1.34: *nec sanctum Hieronymum, quia presbyter fuit, contemnendum arbitreris.*

[82] For the citation of Jerome as an authority in theological debates in fifth-century Gaul, see Ralph Mathisen, 'The Use and Abuse of Jerome in Gaul during Late Antiquity', in Cain and Lössl, *Jerome of Stridon*, Chap. 15.

[83] *C. Iul.* 2.33.

[84] It is worth noting that priests such as Jerome were not the only victims of episcopal elitism. Augustine, as bishop of a provincial North African town, occasionally found himself snubbed by more prestigious episcopal colleagues such as bishop Atticus of Constantinople. See Conrad Leyser, *Authority and Asceticism from Augustine to Gregory the Great* (Oxford, 2000), 3.

discussion, two pertinent questions arise. What did Jerome claim was his right to speak on spiritual matters in the first place and then to set himself up as a guide for others? Along these same lines: how did he attempt to distinguish himself from rival spiritual writers with whom he competed for a following? In the remainder of this chapter, I shall address these two interrelated questions through case studies on three representative letters.

The voice of one *still* calling in the desert

Jerome's brief experiment as a 'desert' monk in the 370s was fundamental to any and all spiritual authority to which he would later lay claim. It is from this arena of metaphorical warfare that he was supposed to have emerged as a tried and tested man of God qualified to give guidance to others on the path to spiritual perfection.[85] According to the 'way of the desert', purity of heart, manifested in righteous deeds, entitled the monk to speak authoritatively on spiritual matters.[86] The post-Chalcis Jerome was a holy man not unlike the veteran *abba* of the eastern desert to whom eager neophyte monks flocked to receive a word of salvation.[87] Indeed, from the early 390s on, Christians throughout the world did flock to him, either in person or through correspondence, to receive words of wisdom about matters of practical spirituality.

Jerome was not the only fourth-century ascetic writer to have spent time in the 'desert'. For example, in the 370s, John Chrysostom withdrew for two years to a secluded mountain retreat and lived a solitary life of prayer and fasting.[88] Nevertheless, it is worth pointing out that Jerome was the first *Latin* ascetic writer to cite this kind of life experience explicitly as a basis for personal spiritual authority. In Chapter 1, we saw how his self-construction in the *Epistularum ad diversos*

---

[85] See Chapter 1.

[86] Gregorio Penco, 'Il concetto di monaco e di vita monastica in Occidente nel secolo VI', *StudMon*, 1 (1959), 37–43; Rousseau, *Ascetics, Authority, and the Church*, 21–32.

[87] On the *abbas*–disciple relationship, see Graham Gould, *The Desert Fathers on Monastic Community* (Oxford, 1993), 26–87.

[88] J. N. D. Kelly, *Golden Mouth: The Story of John Chrysostom: Ascetic, Preacher, Bishop* (Grand Rapids, Mich., 1995), 32–5.

liber as the quintessential monk was intended to ingratiate him as a would-be spiritual mentor to the women of the 'Aventine circle'. After leaving Rome, he continued to make a similarly embellished version of the story of his desert sojourn accessible to as wide a reading audience as possible. In 393, he immortalized the *Epistularum ad diversos liber* in his auto-bibliography (*Vir. ill.* 135) and thereby took steps to insure that he would be known, for all time to come, as a desert 'saint'. Furthermore, in his later correspondence he reminded readers of *Ep.* 14 to Heliodorus,[89] which he had written from Chalcis, as well as *Ep.* 22 to Eustochium,[90] in which he had included a vivid account of his time in the Syrian 'wilderness'.[91] Jerome inserted reminiscences of his years as an 'anchorite' also into letters of spiritual advice to Nepotian and the Gallic monk Rusticus. In the two sections to follow, I shall argue that he did so for strategic purposes: to define himself as an authoritative teacher of the ascetic life in contradistinction to certain rival teachers at whom he takes aim at the subtextual level.

Ep. 52 to Nepotian

Nepotian was the nephew of Jerome's old friend Heliodorus, bishop of the small town of Altinum in northern Italy near Aquileia from *c.*380 until *c.*400. He served for a time in the palace guard but resigned his post and became a monk, selling off his property and giving the proceeds to the poor.[92] He also was ordained a priest by Heliodorus, and it was undoubtedly at the latter's prompting that Nepotian wrote to Jerome, apparently on a number of occasions,[93] requesting advice about how to live his vocation as a monk–cleric to the

---

[89] *Epp.* 52.1; 77.9.   [90] *Epp.* 49.18; 52.17; 123.17; 130.19.

[91] See above, pp. 38–9. In addition, in a letter (*Ep.* 18*) he wrote in Rome in 384, he spoke as a weathered veteran of the desert when urging the deacon Praesidius to forsake his home, family, and ecclesiastical office and flee to the wilderness and lead a life of prayerful solitude.

[92] *Ep.* 60.10: *balteo posito habituque mutato, quidquid castrensis peculii fuit in pauperes erogavit.* See *PCBE*, ii. 1535–6 ('Nepotianus').

[93] *Ep.* 52.1: *petis, Nepotiane carissime, litteris transmarinis et crebro petis, ut tibi brevi volumine digeram praecepta vivendi.*

fullest.[94] In 393,[95] Jerome sent a polished epistolary treatise (*Ep.* 52) in which he promised to 'guide you from the cradle of faith to spiritual manhood and, by laying down step-by-step precepts for living, instruct others by instructing you'.[96] From the last clause of this passage it is evident that Jerome did not intend this handbook solely for the private edification of Nepotian. He meant it to circulate widely and to be of use to Christian clerics throughout northern Italy and the west.

Jerome vows to teach Nepotian what it takes to be a priest, while Heliodorus is delegated the task of teaching him how to be a good monk.[97] At first glance, this is an unexpected reversal of roles. A bishop who could not stomach life in the desert[98] is now called upon to be a model for monks, and a card-carrying monk who does not practise his priesthood puts himself in charge of instructing on the cleric's duties. The role-reversal makes good sense, though, when considered in the context of Jerome's agenda in the letter. He argues that exemplary personal sanctity achieved through ascetic self-discipline should be *the* defining feature of the clergy.[99] He envisages what is essentially a monastic clergy, one in which true ecclesiastical *dignitas* does not consist in rank per se but in the piety of the office-holder. As a result, rank itself becomes secondary and even the traditional hierarchical distinction between priest and bishop theoretically disappears, because 'as there is one Lord and one temple, so also should there be one ministry'.[100]

---

[94] Not more than three years later, Nepotian died and Jerome sent Heliodorus a letter of consolation (*Ep.* 60). For a commentary on this letter, see J. H. D. Scourfield, *Consoling Heliodorus: A Commentary on Jerome, Letter 60* (Oxford, 1993).

[95] Nautin, 'Études de chronologie hiéronymienne (393–397), iv. Autres lettres de la période 393–396', *REAug*, 20 (1974), 251–3.

[96] *Ep.* 52.4: *te ab incunabulis fidei usque ad perfectam ducat aetatem et per singulos gradus vivendi praecepta constituens in te ceteros erudiat.*

[97] *Ep.* 52.4: *suscipe et libellum hunc libello illius copulato, ut, cum ille* [sc. Heliodorus] *te monachum erudierit, hic clericum doceat esse perfectum.*

[98] *Ep.* 14.1–2.

[99] Rousseau, *Ascetics, Authority, and the Church*, 125–32; Ralph Hennings, 'Hieronymus zum Bischofsamt', *ZKG*, 108 (1997), 1–11. See also Pierre Hamblenne, 'Jérôme et le clergé du temps: idéaux et réalités', *Augustinianum*, 37 (1997), 351–410.

[100] *Ep.* 52.7: *unus dominus, unum templum, unum sit etiam ministerium.* See also *Ep.* 146 to Evangelus.

In his reconceptualization of the institutional hierarchy in wholly monastic terms Jerome is not so much replacing episcopal elitism with a more egalitarian view that all clerics are on the same level as he is advocating another kind of elitism that privileges the full-time ascetic. Furthermore, if clerics must now become ascetics, then to whom can they turn for instruction except to an acclaimed expert on the ascetic life? Enter Jerome, who as we saw above offers his services to Nepotian and to 'others'. But before proposing his controversial notion of the monastic clergy Jerome cites his spiritual credentials, alluding briefly but poignantly to his tenure in the desert:

When I was a young man (*adulescens*), or rather almost still a boy (*puer*), and was curbing the first attacks of lascivious youth with the austerity of the desert, I wrote to your uncle, the holy Heliodorus, a letter of exhortation that was full of tears and complaints and that showed the deep affection of the comrade he had deserted.[101]

Jerome says first that he was a 'young man' (*adulescens*) and then clarifies that he was almost 'a boy' (*puer*). In Hieronymian parlance an '*adulescens*' is anyone under thirty-three years of age, while a '*puer*' is a male up to the age of nineteen years.[102] It is historical fact that Jerome was in his early thirties during his stay in Chalcis in the middle 370s. This means that he was already at least a decade removed from *pueritia* and at the tail end of his *adulescentia*. In the passage above, he creatively adjusts the chronology of his own life to make himself sound like an ascetic 'boy wonder'. While his peers were revelling in teenage vices, he 'was curbing the first attacks of lascivious youth with the austerity of the desert'.[103]

The letter-treatise dedicated to Nepotian was not the only one of its kind in circulation in the late fourth century. Sometime between 388 and 390 bishop Ambrose of Milan released his own

---

[101] *Ep.* 52.1: *dum essem adulescens, immo paene puer, et primos impetus lascivientis aetatis heremi duritia refrenarem, scripsi ad avunculum tuum, sanctum Heliodorum, exhortatoriam epistulam plenam lacrimis querimoniisque et quae deserti sodalis monstraret affectum.*

[102] Hamblenne, 'La Longévité de Jérôme: Prosper avait-il-raison?', *Latomus*, 28 (1969), 1081–119.

[103] Cf. in *Ep.* 50.1 Jerome speaks of his 'daily study of the Law, the Prophets, the Gospels, and the Apostles from my youth up until now' (*ab adulescentia usque ad hanc aetatem cotidiana in lege, prophetis, evangeliis apostolisque meditatio*).

monumental handbook on clerical ethics in three books under the title *De officiis*.[104] In the preface, he makes the following candid confession:

Having been whisked into the priesthood from a career at the tribunes and from the distinctions of administrative office, I began to teach you what I did not learn myself. It has been the case then that I began to teach before learning. Therefore, I must simultaneously learn and teach, seeing that I did not have time beforehand to learn.[105]

Ambrose alludes to the complete lack of advance preparation he had received upon assuming his pastoral duties as bishop of Milan.[106] A week prior to his ordination (7 December 374) and instalment into one of the premier western bishoprics he had been an unbaptized catechumen with no formal theological training to speak of.[107] In a letter to his Roman friend Oceanus, which dates to late 395 or early 396, Jerome satirizes one such overnight promotion: 'Yesterday a catechumen, today a bishop; yesterday in the amphitheatre, today in the church; in the circus in the evening and in the morning at the altar; once the patron of actors, now the consecrator of virgins.'[108] This may well be one of many veiled attacks on Ambrose that litter Jerome's writings.[109] The exact reason behind his contempt for the bishop

---

[104] See Ivor Davidson, 'Ambrose's *De Officiis* and the Intellectual Climate of the Late Fourth Century', *VChr*, 49 (1995), 313–33; id., *Ambrose: De officiis. Introduction, Text, Translation, and Commentary* (2 vols., Oxford, 2001).

[105] *Off.* 1.4: *ego enim raptus de tribunalibus atque administrationis infulis ad sacerdotium, docere vos coepi quod ipse non didici. itaque factum est ut prius docere inciperem quam discere. discendum igitur mihi simul et docendum est quoniam non vacavit ante discere.*

[106] Ambrose's frankness in this passage, which goes beyond conventional Christian self-deprecation, is discussed by Hervé Savon, 'Les Intentions de saint Ambroise dans la préface du *De officiis*', in Michel Soetard (ed.), *Valeurs dans le stoïcisme, du portique à nos jours. Textes rassemblés en hommage à Michel Spanneut* (Lille, 1993), 155–69.

[107] For the sequence of events leading up to his ordination, see Neil McLynn, *Ambrose of Milan: Church and State in a Christian Capital* (Berkeley, Calif., 1994), 1–13.

[108] *Ep.* 69.9: *heri catechumenus, hodie pontifex; heri in amphitheatro, hodie in ecclesia; vespere in circo, mane in altari; dudum fautor strionum, nunc virginum consecrator.* For a close analysis of this passage, see Adkin, ' "Heri catechumenus, hodie pontifex" (Jerome, *Epist.*, 69.9.4)', *AClass*, 36 (1993), 113–17.

[109] The possible and certain references by Jerome to Ambrose have been assembled in the following studies: Angelo Paredi, 'S. Gerolamo e s. Ambrogio', in *Mélanges Eugène Tisserant, Studi e Testi 235* (Vatican City, 1964), 183–98; Gérard Nauroy,

remains a subject of scholarly debate. Angelo Paredi suggested on shaky grounds that he began resenting Ambrose in the late summer of 385 because he allegedly blamed him for not using his influence to rescue him from certain condemnation by the Roman church.[110] Neil Adkin has suggested that Jerome's ill will was motivated by a sense of professional rivalry and that it manifested itself as far back as 384, in the form of a mock tribute to Ambrose's *De virginibus* in his own *libellus* on virginity (*Ep.* 22).[111] Whatever the case, it is clear that Jerome had little if any respect for Ambrose as a biblical exegete and as an ascetic theorist.[112]

Jerome seems to have known Ambrose's *De officiis* first-hand. In fact, it has been argued that he formulated *Ep.* 52 in part as a veiled refutation of this work.[113] In view of the intriguing possibility that he intended his letter-treatise to supplant Ambrose's, Jerome's furnishing of his monastic credentials in the opening of *Ep.* 52 assumes fresh significance. While Ambrose frankly admitted that he had taught men how to be godly clerics before first learning the clerical ropes himself, Jerome presumed to offer such instruction only because he was a committed ascetic who had what he implied to be a *lifetime* of rigorous spiritual training under his belt. The contrast between the two men's qualifications, which would have been readily apparent to

'Jérôme, lecteur et censeur de l'exégèse d'Ambroise', in Duval (ed.), *Jérôme entre l'Occident et l'Orient*, XVIe centenaire du départ de saint Jérôme de Rome et de son installation à Bethléem. Actes du colloque de Chantilly, Sept. 1986 (Paris, 1988), 173–203; Steven Oberhelman, 'Jerome's Earliest Attack on Ambrose: *On Ephesians*, Prologue (ML 26: 469D–70A)', *TAPhA*, 121 (1991), 377–401; Adkin, 'Jerome on Ambrose: The Preface to the Translation of Origen's Homilies on Luke', *Rbén*, 107 (1997), 5–14.

[110] 'S. Gerolamo e S. Ambrogio'. For a brief refutation of Paredi's thesis, see Cain, 'In Ambrosiaster's Shadow: A Critical Re-evaluation of the Last Surviving Letter-exchange between Pope Damasus and Jerome', *REAug*, 51 (2005), 266–7.

[111] 'Ambrose and Jerome: The Opening Shot', *Mnemosyne*, 46 (1993), 364–76.

[112] The feeling evidently was mutual. Ambrose, in a letter written near the end of life, criticized certain of Jerome's theological opinions. See Hunter, 'The Raven Replies: Ambrose's *Letter to the Church at Vercelli (Ep. ex. coll. 14)* and the Criticisms of Jerome', in Cain and Lössl, *Jerome of Stridon*, Chap. 14.

[113] For this suggestion, see Maurice Testard, 'Jérôme et Ambroise. Sur un "aveu" du *De officiis* de l'évêque de Milan', in Duval, *Jérôme entre l'Occident et l'Orient*, 227–54; Ivor Davidson, 'Pastoral Theology at the End of the Fourth Century: Ambrose and Jerome', *StudPatr*, 33 (1997), 295–301. Cf. Adkin, 'Jerome, Ambrose and Gregory Nazianzen', *Vichiana*, 4 (1993), 294–300.

any ancient reader because of their placement at the front of each treatise, could not be any more glaring. This, I suggest, is precisely the effect for which Jerome was aiming.

Ep. 125 to Rusticus

In 412, Jerome wrote an epistolary manifesto (*opusculum*[114]) on the monastic life and addressed it to Rusticus, a classically educated monk living in Marseilles (*Ep.* 125).[115] He may have been the same Rusticus who on 9 October 427 succeeded Hilarius as bishop of Narbonne and went on to become one of the most prominent Gallic bishops of the day.[116] If this identification is correct, then an important piece of epigraphical evidence throws some light on the *cursus* that the ecclesiastical-monastic career of Jerome's addressee followed. An inscription dated to 29 November 445, in the nineteenth year of Rusticus' episcopate, shows that he belonged to an ecclesiastical dynasty: both his father Bonosus and uncle Arator had been bishops. The inscription also places him and Venerius, the future bishop of Marseilles (*c.*431–*c.*451), as fellow priests in a monastery at Marseilles in the early 420s.[117] In the letter he wrote to Jerome requesting a treatise about the virtues of the coenobitic monastic life, Rusticus

[114] *Ep.* 125.17: *in praesenti opusculo*.

[115] On the monastic communities in late antique Marseilles, see Élie Griffe, 'Saint Martin et le monachisme gaulois', *Saint Martin et son temps. Mémorial du XVIe centenaire des débuts du monachisme en Gaule 361–1961* (Studia Anselmiana, 46) (Rome, 1961), 17–18; Jean-Remy Palanque, *Le Diocèse de Marseilles* (Paris, 1967); Simon Loseby, 'Marseilles: A Late Antique Success Story?', *JRS*, 82 (1982), 165–85. On the 'ascetic invasion' of late antique Gaul more generally, see Markus, *End of Ancient Christianity*, Chap. 13.

[116] So Hartmut Atsma, 'Die Christlichen Inschriften Galliens als Quelle für Klöster und Klosterbewohner bis zum Ende des 6. Jahrhunderts', *Francia*, 4 (1976), 10–17; Martin Heinzelmann, *Bischofsherrschaft in Gallien: Zur Kontinuität römischer Führungsschichten vom 4. bis zum 7. Jahrhundert* (Munich, 1976), 106–8; Rousseau, *Ascetics, Authority, and the Church*, 122.

[117] The relevant portion reads: *Rusticus ep[iscopu]s Bonosi filius / ep[iscop]i Aratoris de sorore nepus / ep[iscop]i Veneri soci[us] in monasterio / conpr[es]b[yteri] eccle[siae] Massiliens[is]*. See Henri-Irénée Marrou, 'Le Dossier épigraphique de l'évêque Rusticus de Narbonne', *RACr*, 3–4 (1970), 331–49.

evidently mentioned a desire to enter the clergy.[118] At the time of writing he was still a lay monk probably living in the monastery presided over by Proculus, the influential bishop of Marseilles from 381 until *c*.431.[119] In his reply to Rusticus Jerome praises Proculus as '*sanctus*' and '*doctissimus*' and exhorts the young monk to stay close to his bishop, who can 'outdo my written sheets with his living and present voice and direct your path by his daily homilies'.[120] This gesture of collegial deference may have been motivated by at least two practical considerations besides Jerome's sincere sense of Christian charity. Because by virtue of his letter to Rusticus he was taking charge of advising someone probably already under the direct spiritual care of Proculus, he may have wanted to assure the bishop that he had no intention of undermining his jurisdiction, which would have been considered a serious offence in late antique Gaul.[121] The flattering overture can also be read similarly as Jerome's way of making sure he stayed in the bishop's good graces. For getting off on the wrong foot with Proculus, however unintentionally, might have resulted in his being blackballed in some of the most important Christian circles at Marseilles.[122]

With due *politesse* accorded Rusticus' bishop, Jerome assumes the role of mentor-from-afar to his young protégé. He invokes the language of kinship and makes Rusticus play the son to his spiritual father (*fili Rustice*[123]), declaring that he is responsible for presenting him 'without spot or wrinkle as a chaste virgin, holy in mind as well

---

[118] At *Ep.* 125.8, Jerome directs Rusticus to *Ep.* 52 in the event that he enters the priesthood: *habeant illi ordinem et gradum suum, quem si tenueris, quomodo tibi in eo vivendum sit, editus ad Nepotianum liber docere te poterit.*

[119] On Proculus' ecclesiastical career, see Ralph Mathisen, *Ecclesiastical Factionalism and Religious Controversy in Fifth–century Gaul* (Washington, DC, 1989), 21–4, 52–60.

[120] *Ep.* 125.20: *habes ibi sanctum doctissimumque pontificem Proculum, qui viva et praesenti voce nostras scidulas superet cotidianisque tractatibus iter tuum dirigat.*

[121] See Mathisen, *Ecclesiastical Factionalism, passim.*

[122] Jerome is known to have worried about clerics using their influence to turn their flocks against him. For example, he wrote to Augustine (*Ep.* 112.18): 'You must not incite the ignorant rabble against me, those who revere you as their bishop and who welcome you, when you preach in church, with the esteem owed to the bishopric' (*neque mihi inperitorum plebeculam concites, qui te venerantur ut episcopum et in ecclesia declamantem sacerdotii honore suscipiunt*).

[123] *Ep.* 125.1.

as in body.[124] Jerome introduces a nautical metaphor to dramatize
the difficulty of the journey that lies ahead[125] and to impress upon
Rusticus that he must rely on his seafaring expertise: 'Like a skilled
sailor who has been through many shipwrecks, I am anxious to cau-
tion an inexperienced passenger.'[126] What 'shipwrecks' has the 'skilled
sailor' endured? He answers this question later in the letter when
he conjures up a haunting still-life portrait of his days as a desert
monk:

When I was a young man and the deserted haunts of the wilderness impris-
oned me, I was not able to handle the allurements of vice and the heat
of my passions. Although I tried to break the force of both with frequent
fasts, my mind still welled up with unclean thoughts. To bring my wayward
mind under control I committed myself to a certain brother, an ex-Jew, to
teach me Hebrew, so that after the pointedness of Quintilian, the rivulets of
Ciceronian eloquence, the weightiness of Fronto, and the mildness of Pliny,
I learned the alphabet all over again and mulled over words that were both
harsh-sounding and guttural. What effort I expended on this, what hardship
I went through, how often I lost all hope, and how often I threw my hands
up in the air and then went back to it out of an eagerness to learn—I who
suffered through all of this and those who lived with me can attest to what I
say. I give thanks to the Lord that from this bitter seed of learning I now pick
sweet fruits.[127]

---

[124] *Ep.* 125.20: *sine ruga et macula quasi pudicam virginem exhibeam sanctamque
tam mente quam corpore.*

[125] The proverbial perilousness of ancient sea travel provided material for a
metaphor, often invoked by Jerome in his letters (*Epp.* 14.6; 43.3; 77.6; 147.11), about
the hidden pitfalls of the spiritual life. See Henri Rondet, 'Le Symbolisme de la mer
chez saint Augustin', Congrès international augustinien, *Augustinus Magister* (3 vols.,
Paris, 1954), ii. 691–711; Bernard McGinn, 'Ocean and Desert as Symbols of Mystical
Absorption in the Christian Tradition', *JR*, 74 (1994), 155–81.

[126] *Ep.* 125.2: *quasi doctus nauta post multa naufragia rudem conor instruere vec-
torem.*

[127] *Ep.* 125.12: *dum essem iuvenis et solitudinis me deserta vallarent, incentiva vitio-
rum ardoremque naturae ferre non poteram; quae cum crebris ieiuniis frangerem, mens
tamen cogitationibus aestuabat. ad quam edomandam cuidam fratri, qui ex Hebraeis
crediderat, me in disciplinam dedi, ut post Quintiliani acumina Ciceronisque fluvios
gravitatemque Frontonis et lenitatem Plinii alphabetum discerem, stridentia anhelan-
tiaque verba meditarer. quid ibi laboris insumpserim, quid sustinuerim difficultatis,
quotiens desperaverim quotiensque cessaverim et contentione discendi rursus inceperim,
testis est conscientia tam mea, qui passus sum, quam eorum, qui mecum duxere vitam.
et gratias ago domino, quod de amaro semine litterarum dulces fructus capio.*

Jerome presents himself as the consummate monk–scholar. He is a
battled-scarred ascetic athlete who knows first-hand what it is like
to struggle against temptation. He is a conscientious prose stylist
and man of letters whose literary refinement is bound to appeal
to the classically trained Latin monk—the very demographic subset
he ostensibly addresses in his letter.[128] Last, but not least, he is a
dedicated biblical scholar who sublimated his spiritual travails by
mastering a language as challenging as Hebrew.[129] Finally, lest anyone
should doubt his claim that he really did live the hard life of the
desert, Jerome adds that his lifestyle was witnessed by 'those who lived
with me'.

Jerome follows up the auto-hagiographic memoir quoted above
with an anecdote that has the look and feel of the kind we frequently encounter in the *Apophthegmata patrum*. The story, set in
a monastery in Egypt, concerns a young Greek-speaking monk who
could not get a handle on his passions no matter how much fasting
and other self-mortifications to which he subjected himself.[130] The
abbot wanted to distract him from further psychological torment
and arranged to have a fellow monk spread nasty gossip about him.
Whenever witnesses (who were complicit in the abbot's plot) were
called to hear the accusations they would judge on the side of the
slanderer. Things went on like this for a year, until finally the vic-
timized monk was asked if lustful thoughts still plagued him. He
responded: 'Good gracious, how can I find pleasure in fornication
when I am not allowed so much as to live?' Jerome concludes the story
with a lesson: 'Had he been a solitary hermit, by whose aid could he
have overcome the temptations that assailed him?' Besides infusing
some *variatio* into the letter, this story illustrates one of the running
themes of *Ep*. 125: that the communal life is superior to the solitary
life.[131] Additionally, it serves as another case in point of Jerome's self-
professed familiarity with the monastic east, and more specifically
with Egypt. He introduces the section as follows: 'I shall also mention

---

[128] *Ep*. 125.8: *nunc monachi incunabula moresque discutimus et eius monachi, qui liberalibus studiis eruditus in adulescentia iugum Christi collo suo inposuit.*
[129] Jerome refers to his reading knowledge of Hebrew in other letters of ascetic advice (e.g., *Epp*. 122.2; 130.7).
[130] See *Ep*. 22.33 for a similar-sounding of anecdote set in Egypt.
[131] See esp. section 9.

another thing that I saw in Egypt' (*dicam et aliud, quid in Aegypto viderim*).[132] This '*aliud*' presupposes at least one other thing that he 'saw' in Egypt, and the postpositive '*et*' grammatically points back to the section immediately preceding this one where Jerome speaks of his time as a desert monk. Jerome thus is implying that he has first-hand knowledge of Egyptian desert monasticism.

The irony, of course, is that with the exception of a brief tour of the monasteries of Nitria with Paula in the winter of 385/6[133] Jerome never set foot in Egypt. This fact, however, did not prevent him from speaking of Egyptian monastic customs as if he had an insider's knowledge of them,[134] nor did it stop him from retroactively switching the location of his own monastic experiment in Syria to there. Why did he do this?—because Egypt was regarded by most western Christians as the birthplace of monasticism.[135] Jerome presumably claimed an Egyptian monastic pedigree in order to emphasize that he was as authentic a spiritual master as they came—unlike, for instance, certain monastic authorities in Rusticus' own Gaul who were home-grown on western soil and who had never been to the fabled Egyptian desert, much less lived there for any extended period.[136] There is reason to believe that he had one Gallic monastic celebrity in partic-ular in his sights: St Martin (336–97), the Pannonian soldier turned miracle-working monk and first bishop of Tours. The contemporary case for Martin's sainthood was pressed most forcefully by the Aqui-tanian aristocrat Sulpicius Severus. His *Vita sancti Martini*, released about a year before its subject's death in 397, showcases Martin's thau-maturgical feats, especially his exorcisms.[137] Not a few of Sulpicius'

---

[132] *Ep.* 125.13.　　[133] *Ep. adv. Ruf.* 22; *Ep.* 108.14.

[134] *Epp.* 22.34–6; 125.11; 130.17. For Augustine's reliance on Jerome's *Ep.* 22 for his discussion of the Egyptian monks and their customs in the first book of his *Mor. eccl. cath.*, see John Coyle, *Augustine's De Moribus Ecclesiae Catholicae: A Study of the Work, its Composition and its Sources* (Freiburg, 1978).

[135] See above, pp. 37–8.

[136] This lack of experience in the desert was John Cassian's primary complaint about Gallic monks as well. See Goodrich, *Contextualizing Cassian*, Chapter 3.

[137] For all literary and chronological questions related to Martin and his *V. Mart.*, see Clare Stancliffe, *St Martin and his Hagiographer* (Oxford, 1983). Dated but still useful are Hippolyte Delehaye, 'Saint Martin et Sulpice Sévère', *AB*, 38 (1920), 5–136; Jacques Fontaine, *Sulpice Sévère: vie de saint Martin* (Paris, 1967–9). On the cult of St Martin, see Raymond van Dam, *Saints and their Miracles in Late Antique Gaul* (Princeton, NJ, 1993), 13–28.

fellow Gauls were highly sceptical of these lavish claims,[138] and, as we shall see in a moment, Jerome would seem to have joined in their chorus.

Jerome was no admirer of Sulpicius for a number of plausible reasons. First, Sulpicius was a rival Latin hagiographer pushing a competing ascetic agenda. Second, Sulpicius' friendship with Paulinus of Nola, Rufinus, and Melania during the course of the Origenist controversy in the 390s would have earned him nothing but demerits from Jerome.[139] Finally, around 404, Sulpicius drew what Richard Goodrich convincingly shows to be an unflattering sketch of the monk of Bethlehem in his *Dialogi de virtutibus sancti Martini* (1.8–9, 21).[140] Jerome made unsympathetic references to both Sulpicius and Martin in various writings. One comes from his commentary on Ezekiel (410–14). In his exposition of Ezekiel 36: 1–15, where the prophet foretells a future time of material prosperity for Israel, Jerome rejects the idea that this passage prophesies the millennium, an interpretation advanced by a few Greek and Latin Christian writers, including 'recently our own Severus in the dialogue he has entitled *Gallus*'.[141] The reference is to *Dial.* 2.14, where Martin discusses his eschatological views and the imminent advent of the Antichrist. Paul Antin was the first to suggest what seems to be an odd allusion in Jerome's commentary on Isaiah (408–10) to the famous episode in the *Vita sancti Martini* (3.1–2) where the soldier Martin divides his cloak in two and gives one-half to a beggar at the city gate of Amiens. Jerome compares Isaiah 58: 7 ('If you see a man who is naked, clothe him') with Luke 3: 11 ('the one who has two cloaks should give one to he who has none') and explains that the Lord 'did not order that one cloak be torn and parcelled

[138] Sulpicius, *Ep.* 1; *Dial.* 2.13.7; 3.15.4. See Stancliffe, *St Martin*, 249–61; Van Dam, *Leadership and Community in Late Antique Gaul* (Berkeley, Calif., 1985), 119–20.

[139] Stancliffe, *St Martin*, 300–10; Gerrit van Andel, 'Sulpicius Severus and Origenism', *VChr*, 34 (1980), 278–87.

[140] Goodrich, '*Vir maxime catholicus*: Sulpicius Severus' use and abuse of Jerome in the *Dialogi*', *JEH*, 58 (2007), 189–210. See also Duval, 'Sulpice Sévère entre Rufin d'Aquilée et Jérôme dans les Dialogues 1. 1–9', in *Mémorial Dom Jean Gribomont* (Rome, 1988), 199–222. On the dating of the *Dialogi* to 404, see Jacques Fontaine, *Sulpice Sévère. Gallus: dialogues sur les vertus de saint Martin* (Paris, 2006), 20–2.

[141] *In Hiez.* 9.36.1/15: *nuper Severus noster in dialogo cui 'Gallo' nomen imposuit.*

out, which many do to gain popularity with the masses, but that a second one should not be kept'.[142] In his letter to Rusticus, Jerome makes what seems to be another veiled indictment of Martin and his hagiographer:

I wish for soldiers[143] to emerge from the monastic academies...who do not know how to invent (as certain men do) incredible stories about demons fighting with them in order to build themselves up as heroes among uneducated and simple folk and to make a profit from them.[144]

This criticism fits Sulpicius and Martin perfectly, and it is all the more pointed because it is found in a letter to a *Gallic* audience. Among the many spiritual exploits with which Sulpicius credited his subject, hand-to-hand spiritual combat with demons consistently stands out.[145] Furthermore, Jerome's insinuation that these supernatural tales were invented as part of a moneymaking scheme may have been inspired by Sulpicius' own comment that as soon as the *Vita* had made it to Rome it became an instant sensation and booksellers rejoiced at its high asking price.[146] If some of Martin's most impressive feats turned out to be the stuff of fairy tales,[147] then he would be exposed as a charlatan who did not deserve respect, much

---

[142] *In Es.* 16.58.7: *Si 'videris nudum, operi.' quod et Dominus in evangelio loquebatur: qui habet duas tunicas, det alteram non habenti.' non enim unam iussit scindi et dividi, quod multi popularis aurae causa faciunt; sed alteram non servari.*

[143] Like other patristic writers, Jerome on occasion referred to monks as 'soldiers' using the *militia Christi* metaphor (*Epp.* 14.2; 45.6; 49.7; 52.13; 118.5; 125.8). See Jean Leclercq, 'Militare Deo dans la tradition patristique et monastique', in *Militia Christi e crociata nei secoli XI–XIII* (Milan, 1992), 3–18.

[144] *Ep.* 125.9: *de ludo monasteriorum huiusce modi volumus egredi milites...qui nesciunt secundum quosdam homines daemonum obpugnantium contra se portenta confingere, ut apud inperitos et vulgi homines miraculum sui faciant et exinde sectentur lucra.* For the identification with Martin, see, e.g., Rousseau, *Ascetics, Authority, and the Church,* 122; Rebenich, *Hieronymus und sein Kreis: Prosopographische und sozialgeschichtliche Untersuchungen* (Stuttgart, 1992), 253.

[145] *V. Mart.* 6, 17, 18, 21–2; *Dial.* 1.20, 22; 2.8, 9, 13; 3.6, 8, 15. Martin not coincidentally was appointed an exorcist early on in his ecclesiastical career (see *V. Mart.* 5).

[146] *Dial.* 1.23: *deinde cum tota certatim urbe raperetur, exultantes librarios vidi, quod nihil ab his quaestuosius haberetur, siquidem nihil illo promptius, nihil carius venderetur.*

[147] Jerome's ridiculing of Sulpicius (and Martin) for inventing stories about struggles with demons could easily have been turned around on himself, for in his *V. Hilar.* (4–12) he glamorizes Hilarion's battles with demons.

less a cult following. Turnabout was fair play. Sulpicius alleged in his
Dialogi (e.g., 1.24–5) that Martin stood head and shoulders above
even the most legendary monks of the east by virtue of his sanctity
and thaumaturgy.[148] This means that, even though he never spent any
time whatsoever in the desert, Martin was spiritually superior also
to any westerner such as Jerome who claimed an eastern monastic
pedigree.[149] It goes without saying that Jerome, who had read the
Dialogi by the time he wrote to Rusticus, would not have appreciated
this devaluation of monks of his ilk. If the interpretation of *Ep.* 125
advanced here is correct, one of the reasons why Jerome cited—in
rather dramatic fashion, no less—his monastic training in the 'desert'
was to vindicate his spiritual authority in Gaul against dissenting
voices such as Sulpicius Severus and to impress upon Gallic monks
that they needed a teacher who identified intimately with the venerable monastic tradition of the east.[150]

The mentor of virgins and widows

We have seen examples of Jerome citing his experience in the 'desert'
to corroborate his claim to expertise on the monastic life. When
he wrote letters to virgins and widows exhorting them to chastity,
especially later in his career, he regularly appealed to another type of
experientia: his track record as a spiritual advisor-by-correspondence.
In his letter to Salvina on widowhood, for example, he mentions 'the
many people to whom I have written before about this same subject
matter'.[151] Similarly, he points out to the Gallic widow Geruchia
that, 'I have often written to widows and in exhorting them I have
produced many examples from Holy Scripture and have woven
together the many-coloured flowers of its truths into one garland of

---

[148] For an extensive introduction to this and other themes in the Dialogi, see
Fontaine, *Sulpice Sévère. Gallus*, 17–73.

[149] See Jean Gribomont, 'L'influence du monachisme oriental sur Sulpice Sévère',
Saint Martin et son temps, 135–49.

[150] For an attempt by Jerome to justify his spiritual authority to Gallic Christians
in another context, see Cain, 'Jerome's *Epistula* 117 on the *Subintroductae*'.

[151] *Ep.* 79.1: *multorum...ad quos ante super eadem materia scripseram*.

chastity'.[152] By making statements such as these, Jerome presumably intended to make his readers aware, if they were not aware already, that his services were in great demand. Just as significantly, his experience as a seasoned writer of *ascetica* implied a profound knowledge of Scripture, as he hints with his floral metaphor in the second quotation above.[153] When furnishing his credentials, Jerome often went beyond vague allusions to his other writings and mentioned them by name. At the end of *Ep.* 123 to Geruchia he announces that this letter will become the third instalment of (what turned out to be) a Hieronymian trilogy of epistolary treatises on widowhood. He recommends a shortlist of further reading to her that includes three of his other works on virginity (*Ep.* 22 to Eustochium) and widowhood (*Ep.* 54 to Furia and *Ep.* 79 to Salvina).[154] By earmarking these three as indispensable guidebooks for showing 'how you ought to live in chaste widowhood', Jerome is essentially enshrining them as ascetic classics.[155] Furthermore, because he neglects to mention the writings of other contemporaries on widowhood with which he undoubtedly was familiar, such as Ambrose's *De viduis* (377/8), he gives the impression, intentionally no doubt, that the literary tradition *de servanda viduitate* begins and ends with him. There is at least one instance elsewhere in his correspondence in which Jerome is similarly self-referential and emphasizes his own vast experience in paraenesis in

---

[152] *Ep.* 123.1: *saepe ad viduas scripsimus et in exhortatione earum multa de scripturis sanctis exempla repetentes varios testimoniorum flores in unam pudicitiae coronam texuimus.*

[153] Jerome was quite fond of using this floral metaphor to describe the compositional technique he deployed in his letters of spiritual advice. See *Epp.* 117.12: *de Scripturis pauca perstrinxi nec orationem meam, ut in ceteris libris facere solitus sum, illarum floribus texui*; 122.4: *haec omnia quasi per pulcherrima Scripturarum prata discurrens in unum locum volui congregare et de speciosissimis floribus coronam tibi texere paenitentiae*; 130.9: *haec cursim quasi de prato pulcherrimo sanctarum Scripturarum parvos flores carpsisse sufficiat pro commonitione tui.*

[154] *Ep.* 123.17: *legito, quomodo tibi in viduitate vivendum sit, librum ad Eustochium de virginitate servanda et alios ad Furiam atque Salvinam, quarum altera Probi quondam consulis nurus, altera Gildonis, qui Africam tenuit, filia est. hic libellus 'De monogamia' sub nomine tuo titulum possidebit.*

[155] Further evidence of the special status Jerome accorded *Ep.* 54 and *Ep.* 79 is that when writing in 407 to the Gallic Christian widow Hedibia, he pointed her to these two 'libelli' (*Ep.* 120.1).

order to contrast it with that of a specific rival writer. It is to this letter that we now turn.

Ep. 130 to Demetrias

The last letter of spiritual exhortation to survive from Jerome's pen was written in 414 to Demetrias (*Ep.* 130),[156] a teenage virgin from the *gens Anicia*, which next to the *gens Ceionia* was the most prestigious family in the late Roman west.[157] In the aftermath of the invasion of Rome by the Visigothic chieftain Alaric in 410, Demetrias, her mother Juliana and grandmother Anicia Faltonia Proba[158] fled from Italy as refugees to North Africa, where they were welcomed by bishop Aurelius of Carthage. By 413, Demetrias was engaged to be married to a nobleman who had stayed behind in Italy. For whatever reason, whether at her own prompting or at that of her mother and grandmother, or a combination of the two, the wedding was called off and Demetrias resolved to remain a lifelong virgin. After she had taken the virgin's veil in an elaborate ceremony presided over by Aurelius, Juliana wrote to Jerome and asked him to address a letter to her daughter with counsel that would prepare her for her vocation. Jerome opens his letter to Demetrias by explaining its occasion. He also takes the opportunity to cite his decades-long experience in treating a wide range of subject matters on the ascetic life:

Of all the subjects about which I have written from my youth up until now, either in my own hand or by dictating to secretaries, none is more difficult

[156] *PCBE*, ii. 544–6 ('Demetrias Amnia').

[157] M. T. W. Arnheim, *The Senatorial Aristocracy in the Later Roman Empire* (Oxford, 1972), 50.

[158] *PCBE*, ii. 1169–71 ('Anicia Iuliana 3') and ii. 1831–3 ('Anicia Faltonia Proba 2'). Proba was the widow of Sextus Claudius Petronius Probus and doyenne of the Anician clan. She rather than Faltonia Betitia Proba may have been the famous centonist: see Danuta Shanzer, 'The Anonymous *Carmen contra paganos* and the Date and Identity of the Centonist Proba', *REAug*, 32 (1986), 232–48; ead., 'The Date and Identity of the Centonist Proba', *RecAug*, 27 (1994), 75–96. See also T. S. Mommaerts and David Kelley, 'The Anicii of Gaul and Rome', in John Drinkwater and Hugh Elton (eds.), *Fifth–century Gaul: A Crisis of Identity?* (Cambridge, 1992), 111–21.

than the present work. I am to write to Demetrias, a virgin of Christ, who ranks first in the Roman world in nobility and wealth...Her grandmother and mother are both women of distinction, and they have the authority to command, faithfulness to seek out, and perseverance to obtain what they ask for. They do not indeed request from me anything new or special, I whose talents have often been exercised upon subjects of this sort.[159]

Jerome closes the letter with an even more assertive affirmation of his credentials. The result is a ring composition: he sandwiches the instruction given in the body of the letter between two vivid reminders to the reader about why his word on the subject of virginity should be trusted. He first digresses about the rocky reception of his *Libellus de virginitate servanda* to Eustochium (*Ep.* 22), openly admitting what the Anician women, as prominent members of the Roman ascetic circles in the 380s would already have known—namely, that its satire had offended a great many (secularized) Christians in Rome. As he did elsewhere, so here Jerome defends it on the score that the only ones to lodge a complaint are the 'hypocrites' whose vices he has exposed. Nevertheless, these disgruntled critics come and go, but his book stands the test of time and is here to stay (*liber manet, homines praeterierunt*).[160] Implicit in this bold statement about the permanence of his work is perhaps the hint to Demetrias that she could expect to be immortalized by his pen, just as Eustochium had been.

Further on, Jerome alludes to his other writings on the ascetic life and then situates *Ep.* 130 in the patristic literary tradition *de virginitate*:

I have written short hortatory treatises to several virgins and widows, and all that is able to be said on the subject is set forth in these works. The result is that I either risk redundancy in repeating the same exhortations or injure this treatise by omitting them. The blessed Cyprian has, to be sure, left an outstanding book on virginity, and many others writing in Greek or Latin

[159] *Ep.* 130.1: *inter omnes materias, quas ab adulescentia usque ad hanc aetatem vel mea vel notariorum scripsi manu, nihil praesenti opere difficilius. scripturus enim ad Demetriadem, virginem Christi, quae et nobilitate et divitiis prima est in orbe Romano...tanta est aviae eius et matris, insignium feminarum, in iubendo auctoritas, in petendo fides, in extorquendo perseverantia. neque enim ut novum quiddam et praecipuum a me flagitant, cuius ingenium in huiusce modi materiis saepe detritum est.*
[160] Jerome appropriates the aphoristic-sounding phrase '*liber manet*' from a letter by Pliny the Younger. See Cain, '*Liber manet*: Pliny, *Ep.* 9.27.2 and Jerome, *Ep.* 130.19.5', *CQ*, NS 58 (2008), 708–10.

have done likewise. The virginal life has been praised by the writings and tongues of all nations, especially in the churches. Those who have not yet chosen virginity and need persuading to do so should read these other works so that they may know what it is they must choose. As for me, I advise those who have made their choice. Let us go among scorpions and serpents so that, with our loins girded, our sandals tied, and our staffs in hand, we may navigate the snares and banes of this world and be able to reach the sweet waters of the Jordan and to enter into the land of promise.[161]

This passage has a pronounced magisterial tone. Jerome explicitly states that his body of work contains all that the Christian virgin will ever need to know about her chosen religious profession. He pays homage to Cyprian's *De habitu virginum* and he acknowledges, without naming names, the contributions that many other writers have made to this literary tradition.[162] Nevertheless, he is keen to point out that his own letter-treatises stand in a class of their own, for they offer Demetrias a level of expert instruction, tailor-made to her special needs, that others' writings simply cannot offer. To reinforce his point, Jerome brilliantly typologizes himself as a new Moses ready to lead his prospective disciple into the Promised Land of spiritual perfection.[163] Such a bald assertion of the supremacy of his own writings is unparalleled in his *œuvre*. Is this mere showmanship or is there something more to it? The answer to this question would seem to lie in a careful consideration of the polemical reference point

---

[161] *Ep.* 130.19: *scripsi et ad plerasque virgines ac viduas* σπουδασμάτια *et quiquid dici poterat, in illis opusculis defloratum est, ut aut ex superfluo eadem a nobis repetantur aut nunc praetermissa plurimum noceant. certe et beatus Cyprianus egregium de virginitate volumen edidit et multi alii tam Latino sermone quam Graeco omniumque gentium litteris atque linguis, praecipue in ecclesiis,* ἁγνὴ *vita laudata est. sed hoc ad eas pertineat, quae necdum elegerunt virginitatem et exhortatione indigent, ut sciant, quale sit, quod eligere debeant; nobis electa servanda sunt et quasi inter scorpiones et colubros incedendum, ut accinctis lumbis calciatisque pedibus et adprehensis manu baculis iter per insidias huius saeculi et inter venena faciamus possimusque ad dulces Iordanis pervenire aquas et terram repromissionis intrare.*

[162] Cf. *Ep.* 22.22, where he refers Eustochium to Cyprian's '*volumen egregium*'. On Jerome's admiration for the North African Father, see Simone Deléani, 'Présence de Cyprien dans les œuvres de Jérôme sur la virginité', in Duval (ed.), *Jérôme entre l'Occident et l'Orient*, 61–82.

[163] Note also earlier in the letter (2) how he borrows Pauline phraseology to express his sense of spiritual proprietorship over Demetrias: *in opere praesenti avia quidem materque plantaverint, sed et nos rigabimus et dominus incrementum dabit* (cf. 1 Cor. 3: 6: *ego plantavi, Apollo rigavit, sed Deus incrementum dedit*).

for *Ep.* 130: Jerome's well-documented personal and theological feud with Pelagius.[164]

Juliana wrote separately to Pelagius on behalf of her daughter. At the time, he was living in Jerusalem under the protection of its bishop John, Jerome's old nemesis. Her contacting him was not an unexpected move. Pelagius had enjoyed a longstanding and close association with Demetrias' immediate family and had been supported financially by them during his time in Rome from the early 380s until 410.[165] It is understandable, then, why Juliana turned to him. But why also to Jerome? His reputation as an expert on women's spirituality would most assuredly have preceded him. Since the middle 380s, he had been a household name in Roman ascetic circles. After establishing himself in Bethlehem he went on to become one of the most recognizable figures of the ascetic movement in the west. Juliana's friendship with Augustine, Pelagius' most vocal opponent in North Africa, may also have been a factor in her decision to seek Jerome's opinion. It has been suggested (though there is no evidence to support it) that Augustine nudged her to write to him so that he and Jerome could present a united front against Pelagius.[166] Or, it may be that Juliana began to have second thoughts about Pelagius' theology following his condemnation at a synod at Carthage in 411/12.[167] Whatever the case, it seems clear that she wanted to keep her options open and to give both Jerome and Pelagius the opportunity to plead their respective cases.

Jerome knew from the outset that he was competing with a longtime client of the Anicians for the honour of being Demetrias'

[164] Kelly, *Jerome*, 309–23; Jeanjean, *Jérôme et l'hérésie*, 387–431; id., 'Le *Dialogus Attici et Critobuli* de Jérôme et la prédication pélagienne en Palestine entre 411 et 415', in Cain and Lössl, *Jerome of Stridon*, Chap. 5; Philip Rousseau, 'Jerome on Jeremiah: Exegesis and Recovery', in Cain and Lössl, *Jerome of Stridon*, Chap. 6.

[165] Peter Brown, 'Pelagius and his Supporters: Aims and Environment', *JThS*, NS 19 (1968), 83–114; id., 'The Patrons of Pelagius: The Roman Aristocracy between East and West', *JThS*, NS 21 (1970), 56–72.

[166] Walter Dunphy, 'Saint Jerome and the Gens Anicia (Ep. 130 to Demetrias)', *StudPatr*, 18 (1990), 139–45.

[167] For the debate about the dating, see J. H. Koopmans, 'Augustine's First Contact with Pelagius and the Dating of the Condemnation of Caelestius at Carthage', *VChr*, 8 (1954), 149–53; J. Refoulé, 'Datation du premier concile de Carthage contre les Pélagiens et du *Libellus fidei* de Rufin', *REAug*, 9 (1963), 41–9.

spiritual protector.[168] Scholars have long suspected that he had somehow obtained a copy of his rival's letter[169] to the young girl before
composing his own. Georges de Plinval was the first to advance this
hypothesis.[170] He noted some verbal parallels between the *exordia* of
both letters:

Pelagius, *Ep. ad Dem.* 1.1: *novum ... et ... praecipuum ... quoddam flagitat.*[171]

Jerome, *Ep.* 130.1: *neque ... novum et praecipuum quiddam ... flagitant.*

The collocation of these words, unattested anywhere else in extant
Latin literature, would seem to suggest tentatively that either Jerome
was evoking Pelagius' phraseology or vice versa. Plinval, followed
by J. N. D. Kelly,[172] assumed, without stating reasons, that Jerome
was the one who copied Pelagius' turn of phrase. Adalbert de Vogüé
adduced a number of additional plausible verbal parallels between
the two letters and, on the basis of these, argued persuasively that
Jerome did in fact have access to Pelagius' letter before writing his
own.[173] Furthermore, there are indications internal to *Ep.* 130 that
Jerome conceived his letter in part to be a rebuttal of Pelagius' letter.
His exhortation to Demetrias that she rely completely on the mercy of
God and the free gift of divine grace rather than on her own merits[174]
seems like a calculated rebuff to Pelagius' advice that she recognize
her innate ability to achieve spiritual perfection of her own volition.[175] Pelagius' lengthy warning to Demetrias to beware of flatter-
ers may explain Jerome's numerous—more numerous than usual—
protestations that his praise of her virtues and those of her family was

---

[168] See M. Gonsette, 'Les Directeurs spirituels de Demetrias', *NRTh*, 60 (1933),
783–801; Andrew Jacobs, 'Writing Demetrias: Ascetic Logic in Ancient Christianity',
ChHist, 69 (2000), 719–48.

[169] For the Latin text of Pelagius' letter, see *PL* 30: 15–45. A suitable translation
can be found in Bryn Rees, *Pelagius: Life and Letters* (2 vols., Woodbridge, 1991), ii.
35–70.

[170] *Pélage. Ses écrits, sa vie et sa réforme* (Lausanne, 1943), 246 n. 1.

[171] *PL* 30: 16.   [172] *Jerome*, 313 n. 19.

[173] Vogüé, *Histoire littéraire du mouvement monastique dans l'antiquité* (6 vols.,
Paris, 1991–2003), v. 320–2.

[174] *Ep.* 130.12.   [175] E.g., *Ep. ad Dem.* 2.1.

motivated by only the purest of intentions.[176] Additionally, Jerome's cryptic condemnation of Origenism (16) is a proxy condemnation of Pelagianism, for Jerome saw the latter 'heresy' as arising from the former.[177]

By the middle teens of the 400s, Pelagius had a number of important titles to his credit, including the tracts *De virginitate*[178] and *De natura*[179] and a commentary on St Paul's epistles.[180] Jerome therefore knew that he was squaring off against a rival who was not only an experienced spiritual director but also who had a long personal association with the Anician house. For this reason, he went a step further than simply appealing in vague terms to his advisorial experience, as he did in other comparable letters,[181] and claimed with stunning forthrightness that his writings offered Demetrias a quality and comprehensiveness of instruction she could not find elsewhere. But far more was at stake for Jerome than just the right, a distinct honour in itself though that was, to oversee the spiritual maturation of the girl to whom he dedicated his last great work on virginity. The highly suggestive imagery he used to typecast himself as a latter-day Moses poised to lead Demetrias into the Promised Land (not to mention the explicit typological link he drew between *Ep.* 22 and *Ep.* 130 as the two bookends of his personal library of ascetic masterpieces) makes it abundantly clear that Jerome was grooming the young Anician to become the iconic symbol of Hieronymian-style *virginitas* for the next generation of female ascetics, just as Eustochium, now a woman in her mid-forties, had been for the previous generation. This was a golden opportunity—perhaps Jerome's last, as he was nearing the

[176] E.g., *Ep.* 130.1: *si cuncta virtutibus eius congrua dixero, adulari putabor*; 2: *procul obtrectatio, facessat invidia, nullum in ambitione sit crimen*; 7: *sentio me inimicorum patere morsibus, quod adulari videar nobilissimae et clarissimae feminae.*

[177] Kelly, *Jerome*, 313; Clark, *Origenist Controversy*, 146.

[178] For the Latin text, see CSEL, 1: 224–50. The attribution of this letter to Pelagius has occasionally been disputed, but Robert Evans, *Four Letters of Pelagius* (London, 1968), *passim*, makes a reasonable case for its authenticity.

[179] Duval, 'La Date du *De natura* de Pélage: les premières étapes de la controverse sur la nature de la grâce', *REAug*, 36 (1990), 257–83.

[180] Theodore de Bruyn, *Pelagius's Commentary on St Paul's Epistle to the Romans* (Oxford, 1998).

[181] See above, pp. 158–9.

end of his life—to bid for the patronage of one of the most influential Christian families in the west and, if his efforts met with a positive outcome,[182] to come one step closer to making a lasting mark on Latin Christian spirituality in his own day and beyond.

LEGITIMIZATION

Jerome was but one of many Christian spiritual writers in the late fourth and early fifth centuries who competed for a sympathetic audience. Various problematic aspects of his profile that we surveyed in this chapter overshadowed his efforts to legitimize himself and his fringe cause among the wider Christian community. To make matters worse for him, the open field of competition, of which he was uneasily aware (e.g., he knew that he was not the only one whom Juliana Anicia had consulted), virtually guaranteed that his ascetic authority could never be taken for granted as being absolute and undisputed—and indeed it was not, even (sometimes) by those in his inner circle, as the Jovinianist affair made abundantly clear. Jerome accordingly went to great lengths to convince prospective followers why he was a more competent spiritual director than his many rivals and why his teachings were intrinsically superior to theirs. In the case studies presented in this chapter, I argued that Jerome justified his right to advise on spiritual matters in three different epistolary moments by appealing either to his tenure as a desert monk or to his fulsome bibliography of

---

[182] After 414 we hear of no further contact between Jerome and Demetrias or any member of her immediate family, and a lack of any other pertinent evidence makes it impossible to know to what extent his advice may have influenced her personal spirituality and, conversely, to what extent her family's possible endorsement of his ascetic programme may have impacted on his legacy in the fifth century. There is evidence, though, that she remained in contact with Augustine: see Patrick Laurence, 'Proba, Juliana et Démétrias: Le Christianisme des femmes de la *gens Anicia* dans la première moitié du Ve siècle', *REAug*, 48 (2002), 158–61. We do nevertheless know from a dedicatory inscription for the basilica of Pope St Stephen I (254–7) in Rome, the building of which Demetrias financed later in life, that she was a virgin at her death (the first elegiac diptych reads: *cum mundum linquens Demetrias Amnia virgo/clauderet extremum non moritura diem*). See Maurice Testard, 'Démétrias, une disciple de saint Jérôme, et la *sollicitudo animi*', *BSAF* (1999), 251–5.

ascetica, both of which testified to his vast personal experience living as a committed Christian and to a profound insight into the spiritual life that was implied by this experience. Furthermore, I argued that Jerome's reasons for developing these specific modes of authority are best understood in the context of an antagonistic dialogue he was carrying on at the subtextual level of each letter with formidable authorities on the ascetic life: an imperious bishop (Ambrose); a deceased miracle-working monk–bishop (St Martin) and the hagiographer who kept his legacy alive and well (Sulpicius Severus); and a fellow monk and freelancing Christian writer (Pelagius). In each instance, Jerome tried ever so subtly, drawing from the full range of his impressive rhetorical repertoire, to displace the authority figure in question by trumping that person's supposed inexperience and lack of expertise with his own superabundance of both. All of this was in an attempt to fortify his own standing as a spiritual authority and to make the case that his (ascetic) interpretation of Christianity best preserved the pristine purity of the Gospel message.

6

The Exegetical Letters

Over the course of his long and illustrious scholarly career, Jerome translated into Latin, or revised existing translations of, most of the Bible.[1] He also produced scores of commentaries on individual biblical books. For the New Testament he composed commentaries on Matthew (398) and St Paul's epistles to the Galatians, Ephesians, Titus, and Philemon (386[2]). He defined himself first and foremost as an Old Testament scholar, a preference reflected by his output. He wrote massive *opera* on Isaiah (408–10), Ezekiel (410–14), and Jeremiah (414–16), and smaller-scale commentaries on Ecclesiastes (388/9), Daniel (407), the Psalms (before 393), and the Minor Prophets (393–406).[3] In addition, he composed several other works, such as the *Liber de nominibus hebraicis* (389/91)

---

[1] Between 390 and 405 he translated the canonical Old Testament from the Hebrew: see Pierre Jay, 'La Datation des premières traductions de l'Ancien Testament sur l'hébreu par saint Jérôme', *REAug*, 28 (1982), 208–12. On his revisions and translations of the Psalter, see Arthur Allgeier, *Die altlateinischen Psalterien: Prolegomena zu einer Textgeschichte der hieronymianischen Psalmübersetzungen* (Freiburg, 1928); Colette Estin, *Les Psautiers de Jérôme: à la lumière des traductions juives antérieures* (Rome, 1984). As for the New Testament, Ferdinand Cavallera showed almost a century ago that Jerome did not revise or retranslate Acts, the Pauline epistles, or the Apocalypse; the Gospels were the only portion of the New Testament for which he was responsible: 'Saint Jérôme et la Vulgate des Actes, des Épîtres et de l'Apocalypse', *BLE*, 21 (1920), 269–92. It is now believed that a scholar working in Rome in the late fourth century, perhaps Rufinus the Syrian, was behind the Vulgate version of these books.

[2] Pierre Nautin, 'La Date des commentaires de Jérôme sur les épîtres pauliniennes', *RHE*, 74 (1979), 5–12.

[3] For a recent reassessment of the importance of the Minor Prophets commentaries within Jerome's exegetical corpus, see Megan Hale Williams, *The Monk and the Book: Jerome and the Making of Christian Scholarship* (Chicago, 2006), 97–131.

and the *Quaestiones hebraicae in Genesim* (391/2),[4] to serve as companion pieces for study of the Bible. An often undervalued but none the less important segment of Jerome's work as a biblical scholar is what concerns us in this chapter: his exegetical correspondence.

Biblical exegesis figures in virtually all of Jerome's letters,[5] but certain letters—which all together comprise over one-quarter of his surviving correspondence—consist almost entirely of the close reading and exposition of the biblical text.[6] These letters belong to the literary genre of *quaestiones et responsiones*, in which knotty Scriptural problems were posed and then solved. This genre flourished among Christians in the fourth and fifth centuries.[7] Of Jerome's twenty-six extant exegetical letters, one was written *c*.380 in Constantinople,[8] nine were written in Rome between 383 and 385,[9] and the remaining sixteen were written from Bethlehem to Christians in

[4] Adam Kamesar, *Jerome, Greek Scholarship, and the Hebrew Bible: A Study of the Quaestiones Hebraicae in Genesim* (Oxford, 1993); C. T. R. Hayward, *Jerome's Hebrew Questions on Genesis* (Oxford, 1995).

[5] Barbara Conring, *Hieronymus als Briefschreiber. Ein Beitrag zur spätantiken Epistolographie* (Tübingen, 2001), 225: 'Exegese ist das prägende inhaltliche Element fast eines jeden Briefes von Hieronymus.'

[6] For an inventory of these letters, see below, pp. 218–19.

[7] Gustave Bardy, 'La Littérature patristique des *quaestiones et responsiones* sur l'écriture sainte', *RBi*, 41 (1932), 210–36, 341–69, 515–37; *RBi*, 42 (1933), 14–30, 211–29, 328–52; Lorenzo Perrone, 'Sulla preistoria delle *quaestiones* nella letteratura patristica. Presupposti e sviluppi del genere letterario fino al IV sec.', *AnnSE*, 8 (1991), 485–505; id., 'Perspectives sur Origène et la littérature patristique des *Quaestiones et Responsiones*', in Gilles Dorival and Alain le Boulluec (eds.), *Origeniana Sexta*, Origen et la Bible: Actes du Colloquium Origenianum Sextum, Chantilly, 30 Aug.–3 Sept. 1993 (Leuven, 1995), 151–64; Kamesar, *Jerome, Greek Scholarship, and the Hebrew Bible*, 82–96; Annelie Volgers and Claudio Zamagni (eds.), *Erotapokriseis. Early Christian Question-and-Answer Literature in Context. Proceedings of the Utrecht Colloquium, 13–14 October 2003* (Leuven, 2004); Sophie Lunn-Rockliffe, *Ambrosiaster's Political Theology* (Oxford, 2007), 64–7.

[8] *Ep.* 18A + B. Jerome later dedicated it to Pope Damasus. See Nautin, 'Le *De Seraphim* de Jérôme et son appendice *ad Damasum*', in Michael Wissemann (ed.), *Roma renascens. Beiträge zur Spätantike und Rezeptionsgeschichte. Festschrift Ilona Opelt* (Frankfurt, 1988), 257–93.

[9] To Marcella: *Epp.* 25, 26, 28, 29, 34. To Pope Damasus: *Epp.* 20, 21, 36. To Paula: *Ep.* 30.

Italy,[10] Gaul,[11] and Pannonia.[12] The exegetical letters come in all shapes and sizes. Some are monographs on a specific biblical theme and explanations of a block of Scriptural text.[13] Others deal with technical lexicographical and text-critical questions relating to words or phrases in the Hebrew Bible.[14] Quite a few more, varying widely in length among themselves, answer lists of questions about miscellaneous passages from the Old and New Testaments.[15]

Scholars overwhelmingly access Jerome's exegetical letters from the Bethlehem years in two main capacities: (for their theological content) as scattered pieces in the puzzle of his intellectual biography and (for their prosopographical value) as evidence for whom he was in contact with and when. The fruits of these two approaches, to be sure, have greatly enhanced our knowledge of Jerome's developing profile as a biblical exegete and especially of the composition of his social network during his time in Bethlehem from 386 until his death c.419.[16] There has, however, been no intensive investigation into the absolutely vital propagandistic dimension of the post-Roman exegetical correspondence that explores, in particular, the ways in which Jerome negotiated his contested authority as an interpreter of Scripture. The present chapter aims to begin to fill this void. Here, as in previous chapters, my intention is by no means to reduce the letters

[10] *Ep.* 59 to Marcella (Rome, 395/6); *Ep.* 64 to Fabiola (Rome, 397); *Ep.* 65 to Principia (Rome, 397); *Ep.* 69 to Oceanus (Rome, 397); *Ep.* 73 to Evangelus (Rome, 398); *Ep.* 74 to Rufinus (Rome, 398); *Ep.* 78 to Fabiola (Rome, 400); *Ep.* 85 to Paulinus (Nola, 400); *Ep.* 140 to Cyprian (Rome?, c.417); *Ep.* 146 to Evangelus (Rome, unknown date).

[11] *Ep.* 55 to Amandus (Bordeaux, c.394); *Ep.* 119 to Minervius and Alexander (Toulouse, 406); *Ep.* 120 to Hedibia (Bordeaux, 407); *Ep.* 121 to Algasia (Cahors?, 407); *Ep.* 129 to Claudius Postumus Dardanus (Narbonne, 414).

[12] *Ep.* 72 to Vitalis (398).

[13] *Ep.* 18A + B on Isa. 6; *Ep.* 21 on the parable of the prodigal son; *Ep.* 30 on the alphabetical Psalms; *Ep.* 64 on Aaron's priestly vestments; *Ep.* 65 on Ps. 45; *Ep.* 69 on bishops remarrying; *Ep.* 72 on Solomon and Ahaz; *Ep.* 73 on Melchizedek; *Ep.* 74 on the judgement of Solomon; *Ep.* 78 on Numbers 33; *Ep.* 129 on the Promised Land; *Ep.* 140 on Ps. 90; *Ep.* 146 on equality of deacons and priests.

[14] *Ep.* 20 on the word 'hosanna'; *Ep.* 25 on the ten names of God; *Ep.* 26 on the words 'alleluia', 'amen', 'maranatha'; *Ep.* 28 on the word 'selah'; *Ep.* 29 on the words 'ephod bad' and 'teraphim'; *Ep.* 34 on two phrases in Ps. 127.

[15] Three passages from the Old Testament: *Ep.* 36. Various passages from the New Testament: *Ep.* 55 (3); *Ep.* 59 (5); *Ep.* 85 (2); *Ep.* 119 (2); *Ep.* 120 (12); *Ep.* 121 (11).

[16] See, e.g., Stefan Rebenich's masterful study *Hieronymus und sein Kreis: Prosopographische und sozialgeschichtliche Untersuchungen* (Stuttgart, 1992).

in question to the common denominator of apology and propaganda, as if the exegesis itself were an issue of secondary importance. Rather, I shall suggest some clever but hitherto undetected strategies by which Jerome sought through his epistolography to secure a favourable reception of his biblical scholarship primarily in Rome and southern Gaul, the two main geographical centres of his social contacts for the greater part of his career.

REMEMBERING FABIOLA, DEFENDING HEBREW VERITY

The *raison d'être* of Jerome's Hebrew scholarship was seriously challenged by contemporary Christians—biblical experts and non-specialists alike—in locales as disparate as Rome and the backwoods of North Africa.[17] From the early 380s until the end of his career, Jerome vigorously defended his methodology in the prefaces to his translations of, and commentaries on, individual biblical books,[18] as well as in his correspondence.[19] In Chapter 2, I argued that he initially released his exegetical letter-exchanges with Pope Damasus as a way to assure the Christian community at Rome that his avant-garde work had papal sanction. In Chapter 3, I argued that one of his aims in releasing his selected correspondence to Marcella was to furnish proof to Roman Christians that one of the evidently prominent figures in local ascetic circles enthusiastically supported his scholarly programme. In the section that follows below I shall propose that Jerome made another innovative use of the epistolary medium—a dossier of letters to and about his Roman friend Fabiola—to continue to make his Hebrew scholarship palatable to a Christian audience in Rome long after he had left this city.

---

[17] See above, pp. 64–6.

[18] For an overview of the general content of the prefaces to these works, see Yves-Marie Duval, *Jérôme, Commentaire sur Jonas: introduction, texte critique, traduction et commentaire* (Paris, 1985), 29–42. See also Walter Stade, *Hieronymus in prooemiis quid tractaverit et quos auctores quasque leges rhetoricas secutus sit* (Rostock, 1925).

[19] Stefan Rebenich, 'Jerome: The *vir trilinguis* and the *Hebraica veritas*', VChr, 47 (1993), 68 n. 28 (with bibliography); id., *Jerome* (London and New York, 2002), 101–4; Alfons Fürst, *Hieronymus: Askese und Wissenschaft in der Spätantike* (Freiburg, 2003), 267–82.

Fabiola was a Christian widow from one of the oldest and most distinguished Roman families (*gens Fabia*).[20] What sparse details we know about her life come almost exclusively from the epitaph on her (*Ep.* 77) that Jerome wrote in 400 and addressed to their mutual Roman friend Oceanus. Like his other epistolary *epitaphia*, this one is a polished composition[21] meant not just for the eyes of its dedicatee but for a broad audience as well.[22] Indeed, it was a masterpiece in the estimation of its author. Jerome begins it by constructing a *consolatio* tradition populated entirely by his own letters[23] and then he proceeds to induct *Ep.* 77 into this literary hall of fame.[24]

Fabiola had been married twice. Her first husband was so miserable that not even a slave or prostitute would have been able to live with him.[25] She divorced him and remarried before he was dead; this made her an adulteress by strict Christian standards.[26] Jerome, who condemned second marriages,[27] frankly acknowledges that he has his eulogistic work cut out for him, and he vows to clear Fabiola of the charge of adultery before venturing to build the case for her exemplary sanctity.[28] To this end, he devotes one-third of the letter to

[20] *PCBE*, ii. 734–5 ('Fabiola I'). This is not the Fabiola who lived in North Africa and to whom Augustine addressed his *Ep.* 267 (402) and also to whom Jerome dedicated the first two books of his commentary on Ezekiel (411).

[21] Steven Oberhelman, *Rhetoric and Homiletics in Fourth-century Christian Literature* (Atlanta, Ga., 1991), 84, notes the stylistic finesse of this letter as reflected in its prose rhythm.

[22] e.g., at *Ep.* 77.5 he refers to his 'readers' (*legentibus*). For a catalogue of Jerome's references to the general reader in his works, see Paul Antin, 'Saint Jérôme et son lecteur', *RSR*, 34 (1947), 82–99.

[23] *Ep.* 39 to Paula on Blesilla; *Ep.* 60 to Heliodorus on Nepotian; *Ep.* 66 to Pammachius on Paulina.

[24] For Jerome's place in the ancient consolatory tradition, see Giuseppe Guttilla, 'Tematica cristiana e pagana nell'evoluzione finale della *consolatio* di san Girolamo', *ALGP*, 17–18 (1980–1), 87–152; J. H. D. Scourfield, *Consoling Heliodorus: A Commentary on Jerome, Letter 60* (Oxford, 1993), 15–33.

[25] *Ep.* 77.3: *tanta prior maritus vitia habuisse narratur, ut ne scortum quidem et vile mancipium ea sustinere posset.*

[26] See Charles Munier, 'Divorce, remariage et pénitence dans l'Église primitive', *RSR*, 52 (1978), 97–117.

[27] Giacomo Violardo, *Il pensiero giuridico di san Girolamo* (Milan, 1937), 154–71.

[28] *Ep.* 77.3: *et quia statim in principio quasi scopulus quidam et procella mihi obtrectatorum eius opponitur, quod secundum sortita matrimonium prius reliquerit, non laudabo conversam, nisi ream absolvero.*

a sympathetic explanation of her conduct.[29] He further emphasizes how after her second husband's death a penitent Fabiola publicly confessed her sin in a ceremony in the Lateran. Once restored to full communion with the church, she began living a life of chaste widow-hood and devoted herself to almsgiving and other charitable work.

In the autumn of 394, Fabiola undertook a pilgrimage to the Holy Land. In his epitaph on her Jerome makes it sound as if the real purpose of her trip was not so much to tour the sacred sites as to study the Bible with him in person in Bethlehem, for the only activ-ities of hers that his highly selective narrative mentions are private Scriptural lessons under his watchful eye.[30] Fabiola fell in love with 'Mary's inn'—the pilgrim hostelry run by Paula and Jerome[31]—and she had every intention of making Bethlehem her permanent home.[32] Given her philanthropic ambitions (see below), it seems likely that she planned either to become a financial partner in this hostelry or to start her own.[33] By the summer of 395, however, Fabiola had experienced a sudden change of heart and was on a ship back to Italy. Jerome attributes her awkwardly abrupt departure to trepida-tion about the Huns' rapidly advancing armies. He also mentions in passing 'a certain disagreement among us' (*quaedam apud nos dissensio*), an allusion to the Origenist controversy.[34] Even though Fabiola may have feared the Huns, it is probably the case that she

---

[29] *Ep.* 77.3–5.   [30] *Ep.* 77.7.

[31] Jerome often spoke of the hostelry in biblical terms, presumably in order to magnify the charitable work being done there. See, e.g., *Epp.* 66.14: *in ista provin-cia aedificato monasterio et diversorio proper extructo, ne forte et modo Ioseph cum Maria Bethlehem veniens non inveniat hospitium*; 108.14: *diversorium peregrinorum iuxta viam conderet, quia Maria et Ioseph hospitium non invenerant*; *Ep. adv. Ruf.* 17: *nobis in monasterio hospitalitas cordi est omnesque ad nos venientes laeta human-itatis fronte suscipimus. veremur enim ne Maria cum Ioseph locum non inveniat in diversorio*.

[32] *Ep.* 77.8; cf. *Ep.* 64.8: *tu quidem optato frueris otio et iuxta Babylonem Bethlemit-ica forsitan rura suspiras*.

[33] Jerome would undoubtedly have welcomed Fabiola's pecuniary assistance, for the building and maintenance costs of his and Paula's monasteries and their hostelry were underwritten almost entirely by Paula's fortune. By the late 390s, these financial resources had all but dried up and Jerome, in desperate need of funds, sent his younger brother Paulinian to Italy and Dalmatia to liquidate what was left of their family estates (*Ep.* 66.14).

[34] *Ep.* 77.8.

wanted to avoid becoming an unwitting pawn in this acrimonious theological dispute.[35]

After returning to Italy in the summer of 395, Fabiola remained as much Jerome's disciple as ever; this, at any rate, is what he would have us believe. She memorized his hortatory letter to Heliodorus (*Ep.* 14) and looked to it as a constant source of comfort and guidance.[36] She also nourished herself on a steady diet of Scripture, turning to the sage of Bethlehem for her exegetical needs. In 396, she wrote to him and requested a discussion of the priestly vestments described in the Pentateuch. He replied with an immensely detailed epistolary treatise (*Ep.* 64) in which he went above and beyond the call of duty and commented on other aspects of the priesthood as well.[37] The work stands out as much for its allegorical creativity in explaining the mystical significance of the priest's accoutrements as it does for its extensive display of Hebrew learning.[38] It took almost no time to write, according to Jerome: 'I have dictated these things hastily and from memory in one night, as the ship's rope was being untied from the shore and as the sailors were insisting ever more frequently that they leave.'[39] Given the tract's length (it comes to just under thirty pages in Hilberg's edition) and the sheer effort that evidently went into it, his claim that he nonchalantly wrote it in such a short space of time seems highly suspect.[40] The supposed ability instantaneously to dictate lengthy, information-packed, and stylistically impeccable works—be they letters, biblical commentaries, or theological treatises—was one

---

[35] See E. D. Hunt, *Holy Land Pilgrimage in the Later Roman Empire, AD 312–460* (Oxford, 1982), 191.

[36] *Ep.* 77.9: *librum, quo Heliodorum quondam iuvenis ad heremum cohortatus sum, tenebat memoriter et Romana cernens moenia inclusam se esse plangebat.*

[37] *Ep.* 64.8: *conpulisti me, Fabiola, litteris tuis, ut de Aaron tibi scriberem vestimentis. ego plus obtuli, ut de cibis et praemiis sacerdotum et de observatione pontificis praefatiunculam struerem.* For its epistolary nature, see *Ep.* 64.21: *ego iam mensuram epistulae excedere me intellego.*

[38] C. T. R. Hayward, 'St Jerome and the Meaning of the High-priestly Vestments', in William Horbury (ed.), *Hebrew Study from Ezra to Ben-Yehuda* (Edinburgh, 1999), 90–105.

[39] *Ep.* 64.22: *haec ad unam lucubratiunculam, cum iam funis solveretur e litore et nautae crebrius inclamarent, propero sermone dictavi, quae memoria tenere poteram.*

[40] Cf. *Ep.* 33 to Paula, which contains a near-exhaustive listing of Origen's works. Jerome says (6) that he dictated it 'quickly and not carefully' (*cito, sed non cauto sermone*). In *Apol. c. Hier.* 2.21 Rufinus quotes this very passage and questions the truthfulness of his claim with a sarcastic 'as you say' (*ut ais*).

of Jerome's favourite conceits.[41] Often in his correspondence (as here) he couples this hasty-dictation *topos* with the *lucubratio* one. This latter had been a *topos* in Latin literature long before Jerome's time.[42] Previous writers had made use of it mainly to demonstrate their own diligence by appealing to 'a popular conception of men of learning sitting at night and working by candlelight when the rest of the world was asleep'.[43] Jerome similarly invoked this *topos* frequently in his own writings, such as in *Ep.* 64 to Fabiola, in order to portray himself as an indefatigable scholar.

Several years after sending Fabiola this letter-treatise, Jerome composed a second one for her (*Ep.* 78). This one, longer than its predecessor, at thirty-eight pages in Hilberg's edition, is an exposition of the Israelites' forty-two stops (*mansiones*) on their way from Egypt to the Promised Land as documented in Numbers 33.[44] Jerome renders the Hebrew place names of the *mansiones* into Latin, often giving *faux* etymologies, and interprets this biblical chapter as an allegory for the Christian's pilgrimage from earth to heaven. He informs the reader that in the course of completing the project he studied the Old Testament in its original Hebrew, for the Greek and Latin codices

---

[41] See, e.g., *Epp.* 33.6; 57.2; 84.12; 99.1; 108.32; 114.1; 117.12; 118.1; 127.14; 128.5; *C. Vigil.* 17; *In Math.*, prologue. For further discussion and references, see Alfred Wikenhauser, 'Der heilige Hieronymus und die Kurzschrift', *TQ*, 29 (1910), 50–87; Evaristo Arns, *La Technique du livre d'après saint Jérôme* (Paris, 1953), 37–50; Harald Hagendahl, 'Die Bedeutung der Stenographie für die spätlateinische Christliche Literatur', *JbAC*, 14 (1971), 29–33; Conring, *Hieronymus als Briefschreiber*, 106–18.

[42] James Ker, 'Nocturnal Writers in Imperial Rome: The Culture of *lucubratio*', *CPh*, 99 (2004), 209–42.

[43] Tore Janson, *Latin Prose Prefaces: Studies in Literary Conventions* (Stockholm, 1964), 97; see also Jan Ziolkowski, 'Classical Influences on Medieval Latin Views of Poetic Inspiration', in Peter Godman and Oswyn Murray (eds.), *Latin Poetry and the Classical Traditio: Essays in Medieval and Renaissance Literature* (Oxford, 1990), 19–20.

[44] While composing this letter he worked very closely from one of Origen's homilies on Numbers, which has been preserved by Rufinus in Latin translation (*Orig. Num.* 27). However, he nowhere so much as alludes to his actual source, doubtless because the Origenist controversy was still in full swing. See Hermann-Josef Sieben, 'Israels Wüstenwanderung (Num 33) in der Auslegung des Hieronymus und des Origenes. Ein Beitrag zur Geschichte der Spiritualität und der origenistischen Streitigkeiten', *Th&Ph*, 77 (2002), 18–22.

contained too many corruptions to be of any real use.[45] In addition, throughout the letter he clarifies that his interpretations are based on a micro-textual reading of the Hebrew text.[46] Hence, *Ep.* 78 is explicitly presented as a thoroughgoing application of 'Hebrew verity'. Fabiola had asked Jerome to write this treatise for her years earlier when she was staying with him in Bethlehem, but he did not get around to it until news of her death reached him. He despatched the finished product to Rome along with the *epitaphium* on her.

Because the dedicatee of *Ep.* 78 was deceased Jerome obviously did not write it for her personal edification. For whom and for what purpose, then, did he write it? By way of answering this question let us consider some interesting features of *Ep.* 77 and *Ep.* 78. There are indications that Jerome composed them with an eye that they circulate together as a tight unit. First of all, the two pieces almost always appear alongside one another in the medieval manuscripts of Jerome's correspondence.[47] Secondly, there is the curiously imper- sonal character of *Ep.* 78. Neither Fabiola nor anyone else for that matter is mentioned or directly addressed in it, and so one could never deduce that it was written for any single person. It also lacks details about the circumstances of its composition that Jerome cus- tomarily inserted into the preface or conclusion to a work. Moreover, *Ep.* 78 does not have the internal look or feel of a stand-alone com- position. At certain points the epitaph foreshadows *Ep.* 78, such that the former can be said to act as a preface of sorts to the latter. In the epitaph Jerome goes on at some length explaining how this exegetical letter-treatise originated.[48] He speaks of how Fabiola, when she was in Bethlehem, would regularly quiz him about various Scriptural problems. He vividly recreates one session in particular in which they were studying the book of Numbers together. He answered a series of her questions about the structure of the book and about the meaning of selected passages. Then they came to chapter 33.

---

[45] *Ep.* 78.11: *prudentem studiosumque lectorem rogatum velim, ut sciat me vertere nomina iuxta Hebraicam veritatem; alioquin in Graecis et Latinis codicibus praeter pauca omnia corrupta repperimus.*

[46] The phrase '*apud Hebraeos*' occurs in 2, 9, 11, 15, 20, 40; cf. '*iuxta Hebraeos*' in 38. See also 28: *in Hebraeo ... legimus*; 35: *legimus in Genesi iuxta Hebraicam veritatem*; 40: *quae Hebraice dicitur.*

[47] See *BHM* 1(B), 775–84.   [48] *Ep.* 77.7.

Fabiola wondered why the Israelites had chosen to camp in the places they did. No impromptu explanation Jerome could furnish satisfied her. She persuaded him to promise (*pollicerer*) that he would write a treatise for her on this topic. He concludes the section by saying that he finally has made good on his promise:[49]

As I now understand it, this work which has been delayed up until now by the will of the Lord is offered up to her memory, in such a way that she who put on the priestly clothing of the first treatise (= *Ep.* 64) dedicated to her may rejoice that she at last has come through the desert of this world to the land of promise.[50]

This passage serves as a nexus between the two epistolary treatises dedicated to Fabiola. The first one is sentimentally recalled and the newest one is introduced. Indeed, the entire seventh section is an elaborate build-up that whets the reader's appetite for the exegetical delight that is to come as soon as the epitaph ends. *Ep.* 77 winds down with several Scriptural one-liners, one of which seems particularly apropos as a lead-in to a discussion of '*mansiones*': 'In my Father's house are many dwelling places (*mansiones*)' (John 14: 2).[51]

Jerome, then, conceived *Ep.* 77 and *Ep.* 78 to be read in tandem.[52] But why? *Ep.* 78 seems an arduous read for all but the specialist: it is an extremely technical treatment of a fairly obscure topic in one of the least charted books of the Old Testament. One of the challenges facing Jerome, of which he was painfully aware,[53] was to convince educated Christians that his Hebrew exegesis was not a tedious and inconsequential intellectual exercise but that it had application to everyday life. *Ep.* 78, read in conjunction with *Ep.* 77, demonstrates the practical nature of such exegetical work. For *Ep.* 78 decodes Numbers 33 and uses it as a guide for the ascetic Christian's earthly

---

[49] Cf. *Ep.* 78.1: *sed iam tempus est, ut promissa conplentes mansionum Israhel ordinem persequamur.*

[50] *Quod* [*opus*] *usque in praesens tempus, ut nunc intellego, domini voluntate dilatum redditur memoriae illius, ut sacerdotalibus prioris ad se voluminis induta vestibus per mundi huius solitudinem gaudeat se ad terram repromissionis aliquando venisse.*

[51] Note that Jerome plays on two slightly different meanings of the word '*mansio*': a travel inn (Num. 33) and a permanent dwelling (John 14: 2).

[52] Jerome perhaps sent a separate letter of friendship to Oceanus in the same dispatch containing *Epp.* 77–8 more explicitly expressing his wish that they circulate together.

[53] See above, pp. 82–4.

pilgrimage to the heavenly Promised Land. As the honorary addressee of *Ep*. 78, and as the hagiographic subject of its companion piece (*Ep*. 77), Fabiola is presented as the archetypal pilgrim who reached her final destination precisely because she had followed Jerome's spiritual direction. Jerome ever so delicately implies that acceptance of his exegetical programme is a matter of eternal salvation.[54] Christian readers of this epistolary packet are accordingly invited to imitate Fabiola's example in recognizing the relevance and the necessity of Jerome's scholarly and spiritual expertise.

If Jerome expected Fabiola's 'celebrity endorsement' of his Scriptural programme to resonate with Christians at Rome, it was for good reason. During the decade prior to her death *c*.399 she had maintained a relatively high profile there, if by nothing else than by her philanthropy. She funded out of her own pocket the construction of the first civilian public hospital in Rome.[55] In 396, she partnered with the senator Pammachius to open the first Christian-owned and -operated travellers' inn (*xenodochium*) at the nearby harbour town Portus. Jerome claims that thousands turned out for her funeral to pay their last respects, and people even crowded onto rooftops to gain a passing glimpse of her bier.[56] In short, Fabiola apparently had just the kind of respectability and popularity that made her an ideal spokesperson, even from beyond the grave, for Jerome's cause, to help mainstream his Old Testament scholarship among intellectually minded aristocratic Christians in Rome and farther afield, once the epistolary couplet had a chance to circulate throughout Italy and elsewhere.

FROM BETHLEHEM TO THE FURTHEST REACHES
OF GAUL

From Rome we turn to southern Gaul, which second only to Rome was the most important centre for Jerome's contacts during the Bethlehem years.[57] When Christians in Gaul initiated contact with

---

[54] He implies the same in *Ep*. 65 to Principia on Ps. 45. See above, pp. 133–4.
[55] *Ep*. 77.6.   [56] *Ep*. 77.11.
[57] Henri Crouzel, 'Saint Jérôme et ses amis toulousains', *BLE*, 73 (1972), 125–46; id., 'Les Échanges littéraires entre Bordeaux et l'Orient au IVe siècle: saint Jérôme et

Jerome, he did not hesitate to use it as an occasion to extend his influence there.[58] In Chapter 5, I argued that he aimed with his letter-treatise to Rusticus to place a guiding hand over the development of monasticism in Gaul, beginning with Marseilles. Jerome's readiness to inject himself into local affairs is illustrated also by his involvement in a theological (and personal) quarrel with Vigilantius of Calagurris.[59] In late 404, the Aquitanian priest Riparius alerted him that Vigilantius was attacking the cult of relics and other extreme ascetic practices in southern Gaul. In 406, after he had finally obtained the writing(s) in question, Jerome refuted its theses in the short but biting *Adversus Vigilantium*, copies of which he sent to Gaul with the deacon Sisinnius. To undermine Vigilantius' cause, and to bolster his own, he curried the favour of Exuperius, the influential bishop of Toulouse who was a known sympathizer with Vigilantius' teachings.[60]

In a letter of *c*.392 to Aurelius, the newly installed bishop of Carthage, Jerome urged his correspondent, who had written to him first, to do as his episcopal colleagues in Gaul and North Africa had done and to send a copyist to spend the year(!) in Bethlehem transcribing everything he had ever written.[61] This specific claim about Gallic bishops beating down his door already in the early 390s cannot independently be verified, and, indeed, it is most likely an exaggeration. Nevertheless, there is abundant evidence to show that Jerome was inundated with requests for biblical exegesis from lay Christians, priests, and bishops from southern Gaul in the first decade of the fifth century. For instance, in the autumn of 406 alone there came time-sensitive requests from Toulouse from bishop Exuperius (for a commentary on Zechariah), from the lawyers-turned-monks Minervius and Alexander (for a commentary on Malachi and for explanations of

ses amis aquitains', *RFHL*, 3 (1973), 301–26; Rebenich, *Hieronymus und sein Kreis*, 209–59.

[58] Cain, 'Jerome's *Epistula* 117 on the *Subintroductae*: Satire, Apology, and Ascetic Propaganda in Gaul', *Augustinianum*, 49 (2009), forthcoming.

[59] The many sides of Jerome's conflict with Vigilantius are discussed by Rebenich, *Hieronymus und sein Kreis*, 240–51.

[60] David Hunter, 'Vigilantius of Calagurris and Victricius of Rouen: Ascetics, Relics, and Clerics in Late Roman Gaul', *JECS*, 7 (1999), 407–10.

[61] *Ep.* 27*.3: *fac quod alii de Gallia et alii de Italia fratres tui, sancti episcopi, fecerunt, id est mitte aliquem fidum tibi qui unum annum hic faciat me exemplaria tribuente et deferat ad te cuncta quae scripsimus.*

some New Testament passages), and from 'holy brothers and sisters' throughout Gallia Narbonnensis (for elucidations of assorted biblical passages). Jerome was so overwhelmed, in fact, that he was unable to finish all of the replies in time, even though he worked diligently around the clock.[62] The partial reply to two of the questions posed by Minervius and Alexander (*Ep.* 119) is the sole letter from this particular batch of replies to survive. In addition to this one, only four others survive from among the substantial number of replies Jerome must have sent to Christians in Gaul at any time during his more than thirty years in Bethlehem.[63] The earliest one, dated to *c*.394 and addressed to Amandus (*Ep.* 55), possibly the future bishop of Bordeaux, explains three passages from the New Testament. Chronologically, the latest letter (*Ep.* 129), written *c*.414 to the former two-time prefect of Gaul Claudius Postumus Dardanus, discusses the Promised Land. The remaining two were sent in 407 to the noble-women Hedibia (*Ep.* 120) and Algasia (*Ep.* 121) and answer questions about miscellaneous passages from the New Testament.

The letters to Hedibia and Algasia are noteworthy for several reasons. First of all, both span approximately fifty pages in Hilberg's edition. Their length is not simply a function of the sheer volume of questions, for they are still proportionately much longer than Jerome's other surviving exegetical letters that expound lists of biblical passages.[64] Secondly, unlike Jerome's other three extant exegetical letters to Christians in Gaul, they are adorned with literary prefaces of the sort he affixed to his biblical commentaries.[65] Finally, a short time after sending his reply to Hedibia, Jerome alluded to this reply

[62] *Ep.* 119.1: *multas sanctorum fratrum ac sororum de vestra provincia ad me detulit quaestiones, ad quas usque diem epiphaniorum largissimo spatio me responsurum putabam. cumque furtivis noctium lucubratiunculis ad plerasque dictarem et expletis aliis me ad vestram quasi ad difficillimam reservarem, subito supervenit adserens se ilico profecturum.*

[63] I do not include *Ep.* 85 to Paulinus because, even though a Gaul by birth, Paulinus was living in Nola, Italy at the time (399).

[64] *Ep.* 55, four questions in ten pages; *Ep.* 59, five questions in five pages; *Ep.* 85, two questions in two pages. *Ep.* 119, which answers two questions in seventeen pages, is the only exception.

[65] There is evidence to suggest that longer prefaces such as these were composed after Jerome had dictated the body of the letter. In the somewhat elaborate preface to *Ep.* 119, he uses the past tense rather than the future tense to describe his handling of the answers (*sententias protuli et ad verbum pleraque interpretatus sum*).

in his commentary on Isaiah. This would seem to indicate that copies of *Ep.* 120 had already been made available for public consumption. Furthermore, he called this letter an '*opus*',[66] one of the terms he used for epistolary treatises for which he envisaged an indefinitely broad audience that included but also extended well beyond the ostensible addressees.[67] Even though we lack an explicit *testimonium* from Jerome about the status of the letter to Algasia, it is safe to assume, given that it has an identical literary profile to *Ep.* 120, that he thought of it in the same terms. What all of this means, practically speaking, is that Jerome, in addition to sending the replies to those who had requested them, simultaneously released copies of them to members of his literary circle (in Rome and elsewhere), who were expected to facilitate their dissemination through their own channels.[68]

In the discussion of *Ep.* 120 and *Ep.* 121 that follows, I shall confine myself to their literary prefaces. Apart from mining them for prosopographical information, scholars hitherto have failed to extract any meaningful content from them. Nevertheless, I hope to show through a close analysis of their rhetoric that Jerome crafted them in such a way as to define himself as an unrivalled authority to whom Gallic Christians could turn for answers to their questions about the Bible.

EP. 120 TO HEDIBIA (BORDEAUX)

Sometime in 407, a Christian pilgrim by the name of Apodemius, who was probably a lay monk or clergyman, arrived in Bethlehem.[69]

---

[66] *In Es.* 17.63.17–19: *nos in quodam opere perstrinximus* (referring to Rom. 9: 17–18).

[67] Arns, *Technique*, 103–7, 118–22.

[68] See, e.g., *Ep.* 47.3, where Jerome instructs his Roman friend Desiderius to seek copies of his writings from Marcella and Domnio. For the mechanics of textual dissemination in late antiquity, see Gustave Bardy, 'Copies et éditions au Vᵉ siècle', *RSR*, 23 (1949), 38–52; Henri-Irénée Marrou, 'La Technique de l'édition à l'époque patristique', *VChr*, 3 (1949), 208–24; Guglielmo Cavallo, 'Libro e pubblico alla fine del mondo antico', in Guglielmo Cavallo (ed.), *Libri, editori e pubblico nel mondo antico* (Rome, 1977); see also Raymond Starr, 'The Circulation of Literary Texts in the Roman World', *CQ*, 37 (1987), 213–23.

[69] In the prologue to *Ep.* 120 he is called a 'man of God' (*homo dei*), an appellation for monks and clerics: see Mary O'Brien, *Titles of Address in Christian Latin Epistolography to 543 AD* (Washington, DC, 1930), 84. Evidence for Apodemius' trip as a

He brought a letter from the Gallic Christian widow Hedibia asking Jerome for explanations of twelve different passages from the New Testament. Jerome's reply to her has been the subject of controversy among scholars. More than a century ago, the New Testament scholar John Burgon briefly examined it in his book on the authenticity of the last twelve verses of Mark's Gospel.[70] He noted that Hedibia's questions 3–5, which concern apparent discrepancies in the resurrection narrative, and Jerome's corresponding responses, mimic (in the same order and frequently *verbatim*) three questions and their responses by Eusebius of Caesarea in his work on Gospel questions dedicated to Marinus.[71] Burgon, taking into account this importation of material from Eusebius, speculated that *Ep.* 120 was a contrivance in which Jerome posed and answered a series of artificial questions under the guise of a real letter to a real addressee. This reading of *Ep.* 120 was adopted in prominent Hieronymian circles throughout the twentieth century.[72] But, as I have shown elsewhere, there is no reason whatsoever to doubt that *Ep.* 120 was exactly what it purports to be—namely, a genuine reply to a real person who had real questions.[73] As for the Eusebian intertext, it may be accounted for if we reasonably postulate that Hedibia had the Greek Father's work in hand, copied three of the questions from it that piqued her interest, and then sent these as part of her exegetical wish list to get better answers from Jerome.[74] Taking for granted, then, its genuine nature, let us now turn to *Ep.* 120.

At some point before Hedibia wrote to Jerome, her husband had died and left her a childless widow. Her first and therefore presumably most urgent question to him was how it was possible for a widow of her means to obey Christ's mandate to the rich young man to sell all of

pilgrimage is found in *Ep.* 121, prologue: *filius meus Apodemius... quaesivit Bethleem, ut inveniret in ea caelestem panem.* The comment about finding the 'heavenly bread' is a reference to the Hebrew meaning of the word 'Bethlehem' (= 'house of bread'); see Jerome, *Tract. Ps.* 95: *quid dicitur Bethleem? domus panis; Ep.* 66.11: *viculum nostrum, id est domum panis.*

[70] *The Last Twelve Verses of the Gospel According to S. Mark* (Oxford, 1871), 51–5.
[71] For the text of *Mar.*, see PG 22.879–1006.
[72] See, e.g., Donatien de Bruyne, 'Lettres fictives de s. Jérôme', *ZNTW*, 28 (1929), 229–34; Nautin, 'Le Premier [*sic*] échange épistolaire entre Jérôme et Damase: lettres réelles ou fictives?', *FZPhTh*, 30 (1983), 331 n. 1.
[73] Cain, 'Defending Hedibia and Detecting Eusebius: Jerome's Correspondence with Two Gallic Women (*Epp.*, 120–1)', *MP*, 24 (2003), 15–34.
[74] See Cain, 'Defending Hedibia', 28–31.

his possessions and give to the poor in order to be perfect.[75] Jerome's reputation for counselling Christian widows on lifestyle decisions may have induced Hedibia to seek his advice on this matter.[76] So, too, did his reputation as a biblical scholar, for her remaining eleven questions inquire about difficult passages from throughout the New Testament. Significantly, half of her questions (3–7, 9) are about apparent discrepancies in the Gospel narratives. There was a growing demand among Latin Christians in the late fourth and early fifth centuries for written reassurance about the internal unity of the Gospels. At least three aristocratic women, including Hedibia, are known to have asked Jerome to clear up the seeming contradictions.[77] More evidence for this demand is that around 399 Augustine composed his sizeable *De consensu evangelistarum* at the request of 'not a few brothers' (*nonnulli fratres*) who wanted to know how to counter the 'cunning calumnies' (*argutas criminationes*) of sceptics who accused the Gospel writers of disagreeing among themselves.[78] Jerome may have regarded his reply to Hedibia as an opportunity to offer his own authoritative perspective (and that of Eusebius, in Latin translation), albeit on a much smaller scale than Augustine's treatise, on an exegetical dilemma that vexed contemporary Christians.

By the very act of taking her request for biblical exegesis to Jerome, Hedibia was validating his reputation as an expert interpreter of the Bible. It was then up to him to prove, in the form of a learned reply, that her confidence in him was not misplaced. He did not disappoint, as the impressive exegetical content of his thorough reply attests. Equally impressive, rhetorically speaking, is the letter's prologue. It begins as follows:

I have never seen your face, but I know your passionate faith well. From the furthest reaches of Gaul you send a letter with my son, the man of God Apodemius, and prod me, who am hiding out in the countryside of Bethlehem, to answer questions about Holy Scripture. It is as if (*quasi*) you do not have in your own region men who are knowledgeable and perfected

---

[75] *Ep.* 120.1.   [76] See above, pp. 158–66.

[77] In 395/6, Marcella posed one of the same questions as Hedibia (*Ep.* 120.5) about whether Matt. 28: 9 contradicted John 20: 17 (*Ep.* 59.4). A decade later, Algasia (*Ep.* 121.1) wanted to know why Luke (7: 18–19) and John (1: 36) give conflicting reports about a remark made by John the Baptist.

[78] *Cons. evang.* 1.7.10.

184   *The Exegetical Letters*

in the law of God, unless perhaps what you seek from me is a test rather than a teaching and you wish to know what opinions I have concerning the things you have heard from others.[79]

This arresting image of Jerome as a reclusive scholar 'hiding out' in Bethlehem[80] certainly did have truth to it, inasmuch as Bethlehem was a quiet agrarian village located about six miles to the south of Jerusalem[81] and was situated on the western fringe of the Judean desert plateau, a relatively desolate region characterized by sparse rainfall and high temperatures.[82] By the same token, it is important to ask why Jerome might have been motivated to describe himself with this particular rhetoric. I suggest that he juxtaposed Hedibia's and his own remote geographical coordinates in order to set into relief the extraordinary inconvenience to which she, a complete stranger, had gone to track him down in search of a word of knowledge. Owing to the length of time it took for letter-carriers to make the journey by land and sea, as well as Jerome's perpetually busy docket, Christians such as Hedibia would have had to wait up to several months for a reply. This is to say nothing of the problem of finding reliable couriers. What is more, there was no standardized postal system in place to provide at least some reasonable assurance that

[79] *Ignota vultu fidei mihi ardore notissima es. et de extremis Galliae finibus in Bethleemitico rure latitantem ad respondendum provocas de sanctarum quaestiunculis Scripturarum per hominem dei filium meum Apodemium commonitoriolum dirigens, quasi vero non habeas in tua provincia disertos viros et in dei lege perfectos, nisi forte experimentum magis nostri quam doctrinam flagitas et vis scire, quid de his, quae ab aliis audisti, nos quoque sentiamus.*

[80] Jerome was fond of portraying himself in this manner. See, e.g., *Epp.* 57.13: *mihi sufficit... in cellula latitantem diem expectare iudicii*; *Ep.* 27*.1: *latitanti mihi*; 105.3: *senem latitantem in cellula*; 117.1: *incongruum est* [*me*] *latere corpore et lingua per orbem vagari*; *Apol.c.Ruf.* 1.32: *latemus in cellulis*; 3.19: *me latentem*; cf. *Ep.* 75.4: *ob conscientiam peccatorum Bethlemitici ruris saxa incolimus.* The '*saxa*' may be a reference to the numerous cave complexes that surrounded the Bethlehem area: see Félix-Marie Abel, *Géographie de la Palestine* (2 vols., Paris, 1967), i. 440–1. Cf. the '*nuda saxa*' among which Bonosus is said by Jerome to have lived in his retreat off the Dalmatian coast (*Ep.* 3.4).

[81] Bellarmino Bagatti, *Antichi villaggi cristiani della Giudea e del Neghev* (Jerusalem, 1983), 40. Cf. *Ep.* 46.12 for Jerome's claim that the shepherds and farmers in the Bethlehem area whistle the Psalms as they go about their daily chores.

[82] Abel, *Géographie*, 1.104–6; Yizhar Hirschfeld, *The Judean Desert Monasteries in the Byzantine Period* (New Haven, Conn., 1992), 6–10.

correspondence would arrive at its destination in a timely fashion, if at all.[83]

Why, given all of these potentially complicating factors, did Hedibia and others go to the trouble of consulting Jerome rather than local experts in Gaul? Jerome answers this question indirectly in the passage above. He speculates about Hedibia's motives for contacting him by proposing two different scenarios. In the first, he insinuates ever so carefully, using the adverb *quasi*,[84] that there is a dearth of competent biblical experts in Gaul.[85] In the second, he assumes that there *are* local experts and that she consulted them but then approached him for a second opinion, to see how his interpretations stack up against theirs. Thus, Jerome was aware, or at least he strongly suspected, that Hedibia had shopped around for answers to her questions. In either one of these two scenarios, proposed with brilliant subtlety, Jerome emerges as a Scriptural authority superior to indigenous Gallic authorities. For, either the exegetical scene in Gaul is so impoverished that Christians there must contact an out-of-town expert, or there is something so deficient about the answers they do receive from regional authorities that they are forced to rely on Jerome to be the voice of reason.

What is it that Jerome is able to offer Gallic Christians that they cannot find in their own homeland? He provides the answer in the second part of the preface:

[83] As a famous case in point, Augustine's first letter to Jerome (*Ep.* 28) did not make it to Bethlehem because its carrier, Profuturus, never left North Africa (he had stopped off in Cirta, was made a bishop there, and died soon thereafter). By late 398 or early 399, Augustine, realizing the fate of his letter, sent another one (*Ep.* 40), though it did not reach Bethlehem either, at least not right away. Unbeknownst to Augustine, it had been carried to Rome, where it was copied and then disseminated throughout Italy. For a sorting out of the chronology of the Augustine–Jerome correspondence, see Carolinne White, *The Correspondence (394–419) between Jerome and Augustine of Hippo* (Lampeter, 1990), 19–34.

[84] For examples of Jerome's other usages of '*quasi*', see Henri Goelzer, *Étude lexicographique et grammaticale de la latinité de saint Jérôme* (Paris, 1884), 429–30.

[85] Jerome treads lightly with his rhetoric out of fear of offending local Gallic authorities, such as Amandus, the reigning bishop of Bordeaux. This is perhaps the same Amandus who, around 393, when he was still a priest, wrote to Jerome asking him to explain some New Testament passages (Jerome's reply is *Ep.* 55). For the dating of Amandus' episcopate, see Louis Duchesne, *Fastes épiscopaux de l'ancienne Gaule* (2 vols., Paris, 1894), ii. 60.

Your ancestors Patera[86] and Delphidius,[87] one of whom taught rhetoric at
Rome before I was born and the other of whom used his literary talents to
honour all of Gaul in prose and verse while I was a young man, are now dead,
yet they silently rebuke me—and rightly so, because I have the audacity to
mutter a peep to the offspring of their family. Although I concede to them
the grandeur of eloquence and the learning of secular literature, I rightly
remove from their grasp knowledge of the law of God, which no one is able
to have except it be granted by the Father of lights (cf. Jas. 1: 17), who brings
light to every man coming into the world (cf. John 1: 9) and stands in the
midst of believers who have been gathered together in his name (cf. Matt.
18: 20). Therefore I declare openly—and I do not fear the charge of pride—
that I write not in the educated words of human wisdom, which God will
destroy (cf. 1 Cor. 1: 19), but in the words of faith, expressing spiritual truths
in spiritual terms (cf. 1 Cor. 2: 13), so that the deep of the Old Testament may
call upon the deep of the New Testament in the roar of their waterfalls (cf. Ps.
42: 7), that is of their prophets and apostles, and so that the Lord's truth may
come to the clouds (cf. Ps. 107: 5) that were ordered not to pour down rain
on an unbelieving Israel (cf. Isa. 5: 6) but to moisten the fields of the Gentiles
and to sweeten the dense thickets of thorns and the Dead Sea (cf. Joel 3: 18).
Pray, therefore, that the true Elisha may make alive barren and dead waters
in me (cf. 2 Kgs 2: 19–22) and that he may season my little gift with the salt
of the apostles to whom he said, 'You are the salt of the earth' (Matt. 5: 13),
for every sacrifice which is without salt is not offered to the Lord (cf. Lev. 2:
13). Do not take pleasure in the flashiness of worldly eloquence which Jesus
saw fall from heaven like lightning (cf. Luke 10: 18), but rather receive him
who does not have beauty or a visible face, a man who is overcome with
blows yet who knows how to hold up under suffering (cf. Isa. 53: 2–3). You
should know that whatever responses I give to your questions I give not out

---

[86] Attius Patera, a native of Bayeux, was a noted teacher of rhetoric at Rome around
336 before he settled in Bordeaux. See Ausonius, *Prof.* 15; *PLRE*, i. 669–70 ('Attius
Patera').

[87] Patera's son, Attius Tiro Delphidius, was born in Bordeaux and later taught
rhetoric at the famous university there. See Ausonius, *Prof.* 5.7.14; *PLRE*, i. 246
('Attius Tiro Delphidius'); cf. A. D. Booth, 'Notes on Ausonius' *Professores*', *Phoenix*, 32
(1978), 236–9. Delphidius' widow Euchrotia and daughter Procula hosted Priscillian
and company at their lavish estate when the latter passed through Bordeaux in 381.
Priscillian and Procula were rumoured to have had an immoral sexual relationship;
and Euchrotia was executed alongside Priscillian at Trier on the charge of sorcery. See
John Matthews, *Western Aristocracies and Imperial Court AD 364–425* (Oxford, 1975),
163; Dennis Trout, *Paulinus of Nola. Life, Letters, and Poems* (Berkeley, Calif., 1999),
73–4. If Jerome was aware of Hedibia's family's past sympathies with the Priscillianist
heresy, he did not let on about them in his letter to her.

of confidence in my own words but out of the faith of him who promised: 'Open your mouth and I shall fill it' (Ps. 80: 11).[88]

The brief appearance by two of Hedibia's renowned relatives serves another vital function within the narrative besides reminding the reader that Jerome is the personal Scriptural advisor to one of Gaul's distinguished bloodlines. While these rhetoricians are made to stand for the folly of worldly learning and eloquence without the knowledge of God, Jerome puts his trust in the wisdom that comes from above. Ironically, he employs eloquence to decry *eloquentia*. His prose, which is richly descriptive and marked by a series of periodic sentences that are intricate without being convoluted, is unmistakably the product of a highly educated and stylistically self-conscious writer. Jerome's condemnation of secular learning here plays into his argument that knowledge of the law of God (*scientia legis dei*) is a prerequisite of biblical exegesis. By implying that he possesses such rare knowledge, which is granted only by God's grace, he is making a bold claim about the divine source for his authority as an interpreter of the Bible. His compositional technique reinforces this point. The excerpt above is mostly a collage of fifteen verses and verse-fragments from the Old and New Testaments. Jerome introduces three of the passages as direct quotations and integrates the other twelve into the natural flow of

---

[88] *Maiores tui Patera atque Delphidius, quorum alter, antequam ego nascerer, rhetoricam Romae docuit, alter me iam adulescentulo omnes Gallias prosa versuque suo inlustravit ingenio, iam dormientes et taciti me iure reprehendunt, quod audeam ad stirpem generis sui quippiam musitare. licet concedens eis eloquentiae magnitudinem et doctrinam saecularium litterarum merito subtraham scientiam legis dei, quam nemo accipere potest, nisi ei data fuerit a patre luminum, qui inluminat omnem hominem venientem in mundum et stat medius credentium, qui in nomine eius fuerint congregati. unde libere profiteor—nec dictum superbiae pertimesco—me scribere tibi non in doctis humanae sapientiae verbis, quam deus destructurus est, sed in verbis fidei spiritalibus spiritalia conparantem, ut abyssus veteris testamenti invocet abyssum evangelicam in voce cataractarum, id est prophetarum et apostolorum suorum, et veritas domini perveniat usque ad nubes, quibus mandatum est, ne super incredulum Israhel imbrem pluerent, sed ut rigarent arva gentilium et torrentem spinarum ac mare mortuum dulcorarent. ora igitur, ut verus Heliseus steriles in me et mortuas aquas vivificet et apostolorum sale, quibus dixerat: vos estis sal terrae, meum munusculum condiat, quia omne sacrificium, quod absque sale est, domino non offertur. nec fulgore saecularis eloquentiae delecteris, quam vidit Iesus quasi fulgur cadentem de caelo, sed potius eum recipe, qui non habet decorem nec faciem, homo in plagis positus et sciens ferre infirmitatem, et quicquid ad proposita respondero, scias me non confidentia respondisse sermonis, sed eius fide, qui pollicitus est: aperi os tuum et implebo illud.*

his prose in such a way as to collapse the boundary between his own authorial voice and the voice of Scripture.[89] He fittingly closes the preface and leads directly into the answers portion of his letter with an appropriate biblical intertext by which he assures Hedibia that his interpretations can be trusted: 'You should know that whatever responses I give to your questions, I give not out of confidence in my own words but out of the faith of him who promised: "Open your mouth and I shall fill it".'

EP. 121 TO ALGASIA (CAHORS?)

When Apodemius arrived in Bethlehem he brought correspondence also from Algasia. In the preface to his reply to her (*Ep.* 121), Jerome mentions that Apodemius travelled 'from the ocean's shore and from the furthest reaches of Gaul' (*de oceani litore atque ultimis finibus Galliarum*).[90] Because the description 'from the ocean's shore and from the furthest reaches of Gaul' fits Bordeaux well,[91] and because it mirrors phraseology in the letter to Hedibia (*de extremis Galliae finibus*), scholars often assume that Algasia lived there.[92] There is

---

[89] For a larger-scale display of this stylistic flourish, see *Ep.* 122, in which Jerome rebukes the Gallic Christian Rusticus for having broken a vow of continence with his wife Artemia. Apart from a few short sentences at the beginning of the letter whereby Jerome introduces himself, this lengthy letter filling fifteen pages in Hilberg's edition is a running inventory of Scriptural passages about repentance, with brief commentaries on select passages by Jerome serving as the connective tissue holding the textual tapestry together.

[90] Jerome also takes the opportunity to pun on the meaning of Apodemius' name in Greek ἀπόδημος = adj. 'away from home'): *interpretationem nominis sui longa ad nos veniens navigatione signavit*. On Jerome's fondness for punning on people's names in his letters, see Francesco Trisoglio, 'Note stilistiche sull'epistolario di Girolamo', *VetChr*, 30 (1993), 276; Cain, 'Miracles, Martyrs, and Arians: Gregory of Tours' Sources for his Account of the Vandal Kingdom', *VChr*, 59 (2005), 422–3.

[91] A passage in Pacatus Drepanius' panegyric (*Pan.* 2/12.2) on Theodosius I (398) suggests that Jerome was using stock terminology for plotting Bordeaux's coordinates. Pacatus, a native of Agen (100 miles south-west of Bordeaux), discusses the circumstances that led him to make the long trek to Rome from Bordeaux, where he had been teaching rhetoric: *sed cum admiratione virtutum tuarum ab ultimo Galliarum recessu, qua litus Oceani cadentem excipit solem et deficientibus terris sociale miscetur elementum, ad contuendum te adorandumque properassem.*

[92] See, e.g., Rebenich, *Hieronymus und sein Kreis*, 276.

reason to question this assumption. In the preface to Algasia's letter, Jerome says that, 'you have there a holy man, the priest (*presbyter*) Alethius, who is able to answer your questions "in the living voice" (as the saying goes) and with judiciousness and eloquence'. There are several Alethii attested for fourth- and fifth-century Gaul.[93] The only known cleric by this name was a priest who succeeded his brother Florentius as bishop of Cahors sometime in the first decade of the 400s. Jerome's Alethius was a priest at the time of his writing.[94] If he is to be identified with the bishop,[95] then Jerome's letter, which we can date firmly to 407,[96] provides a valuable *terminus post quem* for his installation into the episcopate.[97] Alethius corresponded with Paulinus of Nola in the early 400s when he was still a priest. Paulinus, writing *c*.402,[98] praised the eloquence (*eloquii suavitas*) of his letters and sermons.[99] This comment squares with Jerome's allusion to *his* Alethius' oratorical finesse (*prudenti disertoque sermone*). Moreover, if (as seems plausible) Jerome's Alethius was the future bishop of Cahors, then Algasia must have been writing from the vicinity of Cahors, which was in southern Aquitania Prima, over 100 miles to the south-east of Bordeaux. When Jerome used the phrase 'from the ocean's shore and from the furthest reaches of Gaul' he may simply have been speaking of the origination point of Apodemius' itinerary—Bordeaux, or conceivably some other city on the western coast of Gaul. This means that Apodemius would have passed

[93] Martin Heinzelmann, 'Gallische Prosopographie 260–527', *Francia*, 10 (1982), 550.

[94] In late antiquity the title 'presbyter' was used occasionally for bishops but it was usually reserved for priests: see O'Brien, *Titles of Address*, 86, 165; Antoon A. R. Bastiaensen, *Le Cérémonial épistolaire des chrétiens latins: origine et premiers développements* (Nijmegen, 1964), 29.

[95] So Georg Grützmacher, *Hieronymus: Eine biographische Studie zur alten Kirchengeschichte* (3 vols., Berlin, 1901–8), iii. 330; Pierre Fabre, *Saint Paulin de Nole et l'amitié chrétienne* (Paris, 1949), 185; Matthias Skeb, *Epistulae: Paulinus von Nola* (2 vols., Freiburg, 1998), i. 86–7.

[96] Rebenich, *Hieronymus und sein Kreis*, 276.

[97] Cf. Duchesne, *Fastes*, 2.44, who on other grounds has Alethius' episcopal reign beginning in or after 407. If Alethius was already bishop, we would expect Jerome to qualify him as such, as he does Exuperius in *Ep.* 125.20 (*sanctus Exuperius, Tolosae episcopus*).

[98] Pierre Fabre, *Essai sur la chronologie de l'œuvre de saint Paulin de Nole* (Paris, 1948), 50.

[99] *Ep.* 33.

through Cahors *en route* to Bethlehem, collecting along the way correspondence to be delivered to Jerome.[100]

Apodemius brought with him eleven 'very big questions written
on a small sheet of paper' (*in parva scidula maximas quaestiones*).
The rhetorical device of antithesis is at work here.[101] Jerome pairs
contrasting adjectives, '*parva*' and the superlative '*maximas*', in order
to emphasize the difficulty of Algasia's questions, thus simultaneously
stoking the fire of her personal sense of intellectual self-worth and
calling attention to his own ability in being able to answer them.[102]
The confidence in his exegetical prowess implied here seems at first
glance to run counter to the self-deprecatory tone Jerome adopts
elsewhere in the preface:

I am quite astonished, seeing that you have a very pure fountain nearby, that
you have sought out the waters of my stream that is so far away, and that
bypassing the waters of Shiloah, which flow with gentle silence (cf. Isa. 8:
6), you desire the waters of Shihor (cf. Jer. 2: 18), which are polluted by the
stormy vices of this world. You have there a holy man, the priest Alethius,
who is able to answer your questions 'in the living voice' (as the saying goes)
and with judiciousness and eloquence—unless perhaps you desire foreign
merchandise[103] and the food seasoned by me tickles your fancy because it
has a different taste.[104]

The formula Jerome uses to direct Algasia to Alethius (*habes ibi sanctum virum Alethium presbyterum, qui viva, ut aiunt, voce et prudenti
disertoque sermone possit solvere, quae requiris*) is virtually identical to

---

[100] On monks and clerics as couriers, see Maribel Dietz, *Wandering Monks, Virgins,
and Pilgrims. Ascetic Travel in the Mediterranean World, AD 300–800* (University Park,
Penn., 2005), 20.

[101] For Jerome's use of antithesis in his letters, see John Hritzu, *The Style of the
Letters of St Jerome* (Washington, DC, 1939), 92–6.

[102] Cf. *Ep.* 59.1: *magnis nos provocas quaestionibus.* For the convention of magnify-
ing a subject, even a trivial one, in order to make it seem of central importance, see
Janson, *Prefaces*, 98–100.

[103] Cf. the preface to his *Quaest. hebr.*, where Jerome refers to this work as 'foreign
merchandise' (*peregrinae merces*).

[104] *Satis miratus sum, cur purissimo fonte vicino nostri tam procul rivuli fluenta
quaesieris et omissis aquis Siloe, quae vadunt cum silentio, desideres aquas Sior, quae
turbidis saeculi huius vitiis sordidantur. habes ibi sanctum virum Alethium presbyterum,
qui viva, ut aiunt, voce et prudenti disertoque sermone possit solvere, quae requiris, nisi
forte peregrinas merces desideras et pro varietate gustus nostrorum quoque condimento-
rum te alimenta delectant.*

the ones he employs on two other occasions in his extant letters ostensibly to refer his advisees to local experts. In his letter to Rusticus, examined in the previous chapter, he acknowledges bishop Proculus' competence as a spiritual guide.[105] In a letter to the North Africans Marcellinus and his wife Anapsychia he recommends that they take their question about the origin of the soul to Augustine.[106] The referrals he gives in the letters to Rusticus and Algasia, however, are not quite as convincing, for Jerome proceeds to mentor each Christian in the form of an extensive reply rather than leave the business of advising to local authorities. He makes a gesture of collegial deference to Alethius and he even goes so far as to contrast Alethius' 'pure fountain' with his own 'polluted' waters,[107] but the subtle implication of his rhetoric is that Algasia, by seeking out 'the waters of my stream that is so far away', has reason to believe that Jerome possesses a level of biblical expertise superior to that of her nearby cleric. This point is made more forceful by the suggestion that Jerome's epistolary voice, projected from faraway Bethlehem, trumps Alethius' '*viva vox*', which Algasia had ready at her disposal.[108] But, so as (no doubt) to avoid offending Alethius, Jerome attributes Algasia's preference for him to a matter of taste, even though the sense of the rhetoric indicates otherwise.

Elsewhere in the preface Jerome utilizes a different strategy for valorizing himself in the eyes of the reader as the pre-eminent international authority on the Bible:

---

[105] *Ep.* 125.20: *habes ibi sanctum doctissimumque pontificem Proculum, qui viva et praesenti voce nostras scidulas superet cotidianisque tractatibus iter tuum dirigat.* See above, p. 152.

[106] *Ep.* 126.1: *habes ibi virum sanctum et eruditum Augustinum episcopum, qui viva, ut aiunt, voce docere te poterit.*

[107] Jerome's phraseology in the preface (*cur purissimo fonte vicino nostri tam procul rivuli fluenta quaesieris et ... desideres aquas Sior, quae turbidis saeculi huius vitiis sordidantur*) seems to be inspired by biblical imagery he employs in his answer to Algasia's second question (*in Iesu volumine torrens appellatur Cane, id est, 'calami', qui aquas habet turbidas ... purissima Iordanis fluenta contemnens ... et desiderans caenosam ac palustrem regionem*). Such phraseological recycling is not surprising given that both letters were written at about the same time.

[108] For examples of '*viva voce*' as a marker for the advantages of live (as opposed to written) communication, see Reinhard Häussler, *Nachträge zu A. Otto, Sprichwörter und sprichwörtliche Redensarten der Römer* (Hildesheim, 1968), 324 (n. 1936); cf. Adkin, 'The Younger Pliny and Jerome', *RPL*, 24 (2001), 36.

Upon reading your questions, I realized that the zeal of the queen of Sheba has been brought to fruition in you. She travelled from the ends of the earth to hear the wisdom of Solomon. I indeed am not Solomon, who surpassed all men before and after him in wisdom, but you are to be regarded as the queen of Sheba, in whose mortal body sin does not reign and who having turned to the Lord with your whole heart will hear from him, 'Turn to me, Sunamite, turn to me'. For, indeed, 'Sheba' in the Latin language means 'to turn towards'. And at the same time it occurred to me that your questions, posed only about the Gospels and St Paul's epistles, show that you either do not read enough or do not sufficiently comprehend the Old Testament, which is shrouded in such great obscurities and typological figures that the whole of it requires interpretation.[109]

Jerome elegantly deploys the rhetorical figure of 'comparison' (*synkrisis*). This device was a staple feature of classical and early Christian encomiastic literature.[110] Encomiasts and biographers used it to glorify their subjects by favourably comparing them to exceptional historical figures; Jerome uses it here to equate Algasia with the queen of Sheba. According to biblical tradition, this unnamed queen, probably the ruler of Ethiopia in the tenth century BC, came in a large caravan to visit King Solomon in Jerusalem because she wanted to put his renowned wisdom to the test.[111] In scripting Algasia as a modern-day queen of Sheba, Jerome casts himself by implication as a modern-day

---

[109] *Ad quarum lectionem intellexi studium reginae Saba in te esse conpletum, quae de finibus terrae sapientiam venit audire Salomonis. non quidem ego Salomon, qui et ante se et post se cunctis hominibus praefertur in sapientia, sed tu regina apellanda es Saba, in cuius mortali corpore non regnat peccatum et quae ad dominum tota mente conversa audies ab eo: convertere, convertere, Sunamitis. etenim Saba in lingua nostra 'conversionem' sonat. simulque animadverti, quod quaestiunculae tuae de evangelio tantum et de apostolo positae indicant te veterem Scripturam aut non satis legere aut non satis intellegere, quae tantis obscuritatibus et futurorum typis involuta est, ut omnis interpretatione egeat.*

[110] Plutarch is the classical writer best known for his use of *synkrisis* (in the *Lives*); see the recent discussion by Timothy Duff, *Plutarch's Lives: Exploring Virtue and Vice* (Oxford, 1999), 243–86. It also appears in the writings of others such as Sallust and Tacitus: see Karl Büchner, 'Zur Synkrisis Cato-Caesar in Sallusts' *Catilina*', *GB*, 5 (1976), 37–57; Brian McGing, 'Synkrisis in Tacitus' Agricola', *Hermathena*, 132 (1982), 15–25. For Eusebius' use of *synkrisis*, see Michael Hollerich, 'Myth and History in Eusebius', *De vita Constantini: Vit. Const* 1. 12 in its Contemporary Setting', *HThR*, 82 (1989), 423–7.

[111] 1 Kgs 10: 1–13; 2 Chr. 9: 1–12.

Solomon. This *synkrisis* seems particularly apt, given that Solomon and Jerome were situated in virtually the same geographical space in Palestine and were visited—Solomon literally and Jerome figuratively, through correspondence—by female admirers-from-afar: the queen of Sheba 'from the ends of the earth' (*de finibus terrae*) and Algasia 'from the furthest reaches of Gaul' (*de ultimis finibus Galliarum*). Jerome's qualifying of Algasia's questions as '*maximas*' therefore becomes even more significant.

I suggest that Jerome introduced this comparison for another reason: to remind readers that his exegetical expertise comprehensively bridges *both* Testaments. This would explain why he furnishes the superfluous etymology of the Hebrew word 'Sheba'[112] as well as why he incorporates a multitude of quotations from the Old Testament, many of them gratuitous, into his answers to most of her questions.[113] He also provides examples of his Old Testament scholarship in action. For example, he turns his answer to her second question about the meaning of an odd messianic verse that Matthew (12: 20) borrowed from Isaiah (42: 3) into a case study in how one should use comparative readings from the Septuagint and the Hebrew Old Testament to elucidate hermeneutical problems in the New Testament; he concludes, not surprisingly, that the Hebrew truth always prevails.[114] Furthermore, he closely links—using the enclitic '-*que*'—the *synkrisis* and his gentle reproof of Algasia for asking questions only about the New Testament (*simulque animadverti...*). This rebuke is a cue to her thenceforth to make study of the Old Testament a priority. He describes such study as a tangly venture for which she requires a trained guide (*tantis obscuritatibus et futurorum typis involuta est,*

---

[112] Later in the letter (10) he gives the meaning of the Hebrew word '*sabaoth*'.

[113] See esp. sections 1, 2, 8, 9, 11.

[114] *Hoc non solum in praesenti loco, sed, ubicumque de veteri instrumento evangelistae et apostoli testimonia protulerunt, diligentius observandum est non eos verba secutos esse, sed sensum et, ubi Septuaginta ab Hebraico discrepant, Hebraeum sensum suis expressisse sermonibus.* Besides implying in his answer to her second question that he has a fluent reading knowledge of Hebrew and Greek, he even hints at having an acquaintance with Syriac (6: *iniquus autem mamona non Hebraeorum, sed Syrorum lingua divitiae nuncupantur*). His actual knowledge of Syriac, however, was minimal: see Daniel King, '*Vir quadrilinguis?* Syriac in Jerome and Jerome in Syriac', in Andrew Cain and Josef Lössl (eds.), *Jerome of Stridon: His Life, Writings and Legacy* (Aldershot, 2009), Chap. 16.

ut omnis interpretatione egeat[115]). This letter, then, in addition to resolving difficulties in the New Testament, is a veiled invitation to both Algasia and other Gallic readers perhaps minimally (or not at all) aware of Jerome's Old Testament scholarship to avail themselves of it.

CULTIVATED IMAGE

In this chapter, I have tried to show that there is much more to Jerome's post-Roman exegetical epistolography than previous scholarly treatments have granted. In the case of the letters examined, Jerome was not simply answering questions put to him by admirers. He ambitiously used these letters as a textual platform from which to shape the Latin Christian world's perception of him as an unquestioned authority on the Bible. Yet, an unquestioned authority he was not. Few contemporary Christians outside his inner circle evidently saw the merit to his Hebrew scholarship. The grudging realization of the generally hostile reception of his life's work as a biblical translator and interpreter drove him to formulate elegant and creative defences of it. As a case in point, I argued that Jerome attempted to tie his scholarship inextricably to the legacy of Fabiola, just as he had done with Pope Damasus and Marcella. He composed an epistolary *vita* on her in which he glorified her as his precocious Scriptural student. He then paired it with a detailed exposition of an Old Testament text taken as an allegory for the Christian's earthly pilgrimage to heavenly rest, in order to emphasize that his style of exegesis was in demand among the spiritual elite because of its salvific effects.

One of the reasons why Jerome's biblical authority, like his ascetic authority, was not taken for granted by contemporaries had to do with the matter of competition. Jerome may have been one of the more visible authorities of his day, but he was by no means the only

---

[115] See the similar phraseology in *Ep.* 120.10, where Jerome says that the 'obscurities' in Paul's letter to the Romans require expert interpretation: *omnis quidem ad Romanos epistula interpretatione indiget et tantis obscuritatibus involuta est, ut in intellegenda ea spiritus sancti indigeamus auxilio.*

one. There were many experts, from the local parish priest (e.g., Alethius) to internationally renowned writers (e.g., Augustine), who were around to field questions about Scripture. Given the variety of options available to them, what incentive did Christians have to choose Jerome—especially ones in Gaul, who had to go to considerable inconvenience to solicit his help? In the prefaces to the letters to Hedibia and Algasia he broached this question and presented himself with tactful subtlety as a better-qualified, and even divinely inspired, alternative to regional experts in Gaul. For heightened effect he held up these two women as model seekers-from-afar to be imitated by their fellow Christian country(wo)men. The letters to them are substantial specimens of exegesis with elaborate literary prefaces. As such, they have the look and feel of the commentaries Jerome wrote on individual biblical books, except that *Epp.* 120–1 are topical in nature.[116] This topical format enabled Jerome to display, to his immediate addressee as well as to the general reader, his scholarly versatility in explicating a range of mostly unrelated passages. I argued that these letters served at least two purposes simultaneously (as envisaged by their author): a didactic one, in providing expert guidance in the interpretation of selected New Testament *cruces*; and a propagandistic one, in supplying Jerome with a forum for advertising his scholarly services to the Gallic Christian community *writ large.* For to make his work as widely accessible as possible he needed a continually growing nucleus of patrons and followers to facilitate the circulation of his writings in their own locales within Gaul and to give glowing word-of-mouth endorsements of him to Christian friends and acquaintances. In case some readers were unfamiliar with the full spectrum of his exegetical *œuvre*, including especially his work on the Old Testament, he embedded informative 'sound bites' in the prefaces and in his answers to individual questions.[117] To this end, he conscientiously cultivated an image as an orthodox commentator on

[116] From a purely stylistic standpoint at least Jerome evidently regarded his exegetical letters as being more or less on a par with his biblical commentaries, for he used the same prose rhythm (*cursus mixtus*) in both. See Steven Oberhelman, *Rhetoric and Homiletics in Fourth-century Christian Literature* (Atlanta, Ga., 1991), 82–4.

[117] In *Ep.* 120.1 he mentions *Ep.* 54 to Furia and *Ep.* 79 to Salvina and later (8) refers to his commentary on Matthew. In *Ep.* 121 he mentions his commentaries on Amos (10), Matthew (2, 4), and Ephesians (10).

the Bible whose interpretations could be trusted.[118] What, moreover, did Jerome hope to accomplish by all of this? In a word: to convince the wider Latin Christian world—and not just pockets of partisans scattered throughout Gaul and elsewhere—of what he believed to be true—namely, that his body of work afforded Christians a more intellectually and spiritually stimulating encounter with the Bible than they could achieve by any other means.

[118] In both letters he denounces views espoused by a number of heretical sects: Montanists (*Ep.* 120.9); Manichaeans (*Ep.* 120.5, 10); Arians (*Ep.* 121.7); Marcionites (*Ep.* 121.7). Once in each letter he attacks Origen's doctrines without mentioning Origen by name (*Epp.* 120.10; 121.1). In view of the condemnation of Origenism, it is interesting to note that Jerome works from Origen's exegesis in his reply to Algasia: see Caroline Hammond Bammel, 'Philocalia IX, Jerome, Epistle 121, and Origen's Exposition of Romans VII', *JThS*, NS 32 (1981), 50–81. For a fine study of Jerome's heresiology, see Benoît Jeanjean, *Saint Jérôme et l'hérésie* (Paris, 1999).

Conclusion

The past couple of decades have witnessed an efflorescence of new scholarship examining how spiritual and intellectual authority were acquired and negotiated at the personal and institutional levels during the patristic age.[1] Jerome is an intriguing case study in this regard because of the problematic nature of his profile as viewed against the backdrop of his astral career ambitions. In this book, I have charted the contours of his manufactured authority in the two spheres of interest, biblical scholarship and ascetic spirituality, which dominated his life and literary production for nearly half a century. The correspondence has taken centre stage in this investigation, as I have argued it did also in Jerome's contemporary context. My intention has been to explore systematically the largely neglected but none the less fundamental propagandistic dimension of the correspondence and to propose theories about how, and above all *why*, Jerome used individual letters and letter-collections to bid for status as an expert on the Bible and asceticism.

For his time Jerome was a pioneer. He has the distinction of having been the first Latin Christian writer to ground his spiritual authority foremost in his tenure as a monk in the eastern 'desert'. This experience, captured vividly by his revisionist narrative, certified

---

[1] A few of the more recent book titles may be noted: Conrad Leyser, *Authority and Asceticism from Augustine to Gregory the Great* (Oxford, 2000); Theresa Urbainczyk, *Theodoret of Cyrrhus: The Bishop and the Holy Man* (Ann Arbor, Mich., 2002); Claudia Rapp, *Holy Bishops in Late Antiquity: The Nature of Christian Leadership in an Age of Transition* (Berkeley, Calif., 2005); Richard Goodrich, *Contextualizing Cassian: Aristocrats, Asceticism, and Reformation in Fifth-century Gaul* (Oxford, 2007). See also the collected papers in Andrew Cain and Noel Lenski (eds.), *The Power of Religion in Late Antiquity* (Aldershot, 2009).

him as a 'holy man' whose life and teachings were above reproach. Additionally, it made him a credible purveyor of eastern monastic ideals to Latin ascetics from the upper classes whose only exposure to these ideals came perhaps from the *Life of St Antony* or some other second-hand source.[2] Jerome also was the first Latin Christian to root his authority as an orthodox translator, textual critic, and interpreter of the Bible in a reading knowledge of its text in the original languages, notably Hebrew. In championing his 'back to the sources' methodology he sought to do for biblical studies in the Latin-speaking world what Origen, after whom he consciously patterned himself,[3] did for the Greek-speaking one. In the process, he recalibrated how excellence in biblical scholarship was to be measured in the west and obtruded himself as being better equipped than any of his Latin forebears or contemporaries to unlock the mysteries of the Bible and especially of the Old Testament.

In his letters and other writings, Jerome notoriously went to great lengths to create the impression that he was the spiritual and scholarly centre of gravity of the late antique church. Modern scholars tend to explain his apparent bravado cynically, in terms of a character defect or of rhetoric gone awry. This interpretation is too reductive, for it trivializes the complexity of his motives and makes the *a priori* assumption that he lacked self-awareness. Without, of course, discounting Jerome's strong personal conviction about the monumentality of his own work, I have tried to take a more neutral line by seeing his triumphalist rhetoric partly as a function of his realization that his status as an authority was never taken for granted as being absolute and unquestioned, at times not even by those in his inner circle. The overwhelming majority of Jerome's Christian contemporaries opposed, sometimes quite vocally, his extreme ascetic interpretation of the Gospel imperatives and the philological premises that undergirded his programme of biblical scholarship. The decisive challenges with which he met, on many fronts, naturally put him on

[2] See Stefan Rebenich, 'Inventing an Ascetic Hero: Jerome's *Life of Paul the First Hermit*', in Andrew Cain and Josef Lössl (eds.), *Jerome of Stridon: His Life, Writings and Legacy* (Aldershot, 2009), Chap. 1.

[3] Mark Vessey, 'Jerome's Origen: The Making of a Christian Literary *Persona*', *StudPatr*, 28 (1993), 135–45.

the defensive, so much so and so frequently that apology and self-justification necessarily became almost as integral to his teachings and scholarship as the content itself. He was uneasily aware, to a degree not usually conceded in modern scholarship, that he was but one voice among many vying for personal influence and a sympathetic audience to rally behind the various causes he promoted. The burden, then, was on Jerome to convince prospective supporters why the spiritual and Scriptural mentoring he offered was sound and even intrinsically superior to that available from competing Christian authorities.

Jerome's recognition of the tenuousness of his own position was not the only impetus behind the many epistolary campaigns he waged throughout his years in Rome and Bethlehem. During the course of this study, I have plotted the trajectory of Jerome's career simultaneously on another set of coordinates in order to situate it in its late antique sociocultural milieu. Jerome was a provincial *parvenu* of obscure lineage from a virtually unknown town on the border of Pannonia and Dalmatia. The pedigree secondary education he received in Rome is an indicator of the high hopes his father Eusebius, a local landowning *curialis*, had for him to pursue a lucrative career in law or government. By the late 360s, when he was in his mid-twenties, Jerome was employed as an official courier (*agens in rebus*) in the Gallic city of Trier, which at that time was an administrative centre of the west and residence of the emperor Valentinian. At some point, he experienced a religious conversion and abandoned his potentially promising career in the imperial bureaucracy. When he resigned his post, Jerome was not relinquishing his professional ambitions; he simply was turning them in another direction, from the secular to the sacred. The fourth-century church offered attractive career prospects that in some instances rivalled those in the civic sphere. The episcopate in particular was a viable option for Christian converts of rank such as Ambrose who previously had held prestigious government posts.[4] Even provincial upstarts such as Augustine and his friend Alypius could—with the right connections and a stubborn

---

[4] On the intersection of civic and ecclesiastical career paths in late antiquity, see Michele Salzman, *The Making of a Christian Aristocracy: Social and Religious Change in the Western Roman Empire* (Cambridge, Mass., 2002), 107–37.

determination to succeed—advance respectably far in the ecclesiastical *cursus*.[5] Jerome's aspirations, however, lay elsewhere. Through much trial and error, he forged for himself a two-pronged vocation as an ascetic monk and biblical scholar.

For *novi homines* in Roman antiquity such as Jerome,[6] professional (and social) advancement often was a daunting challenge. Because he was not independently wealthy, Jerome was unable to finance his own scholarly career. The fact remains that the vocation he chose for himself would never have materialized, or at least not in the way he presumably envisaged, without powerful patrons to underwrite the expenses of his labours, to provide for his general well-being, and to facilitate the dissemination of his writings through their own networks. This certainly held true when Jerome arrived in Rome in 382, for the second time since his student days, as an aspiring but undistinguished Christian writer eager to avail himself of new opportunities to further his monastic and scholarly agenda. His experience as a 'desert' monk and his growing expertise in biblical exegesis ingratiated him with Pope Damasus as well as with Marcella, Paula, and their female friends. He resourcefully maximized his connections with these people and intimately associated them (and later others, such as Fabiola) with his controversial ascetic and scholarly programmes in an effort to bring greater visibility and legitimacy to them, and an enhanced authoritative status to himself, among Christians outside his immediate circle. None of this, of course, is meant to play down the sincerity of Jerome's passionate religiosity or to morph him, however insinuatively, into a caricature of careerist excess for whom monastic and academic pursuits were subservient or even incidental to his upward mobility. To the contrary, it is only to acknowledge that Jerome was a product of his status-conscious times and that he needed to be pragmatically minded, and tenacious, about attaining the goals he had set for himself.

[5] See Claude Lepelley, 'Quelques parvenus de la culture de l'Afrique romaine tardive', in Louis Holtz and Jean-Claude Fredouille (eds.), *De Tertullien aux Mozarabes: mélanges offerts à Jacques Fontaine, à l'occasion de son 70ᵉ anniversaire, par ses élèves, amis et collègues* (2 vols., Paris, 1992), i. 583–94.

[6] A late republican analogue to Jerome is Cicero. See John Dugan, *Making a New Man: Ciceronian Self-fashioning in the Rhetorical Works* (Oxford, 2005).

An abundance of modern scholarly studies on the stylistic and other related aspects of Jerome's correspondence leaves us in no doubt as to his sophistication as a letter-writer.[7] In my discussions of individual letters, as well as in the overview of his epistolary corpus provided in Appendix I, I have aimed to reinforce this already glowing assessment by identifying some hitherto unnoticed contributions by Jerome to the Latin epistolographic tradition. As is demonstrated by the new taxonomy outlined in Appendix I, Jerome had a comprehensive working knowledge of a wide range of ancient epistolary types. His innovative application of two types in particular stands out. His reproach letters are impressive for their stylish *variatio* on a theme that remained one-dimensional in the hands even of Cicero and Pliny. Even more noteworthy is Jerome's application of the exegetical type. Other contemporary Latin Christian letter-writers, such as Ambrose and Augustine, experimented with the *epistula* as a vehicle for biblical exegesis. Jerome, however, developed it, prolifically and often creatively, into a full-blown epistolary type useful for communicating specialist knowledge about the Bible, and encompassing purely exegetical content as well as matters of biblical textual criticism and translation, and, of course, finer points of Hebrew philology. Some of his exegetical letters—e.g., *Ep.* 36 to Pope Damasus, *Ep.* 120 to Hedibia, and *Ep.* 121 to Algasia—approximate his biblical commentaries in that they are weighty pieces of exegesis prefaced by elaborate literary prologues, an indication of their elevated status in their author's eyes. Arguably, Jerome's most substantial contribution to the Latin epistolographic tradition takes the form of his two collections of personal correspondence to miscellaneous people and to Marcella. These literary monuments are remarkable not only for Jerome's attention to detail in painting a stunning self-portrait on a textual canvas, but also for his insight into how episodic 'lives-in-letters' such as these, once released, could help him to achieve extra-textual objectives—namely, to fortify his standing among target readerships as a spiritual and intellectual authority.

Ancient rhetoric, at least in its classical Roman expression, had a threefold function—to instruct (*docere*), to entertain (*delectare*), and

[7] See Introduction for a full bibliography.

most of all to persuade (*persuadere*). Jerome, heir par excellence to
the Roman rhetorical tradition, understood well how to use rhetoric
to shape his readers' opinions about a given subject matter, and to
do so in an aesthetically pleasing manner. Take, for example, his dramatic self-portrayal as a long-haired, chain-wearing desert monk who
braved the scorching heat of the sun (and of his passions) in complete
solitude. Advances in recent scholarship have attuned us to the gaping
disconnect between the historical reality of Jerome's actual experience
and his embellished, and indeed quasi-hagiographic, recreation of it.
If we are left with a sense of rhetorical vacuity, it is because we as
modern readers make demands of this narrative that are inconsonant
with the expectations that its author placed upon it. Jerome's intention was to provide not a factual, true-to-life account of his time in
the 'desert' (of the sort that would be satisfying to the historicist sensibilities of modern biographers) but an account that, in conformity
to the tripartite aim of classical rhetoric, instructed Christian readers
by example about authentic monastic piety, captivated them with a
picturesque snapshot of life in the (to western urbanites) haunting
eastern wilderness, and, most importantly of all, persuaded them
that he had the credentials necessary to bolster his claims to spiritual
authority.

In the centuries following Jerome's death *c*.419, as history grad-
ually gave way to legend, an enormously popular cult in his honour
proliferated, resulting in the transformation of the historical Eusebius
Hieronymus Stridonensis into a larger-than-life symbol of Christian
piety and scholarship and, eventually, into one of the four great
doctors of the Latin church.[8] Thus, in posterity, Jerome achieved the
recognition that most of his contemporaries had been unwilling to
grant him. Of the many factors that contributed to the development
of the 'Saint Jerome legend',[9] we must not overlook Jerome's magnif-
icent talents as a self-portraitist, which we see on display especially
in his letters (as well as in the prefaces to his biblical commentaries and translations[10]). So compelling were the literary identities

[8] This honour was conferred upon him by Pope Boniface VIII on 20 Sept. 1295.
[9] Its main lines of development are discussed by Eugene Rice, *Saint Jerome in the Renaissance* (Baltimore, Md., 1985).
[10] See Charles Favez, *Saint Jérôme peint par lui-même* (Brussels, 1958).

he fashioned for himself that they inspired a rich tradition of late medieval and Renaissance iconography that glorified him alternately as a self-flagellating penitent in the wilderness and as a bookish monk holed away in his study. This book has aimed to pay its own tribute to Jerome by appreciating the complexity of his literary artistry, first on its own terms and then in the broader context of his life and work.

Appendices

APPENDIX I

Classifying the Letters: A New Taxonomy

There are 123 genuine letters by Jerome that have survived.[1] All but two of these are printed in Isidor Hilberg's three-volume critical edition of the correspondence.[2] These remaining two were not included by Margit Kamptner, either, in her 1996 reprint of Hilberg's edition,[3] and so they should be mentioned briefly here. The first (*Ep.* 18*) was written from Rome around 384 to Praesidius, a deacon in Piacenza in northern Italy. It circulated among Jerome's correspondence for several centuries but was rejected by scholars as apocryphal beginning in the 1500s. In the late nineteenth century, Germain Morin made a compelling case on stylistic grounds for reinstating its Hieronymian authorship.[4] Scholars since then have for the most part accepted Morin's findings with confidence.[5] The second letter (*Ep.* 27*), addressed to bishop Aurelius of Carthage in the early 390s, surfaced in the last quarter of the twentieth century.[6] No one had so much as suspected its

---

[1] Alfons Fürst, *Hieronymus: Askese und Wissenschaft in der Spätantike* (Freiburg, 2003), 286 and Stefan Rebenich, *Jerome* (London and New York, 2002), 142, include among Jerome's genuine correspondence the *Epistula ad Sophronium de ecclesia Lyddensi*, a letter purportedly written by Jerome and preserved only in a Georgian translation. For a French translation and discussion of this letter, see Michel van Esbroeck, 'L'histoire de l'église de Lydda dans deux textes géorgiens', *BKR*, 35 (1977), 111–31. This idiosyncratic letter is full of anachronisms, and van Esbroeck's argument for Hieronymian authorship remains decidedly unconvincing. Therefore, I see no reason to regard the letter as genuine.

[2] Hilberg, *Sancti Eusebii Hieronymi epistulae* (CSEL, 54–6) (Vienna and Leipzig, 1910–18).

[3] Reviewers were quick to point out Kamptner's puzzling oversight. See, e.g., Henry Chadwick in *JEH*, 49 (1998), 707, and Stefan Rebenich in *Gymnasium*, 106 (1999), 77–8.

[4] Morin, 'Un écrit méconnu de s. Jérôme: la 'Lettre à Présidius' sur le cierge pascal', *RBén*, 8 (1891), 20–7; id., 'La Lettre de saint Jérôme sur le cierge pascal: réponse à quelques difficultés de M. l'abbé Duchesne', *RBén*, 9 (1892), 392–7; id., 'Pour l'authenticité de la lettre de s. Jérôme à Présidius', *BALAC*, 3 (1913), 52–60.

[5] e.g., J. N. D. Kelly, *Jerome. His Life, Writings, and Controversies* (London, 1975), 111; Rebenich, *Hieronymus und sein Kreis: Prosopographische und sozialgeschichtliche Untersuchungen* (Stuttgart, 1992), 170.

[6] For the text, see CSEL, 88: 130–3. Cf. a slightly emended text in Johannes Divjak, *Œuvres de saint Augustin 46B: Lettres 1*–29** (Paris, 1987), 394–401, with a commentary by Yves-Marie Duval at 560–8.

existence before the Austrian scholar Johannes Divjak found it embedded in a *corolla* of over two dozen previously unknown letters by Augustine that he had discovered by accident in 1975.[7]

Some scholars have questioned how many of Jerome's 123 genuine letters are really 'letters' as opposed to ascetic or exegetical 'treatises' with dedicatees.[8] However, we must bear in mind that in the ancient world the 'letter' was an elastic literary form that accommodated everything from Cicero's personal correspondence with Atticus to Seneca's topical essays on philosophy, the *Epistulae morales* to Lucilius. Christian letter-writers certainly were aware of this open-ended application for the epistolary medium.[9] Jerome was no different; hence, the interchangeable terminology he used when referring, for example, to *Ep.* 22 to Eustochium on preserving virginity ('*epistula*', '*liber*', '*libellus*'[10]). Similarly, he specifically designated some of his inordinately long exegetical compositions, such as *Ep.* 64 to Fabiola on the priestly vestments, by the term '*epistula*'.[11]

To give readers a bird's-eye view of Jerome's epistolary corpus, modern scholars traditionally have devised taxonomies that divide the letters into groups based on their primary subject matter. Jérôme Labourt's schema is typical. He reduced the letters to the following catch-all headings: 'morale pratique, dogme, exégèse biblique, polémique, éloges ou oraisons funèbres, lettres familières'.[12] Labourt conceded that this hotchpotch taxonomy is

---

[7] As to how this letter came to be transmitted among Augustine's, Divjak, 'Die neuen Briefe des hl. Augustinus', *WHB*, 19 (1977), 15, sensibly suggests that Aurelius forwarded it to Augustine for information's sake ('zur Information') and that the letter owes its initial survival to having escaped from Augustine's episcopal archive in Hippo.

[8] e.g., Aline Canellis, 'La Lettre selon saint Jérôme: l'épistolarité de la correspondance hiéronymienne', in Léon Nadjo and Élisabeth Gavoille (eds.), *Epistulae antiquae*, ii. *Actes du IIe colloque 'Le genre épistolaire antique et ses prolongements européens'* (Université François-Rabelais, Tours, 28–30 Sept. 2000) (2 vols., Louvain-Paris, 2002), ii. 313–14; Barbara Conring, *Hieronymus als Briefschreiber. Ein Beitrag zur spätantiken Epistolographie* (Tübingen, 2001), 100–5.

[9] See Stanley Stowers, *Letter Writing in Greco-Roman Antiquity* (Philadelphia, 1986). Cf. Henri-Irénée Marrou, 'La Technique de l'édition à l'époque patristique', *VChr*, 3 (1949), 221–2, on 'la frontière indécise qui, dans la littérature patristique, sépare lettres et traités'.

[10] *Apol. c. Ruf.* 1.30; *Adv. Iov.* 1.13; *Epp.* 22.22; 48.18; 130.19. See Evaristo Arns, *La Technique du livre d'après saint Jérôme* (Paris, 1953), 100–1.

[11] *Ep.* 64.21: *ego iam mensuram epistulae excedere me intellego.*

[12] Labourt, *Jérôme: Lettres* (8 vols., Paris, 1949–63), i. pp. xli–xlii. Cf. Berthold Altaner and Alfred Stuiber, *Patrologie. Leben, Schriften und Lehre der Kirchenväter* (Freiburg, 1978), 401: 'Es sind Briefe persönlich-familiären Charakters, aber auch viele Briefe, die sich mit aszetischen, polemischen, apologetischen, exegetischen und didaktischen Fragen beschäftigen'. And, more recently, Michael Trapp, *Greek and Latin Letters. An Anthology, with Translation* (Cambridge, 2003), 20: '[The letters] can be

'nécessairement artificielle'. Its main weakness, however, is not artificiality but rather its oversimplification of Jerome's mastery of a broad range of epistolary genres. A more nuanced taxonomy is needed, one that demonstrates this range by locating the letters in their ancient rhetorical context.

For guidance in developing a more satisfactory classification system I suggest that we turn to the two most comprehensive letter-writing handbooks to survive from the Greco–Roman world, pseudo-Demetrius' *Typoi epistolikoi* (100 BC–AD 200) and pseudo-Libanius' *Epistolimaioi characteres* (AD 300– 500).[13] Both manuals include descriptions and brief samples of epistolary types in use in antiquity. Even though they were written at different times and by different authors who applied the particulars of epistolary practice in somewhat different ways, taken together they would seem to provide a useful basis for classifying Jerome's letters. We would be naive, of course, to expect all of his letters to conform rigidly to the templates articulated in these two handbooks, as if Jerome composed his correspondence while consulting them closely. Nevertheless, his extant letters do show that he worked very consciously within an established epistolographic tradition that recognized distinct epistolary types such as the ones conveniently outlined by pseudo-Demetrius and pseudo-Libanius. Leaving aside, then, the anachronistic classification systems devised by modern scholars, we may assign Jerome's surviving letters to the following seventeen groups:[14]

Apologetic (ἀπολογητικός)

According to pseudo-Demetrius, the 'apologetic type is that which adduces, with proof, arguments which contradict charges that are being made'.[15] Apologetic letters usually begin with a list of charges brought against the writer followed by his rebuttal. In his fourteen extant letters of this kind, Jerome defends his moral, theological, and scholarly integrity against challenges from critics.

---

roughly categorized as eleven on points of dogma, twenty-four exegetic, thirty on moral issues, eleven funeral orations (obituaries), thirty-one polemical, and a few private letters to friends.'

[13] For a critical edition of these two works, see Valentin Weichert, *Demetrii et Libanii qui feruntur ΤΥΠΟΙ ΕΠΙΣΤΟΛΙΚΟΙ et ΕΠΙΣΤΟΛΙΜΑΙΟΙ ΧΑΡΑΚΤΗΡΕΣ* (Leipzig, 1910). English translations of both works are taken from Abraham Malherbe, *Ancient Epistolary Theorists* (Atlanta, Ga., 1988).

[14] Where applicable, I include references to published studies on individual letters. I do not, however, systematically provide references to the places in the present book in which I discuss many of these letters.

[15] Malherbe, *Ancient Epistolary Theorists*, 41. See Stowers, *Letter Writing*, 167–70.

Ep. 17 to Mark: Trinitarian heresy
Ep. 27 to Marcella: revision of the Gospels according to the Greek
Ep. 45 to Asella: sexual misconduct and opportunism[16]
Ep. 48 to Pammachius: *Adversus Iovinianum*
Ep. 49 to Pammachius: *Adversus Iovinianum*
Ep. 57 to Pammachius: translation methodology[17]
Ep. 61 to Vigilantius: heresy (Origenism)
Ep. 70 to Magnus: quoting from the Latin classics
Ep. 82 to Theophilus: heresy (Origenism)
Ep. 84 to Pammachius and Oceanus: heresy (Origenism)
Ep. 97 to Pammachius and Marcella: heresy (Origenism)
Ep. 106 to Sunnia and Fretela: Jerome's Latin translation of the Psalter[18]
Ep. 112 to Augustine: biblical exegesis and translation
Ep. 124 to Avitus: heresy (Origenism)

Consulting (ἀναθετικός)

Pseudo-Libanius defines the consultation letter as 'that in which we communicate our own opinion to one of our friends and request his advice on the
matter'.[19] Jerome comes through in his letters as a magisterial figure perfectly
comfortable with dispensing advice about the spiritual life and the Bible.
However, on two notable occasions in his surviving correspondence he is
the one asking for guidance rather than the one offering it.

Ep. 2 to Theodosius: guidance about monastic life
Ep. 15 to Pope Damasus: communicating with schismatic bishops;
        Trinitarian theology[20]

---

[16] See above, pp. 106–8.
[17] G. J. M. Bartelink, *Hieronymus, Liber de optimo genere interpretandi (Epistula 57). Ein Kommentar* (Leiden, 1980).
[18] Donatien de Bruyne, 'La Lettre de Jérôme à Sunnia et Fretela sur le Psautier', *ZNTW*, 28 (1929), 1–13; Arthur Allgeier, 'Der Brief an Sunnia und Fretela und seine Bedeutung für die Textherstellung der Vulgata', *Biblica*, 11 (1930), 80–107; id., *Die Psalmen der Vulgata* (Paderborn, 1940), 63–8; Jacques Zeiller, 'La Lettre de saint Jérôme aux Goths Sunnia et Frétela', *CRAI* (1935), 238–50; Berthold Altaner, 'Wann schrieb Hieronymus seine Ep. 106 ad Sunniam et Fretelam de Psalterio?', *VChr*, 4 (1950), 246–8.
[19] Malherbe, *Ancient Epistolary Theorists*, 71.
[20] Thomas Lawler, 'Jerome's First Letter to Damasus', in Patrick Granfield and Josef Jungmann (eds.), *Kyriakon. Festschrift Johannes Quasten* (2 vols., Münster, 1970), ii. 548–52; Rebenich, *Jerome*, 70–4; Conring, *Hieronymus als Briefschreiber*, 198–215.

Recommending (συστατικός)

The letter of recommendation is one 'which we write on behalf of one person to another, mixing in praise, at the same time also speaking of those who had previously been unacquainted as though they were (now) acquainted'.[21] Such letters in antiquity normally included a brief and glowing character sketch of the recommendee that aimed to convince the recipient(s) to receive him with goodwill and to bestow upon him employment, patronage, or some other benefit.[22] In contrast to some other ancient epistolary corpora such as Cicero's and Symmachus',[23] Jerome's contains a very small percentage of recommendation letters. This need not be taken as a negative reflection of his contemporary influence or of the breadth of his social network; it is, rather, probably more a function of the incompleteness of his surviving correspondence.[24]

Ep. 103 to Augustine: the deacon Praesidius
Ep. 115 to Augustine: the priest Firmus

Consolatory (παραμυθητικός)

Consolatory letters, broadly defined, were 'written to people who are grieving because something unpleasant has happened [to them]',[25] be it the death of a friend or loved one or some other misfortune. Jerome occupies a time-honoured place in the Christian *consolatio* tradition.[26] In fact, his many consolation letters are among the best representatives of this rich tradition. In two of them, he offers comforting words to correspondents suffering from blindness and in the rest he consoles Christians for the deaths of friends or family members.

[21] Malherbe, *Ancient Epistolary Theorists*, 33. See Stowers, *Letter Writing*, 153–65.

[22] Koenraad Verboven, *The Economy of Friends. Economic Aspects of Amicitia and Patronage in the Late Republic* (Brussels, 2002), 287–329.

[23] Book 13 of Cicero's *Epistulae ad familiares* consists almost entirely of over seventy commendatory letters. Book 9 of Symmachus' letters also contains an unusually high proportion of *epistulae commendaticiae*. See Sergio Roda, 'Polifunzionalità della lettera *commendaticia*: teoria e prassi nell'epistolario Simmachiano', in F. Paschoud (ed.), *Actes du Colloque pour le 1600ᵉ anniversaire du débat autour de l'Autel de la Victoire, Genève 1984* (Paris, 1986), 177–202.

[24] See Appendix II.   [25] Malherbe, *Ancient Epistolary Theorists*, 35.

[26] Giuseppe Guttilla, 'Tematica cristiana e pagana nell'evoluzione finale della *consolatio* di san Girolamo', *ALGP*, 17–18 (1980–1), 87–152. See also Charles Favez, *La Consolation latine chrétienne* (Paris, 1937); Peter von Moos, *Consolatio. Studien zur mittellateinischen Trostliteratur über den Tod und zum Problem der Christlichen Trauer* (4 vols., Munich, 1971–2).

Ep. 23 to Marcella: death of Lea (friend)
Ep. 39 to Paula: death of Blesilla (daughter)[27]
Ep. 60 to Heliodorus: death of Nepotian (nephew)[28]
Ep. 66 to Pammachius: death of Paulina (wife)[29]
Ep. 68 to Castrician: Castrician's blindness
Ep. 75 to Theodora: death of Lucinus (husband)
Ep. 76 to Abigaus: Abigaus' blindness[30]
Ep. 77 to Oceanus: death of Fabiola (friend)[31]
Ep. 79 to Salvina: death of Nebridius (husband)
Ep. 108 to Eustochium: death of Paula (mother)[32]
Ep. 118 to Julian: death of several family members
Ep. 127 to Principia: death of Marcella (friend)[33]

Reporting (ἀπαγγελτικός)

The purpose of a reporting letter is quite simply to 'give some report of the things that have transpired'.[34] No matter what type of letter they happened to be writing, friends in antiquity would almost invariably insert titbits of news about themselves or mutual friends. It is a reporting letter proper, though, when this news giving takes centre stage.

Ep. 3 to Rufinus: update on the travels of Bonosus and Jerome
Ep. 32 to Marcella: progress report about recent research activities
Ep. 142 to Augustine: Christians persisting in heresy
Ep. 143 to Alypius and Augustine: Jerome's plan to write a refutation of Pelagianism

---

[27] Barbara Feichtinger, 'Konsolationstopik und Sitz im Leben: Hieronymus' ep. 39 ad Paulam de obitu Blesillae im Spannungsfeld zwischen Christlicher Genusadaption und Lesermanipulation', *JbAC*, 38 (1995), 75–90.

[28] J. H. D. Scourfield, *Consoling Heliodorus: A Commentary on Jerome, Letter 60* (Oxford, 1993).

[29] Pierre Nautin, 'La Date de la mort de Pauline, de l'épître 66 de Jérôme et de l'épître 13 de Paulin de Nole', *Augustinianum*, 18 (1978), 547–50.

[30] Fernando Lillo Redonet, 'La *consolatio de caecitate* en la literatura latina', *Helmantica*, 54 (2003), 369–90.

[31] See above, pp. 172–8.

[32] Cain, 'Jerome's *Epitaphium Paulae*: Hagiography, Pilgrimage, and the Cult of Saint Paula', *JECS*, 18 (2010), forthcoming.

[33] Id., 'Rethinking Jerome's Portraits of Holy Women', in Cain and Josef Lössl (eds.), *Jerome of Stridon: His Life, Writings and Legacy* (Aldershot, 2009), Chap. 4.

[34] Malherbe, *Ancient Epistolary Theorists*, 71.

Congratulatory (συγχαρητικός)

'The congratulatory style is that in which we congratulate someone who is experiencing good fortune'.[35] Jerome's letter in which he compliments Pope Boniface I on his promotion to the pontificate is the one clear-cut example of this particular epistolary type among the extant correspondence.

Ep. 153 to Pope Boniface I

Supplicatory (ἀξιωματικός)

True to its name, the supplicatory letter 'consists of requests, supplications and so-called entreaties'.[36] The requests may be for any number of favours or services.

Ep. 4 to Florentinus: request to have a letter (*Ep.* 3) forwarded to Rufinus
Ep. 5 to Florentinus: book borrowing
Ep. 10 to Paul of Concordia: book borrowing

Reproaching (ὀνειδιστικός)

In this letter, 'we reproach, with accusations, someone whom we had earlier benefited, for what he has done'.[37] In his eight examples of this epistolary type, Jerome accuses friends of neglect for failing to respond to him either in a timely fashion or at all. These are the finest specimens to survive from the classical and Christian Latin epistolographic traditions.[38]

Ep. 6 to Julian
Ep. 7 to Chromatius, Jovinus, and Eusebius
Ep. 8 to Niceas
Ep. 9 to Chrysocomas
Ep. 11 to some virgins at Aemona
Ep. 12 to Antony
Ep. 13 to Castorina
Ep. 16 to Pope Damasus

---

[35] Ibid., 69.   [36] Ibid., 37.
[37] Ibid., 35. See Stowers, *Letter Writing*, 139–41.
[38] Cain, '*Vox clamantis in deserto*: Rhetoric, Reproach, and the Forging of Ascetic Authority in Jerome's Letters from the Syrian Desert', *JThS*, NS 57 (2006), 500–25; see above, pp. 25–30.

Censuring (ἐπιτιμητικός)

Pseudo-Demetrius describes the letter of censure as 'that written with rebukes on account of errors that have already been committed'.[39] These errors may have a moral dimension (e.g., when Jerome censures the deacon Sabinian for seducing a nun). In the majority of cases, the censuring takes place in a theological context, such as when Jerome condemns opposing theological systems and their adherents.

> *Ep.* 37 to Marcella: Reticius of Autun's commentary on the Song of Songs
> *Ep.* 41 to Marcella: Montanism
> *Ep.* 42 to Marcella: Novatianism
> *Ep.* 109 to Riparius: Vigilantius' teachings[40]
> *Ep.* 133 to Ctesiphon: Pelagianism
> *Ep.* 147 to Sabinian: seducing a nun
> *Ep.* 154 to Donatus: Pelagianism

Exhorting (παραινετικός)

'The paraenetic style is that in which we exhort someone by urging him to pursue something or to avoid something'.[41] In this type of letter, the writer recommends that the recipient adopt a specific behaviour or lifestyle.[42] Jerome's experiments with it number to twenty-one extant letters. In almost all of them, he urges correspondents to embrace a life of self-renunciation, but in a few cases his exhortation takes the form of invitations to friends and acquaintances to come on pilgrimage to the Holy Land and specifically to Bethlehem.

> *Ep.* 14 to Heliodorus: the desert monastic life
> *Ep.* 18* to Praesidius: the ascetic life[43]
> *Ep.* 22 to Eustochium: preserving virginity[44]
> *Ep.* 27* to Aurelius of Carthage: procuring copies of Jerome's writings[45]

---

[39] Malherbe, *Ancient Epistolary Theorists*, 35.

[40] Conring, *Hieronymus als Briefschreiber*, 215–29.

[41] Malherbe, *Ancient Epistolary Theorists*, 69.

[42] Stowers, *Letter Writing*, 94–106.

[43] Yves-Marie Duval, 'Sur trois lettres méconnues de Jérôme concernant son séjour à Rome (382–385)', in Cain and Lössl, *Jerome of Stridon*, Chap. 2.

[44] Adkin, *Jerome on Virginity. A Commentary on the Libellus de virginitate servanda (Letter 22)* (Cambridge, 2003).

[45] Ilona Opelt, 'Aug.*Epist.*, 27* Divjak: ein Schreiben des Hieronymus an Bischof Aurelius von Karthago', *Augustiniana*, 40 (1990), 19–25. See also Duval's historical

Ep. 38 to Marcella: Blesilla as holy *exemplum*
Ep. 43 to Marcella: the rural monastic life
Ep. 46 to Marcella: invitation to Bethlehem[46]
Ep. 47 to Desiderius: invitation to Bethlehem
Ep. 52 to Nepotian: monasticism and the priesthood
Ep. 53 to Paulinus: Scriptural study[47]
Ep. 54 to Furia: chaste widowhood[48]
Ep. 58 to Paulinus: the ascetic life
Ep. 71 to Lucinus: the ascetic life; procuring copies of Jerome's writings
Ep. 107 to Laeta: religious education of the young
Ep. 117 to a mother and daughter in Gaul: 'spiritual marriage' (*subintroductio*)[49]
Ep. 122 to Rusticus: repentance
Ep. 123 to Geruchia: chaste widowhood
Ep. 125 to Rusticus:[50] the monastic life
Ep. 128 to Gaudentius: religious education of the young
Ep. 130 to Demetrias: preserving virginity
Ep. 145 to Exuperantius: invitation to Bethlehem

Thankful (εὐχαριστικός)

'The thankful style is that in which we express thanks to someone for something.'[51] In one of Jerome's two surviving letters of thanks, he expresses

commentary on this letter in *Œuvres de saint Augustin 46B: Lettres 1*-29** (Paris, 1987), 560-8.

[46] Nautin, 'La Lettre de Paule et Eustochium à Marcelle (Jérôme, Ep. 46)', *Augustinianum*, 24 (1984), 441-8; Adkin, 'The Letter of Paula and Eustochium to Marcelle: Some Notes', *Maia*, 51 (1999), 97-110.

[47] Pierre Courcelle, 'Paulin de Nole et Saint Jérôme', *REL*, 25 (1947), 250-80; Nautin, 'Études de chronologie hiéronymienne (393-397), iii. Les Premières Relations entre Jérôme et Paulin de Nole', *REAug*, 19 (1973), 213-39; Duval, 'Les Premiers rapports de Paulin de Nole avec Jérôme: moine ou philosophe? poète ou exégète?', *StudTard*, 7 (1989), 177-216; Guttilla, 'Paolino di Nola e Girolamo', *Orpheus*, NS 13 (1992), 278-94. See also Canellis, 'Les Rapports de Paulin de Nole avec Jérôme au-delà de 400: la *Lettre* 39 de Paulin et le *Commentaire sur Joël* 1, 4 de Jérôme', *Augustinianum*, 39 (1999), 311-35; Dennis Trout, *Paulinus of Nola. Life, Letters, and Poems* (Berkeley, Calif., 1999).

[48] Conring, *Hieronymus als Briefschreiber*, 170-98.

[49] Cain, 'Jerome's *Epistula* 117 on the *Subintroductae*: Satire, Apology, and Ascetic Propaganda in Gaul', *Augustinianum*, 49 (2009), forthcoming. See also Lössl, 'Satire, Fiction and Reality in Jerome's *Epistula* 117', *VChr*, 52 (1998), 172-92.

[50] Not the addressee of *Ep.* 122.

[51] Malherbe, *Ancient Epistolary Theorists*, 69.

appreciation to Eustochium for sending some trifles on the occasion of St
Peter's feast day, and in the other he thanks Marcella, on behalf of Paula and
Eustochium, for some miscellaneous articles she sent to them.

> *Ep.* 31 to Eustochium: bracelets, doves, basket of cherries[52]
> *Ep.* 44 to Marcella: sackcloth, chairs, wax tapers, goblets, fly-flaps

Conciliatory (θεραπευτικός)

Pseudo-Libanius defines this epistolary type as the one 'in which we concil-
iate someone who has been caused grief by us for some reason'.[53] Only one
of Jerome's extant letters fits neatly under this rubric. In this short note he
extends the olive branch to Rufinus after their relations soured during the
Origenist controversy.

> *Ep.* 81 to Rufinus: renewed friendship

Mocking (σκωπτικός)

'The mocking style is that in which we mock someone for something'.[54]
Satire is an integral component of Jerome's polemical technique.[55] While
satiric barbs are interspersed throughout many of his letters, two letters in
particular seem best to exemplify the mocking style. In one, Jerome attacks
a legacy-hunting priest ('Onasus') and in the other a monk who may have
been Pelagius.

> *Ep.* 40 to Marcella: 'Onasus of Segesta'[56]
> *Ep.* 50 to Domnio: Pelagius(?)[57]

---

[52] Rebenich, *Jerome*, 79–81.
[53] Malherbe, *Ancient Epistolary Theorists*, 69.   [54] Ibid., 71.
[55] David Wiesen, *Saint Jerome as a Satirist: A Study in Christian Latin Thought and
Letters* (Ithaca, NY, 1964). See also J. Brochet, *Saint Jérôme et ses ennemis. Étude sur la
querelle de Saint Jérôme avec Rufin d'Aquilée et sur l'ensemble de son œuvre polémique*
(Paris, 1906); Ilona Opelt, *Hieronymus' Streitschriften* (Heidelberg, 1973).
[56] Jean-Georges Préaux, 'Procédés d'invention d'un sobriquet par saint Jérôme',
Latomus, 17 (1958), 659–64; Giuseppe Nenci, 'Onasus Segestanus in Girolamo, *Ep.* 40',
RFIC, 123 (1995), 90–4.
[57] Duval, 'Pélage est-il le censeur inconnu de l'*Adversus Iovinianum* à Rome en 393?
ou: du "portrait–robot" de l'hérétique chez s. Jérôme', *RHE*, 75 (1980), 525–57.

Praising (ἐπαινετικός)

According to pseudo-Libanius, this genre is used 'to praise someone eminent in virtue'.[58] In nearly all of his praising letters, Jerome celebrates friends' steadfastness and success in their personal campaigns against 'heresies' such as Origenism and Pelagianism. Two exceptions are letters he wrote in praise of Asella's virginity and the immense learning and admirable work ethic of Origen.

> *Ep.* 1 to Innocentius: glorification of a Christian woman falsely accused of adultery and condemned to death; praise of Evagrius of Antioch's political influence[59]
> *Ep.* 24 to Marcella: Asella's virtues
> *Ep.* 33 to Paula: Origen's scholarly productivity[60]
> *Ep.* 62 to Tranquillinus: Origen's biblical commentaries
> *Ep.* 63 to Theophilus: Theophilus' opposition to Origenism
> *Ep.* 86 to Theophilus: Theophilus' opposition to Origenism
> *Ep.* 88 to Theophilus: Theophilus' opposition to Origenism
> *Ep.* 99 to Theophilus: Theophilus' paschal letter
> *Ep.* 114 to Theophilus: Theophilus' theological writings
> *Ep.* 138 to Riparius: Riparius' zeal against Pelagianism
> *Ep.* 139 to Apronius: Apronius' zeal against Pelagianism
> *Ep.* 141 to Augustine: Augustine's orthodoxy
> *Ep.* 151 to Riparius: Riparius' zeal against Pelagianism
> *Ep.* 152 to Riparius: Riparius' zeal against Pelagianism

Accounting (αἰτιολογικός)

The accounting type gives 'the reasons why something has not taken place or will not take place'.[61] This definition would seem to apply well to two

[58] Malherbe, *Ancient Epistolary Theorists*, 71.

[59] André Chastagnol, 'Le Supplice inventé par Avidius Cassius: remarques sur l'histoire Auguste et la lettre 1 de Saint Jérôme', *Bonner Historia-Augusta-Colloquium* (Bonn, 1970), 95–107; J. H. D. Scourfield, 'A Literary Commentary on Jerome, Letters 1, 60, 107', dissertation (Oxford, 1983), 32–138; Filippo Capponi, 'Aspetti realistici e simbolici dell'epistolario di Gerolamo', in Aldo Ceresa-Gastaldo (ed.), *Gerolamo e la biografia letteraria* (Genoa, 1989), 81–103; Johannes Schwind, 'Hieronymus' Epistula ad Innocentium (epist 1)—ein Jugendwerk?', WS, 110 (1997), 171–86; Hildegund Müller, 'Der älteste Brief des heiligen Hieronymus. Zu einem aktuellen Datierungsvorschlag', WS, 111 (1998), 191–210; Rebenich, *Jerome*, 63–9.

[60] Opelt, 'Origene visto da san Girolamo', *Augustinianum*, 26 (1986), 217–22; Cain, 'Origen, Jerome, and the *senatus Pharisaeorum*', *Latomus*, 65 (2006), 727–34.

[61] Malherbe, *Ancient Epistolary Theorists*, 39.

letters in which Jerome declines for various reasons to commit certain of his theological opinions to writing.

> *Ep.* 126 to Marcellinus and Anapsychia: origin of the soul
> *Ep.* 134 to Augustine: origin of the soul

Threatening (ἀπειλητικός)

'It is the threatening type when with intensity we instil fear in people for what they have done or would do'.[62] Two letters Jerome wrote to Augustine at a time when their relations were severely strained fit this profile. In both Jerome warns him to desist from attacking him behind his back.

> *Ep.* 102 to Augustine
> *Ep.* 105 to Augustine

Exegetical (ἐξηγητικός)

To account for the remaining letters, which compromise about one-quarter of Jerome's surviving correspondence, it is necessary to devise a rubric not used by either pseudo-Demetrius or pseudo-Libanius. I shall call it the 'exegetical' type. It is a letter devoted to the interpretation of the Bible, broadly speaking. Jerome's exegetical letters, the natural outgrowth of the largest branch of his literary corpus (the biblical commentaries), come in all shapes and sizes and exhibit his enormous breadth of erudition and technical expertise. Some, varying widely in length among themselves, answer lists of randomly selected biblical passages sent to him by friends and admirers. Several are monographs on one particular biblical passage or topic. Still others, notably his letters to Marcella, address lexicographical and etymological questions relating to the Hebrew Old Testament.

> *Ep.* 18A + B to Pope Damasus: vision of Isaiah 6[63]
> *Ep.* 20 to Pope Damasus: the word '*hosanna*'
> *Ep.* 21 to Pope Damasus: parable of the prodigal son
> *Ep.* 25 to Marcella: the ten names of God
> *Ep.* 26 to Marcella: the words 'alleluia', 'amen', and '*maranatha*'

---

[62] Ibid., 37.

[63] Nautin, 'Le *De Seraphim* de Jérôme et son appendice *ad Damasum*', in Michael Wissemann (ed.), *Roma renascens. Beiträge zur Spätantike und Rezeptionsgeschichte. Festschrift Ilona Opelt* (Frankfurt, 1988), 257–93; Fürst, 'Jerome Keeping Silent: Origen and his Exegesis of Isaiah', in Cain and Lössl, *Jerome of Stridon*, Chap. 11.

Ep. 28 to Marcella: the word '*selah*'
Ep. 29 to Marcella: the words '*ephod bad*' and '*teraphim*'
Ep. 30 to Paula: the alphabetical Psalms
Ep. 34 to Marcella: two phrases in Psalm 127[64]
Ep. 36 to Pope Damasus: three Old Testament passages[65]
Ep. 55 to Amandus: three New Testament passages
Ep. 59 to Marcella: five New Testament passages
Ep. 64 to Fabiola: Aaron's priestly vestments[66]
Ep. 65 to Principia: Psalm 45[67]
Ep. 69 to Oceanus: can bishops remarry?
Ep. 72 to Vitalis: Solomon and Ahaz
Ep. 73 to Evangelus: Melchizedek
Ep. 74 to Rufinus: the judgement of Solomon
Ep. 78 to Fabiola: Numbers 33[68]
Ep. 85 to Paulinus: two New Testament passages
Ep. 119 to Minervius and Alexander: two New Testament passages
Ep. 120 to Hedibia: twelve New Testament passages[69]
Ep. 121 to Algasia: eleven New Testament passages[70]
Ep. 129 to Dardanus: the Promised Land
Ep. 140 to Cyprian: Psalm 90
Ep. 146 to Evangelus: equality of deacons and priests

[64] Conring, *Hieronymus als Briefschreiber*, 142–70.
[65] Cain, 'In Ambrosiaster's Shadow: A Critical Re-evaluation of the Last Surviving Letter-exchange between Pope Damasus and Jerome', *REAug*, 51 (2005), 257–77. See also Nautin, 'Le Premier [*sic*] échange épistolaire entre Jérôme et Damase: lettres réelles ou fictives?', *FZPhTh*, 30 (1983), 331–44.
[66] C. T. R. Hayward, 'St Jerome and the Meaning of the High-priestly Vestments', in William Horbury (ed.), *Hebrew Study from Ezra to Ben-Yehuda* (Edinburgh, 1999), 90–105.
[67] David Hunter, 'The Virgin, the Bride, and the Church: Reading Psalm 45 in Ambrose, Jerome, and Augustine', *ChHist*, 69 (2000), 281–303.
[68] Hermann-Josef Sieben, 'Israels Wüstenwanderung (Num 33) in der Auslegung des Hieronymus und des Origenes. Ein Beitrag zur Geschichte der Spiritualität und der origenistischen Streitigkeiten', *Th&Ph*, 77 (2002), 1–22.
[69] Cain, 'Defending Hedibia and Detecting Eusebius: Jerome's Correspondence with Two Gallic Women (*Epp.*, 120–1)', *MP*, 24 (2003), 15–34.
[70] Ibid.; Caroline Hammond Bammel, 'Philocalia IX, Jerome, Epistle 121, and Origen's Exposition of Romans VII', *JThS*, NS 32 (1981), 50–81.

Lost Letters of Jerome

Considering Jerome's otherwise prolific literary output and the size of his social network, his 123 extant letters are bound to represent only the tiniest fraction of all of the letters he wrote during his long career.[1] Certain years are represented by scores of correspondence (though admittedly still far below the number we might expect), while stretches of other years are represented by none. For example, twenty-five letters (*Epp.* 20–34, 36–45) date to his second stay in Rome (382–5), but only five (*Epp.* 46–9 and *Ep.* 27*) survive from the first seven years of his stay in Bethlehem (386–93). Ferdinand Cavallera attributed this seven-year virtual silence in Jerome's epistolary record to an unproductive period of literary activity.[2] However, this hypothesis is insufficient because Jerome was in fact engaged in a massive flurry of research and writing during this time.[3] Furthermore, given his documented aggressiveness in trying to recruit Italian friends for his monastic enterprise at Bethlehem in the late 380s and early 390s, we should assume that he sent out many more letters of invitation to the Holy Land than the two that survive.[4]

The earliest lost letters of which we are aware date to Jerome's stay in Chalcis/Maronia (*c*.375–*c*.377): an unspecified number of letters to some nuns at Aemona[5] and to the monk Antony[6] as well as a letter or series

---

[1] In terms of the number of surviving letters, Jerome's epistolary corpus compares favourably with some Christian corpora but not so favourably with others: Ambrose, 93; Paulinus, 59; Augustine, 252; Sidonius Apollinaris, 147; Synesius of Cyrene, 156; Theodoret of Cyrrhus, 230; Gregory Nazianzen, 243; Basil, 365.

[2] Cavallera, *Saint Jérôme: sa vie et son œuvre* (2 vols., Paris, 1922), i. 130.

[3] He composed the following: commentaries on Galatians, Ephesians, Titus, Philemon (386); *Vita Malchi* (386); translation of Didymus' *On the Holy Spirit* (387); commentary on Ecclesiastes (388); *Liber de nominibus hebraicis* (389); *Liber de situ et nominibus locorum hebraicorum* and *Vita Hilarionis* (390); *Quaestiones hebraicae in Genesim* (391); translations of Origen's thirty-nine homilies on Luke and seven *tractatus* on Pss. 10–16 (392); and, last but not least, *De viris illustribus* (393). See Pierre Nautin, 'L'activité littéraire de Jérôme de 387 à 392', *RThPh*, 115 (1983), 247–59.

[4] *Ep.* 46 to Marcella and *Ep.* 47 to Desiderius and Serenilla.

[5] *Ep.* 11: *ne unum quidem apicem totiens vobis tribuenti officium praestitistis.*

[6] *Ep.* 12: *decem iam, nisi fallor, epistulas plenas tam officii quam precum misi.*

of letters to his estranged maternal aunt Castorina.[7] The recipients of lost letters from later periods in his career include: Didymus the Blind;[8] Marcellinus and his wife Anapsychia;[9] Augustine;[10] the priest Firmus;[11] and an otherwise unknown Abundantius.[12] With his priest-friend Riparius, Jerome maintained a steady correspondence '*per singulos annos*',[13] yet only four letters from Jerome survive.[14] Rufinus claimed to possess a copy of a biting letter in which Jerome allegedly attacked Ambrose, but it has not survived.[15] Then there is the batch of exegetical letters he sent to 'many holy brothers and sisters' in Gaul in the first decade of the fifth century;[16] the only one from this group to survive is *Ep.* 119 to Minervius and Alexander. Cassiodorus recommended that his monks read 'the letter by Saint Jerome to Chromatius and Heliodorus', in which they would find out about the lives of the Fathers, the confessions of the faithful, and the passions of the martyrs.[17] Finally, a lost epistolary treatise entitled *Ad Sofronium praeinvectio in detractorem pseudochristianum* is mentioned in a late sixth-century manuscript of Jerome's *De viris illustribus*, though its authenticity cannot be confirmed.[18]

[7] *Ep.* 13: *ante annum prioribus litteris rogaveram.*

[8] *Ep.* 84.3: *litteras meas ad Didymum.*

[9] *Ep.* 126.1: *vobis epistulas meas frequenter ingessi.*

[10] See J. N. D. Kelly, *Jerome. His Life, Writings, and Controversies* (London, 1975), 218–19.

[11] *Ep.* 134.2: *litteras quoque meas ad sanctum presbyterum Firmum direxi.*

[12] According to Cassiodorus (*Instit.* 1.2.6), it was an exegetical letter that addressed '*obscurissimas quaestiones*' about three Old Testament passages.

[13] *Ep.* 151.2.   [14] *Epp.* 109, 138, 151–2.

[15] *Apol. c. Hier.* 2.23: [*Hieronymus*] *scit me habere epistulam suam in qua hoc ipsum excusans, in illum* [*Ambrosium*] *convertit suspicionem. Verum... epistula illa etiam secretiora quaedam continet, quae interim modo publicari nolo ante tempus.*

[16] *Ep.* 119.1, 12: *multas sanctorum fratrum ac sororum de vestra provincia ad me detulit quaestiones... a fratre Sisinnio admonitus sum, ut et ad vos et ad ceteros sanctos fratres... litteras scriberem.*

[17] *Instit.* 1.32.4: *et ideo futurae beatitudinis memores, vitas patrum, confessiones fidelium, passiones martyrum legite constanter, quas inter alia in epistulae sancti Hieronymi ad Chromatium et Heliodorum destinata procul dubio reperitis...* It is possible, given in particular his injunction to 'read the passions of the martyrs constantly', that Cassiodorus is referring to one of the two forged letters that comprised the preface to the *Martyrologium Hieronymianum*. In the letter pseudo-Chromatius and pseudo-Heliodorus ask Jerome to draw up a list of the martyrs' feast days; in his reply pseudo-Jerome accepts the commission and outlines his methodology. This two-part epistolary preface, which was present in the earliest, fifth-century redaction of the *Martyrologium*, is found in all of its manuscripts.

[18] On this manuscript and its contents, see Alfred Feder, 'Zusätze zum Schriftstellerkatalog des hl. Hieronymus', *Biblica*, 1 (1920), 500–13.

The most regrettable gaps in Jerome's surviving epistolary record are the missing letters he addressed to his two closest monastic companions of the Bethlehem years: only three letters each to Paula[19] and Eustochium[20] have come down to us. In his auto-bibliography, Jerome speaks of the untold numbers of letters he would exchange with them on a daily basis in Bethlehem.[21] One possible explanation for why this vast correspondence has (as far as we know) been irretrievably lost relates to the physical form that it might have taken. If, as seems likely, the bulk of it consisted of informal notes that dealt with the day-to-day administrative business of their monastic complex, and other mundane topics, then these letters, which were not meant for public release, would probably have been written on wax *tabulae* and not on costly papyrus or parchment, and thus no permanent archival copies would have been kept of them.

---

[19] *Epp.* 30, 33, 39.   [20] *Epp.* 22, 31, 108.

[21] *Vir. ill.* 135: *epistularum autem ad Paulam et Eustochium, quia cottidie scribuntur, incertus est numerus.* Elsewhere in *Vir. ill.* (58.8) he refers to the 'volumes of letters' (*volumina epistularum*) he wrote to Paula.

The Manuscript Tradition

As we saw in the first three chapters of this book, in his auto-bibliography Jerome earmarked certain of his pre-393 correspondence to circulate as collections (*Epistularum ad diversos liber* and *Ad Marcellam epistularum liber*), smaller cohesive groupings (mutual exchanges with Pope Damasus), and as stand-alone literary showpieces (*Epp.* 14, 22, 39). But what about the rest of his letters, particularly those written after 393? In what form(s) did he intend them to circulate? Jerome has left behind no blueprint, and it would be fruitless to speculate in the complete absence of evidence. It may, nevertheless, be safely assumed that Jerome, who by 393 and perhaps much earlier regarded himself as a public literary figure in the loftiest of terms,[1] did in fact expect the vast majority of his correspondence to be copied and read by an audience that included but at the same time extended well beyond the immediate addressees.[2] Let us therefore pose the question above differently. In what form(s) did Jerome's post-393 correspondence actually circulate in his own day and in subsequent centuries: as one monolithic corpus, as individual pieces, in compact groupings akin to his two known pre-393 *libri epistularum*—or in a combination of these last two forms? There are no ancient *testimonia*, either from Jerome[3] or from contemporary or near-contemporary sources,[4] to help us to arrive at an answer. We therefore

---

[1] Cf. his lament to Pammachius in *Ep.* 48.2 about how his friends and enemies alike disseminate his writings as soon as he releases them (*statim ut aliquid scripsero, aut amatores mei aut invidi diverso quidem studio, sed pari certamine in vulgus nostra disseminant*).

[2] See above, pp. 180–1. See also Cain, 'Jerome's *Epistula* 117 on the *subintroductae*': Satire, Apology and Ascetic Propaganda in Gaul', *Augustinianum*, 49 (2009), forthcoming; id., 'Jerome's *Epitaphium Paulae*: Hagiography, Pilgrimage, and the Cult of Saint Paula', *JECS*, 18 (2010), forthcoming.

[3] According to Feder, Jerome may have made minor later additions to his autobibliography. See Feder, 'Zusätze zum Schriftstellerkatalog des hl. Hieronymus', *Biblica*, 1 (1920); id., *Studien zum Schriftstellerkatalog des heiligen Hieronymus* (Freiburg, 1929), 158–60. Nevertheless, none of these apparent alterations has provided clues as to how he might have structured his post-393 correspondence.

[4] By contrast, we do have one such *testimonium* about the posthumous circulation of the letters of the third-century Carthaginian bishop Cyprian. Rufinus, writing in the late fourth century, tells us that 'the entire body of correspondence of the holy martyr Cyprian is usually contained in one codex' (*Adult. libr. Orig.* 12). On the

must turn to the manuscript tradition; though here, too, we encounter some complications, at least initially.

The definitive analysis of the manuscript tradition of Jerome's letters is still waiting to be written. Such studies are not lacking for other major and minor epistolary corpora from Christian late antiquity—those of Ambrose,[5] Augustine,[6] Ennodius,[7] Avitus,[8] and Ruricius,[9] to name but a few. Thus, it seems especially striking that none yet exists for a cornerstone collection such as Jerome's.[10] Isidor Hilberg had promised a fourth volume of explanatory *prologomena* to cap his three-volume critical edition of the letters, but the political turmoil of the First World War prevented him from delivering on his promise.[11] As a result, we have no explanation from him of his collation methodology and no knowledge of any *stemmata* that he devised during the course of his research.[12] We do know the identity of the 139 manuscripts that he and his collabourators at the Vienna *Corpus Scriptorum Ecclesiasticorum Latinorum* consulted, but not what their exact reasons were for privileging some of the manuscripts over others. Furthermore, even if this information were available to us now, it would be of limited use because Hilberg and his colleagues did not have ready access

---

primitive collections of the Cyprianic epistolary corpus, see Chanoine Bayard, *Saint Cyprien: Correspondance* (2 vols., Paris, 1962), i. pp. xlvi–xlviii.

[5] Micaela Zelzer, CSEL, 82/3 (1982), pp. xi–cli (a continuation of Faller's work).

[6] Alois Goldbacher, CSEL, 58 (1923), pp. v–xciv. See also Rudolf Maurer, 'Strukturelle Untersuchungen zu den Augustinischen Briefkorpora', dissertation (Vienna, 1991). For a discussion of more recent scholarly developments, see Johannes Divjak's article 'Epistulae', in Cornelius Mayer (ed.), *Augustinus-Lexikon* (Basle, 1986–), ii. 5/6.893–1028 (with bibliography).

[7] Friedrich Vogel, MGH AA 7 (1885), pp. xxix–xlviii.

[8] Danuta Shanzer and Ian Wood, *Letters and Selected Prose of Avitus of Vienne* (Liverpool, 2002), 28–57 (a revision of Peiper's work).

[9] Ralph Mathisen, *Ruricius of Limoges and Friends: A Collection of Letters from Visigothic Gaul* (Liverpool, 1999), 51–76.

[10] So F. Nuvolone, 'Notulae manuscriptae', *FZPhTh*, 26 (1979), 254: 'On connaît, malheureusement, le manque de toute étude précise sur la tradition manuscrite des Lettres de Saint Jérôme et, en conséquence, aussi sur les différents "types" d'Epistolaire du même'. There are, however, a few article-length studies of individual manuscripts containing the letters. See Nuvolone, 'Notulae manscriptae'; Pierre Lardet, 'Epistolaires médiévaux de s. Jérôme: Jalons pour un classement', *FZPhTh*, 28 (1981), 271–89; Janet Blow, 'Codex Vaticanus 355 + 356 and the Text of Jerome's Letters in South Italy', *Monastica*, 4 (1984), 69–83.

[11] Jérôme Labourt, *Jérôme: Lettres* (8 vols., Paris, 1949–63), i. pp. xliii–xlvi.

[12] This was lamented by the reviewers of Hilberg's edition, e.g., Alberto Vaccari in *Biblica*, 1 (1920), 386–91 and Aurelio Amatucci, 'Per un edizione delle *Epistole* di s. Girolamo', *Arcadia*, 2 (1950), 87–8 in his review of the first volume (1949) of Labourt's revised critical text and French translation of the correspondence.

to many important manuscripts. Since then, most of the more than 7,000 medieval and Renaissance manuscripts containing Jerome's correspondence have been catalogued.[13] However, no systematic study comparable to what exists for other late antique Latin letter-writers has yet been undertaken. In what follows I shall begin to fill this enormous gap in the scholarship by offering some preliminary observations about the circulation patterns of Jerome's letters in the centuries following his death. From these findings, I shall then draw conclusions about the state of the epistolary corpus in the early fifth century.

The earliest surviving manuscripts containing any of Jerome's letters date to the sixth century. Six are known: three have one letter or fragment of a letter;[14] one contains four letters;[15] and two others have two letters each.[16] In the seventh century Jerome's letters apparently continued to circulate individually[17] and in small dossiers.[18] There is, however, evidence of larger groupings as well. For instance, the codex Bibl.Naz.VI.D.59 in Naples contains a block of twenty-two letters that comprise the largest known Hieronymian collection up to that point:

$$52 + 10 + 14 + 61 + 147 + 122 + 59 + 39 + 53 + 45 + 146 + 83 + 84$$
$$+ 55 + 54 + 60 + 66 + 30 + 14 + 125 + 46 + 121.$$

There are indications that this assemblage is an amalgamation of several smaller collections. First of all, there is the duplication of *Ep.* 14. The pairing of *Ep.* 61 and *Ep.* 147 may derive from either the earlier Verona.Bibl.Cap.XVII (15), which contains the sequence 48 + 49 + 61 + 147, or a lost manuscript in its family. Within the group of twenty-two letters, there are four readily

---

[13] See Bernard Lambert's inventory, published as the first two instalments of his *BHM*. This register is an indispensable resource, the best one in fact currently at our disposal for the study of the manuscript tradition of Jerome's letters. It does, however, have some *lacunae*: Ilona Opelt, for instance, spells out some of these omissions in her review of Lambert's work in *Gnomon*, 45 (1973), 46–50. Lambert's listing has been supplemented by other smaller studies, notably Johannes Divjak and Franz Römer, 'Ergänzungen zur Biblotheca Hieronymiana Manuscripta', *Scriptorium*, 30 (1976), 85–113. I have used Lambert's catalogue as the main reference guide for the research presented here.

[14] Gent. Universiteitsbibliotheek. 246: 147 (fr.); Rome. Bibl. Naz. Vitt. Em. II, Sess.55: 108; Karlsruhe. Landesbibliothek. 339: 2 (fr.).

[15] Verona. Bibl. Cap.XVII (15): 48 + 49 + 61 + 147.

[16] Milan. Bibl. Ambr. O.210. Sup.: 131 + 134; Leningrad. Publ. Bibl. Q.v.I.6–10: 78 + 130.

[17] e.g., Lyons. Bibl. 602(519): 153; Verona. Bibl. Cap.XXXIII(31): 110 (fr.).

[18] e.g., Escorial. Bibl. Mon. Lat. R.II.18: 59 + 121 + 22; Leningrad. Publ. Bibl. Q.v.I.13: 125 + 17 + 147.

discernible clusters. One consists of a letter from Pammachius and Oceanus about the teachings of Origen and Jerome's reply (83 + 84). The other three clusters are arranged by theme as follows: exhortations to repentance (147 + 122); consolations (60 + 66); and exhortations to the monastic life (14 + 125). It is possible that there is another dossier at the beginning of the series based loosely on correspondent: *Ep.* 52 to Nepotian and *Ep.* 14 to Nepotian's uncle Heliodorus. Nevertheless, if these two made up a viable couplet, one can only wonder why a scribe interrupted it with another letter (*Ep.* 10) that has nothing in common with it in the way of chronology, theme, or correspondent. Aside from these few self-contained dossiers, there are no visible signs of a scribal attempt at internal organization.

In the eighth century Jerome's correspondence seems to have begun to circulate for the first time in more robust groupings of forty to close to eighty letters. Two collections dating to the middle to late eighth century containing sixty-four and seventy-five letters and fragments, respectively, typify this trend.[19] These collections not only contain far greater quantities of letters than do ones from the previous two centuries, but they also exhibit a far greater sense of internal orderliness. A good representative example is the series of forty-three letters found in the late eighth-century codex Escorial Bibl.Mon.Lat.&.I.14:

121 + 120 + 101 + 102 + 103 + 111 + 110 + 56 + 105 + 67 + 104 + 112
+ 115 + 116 + 131 + 132 + 134 + 141 + 47 + 6 + 8 + 9 + 12 + 73 + 146
+ 87 + 88 + 93 + 89 + 63 + 86 + 91 + 71 + 126 + 90 + 153 + 154 + 62
+ 2 + 4 + 109 + 152 + 151.

This is a highly structured collage with eight noticeable dossiers and a minimum of stray letters not belonging to any particular cluster. Proceeding in the order in which they appear above, we note first two exegetical letters (121 + 120) written at the same time to women who lived in southern Gaul. A copyist may originally have coupled them on the basis of shared subject matter or the gender or geographical location of the addressees. The next dossier (101–41) is the largest in the collection and includes sixteen items from the Jerome–Augustine correspondence. Then there are two groupings of pre-Roman letters (6 + 8 + 9 + 12 and 2 + 4) that are the remnants of Jerome's archetypal *Epistularum ad diversos liber*.[20] Next to the Jerome–Augustine dossier, the most substantial one in this codex is the series of eight

---

[19] Cologne. Dombibl. 35. Darmst. 2031: 64 letters; Karlsruhe. Bad. Landesbibl. Aug. Perg. CV: 75 letters.
[20] See above, pp. 13–17.

letters (87 + 88 + 93 + 89 + 63 + 86 + 91) about the Origenist controversy written by or to bishop Theophilus of Alexandria. Two letters (*Ep.* 90 and *Ep.* 62) that follow shortly thereafter belong to this dossier thematically, even though they are not physically within its bounds. Two other clusters are correspondent-based, one for Evangelus (73 + 146) and the other for Riparius (152 + 151). The remaining cluster (153 + 154) to be accounted for contains letters to Pope Boniface and an otherwise unknown Donatus. Only four (*Epp.* 47, 71, 126, 109) of the forty-three items are free-floaters that seem to be situated haphazardly among clusters with which they have nothing in common. These apparent anomalies notwithstanding, the collection shows an unprecedented attempt at internal organization.

Collections of Jerome's correspondence verging on eighty or more letters began to materialize in the ninth century. Paris Bibl.Nat.Lat.1869 contains the largest, with ninety-three full-text letters plus fragments of others.[21] Most of these ninth-century collections exhibit a degree of internal organization comparable to that found in eighth-century codices such as Escorial Bibl.Mon.Lat.&.I.14, in part no doubt because ninth-century scribes copied from and augmented some of them.

A clear pattern has now emerged. In the roughly four centuries following Jerome's death, his letters circulated in a plurality of relatively small free-floating dossiers. These eventually served as the building blocks for partial compilations (forty or more letters) that began to proliferate in the eighth century as well as for substantial compilations (seventy or more letters) that made their debut in the ninth century. Moreover, there was no late antique or early medieval archetype of Jerome's complete or even near-complete correspondence. In general, it seems that during his lifetime and for over a century following his death, his letters circulated as *disiecta membra* and never *en masse* as did those of Pliny, Ambrose, and Sidonius.[22] Unlike some of his fellow Latin epistolographers, Jerome did not compile his complete letters for publication in his mature years.

There also is no evidence that Jerome had an associate akin to Possidius to act as the caretaker of his archive and to take charge of assembling his collected correspondence following his death.[23] Even if there had been such a person and even if he had had the will, he probably would not have had the way due to the near-destruction in 416 of Jerome's two Bethlehem

---

[21] See *BHM* 1(A), 242.

[22] The exceptions would presumably have been the letters that constituted the *Epistularum ad diversos liber* and the *Ad Marcellam epistularum liber.*

[23] So Harald Hagendahl and Jan Hendrik, 'Hieronymus', *RAC*, 15 (1989), 123. On Possidius, see now Erika Hermanowicz, *Possidius of Calama: A Study of the North African Episcopate in the Age of Augustine* (Oxford, 2008).

monasteries by a band of marauders. According to Augustine's graphic sec-
ondhand account at the end of *De gestis Pelagii*, which he wrote within weeks
of the attack, the brigands, whom he identifies as followers of Pelagius,[24]
brought horrible bloodshed (*sceleratissima caede*) on the monks and nuns
and even killed one deacon. The monasteries' satellite buildings sustained
extensive fire damage, and the octogenarian Jerome fled and took refuge
in a secure tower (*turris munitior*). Writing to his friend Apronius a year
after the sack, Jerome mourned that his monastery had been left in shambles
(*penitus eversa*) as far as its worldly possessions were concerned (*secundum
carnales opes*).[25] The separate accounts by Augustine and Jerome, read in
conjunction, imply that the monasteries had for all practical purposes been
left uninhabitable. It is possible but not provable that one of the buildings
destroyed either partially or totally in the fire was Jerome's personal study,
where his epistolary archive would have been housed. If this archive went
up in flames, then it follows that an indeterminate amount of Jerome's
file copies of both his own outgoing correspondence and others' incoming
correspondence may have been lost in the fire.

[24] *Gest. Pel.* 66. See Josef Lössl, 'Who Attacked the Monasteries of Jerome and Paula
in 416 AD?', *Augustinianum*, 44 (2004), 91–112.
[25] *Ep.* 139.

Bibliography

Primary Sources

Ambrose

Ieiun.   *De ieiunio* (CSEL 32/2)
Ios.   *De Ioseph* (CSEL 32/2)
Off.   *De officiis*, ed. and trans. Davidson (Oxford, 2001)
Ep.   *Epistulae* (CSEL 82/1–3)
Psal.   *Expositio de psalmo* CXVIII (CSEL 62)
Vid.   *De viduis*, ed. Gori (Milan, 1989)
Virg.   *De virginibus*, ed. Gori (Milan, 1989)

Ambrosiaster

In Rom.   *Commentarius in epistulam Pauli ad Romanos* (CSEL 81/1)
Quaest.   *Quaestiones veteris et novi testamenti* (CSEL 50)

Ammianus Marcellinus

Rer. gest. lib.   *Rerum gestarum libri*, ed. Seyfarth (Leipzig, 1978)

Athanasius

V. Ant.   *Vita Antoni*, ed. Bartelink, SC 400 (Paris, 1994)

Augustine

C. Iul.   *Contra Iulianum* (PL 44)
Civ. dei   *De civitate dei* (CCSL 48)
Conf.   *Confessiones* (CCSL 27)
Cons. evang.   *De consensu evangelistarum* (CSEL 43)
Ep.   *Epistulae* (CSEL 34/1–2, 44, 57)
Gest. Pel.   *De gestis Pelagii* (CSEL 42)
Grat. Chr.   *De gratia Christi* (CSEL 42)
Mor. eccl. cath.   *De moribus ecclesiae catholicae* (CSEL 90)
Retract.   *Retractationes* (CCSL 57)
Serm. dom. mon. *De sermone domini in monte* (CCSL 35)

Ausonius

Prof.   *Professores*, ed. Green, OCT (1999)

Basil of Caesarea

Ep.   *Epistulae*, ed. and trans. Courtonne (Paris, 1957–61)

John Cassian

Instit. coen.   *De institutis coenobiorum* (CSEL 17)

Cassiodorus

Instit.   *Institutiones divinarum et saecularium litterarum*, ed.
          Mynors (Oxford, 1937)

Cicero

Att.   *Epistulae ad Atticum*, ed. Shackleton-Bailey (1999)
Amic.   *De amicitia*, ed. and comm. Powell (Warminster, 1990)
Fam.   *Epistulae ad familiares*, ed. Shackleton-Bailey (1977)
Tusc.   *Tusculanae disputationes*, ed. Pohlenz (Leipzig, 1918)

Cyprian

Ep.   *Epistulae* (CSEL 3)
Hab. virg.   *De habitu virginum* (CSEL 3)

Ennodius

Ep.   *Epistulae* (MGH AA 7)

Eusebius of Caesarea

Mar.   *Quaestiones ad Marinum* (PG 22)

Gregory Nazianzen

Ep.   *Epistulae*, ed. and trans. Gallay (1964–7)

Jerome

Adv. Helv.   *De Mariae virginitate perpetua adversus Helvidium*
                   (PL 23)
Adv. Iov.   *Adversus Iovinianum* (PL 23)
Apol. c. Ruf.   *Apologia contra Rufinum* (CCSL 79)
Alt. Luc.   *Altercatio Luciferiani et orthodoxi* (CCSL 79B)
C. Vigil.   *Contra Vigilantium* (CCSL 79C)
C. Ioh. Hier.   *Contra Iohannem Hierosolymitanum* (CCSL 79A)
Chron.   *Chronicon* (GCS 47)
Dial. adv. Pelag. *Dialogus adversus Pelagianos* (CCSL 80)
Didym. spir. sanct. *Didymi liber de spiritu sancto* (SC 386)

Ep.	*Epistulae* (CSEL 54–6)
Ep. 27*	*Epistula ad Aurelium* (CSEL 88)
Ep. adv. Ruf.	*Epistula adversus Rufinum* (CCSL 79)
In Dan.	*Commentarius in Danielem* (CCSL 75A)
In Eccl.	*Commentarius in Ecclesiasten* (CCSL 72)
In Eph.	*Commentarius in epistulam Pauli ad Ephesios* (PL 26)
In Es.	*Commentarius in Esaiam* (CCSL 73–73A)
In Gal.	*Commentarius in epistulam Pauli ad Galatas* (CCSL 77A)
In Hier.	*Commentarius in Hieremiam* (CCSL 74)
In Hiez.	*Commentarius in Hiezechielem* (CCSL 75)
In Ion.	*Commentarius in Ionam* (SC 323)
In Math.	*Commentarius in Matheum* (CCSL 77)
In Psalm.	*Commentariolus in Psalmos* (CCSL 72)
In Soph.	*Commentarius in Sophoniam* (CCSL 76A)
Lib. nom. hebr.	*Liber de nominibus hebraicis* (CCSL 72)
Lib. sit. loc.	*Liber de situ et nominibus locorum hebraicorum* (GCS 11/1)
Orig. Cant.	*Origenis in Canticum Canticorum homiliae* (SC 37)
Orig. Es.	*Origenis in Esaiam homiliae* (GCS 33)
Orig. Hiez.	*Origenis in Hiezechielem homiliae* (SC 352)
Orig. Luc.	*Origenis in Lucam homiliae* (GCS 49)
Quaest. hebr.	*Quaestiones hebraicae in Genesim* (CCSL 72)
Tract. Ps.	*Tractatus in Psalmos* (CCSL 78)
V. Hilar.	*Vita Hilarionis* (SC 508)
V. Mal.	*Vita Malchi* (SC 508)
V. Paul.	*Vita Pauli* (SC 508)
Vir. ill.	*De viris illustribus*, ed. Ceresa-Gastaldo (Florence, 1988)

Miscellaneous

Apoph. patr.	*Apophthegmata patrum* (SC 387, 474, 498)
C. Th.	*Codex Theodosianus*, ed. Mommsen (1904; repr. 1990)
Cons. Zacc. Apoll.	*Consultationes Zacchaei et Apollonii* (SC 401–2)

Orosius

Hist. adv. pag.	*Historia adversus paganos*, ed. and trans. Arnaud-Lindet (Paris, 1991–2)

Pacatus Drepanius

Pan.	*Panegyricus*, ed. Mynors, OCT (1964)

Palladius

Hist. laus.   *Historia lausiaca*, ed. Bartelink (Milan, 1974)
Dial.   *Dialogus de vita sancti Iohannis Chrysostomi* (SC 341–2)

Paulinus of Milan

V. Ambr.   *Vita sancti Ambrosii*, ed. Pellegrino (Rome, 1961)

Paulinus of Nola

Ep.   *Epistulae* (CSEL 29)

Pelagius

Ep. ad Marc.   *Epistula ad Marcellam* (CSEL 29)
Ep. ad Dem.   *Epistula ad Demetriadem* (PL 30)
Virg.   *De virginitate* (CSEL 1)

Petronius

Sat.   *Satyricon*, ed. Müller (Leipzig, 1995)

Pliny

Ep.   *Epistulae*, ed. Mynors, OCT (1992)

Rufinus

Adult. libr. Orig.   *De adulteratione librorum Origenis* (CCSL 20)
Apol. c. Hier.   *Apologia contra Hieronymum* (CCSL 20)
Orig. Num.   *Origenis in Numeros homiliae* (GCS 30)

Ruricius

Ep.   *Epistulae* (CCSL 64)

Sidonius Apollinaris

Ep.   *Epistulae*, ed. and trans. Anderson, LCL (1939, 1965)

Pope Siricius

Ep.   *Epistulae* (CSEL 82/3)

Sulpicius Severus

Dial.   *Dialogi de virtutibus sancti Martini* (SC 510)
Ep.   *Epistulae* (CSEL 1)
V. Mart.   *Vita sancti Martini* (SC 133–5)

Symmachus

Ep.   *Epistulae*, ed. Callu (Paris, 1972–95)

Synesius of Cyrene

Ep.   *Epistulae*, ed. Garzya (Rome, 1979)

Theodoret of Cyrrhus

Hist. rel.   *Historia religiosa*, ed. and trans. Canivet (Paris, 1977–9)

Vincent of Lérins

Comm.   *Commonitorium* (CCSL 64)

Secondary Sources

Abel, Félix-Marie, 'Saint Jérôme et Jérusalem', *Miscellanea Geronimiana. Scritti varii pubblicati nel XV centenario dalla morte di San Girolamo* (Rome, 1920), 131–55.
—— *Géographie de la Palestine* (2 vols., Paris, 1967).
Adkin, Neil, 'Gregory of Nazianzus and Jerome: Some Remarks', in Michael Flower and Mark Toher (eds.), *Georgica: Greek Studies in Honour of George Cawkwell* (London, 1991), 13–24.
—— 'Ambrose and Jerome: The Opening Shot', *Mnemosyne*, 46 (1993), 364–76.
—— ' "Heri catechumenus, hodie pontifex" (Jerome, *Epist.*, 69.9.4)', *AClass*, 36 (1993), 113–17.
—— 'Jerome, Ambrose and Gregory Nazianzen', *Vichiana*, 4 (1993), 294–300.
—— 'Is the Marcellina of Jerome, *Epist.*, 45.7 Ambrose's Sister?', *Phoenix*, 49 (1995), 68–70.
—— 'Jerome's Use of Scripture Before and after his Dream', *ICS*, 20 (1995), 183–90.
—— 'Pope Siricius' "Simplicity" (Jerome, *Epist.*, 127.9.3)', *VetChr*, 33 (1996), 25–38.
—— 'Jerome on Ambrose: The Preface to the Translation of Origen's Homilies on Luke', *Rbén*, 107 (1997), 5–14.
—— 'Jerome's Vow "Never to Reread the Classics": Some Observations', *REA*, 101 (1999), 161–7.
—— 'The Letter of Paula and Eustochium to Marcella: Some Notes', *Maia*, 51 (1999), 97–110.
—— 'The Younger Pliny and Jerome', *RPL*, 24 (2001), 31–47.

Adkin, Neil, 'A Further Misunderstood Passage in Jerome's Eulogy of Lea (*Epist.*, 23.1.2)', *Eranos*, 101 (2003), 1–5.

—— *Jerome on Virginity. A Commentary on the Libellus de virginitate servanda (Letter 22)* (Cambridge, 2003).

—— 'Whose Nose and Whose Knees? Two Notes on St Jerome', *Orpheus*, NS 24 (2003), 1–6.

—— 'Tertullian in Jerome's Consolation to Heliodorus (*Epist.*, 60)', in Andrew Cain and Josef Lössl (eds.), *Jerome of Stridon: His Life, Writings and Legacy* (Aldershot, 2009), Chap. 3.

Adler, Judith, 'The Holy Man as Traveler and Travel Attraction: Early Christian Asceticism and the Moral Problematic of Modernity', in William Swatos and Luigi Tomasi (eds.), *From Medieval Pilgrimage to Religious Touris: The Social and Cultural Economics of Piety* (London, 2002), 25–50.

Albert, Gerhard, *Goten in Konstantinope: Untersuchungen zur oströmischen Geschichte um das Jahr 400 n. Chr.* (Paderborn, 1984).

Alföldy, Géza, *Die Personennamen in der römischen Provinz Dalmatia* (Heidelberg, 1969).

Allgeier, Arthur, *Die altlateinischen Psalterien: Prolegomena zu einer Textgeschichte der hieronymianischen Psalmübersetzungen* (Freiburg, 1928).

—— 'Der Brief an Sunnia und Fretela und seine Bedeutung für die Textherstellung der Vulgata', *Biblica*, 11 (1930), 80–107.

—— *Die Psalmen der Vulgata* (Paderborn, 1940).

—— 'Haec vetus et vulgata edition: Neue wort- und begriffsgeschichtliche Beiträge zur Bibel auf dem Tridentum', *Biblica*, 29 (1948), 353–90.

Altaner, Berthold, 'Wann schrieb Hieronymus seine Ep. 106 ad Sunniam et Fretelam de Psalterio?', *VChr*, 4 (1950), 246–8.

—— and Alfred Stuiber, *Patrologie. Leben, Schriften und Lehre der Kirchenväter* (Freiburg, 1978).

Altman, Janet, *Epistolarity: Approaches to a Form* (Columbus, Ohio, 1982).

—— 'The Letter Book as a Literary Institution, 1539–1789: Toward a Cultural History of Published Correspondences in France', *YFS*, 71 (1986), 17–62.

Amat, Jacqueline, *Songes et visions: l'au-delà dans la littérature latine tardive* (Paris, 1985).

Amatucci, Aurelio, 'Per un edizione delle *Epistole* di s. Girolamo', *Arcadia*, 2 (1950), 87–94.

Andel, Gerrit van, 'Sulpicius Severus and Origenism', *VChr*, 34 (1980), 278–87.

Anderson, Graham, *Sage, Saint and Sophist: Holy Men and their Associates in the Early Roman Empire* (London, 1994).

André, Jean-Marie, and Marie-Françoise Baslez, *Voyager dans l'antiquité* (Paris, 1993).

André-Delastre, Louise, *Saint Damase 1er: défenseur de la doctrine de la primauté de Pierre, des saintes écritures et patron des archéologues* (Paris, 1965).

Antin, Paul, 'Saint Jérôme et son lecteur', *RSR*, 34 (1947), 82–99; repr. in his *Recueil sur Saint Jérôme* (Brussels, 1968) (xxviii).

—— 'Jérôme, Ep. 125, 18, 2–3', *RBén*, 69 (1959), 342–8; repr. in his *Recueil sur Saint Jérôme* (Brussels, 1968) (xiv).

—— 'La Ville chez saint Jérôme', *Latomus*, 20 (1961), 298–311; repr. in his *Recueil sur Saint Jérôme* (Brussels, 1968) (xxxii).

—— 'Solitude et silence chez s. Jérôme', *RAM*, 40 (1964), 265–76; repr. in his *Recueil sur Saint Jérôme* (Brussels, 1968) (xxiii).

—— *Recueil sur Saint Jérôme* (Brussels, 1968).

Arjava, Antti, 'Paternal Power in Late Antiquity', *JRS*, 88 (1988), 147–65.

—— 'Jerome and Women', *Arctos*, 23 (1989), 5–18.

—— *Women and Law in Late Antiquity* (Oxford, 1996).

Arnheim, M. T. W., *The Senatorial Aristocracy in the Later Roman Empire* (Oxford, 1972).

Arns, Evaristo, *La Technique du livre d'après saint Jérôme* (Paris, 1953).

Asdrubali Pentiti, G., and Maria Carla Spadoni Cerroni (eds.), *Epistolari cristiani (secc. I–V). Repertorio bibliografico II. Epistolari Latini (secc. IV–V)* (Rome, 1990).

Atsma, Hartmut, 'Die Christlichen Inschriften Galliens als Quelle für Klöster und Klosterbewohner bis zum Ende des 6. Jahrhunderts', *Francia*, 4 (1976), 1–57.

Attwater, Donald, and Herbert Thurston (eds.), *Butler's Lives of the Saints* (4 vols., New York, 1956).

Avi-Yonah, Michael, 'The Economics of Byzantine Palestine', *IEJ*, 8 (1958), 39–51.

Baedeker, Karl, *Jerusalem and its Surroundings* (Jerusalem, 1973).

Bagatti, Bellarmino, *Gli antichi edifici sacri di Betlemme* (Jerusalem, 1952).

—— 'Recenti scavi a Betlemme', *LASBF*, 18 (1968), 181–237.

—— *Église de la gentilité en Palestine (Ier–XIe siècles)* (Jerusalem, 1968).

—— *Antichi villaggi cristiani della Giudea e del Neghev* (Jerusalem, 1983).

Baldovin, John, *Liturgy in Ancient Jerusalem* (Nottingham, 1989).

Bardy, Gustave, 'La Littérature patristique des *quaestiones et responsiones* sur l'écriture sainte', *RBi*, 41 (1932), 210–36, 341–69, 515–37; *RBi*, 42 (1933), 14–30, 211–29, 328–52.

—— 'St Jérôme et ses maîtres hébreux', *RBén*, 46 (1934), 145–64.

Bardy, Gustave, 'Faux et fraudes littéraires dans l'antiquité chrétienne', *RHE*, 32 (1936), 5–23, 275–302.

—— 'Pèlerinages à Rome vers la fin du IVe siècle', *AB*, 67 (1949), 225–35.

—— 'Copies et éditions au Ve siècle', *RSR*, 23 (1949), 38–52.

Barnes, Timothy, 'The Crimes of Basil of Ancyra', *JThS*, NS 47 (1996), 550–4.

Bartelink, G. J. M., 'Een gemeenplaats uit de briefliteratuur bij een Christelijk auteur: Brevitas epistolaris bij Hieronymus', *Lampas*, 10 (1977), 61–5.

—— *Hieronymus, Liber de optimo genere interpretandi (Epistula 57). Ein Kommentar* (Leiden, 1980).

—— (ed.), *Vie d'Antoine—Athanase d'Alexandrie. Introduction, texte critique, et traduction* (Paris, 1994).

Bastiaensen, Antoon A. R., *Le Cérémonial épistolaire des chrétiens latins: origine et premiers développements* (Nijmegen, 1964).

—— 'Augustin commentateur de saint Paul et l'Ambrosiaster', *SEJG*, 36 (1996), 37–65.

—— 'Jérôme hagiographe', in Guy Philippart (ed.), *Hagiographies: histoire internationale de la littérature hagiographique latine et vernaculaire en Occident des origines à 1550* (4 vols., Turnhout, 1994–), i. 97–123.

Bayard, Chanoine, *Saint Cyprien: Correspondance* (2 vols., Paris, 1962).

Benoît, Pierre, 'L'inspiration des Septante d'après les Pères', in *Homme devant Dieu: mélanges P. G. de Lubac* (Paris, 1964), i. 169–87.

Berardino, Angelo di (ed.), *Patrology: The Golden Age of Latin Patristic Literature from the Council of Nicea to the Council of Chalcedon* (Westminster, 1988).

Bergren, Theodore, 'Jerome's Translation of Origen's Homily on Jeremiah 2. 21–22', *RBén*, 104 (1994), 260–83.

Berthollet, Jean, *L'évêché d'Autun* (Autun, 1947).

Beyenka, Mary Melchior, *Consolation in Saint Augustine* (Washington, DC, 1950).

Biarne, Jacques, 'La Bible dans la vie monastique', in Jacques Fontaine and Charles Pietri (eds.), *La Bible de tous les temps*, ii. *Le Monde latin antique et la Bible* (Paris, 1985), 409–29.

Bignami-Odier, Jeanne, 'Une lettre apocryphe de saint Damase à saint Jérôme sur la question de Melchisédech', *MEFRA*, 63 (1951), 183–90.

Binns, John, *Ascetics and Ambassadors of Christ The Monasteries of Palestine, 314–631* (Oxford, 1994).

Bitton-Ashkelony, Brouria, 'Penitence in Late Antique Monastic Literature', in Jan Assmann and Gedaliahu Strousma (eds.), *Transformations of the Inner Self in Ancient Religions* (Leiden, 1999), 179–94.

—— *Encountering the Sacred: The Debate on Christian Pilgrimage in Late Antiquity* (Berkeley, Calif., 2005).

Blanchard, P., 'La Correspondance apocryphe du pape s. Damase et de s. Jérôme', *EphL*, 63 (1949), 376–88.

Blow, Janet, 'Codex Vaticanus 355 + 356 and the Text of Jerome's Letters in South Italy', *Monastica*, 4 (1984), 69–83.

Bludau, August, *Die Pilgerreise der Aetheria* (Paderborn, 1927).

Bodin, Yvon, *Saint Jérôme et l'église* (Paris, 1966).

Bonnardière, Anne-Marie la, 'Augustin a-t-il utilisé la vulgate de Jérôme?', in Anne-Marie la Bonnardière (ed.), *Saint Augustin et la Bible* (Paris, 1986), 303–12.

Bonner, Gerald, 'Rufinus of Syria and African Pelagianism', *AugStud*, 1 (1970), 31–47.

Booth, A. D., 'Notes on Ausonius' *Professores*', *Phoenix*, 32 (1978), 235–49.

—— 'The Chronology of Jerome's Early Years', *Phoenix*, 35 (1981), 237–59.

Botas, Vicente Bécares, et al. (eds.), *Intertextualidad en las literaturas griega y latina* (Madrid, 2000).

Brakke, David, *Athanasius and the Politics of Asceticism* (Oxford, 1995).

—— *Demons and the Making of the Monk: Spiritual Combat in Early Christianity* (Cambridge, Mass., 2006).

Brochet, J., *Saint Jérôme et ses ennemis: étude sur la querelle de Saint Jérôme avec Rufin d'Aquilée et sur l'ensemble de son œuvre polémique* (Paris, 1906).

Brown, Dennis, *Vir Trilinguis. A Study in the Biblical Exegesis of Saint Jerome* (Kampen, 1992).

Brown, Peter, 'Pelagius and his Supporters: Aims and Environment', *JThS*, NS 19 (1968), 83–114, repr. in his *Religion and Society in the Age of Saint Augustine* (London, 1972), 183–207.

—— 'The Diffusion of Manichaeism in the Roman Empire', *JRS* 59 (1969), 92–103, repr. in his *Religion and Society in the Age of Saint Augustine* (London, 1972), 94–118.

—— 'The Patrons of Pelagius: The Roman Aristocracy between East and West', *JThS*, NS 21 (1970), 56–72, repr. in his *Religion and Society in the Age of Saint Augustine* (London, 1972), 208–26.

—— 'The Rise and Function of the Holy Man in Late Antiquity', *JRS*, 61 (1971), 80–101.

—— *World of Late Antiquity* (London, 1971).

—— *Religion and Society in the Age of Saint Augustine* (London, 1972).

—— *The Cult of the Saints* (Chicago, 1981).

—— *The Body and Society: Men, Women, and Sexual Renunciation in Early Christianity* (New York, 1988).

—— *Power and Persuasion in Late Antiquity: Towards a Christian Empire* (Madison, Wis., 1992).

Brown, Peter, *Augustine of Hippo: A Biography*, rev. edn. (Berkeley, Calif., 2000).

Brown Tkacz, Catherine, '*Labor tam utilis*: The Creation of the Vulgate', *VChr*, 50 (1996), 42–72.

Bruggisser, Philippe, *Symmaque ou le rituel épistolaire de l'amitié littéraire: recherches sur le premier livre de la correspondance* (Freiburg, 1993).

Bruyn, Theodore de, *Pelagius's Commentary on St Paul's Epistle to the Romans* (Oxford, 1998).

Bruyne, Donatien de, 'La Lettre de Jérôme à Sunnia et Fretela sur le Psautier', *ZNTW*, 28 (1929), 1–13.

——'Lettres fictives de s. Jérôme', *ZNTW*, 28 (1929), 229–34.

——'La Correspondance échangée entre Augustin et Jérôme', *ZNTW*, 31 (1932), 233–48.

Büchner, Karl, 'Zur Synkrisis Cato-Caesar in Sallusts' *Catilina*', *GB*, 5 (1976), 37–57.

Bulic, Francesco, 'Stridone luogo natale di s. Girolamo', *Miscellanea Geronimiana. Scritti varii pubblicati nel XV centenario dalla morte di San Girolamo* (Rome, 1920), 253–330.

Buonaiuti, Ernesto, 'Pelagio e l'Ambrosiastre', *RicRel*, 4 (1928), 1–17.

Burrus, Virginia, *The Making of a Heretic: Gender, Authority, and the Priscillianist Controversy* (Berkeley, Calif., 1995).

Burton, Philip, *The Old Latin Gospels: A Study of their Texts and Language* (Oxford, 2000).

Burton-Christie, Douglas, *The Word in the Desert: Scripture and the Quest for Holiness in Early Christian Monasticism* (Oxford, 1993).

Cain, Andrew, 'Defending Hedibia and Detecting Eusebius: Jerome's Correspondence with Two Gallic Women (*Epp.*, 120–1)', *MP*, 24 (2003), 15–34.

——'In Ambrosiaster's Shadow: A Critical Re-evaluation of the Last Surviving Letter-exchange between Pope Damasus and Jerome', *REAug*, 51 (2005), 257–77.

——'Miracles, Martyrs, and Arians: Gregory of Tours' Sources for his Account of the Vandal Kingdom', *VChr*, 59 (2005), 412–37.

——'Origen, Jerome, and the *senatus Pharisaeorum*', *Latomus*, 65 (2006), 727–34.

——'*Vox clamantis in deserto*: Rhetoric, Reproach, and the Forging of Ascetic Authority in Jerome's Letters from the Syrian Desert', *JThS*, NS 57 (2006), 500–25.

——'*Liber manet*: Pliny, *Ep.* 9.27.2 and Jerome, *Ep.* 130.19.5', *CQ*, NS 58 (2008), 708–10.

——'Rethinking Jerome's Portraits of Holy Women', in Andrew Cain and Josef Lössl (eds.), *Jerome of Stridon: His Life, Writings and Legacy* (Aldershot, 2009), Chap. 4.

——'Jerome's *Epistula* 117 on the *subintroductae*: Satire, Apology, and Ascetic Propaganda in Gaul', *Augustinianum*, 49 (2009), forthcoming.

—— St. Jerome, *Commentary on Galatians*, FOTC 120 (Washington, DC, 2010).

—— 'Jerome's *Epitaphium Paulae*: Hagiography, Pilgrimage, and the Cult of Saint Paula', *JECS*, 18 (2010), forthcoming.

—— and Noel Lenski (eds.), *The Power of Religion in Late Antiquity* (Aldershot, 2009).

—— and Josef Lössl (eds.), *Jerome of Stridon: His Life, Writings and Legacy* (Aldershot, 2009).

Callu, Jean-Pierre, *Symmaque, Lettres*, i (Paris, 1972).

Cameron, Alan, 'Paganism and Literature in Late Fourth Century Rome', in Alan Cameron and Manfred Fuhrmann (eds.), *Christianisme et formes littéraires de l'antiquité tardive* (Geneva, 1977), 1–30.

—— and Fuhrmann, Manfred (eds.), *Christianisme et formes littéraires de l'antiquité tardive* (Geneva, 1977).

Cameron, Averil, *Christianity and the Rhetoric of Empire: The Development of Christian Discourse* (Berkeley, Calif., 1991).

Cameron, John, 'The Rabbinic Vulgate?', in Andrew Cain and Josef Lössl (eds.), *Jerome of Stridon: His Life, Writings and Legacy* (Aldershot, 2009), Chap. 9.

Canellis, Aline, 'Les Rapports de Paulin de Nole avec Jérôme au-delà de 400: la *Lettre* 39 de Paulin et le *Commentaire sur Joël* 1, 4 de Jérôme', *Augustinianum*, 39 (1999), 311–35.

—— 'La Lettre selon saint Jérôme: l'épistolarité de la correspondance hiéronymienne', in Léon Nadjo and Élisabeth Gavoille (eds.), *Epistulae antiquae*, ii. *Actes du IIe colloque 'Le genre épistolaire antique et ses prolongements européens'* (Université François-Rabelais, Tours, 28–30 Sept. 2000) (2 vols., Louvain-Paris, 2002), ii. 311–32.

—— (ed.), *Jérôme, Débat entre un Luciférien et un orthodoxe (Altercatio Luciferiani et orthodoxi)* (Paris, 2003).

—— 'L'*In Zachariam* de Jérôme et la tradition alexandrine', in Andrew Cain and Josef Lössl (eds.), *Jerome of Stridon: His Life, Writings and Legacy* (Aldershot, 2009), Chap. 12.

Caner, Daniel, *Wandering, Begging Monks. Spiritual Authority and the Promotion of Monasticism in Late Antiquity* (Berkeley, Calif., 2002).

Capponi, Filippo, 'Aspetti realistici e simbolici dell'epistolario di Gerolamo', in Aldo Ceresa-Gastaldo (ed.), *Gerolamo e la biografia letteraria* (Genoa, 1989), 81–103.

Cardman, Francine, 'The Rhetoric of Holy Places: Palestine in the Fourth Century', *StudPatr*, 17 (1982), 18–25.

Carriker, Anne, 'Augustine's Frankness in his Dispute with Jerome over the Interpretation of Galatians 2: 11–14', in Douglas Kries and Catherine

Tkacz (eds.), *Nova Doctrina Vetusque: Essays in Honor of F. W. Schlatter* (New York, 1999), 121–38.

Cascio, G. lo, *Girolamo da Stridone, studiato nel suo epistolario* (Catania, 1923).

Caspar, Erich, *Geschichte des Papstums von den Anfängen bis zur Höhe der Weltherrschaft* (2 vols., Tübingen, 1930–3).

Casson, Lionel, *Ships and Seamanship in the Ancient World* (Princeton, NJ, 1971).

Catellani, Cristina, 'Il buon uso delle ricchezze nell'epistolario di san Girolamo', *CrSt*, 13 (1992), 47–72.

Cavallera, Ferdinand, 'Saint Jérôme et la Vulgate des Actes, des Épîtres et de l'Apocalypse', *BLE*, 21 (1920), 269–92.

—— *Saint Jérôme: sa vie et son œuvre* (2 vols., Paris, 1922).

Cavallo, Guglielmo, 'Libro e pubblico alla fine del mondo antico', in Guglielmo Cavallo (ed.), *Libri, editori e pubblico nel mondo antico* (Rome, 1977), 83–132.

Ceresa-Gastaldo, Aldo, 'La tecnica biografica del De viris illustribus di Girolamo', *Renovatio*, 14 (1979), 221–36.

—— *Gerolamo. Gli uomini illustri (De viris illustribus)* (Florence, 1988).

—— (ed.), *Gerolamo e la biografia letteraria* (Genoa, 1989).

Chadwick, Henry, *Priscillian of Avila: The Occult and the Charismatic in the Early Church* (Oxford, 1976).

—— 'The Role of the Christian Bishop in Ancient Society', in Center for Hermeneutical Studies, Protocol of the Thirty-fifth Colloquy (Feb. 1979) (Berkeley, Calif., 1980), 1–14.

Chadwick, Owen, *John Cassian* (Cambridge, 1968).

Champlin, Edward, *Final Judgments: Duty and Emotion in Roman Wills, 200 BC–AD 250* (Berkeley, Calif., 1991).

Chastagnol, André, *La Préfecture urbaine à Rome sous le bas-empire* (Paris, 1960).

—— 'Le Supplice inventé par Avidius Cassius: remarques sur l'histoire Auguste et la lettre 1 de Saint Jérôme', *Bonner Historia-Augusta-Colloquium* (Bonn, 1970), 95–107.

Chitty, Derwas, *The Desert a City* (Crestwood, Il., 1966).

Cimma, Maria Rosa, *L'episcopalis audientia nelle costituzioni imperiali da Costantino a Giustiniano* (Turin, 1989).

Cipriani, N., 'Un'altra traccia dell'Ambrosiaster in Agostino (De pecc. mer. remiss. II, 36, 58–9)', *Augustinianum*, 24 (1984), 515–25.

Clark, Elizabeth, 'The Place of Jerome's Commentary on Ephesians in the Origenist Controversy: The Apokatastasis and Ascetic Ideals', *VChr*, 41 (1987), 154–71.

——'Patrons, not Priests: Gender and Power in Late Ancient Christianity', *G&H*, 2 (1990), 253–73.

—— *The Origenist Controversy: The Cultural Construction of an Early Christian Debate* (Princeton, NJ, 1992).

—— *St Augustine on Marriage and Sexuality* (Washington, DC, 1996).

——'Holy Women, Holy Words: Early Christian Women, Social History, and the "Linguistic Turn"', *JECS*, 6 (1998), 413–30.

—— *Reading Renunciation: Asceticism and Scripture in Early Christianity* (Princeton, NJ, 1999).

Clark, Gillian, *Women in Late Antiquity. Pagan and Christian Life–styles* (Oxford, 1993).

Clausi, Benedetto, 'La Bibbia negli scritti polemici di Gerolamo. Problemi e piste di ricerca', in Claudio Moreschini and Giovanni Menestrina (eds.), *Motivi letterari ed esegetici in Gerolamo. Atti del convegno tenuto a Trento il 5–7 dicembre 1995* (Brescia, 1997), 39–79.

Claussen, Martin Allen, 'Pagan Rebellion and Christian Apologetics in Fourth–century Rome: The Consultationes Zacchaei et Apollonii', *JEH*, 46 (1995), 589–614.

Clough, Cecil, 'The Cult of Antiquity: Letters and Letter Collections', in Clough (ed.), *Cultural Aspects of the Italian Renaissance. Essays in Honour of Paul Oskar Kristeller* (Manchester, 1976), 33–67.

Cole-Turner, Ronald, 'Anti–heretical Issues and the Debate over Galatians 2: 11–14 in the Letters of St Augustine to St Jerome', *AugStud*, 11 (1980), 155–66.

Coleiro, Edward, 'St Jerome's Lives of the Hermits', *VChr*, 11 (1957), 161–78.

Congrès international augustinien, *Augustinus Magister* (3 vols., Paris, 1954).

Conring, Barbara, *Hieronymus als Briefschreiber. Ein Beitrag zur spätantiken Epistolographie* (Tübingen, 2001).

Constable, Giles, *Letters and Letter Collections* (Turnhout, 1976).

Conybeare, Catherine, *Paulinus Noster: Self and Symbols in the Letters of Paulinus of Nola* (Oxford, 2000).

Coon, Lynda, *Sacred Fictions: Holy Women and Hagiography in Late Antiquity* (Philadelphia, 1997).

Cottineau, L. H., 'Chronologie des versions bibliques de St Jérôme', *Miscellanea Geronimiana. Scritti varii pubblicati nel XV centenario dalla morte di San Girolamo* (Rome, 1920), 43–68.

Courcelle, Pierre, 'Paulin de Nole et Saint Jérôme', *REL*, 25 (1947), 250–80.

—— *Les Lettres grecques dans l'Occident de Macrobe à Cassiodore* (Paris, 1948).

Courcelle, Pierre, *Recherches sur les 'Confessions' de saint Augustin* (Paris, 1950).

Coyle, John, *Augustine's De Moribus Ecclesiae Catholicae: A Study of the Work, its Composition and its Sources* (Freiburg, 1978).

Crouzel, Henri, 'Saint Jérôme et ses amis toulousains', *BLE*, 73 (1972), 125–46.

——'Les Échanges littéraires entre Bordeaux et l'Orient au IVᵉ siècle: saint Jérôme et ses amis aquitains', *RFHL*, 3 (1973), 301–26.

Curran, John, 'Jerome and the Sham Christians of Rome', *JEH*, 48 (1997), 213–29.

——*Pagan City and Christian Capital. Rome in the Fourth Century* (Oxford, 2000).

Dam, Raymond van, *Leadership and Community in Late Antique Gaul* (Berkeley, Calif., 1985).

——*Saints and their Miracles in Late Antique Gaul* (Princeton, NJ, 1993), 13–28.

Dassmann, Ernst, 'Autobiographie in Hagiographie: Beobachtungen zu den Mönchsviten und einigen Nekrologen des Hieronymus', *AHIg*, 8 (1999), 109–24.

Davidson, Ivor, 'Ambrose's *De Officiis* and the Intellectual Climate of the Late Fourth Century', *VChr*, 49 (1995), 313–33.

——'Pastoral Theology at the End of the Fourth Century: Ambrose and Jerome', *StudPatr*, 33 (1997), 295–301.

——(ed.), *Ambrose: De officiis. Introduction, Text, Translation, and Commentary* (2 vols., Oxford, 2001).

——'*Captatio* in the Fourth-century West', *StudPatr*, 34 (2001), 33–43.

Davis, Raymond, *The Book of Pontiffs (Liber Pontificalis): The Ancient Biographies of the First Ninety Roman Bishops to AD 715* (Liverpool, 2000).

Dawes, Elizabeth, and Norman Baynes, *Three Byzantine Saints* (Crestwood, 1977).

Dekkers, Eligius, *Clavis Patrum Latinorum* (Brepols, 1995).

——'Des prix et du commerce des livres à l'époque patristique', in Maurice Geerard (ed.), *Opes Atticae: Miscellanea philologica et historica Raymondo Bogaert et Hermanno Van Looy oblata* (The Hague, 1990), 99–115.

Deléani, Simone, 'Présence de Cyprien dans les œuvres de Jérôme sur la virginité', in Yves-Marie Duval (ed.), *Jérôme entre l'Occident et l'Orient*, XVIᵉ centenaire du départ de saint Jérôme de Rome et de son installation à Bethléem. Actes du colloque de Chantilly, Sept. 1986 (Paris, 1988), 61–82.

Delehaye, Hippolyte, 'Saint Martin et Sulpice Sévère', *AB*, 38 (1920), 5–136.

Desmulliez, Janine, 'Paulin de Nole: études chronologiques (393–7)', *RecAug,* 20 (1985), 35–64.

Desprez, Vincent, 'Saint Anthony and the Beginnings of Anchoritism', *ABR,* 43 (1992), 61–81, 141–72.

Devos, Paul, 'Égérie à Bethleem', *AB,* 86 (1968), 87–108.

Dietz, Maribel, 'Itinerant Spirituality and the Late Antique Origins of Christian Pilgrimage', in Linda Ellis and Frank Kidner (eds.), *Travel, Communication and Geography in Late Antiquity: Sacred and Profane* (Aldershot, 2004), 125–34.

—— *Wandering Monks, Virgins, and Pilgrims. Ascetic Travel in the Mediterranean World, AD 300–800* (University Park, Penn., 2005).

Divjak, Johannes, 'Die neuen Briefe des hl. Augustinus', *WHB,* 19 (1977), 10–25.

—— *Œuvres de saint Augustin 46B: Lettres 1*–29** (Paris, 1987).

—— 'Epistulae', in Cornelius Mayer (ed.), *Augustinus-Lexikon* (Basle, 1986–), ii. 5/6.893–1028.

—— and Franz Römer, 'Ergänzungen zur Biblotheca Hieronymiana Manuscripta', *Scriptorium,* 30 (1976), 85–113.

Dodaro Robert, and George Lawless (eds.), *Augustine and His Critics: Essays in Honour of Gerald Bonner* (London, 2000).

Doignon, Jean, 'Les Premiers commentateurs latins de l'écriture et l'œuvre exégétique d'Hilaire de Poitiers', in Jacques Fontaine and Charles Pietri (eds.), *La Bible de tous les temps,* ii. *Le Monde latin antique et la Bible* (Paris, 1985), 509–20.

Dorival, Gilles, and Alain le Boulluec (eds.), *Origeniana Sexta,* Origen et the Bible: Actes du Colloquium Origenianum Sextum, Chantilly, 30 Aug.–3 Sept. 1993 (Leuven, 1995).

Dossey, Leslie, 'Judicial Violence and the Ecclesiastical Courts in Late Antique North Africa', in Ralph Mathisen (ed.), *Law, Society, and Authority in Late Antiquity* (Oxford, 2001), 98–114.

Drijvers, Jan Willem, 'Virginity and Asceticism in Late Roman Western Elites', in Josine Blok and Peter Mason (eds.), *Sexual Asymmetry: Studies in Ancient Society* (Amsterdam, 1987), 241–73.

Drinkwater, John, and Hugh Elton (eds.), *Fifth–century Gaul: A Crisis of Identity?* (Cambridge, 1992).

Driver, Steven, 'The Development of Jerome's Views on the Ascetic Life', *RecTh,* 62 (1995), 44–70.

—— 'From Palestinian Ignorance to Egyptian Wisdom: Jerome and Cassian on the Monastic Life', *ABR,* 48 (1997), 293–315.

Duchesne, Louis, *Le Liber pontificalis: texte, introduction et commentaire* (2 vols., Paris, 1886–92).

Duchesne, Louis, *Fastes épiscopaux de l'ancienne Gaule* (2 vols., Paris, 1894).

Dudley, Martin, 'Danger and Glory: Priesthood in the Writings of John Chrysostom', *StudPatr*, 27 (1991), 162–5.

Duff, Timothy, *Plutarch's Lives: Exploring Virtue and Vice* (Oxford, 1999).

Dugan, John, *Making a New Man: Ciceronian Self-fashioning in the Rhetorical Works* (Oxford, 2005).

Dunphy, Walter, 'Saint Jerome and the Gens Anicia (Ep. 130 to Demetrias)', *StudPatr*, 18 (1990), 139–45.

Duval, Yves-Marie, 'Bellepheron et les ascètes chrétiens: melancholia ou otium?', *Caesarodunum*, 3 (1968), 183–90.

—— 'L'originalité du *De virginibus* dans le mouvement ascétique occidental: Ambroise, Cyprien, Athanase', in Yves-Marie Duval (ed.), *Ambroise de Milan: XVIᵉ centeniare de son élection épiscopale* (Paris, 1974), 9–66.

—— 'Pélage est-il le censeur inconnu de l'*Adversus Iovinianum* à Rome en 393? ou: du "portrait–robot" de l'hérétique chez s. Jérôme', *RHE*, 75 (1980), 525–57.

—— *Jérôme, Commentaire sur Jonas: introduction, texte critique, traduction et commentaire* (Paris, 1985).

—— (ed.), *Jérôme entre l'Occident et l'Orient*, XVIᵉ centenaire du départ de saint Jérôme de Rome et de son installation à Bethléem. Actes du colloque de Chantilly, Sept. 1986 (Paris, 1988).

—— 'Sulpice Sévère entre Rufin d'Aquilée et Jérôme dans les Dialogues 1. 1–9', in *Mémorial Dom Jean Gribomont* (Rome, 1988), 199–222.

—— 'Les Premiers rapports de Paulin de Nole avec Jérôme: moine ou philosophe? poète ou exégète?', *StudTard*, 7 (1989), 177–216.

—— 'La Date du *De natura* de Pélage: les premières étapes de la controverse sur la nature de la grâce', *REAug*, 36 (1990), 257–83.

—— 'Gerolamo tra Tertulliano e Origene', in Claudio Moreschini and Giovanni Menestrina (eds.), *Motivi letterari ed esegetici in Gerolamo. Atti del convegno tenuto a Trento il 5–7 dicembre 1995* (Brescia, 1997), 107–35.

—— 'Vers l'In Malachiam d'Origène. Jérôme et Origène en 406', in Wolfgang Bienert and Uwe Kühneweg (eds.), *Origeniana Septima. Origenes in den Auseinandersetzungen des 4. Jahrhunderts* (Leuven, 1999), 233–59.

—— 'Pélage en son temps: données chronologiques nouvelles pour une présentation nouvelle', *StudPatr*, 38 (2001), 95–118.

—— *L'affaire Jovinien: d'une crise de la société romaine à une crise de la pensée chrétienne à la fin du IVᵉ et au début du Vᵉ siècle* (Rome, 2003).

—— *La Décrétale Ad Gallos Episcopos: son texte et son auteur. texte critique, traduction française et commentaire* (Leiden, 2005).

—— 'Rufin d'Aquilée émule de Jérôme de Stridon', in Sylvie Crogniez-Petrequin (ed.), *Dieu(x) et homes: histoire et iconographie des sociétés païennes et chrétiennes de l'antiquité à nos jours. Mélanges en l'honneur de Françoise Thelamon* (Rouen, 2005), 163–85.

—— 'Sur trois lettres méconnues de Jérôme concernant son séjour à Rome (382–385)', in Andrew Cain and Josef Lössl (eds.), *Jerome of Stridon: His Life, Writings and Legacy* (Aldershot, 2009), Chap. 2.

Ebbeler, Jennifer, *Disciplining Christians: Correction and Community in Augustine's Letters* (Oxford and New York, 2009).

Elliott, James, 'The Translations of the New Testament into Latin: The Old Latin and the Vulgate', in Wolfgang Haase (ed.), *Aufstieg und Niedergang der römischen Welt*, II.26.1 (Berlin and New York, 1992), 198–245.

Ellis, Linda, and Frank Kidner (eds.), *Travel, Communication and Geography in Late Antiquity: Sacred and Profane* (Aldershot, 2004).

Elm, Susanna, 'Perceptions of Jerusalem Pilgrimage as Reflected in Two Early Sources on Female Pilgrimage (3rd and 4th centuries AD)', *StudPatr*, 20 (1984), 219–23.

—— *Virgins of God: The Making of Asceticism in Late Antiquity* (Oxford, 1994).

Engelbrecht, August, *Das Titelwesen bei den spätlateinischen Epistolographen* (Vienna, 1893).

Esbroeck, Michel van, 'L'histoire de l'église de Lydda dans deux textes géorgiens', *BKR*, 35 (1977), 111–31.

Estin, Colette, *Les Psautiers de Jérôme: à la lumière des traductions juives antérieures* (Rome, 1984).

Evans, Robert, *Four Letters of Pelagius* (London, 1968).

Evans Grubbs, Judith, *Law and Family in Late Antiquity: The Emperor Constantine's Marriage Legislation* (Oxford, 2000).

Ewing Hickey, Anne, *Women of the Roman Aristocracy as Christian Monastics* (Ann Arbor, Mich., 1987).

Fabre, Pierre, *Essai sur la chronologie de l'œuvre de saint Paulin de Nole* (Paris, 1948).

—— *Saint Paulin de Nole et l'amitié chrétienne* (Paris, 1949).

Favez, Charles, *La Consolation latine chrétienne* (Paris, 1937).

—— *Saint Jérôme peint par lui-même* (Brussels, 1958).

—— 'Saint Jérôme pédagogue', in *Mélanges de philosophie, de littérature et d'histoire anciennes offerts à Pierre Boyancé* (Rome, 1974), 173–81.

Feder, Alfred, 'Zusätze zum Schriftstellerkatalog des hl. Hieronymus', *Biblica*, 1 (1920), 500–13.

—— *Studien zum Schriftstellerkatalog des heiligen Hieronymus* (Freiburg, 1929).

Feichtinger, Barbara, *Apostolae apostolorum. Frauenaskese als Befreiung und Zwang bei Hieronymus* (Frankfurt, 1995).

Feichtinger, Barbara, 'Konsolationstopik und Sitz im Leben: Hieronymus' ep.
39 ad Paulam de obitu Blesillae im Spannungsfeld zwischen Christlicher
Genusadaption und Lesermanipulation', *JbAC*, 38 (1995), 75–90.

Feiertag, Jean-Louis, *Les Consultationes Zacchaei et Apollonii: étude d'histoire
et de sotériologie* (Freiburg, 1990).

Ferguson, John, *Pelagius: A Historical and Theological Study* (Cambridge,
1956).

Ferrari, Leo, 'Young Augustine: Both Catholic and Manichee', *AugStud*, 26
(1995), 109–28.

Ferrua, Antonio, *Epigrammata Damasiana* (Rome, 1942).

Fodor, I., 'Le Lieu d'origine de s. Jérôme: reconsidération d'une vieille controverse', *RHE*, 81 (1986), 498–500.

Fontaine, Jacques, *Sulpice Sévère: vie de saint Martin* (Paris, 1967–9).

—— 'L'aristocratie occidentale devant le monachisme aux IVe et Ve siècles',
RSLR, 15 (1979), 28–53.

—— *Naissance de la poésie dans l'occident chrétien* (Paris, 1981).

—— and Pietri, Charles (eds.), *La Bible de tous les temps*, ii. *Le Monde latin
antique et la Bible* (Paris, 1985).

—— 'Damase poète théodosien: l'imaginaire poétique des *Epigrammata*',
*Saecularia Damasiana. Atti del convegno internazionale per il XVI cente-
nario della morte di Papa Damaso* (Vatican City, 1986), 113–45.

—— 'Un sobriquet perfide de Damase, matronarum auriscalpius', in
Danielle Porte and Jean-Pierre Néraudau (eds.), *Hommages à Henri le
Bonniec: res sacrae* (Brussels, 1988), 177–92.

—— *Sulpice Sévère. Gallus: dialogues sur les vertus de saint Martin* (Paris,
2006).

Frank, Georgia, *The Memory of the Eyes: Pilgrims to Living Saints in Christian
Late Antiquity* (Berkeley, Calif., 2000).

Fridh, Ake, *Terminologie et formules dans les Variae de Cassiodore* (Göteborg,
1956).

Friedmann, Herbert, *A Bestiary for Saint Jerome: Animal Symbolism in European Religious Art* (Washington, DC, 1980).

Fuhrmann, Manfred, 'Die Mönchsgeschichten des Hieronymus', in Alan
Cameron and Manfred Fuhrmann (eds.), *Christianisme et formes littéraires
de l'antiquité tardive* (Geneva, 1977), 41–99.

—— *Rom in der Spätantike: Porträt einer Epoche* (Munich, 1994).

Fürst, Alfons, '*Veritas latina*: Augustins Haltung gegenüber Hieronymus'
Bibelübersetzungen', *REAug*, 40 (1994), 105–26.

—— 'Kürbis oder Efeu? Zur Übersetzung von Jona 4,6 in der Septuaginta
und bei Hieronymus', *BN*, 72 (1994), 12–19.

—— 'Hieronymus über die heilsame Täuschung', *ZAC*, 2 (1998), 97–112.

——*Augustins Briefwechsel mit Hieronymus* (Münster, 1999).

——'Hieronymus. Theologie als Wissenschaft', in Wilhelm Geerlings (ed.), *Theologen der Christlichen Antike. Eine Einführung* (Darmstadt, 2002), 168–83.

——*Hieronymus: Askese und Wissenschaft in der Spätantike* (Freiburg, 2003).

——'Hieronymus', in Cornelius Mayer (ed.), *Augustinus-Lexikon* (Basle, 1986–), II. 1/2.317–36.

——'Jerome Keeping Silent: Origen and his Exegesis of Isaiah', in Andrew Cain and Josef Lössl (eds.), *Jerome of Stridon: His Life, Writings and Legacy* (Aldershot, 2009), Chap. 11.

Gardner, Jane, *Family and Familia in Roman Law and Life* (Oxford, 1998).

Garzya, Antonio, *Il mandarino e il quotidiano. Saggi sulla letteratura tardoantica e bizantina* (Naples, 1983).

Gasparro, Sfameni, 'L'ermetismo nelle testimonianze dei Padri', *StudPatr*, 11 (1972), 58–64.

Ghellinck, Joseph de, *Patristique et moyen âge: études d'histoire littéraire et doctrinale* (2 vols., Paris, 1947).

Gilliard, Frank, 'Senatorial Bishops in the Fourth Century', *HThR*, 77 (1984), 153–75.

Godman, Peter, and Oswyn Murray (eds.), *Latin Poetry and the Classical Traditio: Essays in Medieval and Renaissance Literature* (Oxford, 1990).

Goehring, James, *Ascetics, Society, and the Desert: Studies in Early Egyptian Monasticism* (Harrisburg, Pa., 1999).

Goelzer, Henri, *Étude lexicographique et grammaticale de la latinité de saint Jérôme* (Paris, 1884).

Gonsette, M., 'Les Directeurs spirituels de Demetrias', *NRTh*, 60 (1933), 783–801.

González Marín, Susana, 'Relaciones intertextuales entre la *Vita Pauli* de Jerónimo y la *Vita Antonii* de Atanasio', in Vicente Bécares Botas, et al. (eds.), *Intertextualidad en las literaturas griega y latina* (Madrid, 2000), 319–36.

Goodrich, Richard, *Contextualizing Cassian: Aristocrats, Asceticism, and Reformation in Fifth-century Gaul* (Oxford, 2007).

——'*Vir maxime catholicus*: Sulpicius Severus' Use and Abuse of Jerome in the *Dialogi*', *JEH*, 58 (2007), 189–210.

Gorce, Denys, *Les Voyages, l'hospitalité et le port des lettres dans le monde chrétien des IVe et Ve siècles* (Paris, 1925).

——*La Lectio divina des origines du cénobitisme à saint Benoît et Cassiodore*, i. *Saint Jérôme et la lecture sacrée dans le milieu ascétique romain* (Paris, 1925).

—— 'Die Gastfreundlichkeit der altChristlichen Einsiedler und Mönche', *JbAC*, 15 (1972), 66–91.

—— 'St Jérôme et son environnement artistique et liturgique', *COCR*, 36 (1974), 150–78.

Gordini, Gian Domenico, 'Forme di vita ascetica a Roma nel IV secolo', *ScrTh*, 1 (1953), 9–54.

—— 'Origine e sviluppo del monachesimo a Roma', *Gregorianum*, 37 (1956), 220–60.

—— 'Il monachesimo romano in Palestina nel IV secolo', *Saint Martin et son temps. Mémorial du XVIᵉ centenaire des débuts du monachisme en Gaule 361–1961 (Studia Anselmiana, 46)* (Rome, 1961), 85–107.

—— 'L'opposizione al monachesimo a Roma nel IV secolo', in Mario Fois, Vincenzo Monachino, and F. Litva (eds.), *Dalla Chiesa antica alla Chiesa moderna* (Rome, 1983), 19–35.

Gougaud, Louis, 'Les Critiques formulées contre les premiers moines d'occident', *RMab*, 24 (1934), 145–63.

Gould, Graham, *The Desert Fathers on Monastic Community* (Oxford, 1993).

Granfield, Patrick, and Josef Jungmann (eds.), *Kyriakon. Festschrift Johannes Quasten* (2 vols., Münster, 1970).

Graves, Michael, *Jerome's Hebrew Philology: A Study Based on His Commentary on Jeremiah* (Leiden, 2007).

Gribomont, Jean, 'L'influence du monachisme oriental sur Sulpice Sévère', *Saint Martin et son temps. Mémorial du XVIᵉ centenaire des débuts du monachisme en Gaule 361–1961 (Studia Anselmiana, 46)* (Rome, 1961), 135–49.

—— 'Les Plus anciennes traductions latines', in Jacques Fontaine and Charles Pietri (eds.), *La Bible de tous les temps, ii. Le Monde latin antique et la Bible* (Paris, 1985), 43–65.

Griffe, Élie, 'Saint Martin et le monachisme gaulois', *Saint Martin et son temps. Mémorial du XVIᵉ centenaire des débuts du monachisme en Gaule 361–1961 (Studia Anselmiana, 46)* (Rome, 1961), 1–24.

Grilli, Alberto, 'San Gerolamo: Un dalmata e i suoi corrispondenti', *Aquileia, la Dalmazia e l'Illirico* (2 vols., Udine, 1985), ii. 297–314.

Grimm, Veronika, *From Feasting to Fasting: The Evolution of a Sin* (London, 1996).

Gründel, Roland, 'Des Hieronymus Briefe: Ihre literarische Bestimmung und ihre Zusammengehörigkeit', dissertation (Leipzig, 1958).

Grützmacher, Georg, *Hieronymus: Eine biographische Studie zur alten Kirchengeschichte* (3 vols., Berlin, 1901–8).

Gryson, Roger, 'Les Elections épiscopales en Occident au IVᵉ siècle', *RHE*, 75 (1980), 257–83.

——and Dominique Szmatula, 'Les Commentaires patristiques sur Isaïe d'Origène à Jérôme', *REAug*, 36 (1990), 3–41.

Guillaumont, Antoine, 'Le Dépaysement comme forme d'ascèse dans le monachisme ancien', *AEHE V*, 76 (1968–69), 31–58.

——'La Conception du désert chez les moines d'Égypte', *RHR*, 188 (1975), 3–21.

Guttilla, Giuseppe, 'Tematica cristiana e pagana nell'evoluzione finale della *consolatio* di san Girolamo', *ALGP*, 17–18 (1980–1), 87–152.

——'Paolino di Nola e Girolamo', *Orpheus*, NS 13 (1992), 278–94.

Guyon, Jean, 'Damase et l'illustration des martyrs', in Mathijs Lamberigts and Peter van Deun (eds.), *Martyrium in Multidisciplinary Perspective: Memorial Louis Reekmans* (Leuven, 1995), 157–77.

Haendler, Gert, 'Cyprians Auslegung zu Galater 2,11 ff.', *ThLZ*, 97 (1972), 561–8.

Hagendahl, Harald, *Latin Fathers and the Classics: A Study on the Apologists, Jerome, and Other Christian Writers* (Göteborg, 1958).

——'Die Bedeutung der Stenographie für die spätlateinische Christliche Literatur', *JbAC*, 14 (1971), 24–38.

——and Jan Hendrik Waszink, 'Hieronymus', *RAC*, 15 (1989), 117–39.

Håkanson, Lennart (ed.), *Declamationes XIX maiores Quintiliano falso ascriptae* (Stuttgart, 1982).

Halton, Thomas, *St Jerome: On Illustrious Men* (Washington, DC, 1999).

Hamblenne, Pierre, 'La Longévité de Jérôme: Prosper avait-il-raison?', *Latomus*, 28 (1969), 1081–119.

——'Relectures de philologue sur le scandale du lierre/ricin (Hier. In Ion. 4.6)', *Euphrosyne*, 16 (1988), 183–223.

——'L'apprentissage du grec par Jérôme', *REAug*, 40 (1994), 353–64.

——'Jérôme et le clergé du temps: idéaux et réalités', *Augustinianum*, 37 (1997), 351–410.

Hammond Bammel, Caroline, 'Last Ten Years of Rufinus' Life and the Date of his Move South from Aquileia', *JThS*, NS 28 (1977), 372–429.

——'Philocalia IX, Jerome, Epistle 121, and Origen's Exposition of Romans VII', *JThS*, NS 32 (1981), 50–81.

——'Die Hexapla des Origenes: Die *Hebraica veritas* im Streit der Meinungen', *Augustinianum*, 28 (1988), 125–49.

——'Augustine, Origen and the Exegesis of St Paul', *Augustinianum*, 32 (1992), 341–67.

——'Pauline Exegesis, Manichaeism and Philosophy in the Early Augustine', in Lionel Wickham and Caroline Hammond Bammel (eds.), *Christian Faith and Greek Philosophy in Late Antiquity: Essays in Tribute to George Christopher Stead* (Leiden, 1993), 1–25.

Hammond Bammel, Caroline, 'Die Pauluskommentare des Hieronymus: die ersten wissenschaftlichen lateinischen Bibelkommentare?', in *Cristianesimo latino e cultura greca sino al sec. IV*, XXI Incontro di studiosi dell'antichità cristiana, Rome, 7–9 May 1992, *Augustinianum*, 42 (1993), 187–207.

Harmless, William, *Desert Christians: An Introduction to the Literature of Early Monasticism* (Oxford, 2004).

Harries, Jill, *Law and Empire in Late Antiquity* (Cambridge, 1999).

Harrison, Carol, *Augustine: Christian Truth and Fractured Humanity* (Oxford, 2000).

Harvey, Anthony, 'Melito and Jerusalem', *JThS*, NS 17 (1966), 401–4.

Harvey, Paul, 'Saints and Satyrs: Jerome the Scholar at Work', *Athenaeum*, 86 (1998), 35–56.

—— 'Jerome Dedicates his *Vita Hilarionis*', *VChr*, 59 (2005), 286–97.

Häussler, Reinhard, *Nachträge zu A. Otto, Sprichwörter und sprichwörtliche Redensarten der Römer* (Hildesheim, 1968).

Hayward, C. T. R., 'Jewish Traditions in Jerome's Commentary on Jeremiah and the Targum of Jeremiah', *PIBA*, 9 (1985), 100–20.

—— 'Saint Jerome and the Aramaic Targumim', *JSS*, 32 (1987), 105–23.

—— 'Some Observations on St Jerome's "Hebrew Questions on Genesis" and the Rabbinic Tradition', *PIBA*, 13 (1990), 58–76.

—— *Jerome's Hebrew Questions on Genesis* (Oxford, 1995).

—— 'St Jerome and the Meaning of the High-priestly Vestments', in William Horbury (ed.), *Hebrew Study from Ezra to Ben-Yehuda* (Edinburgh, 1999), 90–105.

Heine, Ronald, 'The Role of the Gospel of John in the Montanist Controversy', *SCent*, 6 (1987), 1–18.

—— 'The Gospel of John and the Montanist Debate at Rome', *StudPatr*, 21 (1989), 95–100.

—— *The Commentaries of Origen and Jerome on St Paul's Epistle to the Ephesians* (Oxford, 2002).

Heinzelmann, Martin, *Bischofsherrschaft in Gallien: Zur Kontinuität römischer Führungsschichten vom 4. bis zum 7. Jahrhundert* (Munich, 1976).

—— 'Gallische Prosopographie 260–527', *Francia*, 10 (1982), 531–718.

Hendrikx, E., 'Saint Jérôme en tant qu'hagiographe', in *La Ciudad de Dios. Homenaje al P. Angel C. Vega* (El Escorial, 1968), 661–7.

Hengel, Martin, and Anna Maria Schwemer (eds.), *Die Septuaginta zwischen Judentum und Christentum* (Tübingen, 1994).

Hennings, Ralph, 'Rabbinisches und Antijüdisches bei Hieronymus Ep. 121.10', in Johannes van Oort and Ulrich Wickert (eds.), *Christliche Exegese zwischen Nicaea und Chalcedon, 325–451* (Kampen, 1992), 49–71.

——*Der Briefwechsel zwischen Augustinus und Hieronymus und ihr Streit um den Kanon des Alten Testaments und die Auslegung von Gal. 2. 11–14* (Leiden, 1994).

——'Hieronymus zum Bischofsamt', *ZKG*, 108 (1997), 1–11.

Hermanowicz, Erika, *Possidius of Calama: A Study of the North African Episcopate in the Age of Augustine* (Oxford, 2008).

Herron, Margaret Clare, *A Study of the Clausulae in the Writings of St Jerome* (Washington, DC, 1937).

Hillner, Julia, '*Domus*, Family, and Inheritance: The Senatorial Family in Late Antique Rome', *JRS*, 93 (2003), 129–45.

Hinson, E. Glenn, 'Women Biblical Scholars in the Late Fourth Century: The Aventine Circle', *StudPatr*, 23 (1997), 319–24.

Hirschfeld, Yizhar, *The Judean Desert Monasteries in the Byzantine Period* (New Haven, Conn., 1992).

Hoffer, Stanley, *The Anxieties of Pliny the Younger* (New York, 1999).

Hohlwein, N., 'Déplacements et tourisme dans l'Égypte romaine', *CE*, 30 (1940), 253–78.

Hollerich, Michael, 'Myth and History in Eusebius', *De vita Constantini: Vit. Const* 1. 12 in its Contemporary Setting', *HThR*, 82 (1989), 421–45.

Holtz, Louis, and Jean-Claude Fredouille (eds.), *De Tertullien aux Mozarabes: mélanges offerts à Jacques Fontaine, à l'occasion de son 70ᵉ anniversaire, par ses élèves, amis et collègues* (2 vols., Paris, 1992).

Honoré, Tony, *Law in the Crisis of Empire, 379–455 AD: The Theodosian Dynasty and its Quaestors* (Oxford, 1998).

Horbury, William (ed.), *Hebrew Study from Ezra to Ben-Yehuda* (Edinburgh, 1999).

Hoven, René, 'Notes sur Érasme et les auteurs anciens', *AC*, 38 (1969), 169–74.

Hritzu, John, *The Style of the Letters of St Jerome* (Washington, DC, 1939).

Humfress, Caroline, *Orthodoxy and the Courts in Late Antiquity* (Oxford, 2007).

Hunt, E. D., *Holy Land Pilgrimage in the Later Roman Empire, AD 312–460* (Oxford, 1982).

——'Gaul and the Holy Land in the Early Fifth Century', in John Drinkwater and Hugh Elton (eds.), *Fifth-century Gaul: A Crisis of Identity?* (Cambridge, 1992), 264–74.

Hunter, David, '*On the Sin of Adam and Eve*: A Little-known Defense of Marriage and Childbearing by Ambrosiaster', *HThR*, 82 (1989), 283–99.

——'Helvidius, Jovinian, and the Virginity of Mary in Late fourth-century Rome', *JECS*, 1 (1993), 47–71.

Hunter, David, 'Vigilantius of Calagurris and Victricius of Rouen: Ascetics, Relics, and Clerics in Late Roman Gaul', *JECS*, 7 (1999), 401–30.

—— 'The Virgin, the Bride, and the Church: Reading Psalm 45 in Ambrose, Jerome, and Augustine', *ChHist*, 69 (2000), 281–303.

—— 'Rereading the Jovinianist Controversy: Asceticism and Clerical Authority in Late Ancient Christianity', *JMEMS*, 33 (2003), 453–70.

—— 'Between Jovinian and Jerome: Augustine and the Interpretation of 1 Corinthians 7', *StudPatr*, 43 (2006), 131–6.

—— *Marriage, Celibacy, and Heresy in Ancient Christianity: The Jovinianist Controversy* (Oxford, 2007).

—— 'The Raven Replies: Ambrose's *Letter to the Church at Vercelli (Ep. ex. coll. 14)* and the Criticisms of Jerome', in Andrew Cain and Josef Lössl (eds.), *Jerome of Stridon: His Life, Writings and Legacy* (Aldershot, 2009), Chap. 14.

Hutchinson, Gregory, *Cicero's Correspondence. A Literary Study* (Oxford, 1998).

Inglebert, Hervé, *Les Romains chrétiens face à l'histoire de Rome* (Paris, 1996).

Ivray, Jehan d', *Saint Jérôme et les dames de l'Aventin* (Paris, 1937).

Jacobs, Andrew, 'Writing Demetrias: Ascetic Logic in Ancient Christianity', *ChHist*, 69 (2000), 719–48.

Janson, Tore, *Latin Prose Prefaces: Studies in Literary Conventions* (Stockholm, 1964).

Jay, Pierre, 'Jérôme auditeur d'Apollinaire de Laodicée à Antioche', *REAug*, 20 (1974), 36–41.

—— 'La Datation des premières traductions de l'Ancien Testament sur l'hébreu par saint Jérôme', *REAug*, 28 (1982), 208–12.

—— *L'exégèse de saint Jérôme d'après son Commentaire sur Isaïe* (Paris, 1985).

—— 'Jérôme et la pratique de l'exégèse', in Jacques Fontaine and Charles Pietri (eds.), *La Bible de tous les temps*, ii. *Le Monde latin antique et la Bible* (Paris, 1985), 523–41.

—— 'Combien Jérôme a-t-il traduit d'homélies d'Origène?', *StudPatr*, 23 (1989), 133–7.

Jeanjean, Benoît, *Saint Jérôme et l'hérésie* (Paris, 1999).

—— and Lançon, Bertrand, *Saint Jérôme, Chronique. Continuation de la Chronique d'Eusèbe années 326–378* (Rennes, 2004).

—— 'Le *Dialogus Attici et Critobuli* de Jérôme et la prédication pélagienne en Palestine entre 411 et 415', in Andrew Cain and Josef Lössl (eds.), *Jerome of Stridon: His Life, Writings and Legacy* (Aldershot, 2009), Chap. 5.

Jerg, Ernst, *Vir Venerabilis. Untersuchungen zur Titulatur der Bischöfe in den Ausserkirchlichen Texten der Spätantike als Beitrag zur Deutung ihrer öffentlichen Stellung* (Vienna, 1970).

Johnston, David, *The Roman Law of Trusts* (Oxford, 1988).

Jones, A. H. M., *The Later Roman Empire, 284–602: A Social, Economic, and Administrative Survey* (2 vols., Oxford, 1964).

Joussard, G., 'La Personnalité d'Helvidius', in *Mélanges J. Saunier* (Lyons, 1944), 139–56.

Jungblut, Renate, *Hieronymus: Darstellung und Verehrung eines Kirchenvaters* (Tübingen, 1967).

Kahlos, Maijastina, 'Vettius Agorius Praetextatus and the Rivalry between the Bishops in Rome in 366–367', *Arctos*, 31 (1997), 41–54.

—— *Vettius Agorius Praetextatu: A Senatorial Life in Between* (Rome, 2002).

Kamesar, Adam, *Jerome, Greek Scholarship, and the Hebrew Bible: A Study of the Quaestiones Hebraicae in Genesim* (Oxford, 1993).

Karlsson, Gustav, *Idéologie et cérémonial dans l'épistolographie byzantine* (Uppsala, 1962).

Kaser, Max, '*Infamia* und *ignominia* in den römischen Rechtsquellen', *ZSS*, 73 (1956), 220–78.

Kaster, Robert, *Emotion, Restraint, and Community in Ancient Rome* (Oxford, 2005).

Kelly, J. N. D., *Jerome. His Life, Writings, and Controversies* (London, 1975).

—— *The Oxford Dictionary of Popes* (Oxford, 1986).

—— *Golden Mouth: The Story of John Chrysostom: Ascetic, Preacher, Bishop* (Grand Rapids, Mich., 1995).

Ker, James, 'Nocturnal Writers in Imperial Rome: The Culture of *lucubratio*', *CPh*, 99 (2004), 209–42.

King, Daniel, '*Vir quadrilinguis*? Syriac in Jerome and Jerome in Syriac', in Andrew Cain and Josef Lössl (eds.), *Jerome of Stridon: His Life, Writings and Legacy* (Aldershot, 2009), Chap. 16.

King, J. Christopher, *Origen on the Song of Songs as the Spirit of Scripture: The Bridegroom's Perfect Marriage-Song* (Oxford, 2005).

Klauck, Hans-Josef, *Die antike Briefliteratur und das neue Testament. Ein Lehr- und Arbeitsbuch* (Paderborn, 1998).

Klingshirn, William, and Linda Safran (eds.), *The Early Christian Book* (Washington, DC, 2007).

Klostermann, Erich, *Die Schriften des Origenes in Hieronymus' Brief an Paula in Sitzungsberichte der königlich preussischen Akademie der Wissenschaften* (Berlin, 1897).

Köhler, Helga, *C. Sollius Apollinaris Sidonius, Briefe Buch I. Einleitung-Text-Übersetzung-Kommentar* (Heidelberg, 1995).

Konstan, David, 'Problems in the History of Christian Friendship', *JECS*, 4 (1996), 87–113.

Koopmans, J. H., 'Augustine's First Contact with Pelagius and the Dating of the Condemnation of Caelestius at Carthage', *VChr*, 8 (1954), 149–53.

Kötting, Bernhard, *Peregrinatio religios: Wallfahrten in der Antike und das Pilgerwesen in der alten Kirche* (Münster, 1980).

Kolb, Anne, *Transport und Nachrichtentransfer im Römischen Reich* (Berlin, 2000).

Krause, Jens-Uwe, 'Überlegungen zur Sozialgeschichte des Klerus im 5./6. Jh. n. Chr.', in Jens-Uwe Krause and Christian Witschel (eds.), *Die Stadt in der Spätantike—Niedergang oder Wandel?* (Stuttgart, 2006), 413–39.

Kries, Douglas, and Catherine Tkacz (eds.), *Nova Doctrina Vetusque: Essays in Honor of F. W. Schlatter* (New York, 1999).

Krueger, Derek, 'Typological Figuration in Theodoret of Cyrrhus's Religious History and the Art of Postbiblical Narrative', *JECS*, 5 (1997), 393–419.

—— *Writing and Holiness: The Practice of Authorship in the Early Christian East* (Philadelphia, 2004).

Krumeich, Christa, *Hieronymus und die Christlichen feminae clarissimae* (Bonn, 1993).

—— *Paula von Rom: christliche Mittlerin zwischen Okzident und Orient. Eine Biographie* (Bonn, 2002).

Kulikowski, Michael, 'Barbarians in Gaul, Usurpers in Britain', *Britannia*, 31 (2000), 325–45.

Labourt, Jérôme, *Jérôme: Lettres* (8 vols., Paris, 1949–63).

Lafferty, Maura, 'Translating Faith from Greek to Latin: *Romanitas* and *Christianitas* in Late Fourth-century Rome and Milan', *JECS*, 11 (2003), 21–62.

Lamberigts, Mathijs, 'A Critical Evaluation of Critiques of Augustine's View of Sexuality', in Robert Dodaro and George Lawless (eds.), *Augustine and His Critics: Essays in Honour of Gerald Bonner* (London, 2000), 176–97.

—— and Peter van Deun (eds.), *Martyrium in Multidisciplinary Perspective: Memorial Louis Reekmans* (Leuven, 1995).

Lambert, Bernard, *Bibliotheca Hieronymiana Manuscripta: la tradition manuscrite des œuvres de Saint Jérôme* (4 vols. in 6 parts, Steenbrugge, 1969–72).

Lamoreaux, John, 'Episcopal Courts in Late Antiquity', *JECS*, 3 (1995), 143–67.

Lampe, G. W. H. (ed.), *The Cambridge History of the Bible*, ii. *The West from the Fathers to the Reformation* (Cambridge, 1975).

Lançon, Bertrand, 'Maladie et médecine dans la correspondance de Jérôme', in Yves-Marie Duval (ed.), *Jérôme entre l'Occident et l'Orient*, XVIe centenaire du départ de saint Jérôme de Rome et de son installation à Bethléem. Actes du colloque de Chantilly, Sept. 1986 (Paris, 1988), 355–66.

Lanham, Carol, *Salutatio Formulas in Latin Letters to 1200: Syntax, Style, and Theory* (Munich, 1975).

Lanzoni, Francesco, 'La leggenda di s. Girolamo', *Miscellanea Geronimiana. Scritti varii pubblicati nel XV centenario dalla morte di San Girolamo* (Rome, 1920), 19–42.

Lapin, Hartmut, *Economy, Geography, and Provincial History in Later Roman Palestine* (Tübingen, 2001).

Lardet, Pierre, 'Epistolaires médiévaux de s. Jérôme: Jalons pour un classement', *FZPhTh*, 28 (1981), 271–89.

—— *L'Apologie de Jérôme contre Rufin: un commentaire* (Leiden, 1993).

Lauer, Philippe, *Bibliothèque nationale: catalogue général des manuscrits latins* (7 vols., Paris, 1940).

Laurence, Patrick, 'Marcella, Jérôme et Origène', *REAug*, 42 (1996), 267–93.

—— *Jérôme et le nouveau modèle féminin: la conversion à la vie parfaite* (Paris, 1997).

—— 'Rome et Jérôme: des amours contrariées', *RBén*, 107 (1997), 227–49.

—— 'L'implication des femmes dans l'hérésie: le jugement de saint Jérôme', *REAug*, 44 (1998), 241–67.

—— 'L'épître 22 de Jérôme et son temps', in Léon Nadjo and Élisabeth Gavoille (eds.), *Epistulae antiquae*, i. *Actes du Ier colloque 'Le genre épistolaire antique et ses prolongements'* (Université François-Rabelais, Tours, 18–19 Sept. 1998) (Louvain–Paris, 2000), 63–83.

—— 'Proba, Juliana et Démétrias: Le Christianisme des femmes de la gens Anicia dans la première moitié du Ve siècle', *REAug*, 48 (2002), 131–63.

Laurita, Leopoldus, *Insegnamenti ascetici nelle lettere di s. Girolamo* (Rome, 1967).

Lavan, Luke, 'The Political Topography of the Late Antique City: Activity Spaces in Practice', in Luke Lavan and William Bowden (eds.), *Theory and Practice in Late Antique Archaeology* (Leiden, 2003), 314–37.

Lavarini, Roberto, *Il pellegrinaggio cristiano dalle sue origini al turismo religioso del XX secolo* (Genoa, 1997).

Lawler, Thomas, 'Jerome's First Letter to Damasus', in Patrick Granfield and Josef Jungmann (eds.), *Kyriakon. Festschrift Johannes Quasten* (2 vols., Münster, 1970), ii. 548–52.

Layton, Richard, 'Plagiarism and Lay Patronage of Ascetic Scholarship: Jerome, Ambrose, and Rufinus', *JECS*, 10 (2002), 489–522.

Leach, Eleanor, 'The Politics of Self-presentation: Pliny's Letters and Roman Portrait Sculpture', *ClAnt*, 9 (1990), 14–39.

Leanza, Sandro, 'Gerolamo e la tradizione ebraica', in Claudio Moreschini and Giovanni Menestrina (eds.), *Motivi letterari ed esegetici in Gerolamo. Atti del convegno tenuto a Trento il 5–7 dicembre 1995* (Brescia, 1997), 17–38.

Leclerc, Pierre, 'Antoine et Paul: métamorphose d'un héros', in Yves-Marie Duval (ed.), *Jérôme entre l'Occident et l'Orient*, XVIe centenaire du départ de saint Jérôme de Rome et de son installation à Bethléem. Actes du colloque de Chantilly, Sept. 1986 (Paris, 1988), 256–65.

—— and Morales, Edgardo (eds. and trans.), *Jérôme: trois vies de moines (Paul, Malchus, Hilarion)* (Paris, 2007).

Leclercq, Jean, '*Militare Deo* dans la tradition patristique et monastique', in *Militia Christi e crociata nei secoli XI–XIII* (Milan, 1992), 3–18.

Lehmann, Tomas, 'Eine spätantike Inschriftensammlung und der Besuch des Papstes Damasus an der Pligerstätte des Hl. Felix in Cimitile/Nola', *ZPE*, 91 (1992), 243–82.

Lenski, Noel, 'Evidence for the *audientia episcopalis* in the New Letters of Augustine', in Ralph Mathisen (ed.), *Law, Society, and Authority in Late Antiquity* (Oxford, 2001), 83–97.

—— 'Empresses in the Holy Land: The Making of a Christian Utopia in Late Antiquity', in Linda Ellis and Frank Kidner (eds.), *Travel, Communication and Geography in Late Antiquity: Sacred and Profane* (Aldershot, 2004), 113–24.

Lepelley, Claude, 'Quelques parvenus de la culture de l'Afrique romaine tardive', in Louis Holtz and Jean-Claude Fredouille (eds.), *De Tertullien aux Mozarabes: mélanges offerts à Jacques Fontaine, à l'occasion de son 70e anniversaire, par ses élèves, amis et collègues* (2 vols., Paris, 1992), i. 583–94.

Letsch-Brunner, Sylvia, *Marcella–Discipula et Magistra. Auf den Spuren einer römischen Christin des 4. Jahrhunderts* (Berlin, 1998).

Lewin, Ariel, *The Archaeology of Ancient Judea and Palestine* (Verona, 2005).

Leyser, Conrad, *Authority and Asceticism from Augustine to Gregory the Great* (Oxford, 2000).

Liebeschuetz, J. H. W. G., *Antioch. City and Imperial Administration in the Later Roman Empire* (Oxford, 1972).

—— 'The Collected Letters of Ambrose of Milan: Correspondence with Contemporaries and with the Future', in Linda Ellis and Frank Kidner (eds.), *Travel, Communication and Geography in Late Antiquity: Sacred and Profane* (Aldershot, 2004), 95–107.

Lieu, Samuel, *Manichaeism in the Later Roman Empire and Medieval China: A Historical Survey* (Manchester, 1985).

Lillo Redonet, Fernando, 'La *consolatio de caecitate* en la literatura latina', *Helmantica*, 54 (2003), 369–90.

Lippold, Adolf, 'Ursinus und Damasus', *Historia*, 14 (1965), 105–28.

Loewe, Raphael, 'The Medieval History of the Latin Vulgate', in G. W. H. Lampe (ed.), *The Cambridge History of the Bible*, ii. *The West from the Fathers to the Reformation* (Cambridge, 1975), 102–54, 514–18.

Lorenz, Rudolf, 'Die Anfänge des abendlandischen Mönchtums im 4. Jahrhundert', *ZKG*, 77 (1966), 1–61.

Loseby, Simon, 'Marseilles: A Late Antique Success Story?', *JRS*, 82 (1982), 165–85.

Lössl, Josef, 'Satire, Fiction and Reality in Jerome's *Epistula* 117', *VChr*, 52 (1998), 172–92.

——*Julian von Aeclanum. Studien zu seinem Leben, seinem Werk, seiner Lehre und ihrer Überlieferung* (Leiden, 2001).

——'A Shift in Patristic Exegesis: Hebrew Clarity and Historical Verity in Augustine, Jerome, Julian of Aeclanum and Theodore of Mopsuestia', *AugStud*, 32 (2001) 157–75.

——'Hieronymus, Epiphanius von Salamis und das spätantike Judentum', *JSJ*, 33 (2002), 411–36.

——'Who Attacked the Monasteries of Jerome and Paula in 416 AD?', *Augustinianum*, 44 (2004), 91–112.

——'Hieronymus: Ein Kirchenvater?', in J. Arnold, et al. (eds.), *Väter der Kirche. Ekklesiales Denken von den Anfängen bis in die Neuzeit. Festgabe für Hermann Josef Sieben SJ zum 70. Geburtstag* (Paderborn, 2004), 431–64.

——'Martin Luther's Jerome: New Evidence for a Changing Attitude', in Andrew Cain and Josef Lössl (eds.), *Jerome of Stridon: His Life, Writings and Legacy* (Aldershot, 2009), Chap. 18.

Ludolph, Matthias, *Epistolographie und Selbstdarstellung. Untersuchungen zu den 'Paradebriefen' Plinius des Jüngerer* (Tübingen, 1997).

Luebeck, Emil, *Hieronymus quos noverit scriptores et ex quibus hauserit* (Leipzig, 1872).

Lunn-Rockliffe, Sophie, *Ambrosiaster's Political Theology* (Oxford, 2007).

Luongo, Gennaro, *Lo specchio dell'agiografo. s. Felice nei carmi XV e XVI di Paolino di Nola* (Naples, 1992).

McGing, Brian, 'Synkrisis in Tacitus' Agricola', *Hermathena*, 132 (1982), 15–25.

McGinn, Bernard, 'Ocean and Desert as Symbols of Mystical Absorption in the Christian Tradition', *JR*, 74 (1994), 155–81.

McLynn, Neil, *Ambrose of Milan: Church and State in a Christian Capital* (Berkeley, Calif., 1994).

——'A Self-made Holy Man: The Case of Gregory Nazianzen', *JECS*, 6 (1998), 463–83.

258

Bibliography

Maier, Harold, 'The Topography of Heresy and Dissent in Late Fourth-century Rome', *Historia*, 44 (1995), 232–49.

—— 'Religious Dissent, Heresy and Households in Late Antiquity', *VChr*, 49 (1995), 49–63.

Malherbe, Abraham, *Ancient Epistolary Theorists* (Atlanta, Ga., 1988).

Mara, Maria Grazia, 'Storia ed esegesi nella *Expositio Epistulae ad Galatas* di Agostino', *AnnSE*, 2 (1985), 93–102.

—— 'Agostino e la polemica antimanichea: Il ruolo di Paolo e del suo epistolario', *Augustinianum*, 32 (1992), 119–43.

Maraval, Pierre, *Lieux saints et pèlerinages d'Orient: histoire et géographie des origines à la conquête arabe* (Paris, 1985).

—— 'Saint Jérôme et le pèlerinage aux lieux saints de Palestine', in Yves-Marie Duval (ed.), *Jérôme entre l'Occident et l'Orient*, XVIᵉ centenaire du départ de saint Jérôme de Rome et de son installation à Bethléem. Actes du colloque de Chantilly, Sept. 1986 (Paris, 1988), 345–53.

—— 'L'attitude des Pères du IVᵉ siècle devant les lieux saints et les pèlerinages', *Irénikon*, 65 (1992), 5–23.

Marcocchi, Massimo, *Motivi umani e cristiani nell'Epistolario di s. Girolamo* (Milan, 1967).

Marcone, Arnaldo, 'Due epistolari a confronto: Corpus pliniano e corpus simmachiano', in *Studi di storia e storiografia antiche per Emilio Gabba* (Pavia, 1988), 143–54.

Marin, Marcello, 'Ilario di Poitiers e Gerolamo', in Claudio Moreschini and Giovanni Menestrina (eds.), *Motivi letterari ed esegetici in Gerolamo. Atti del convegno tenuto a Trento il 5–7 dicembre 1995* (Brescia, 1997), 137–57.

Markschies, Christoph, 'Hieronymus und die *Hebraica Veritas*: ein Beitrag zur Archäologie des protestantischen Schriftverständnisses', in Martin Hengel and Anna Maria Schwemer (eds.), *Die Septuaginta zwischen Judentum und Christentum* (Tübingen, 1994), 131–81.

Markus, Robert, *The End of Ancient Christianity* (Cambridge, 1990).

Marrou, Henri-Irénée, 'La Technique de l'édition à l'époque patristique', *VChr*, 3 (1949), 208–24.

—— 'Le Dossier épigraphique de l'évêque Rusticus de Narbonne', *RACr*, 3–4 (1970), 331–49.

Martini, Caelestinus, 'De ordinatione duarum Collectionum quibus Ambrosiastri "Quaestiones" traduntur', *Antonianum*, 21 (1947), 23–48.

—— 'Le recensioni delle "Quaestiones Veteris et Novi Testamenti" dell'Ambrosiaster', *RicSRel*, 1 (1954), 40–62.

Mathisen, Ralph, *Ecclesiastical Factionalism and Religious Controversy in Fifth–century Gaul* (Washington, DC, 1989).

—— *Ruricius of Limoges and Friends: A Collection of Letters from Visigothic Gaul* (Liverpool, 1999).

—— (ed.), *Law, Society, and Authority in Late Antiquity* (Oxford, 2001).

—— 'Imperial Honorifics and Senatorial Status', in Ralph Mathisen (ed.), *Law, Society, and Authority in Late Antiquity* (Oxford, 2001), 179–207.

—— 'The Use and Abuse of Jerome in Gaul during Late Antiquity', in Andrew Cain and Josef Lössl (eds.), *Jerome of Stridon: His Life, Writings and Legacy* (Aldershot, 2009), Chap. 15.

Matthews, John, *Western Aristocracies and Imperial Court AD 364–425* (Oxford, 1975).

Maurer, Rudolf, 'Strukturelle Untersuchungen zu den Augustinischen Briefkorpora', dissertation (Vienna, 1991).

Mayer, Wendy, 'Constantinopolitan Women in Chrysostom's circle', *VChr*, 53 (1999), 265–88.

Meershoek, G. Q. A., *Le Latin biblique d'après saint Jérôme: aspects linguistiques de la rencontre entre la Bible et le monde classique* (Nijmegen, 1966).

Menestrina, Giovanni, 'Domino dilectissimo Hieronymo Augustinus: riflessioni sul carteggio Agostino–Gerolamo', *Bibbia, liturgia e letteratura cristiana antica* (Brescia, 1997), 89–177.

Mercati, Giovanni, 'Il carme Damasiano *de Davide* e la falsa corrispondenza di Damaso e Girolamo riguardo al Salterio', *Note di letteratura biblica e cristiana antica* (Rome, 1901), 113–26.

Messina, M. T., 'Hier. *Epist.*, 49.19: Il numero dispari e gli scrittori cristiani', *Sileno*, 28–9 (2002), 61–80.

Metz, René, *La Consécration des vierges dans l'église romaine* (Paris, 1954).

Metzger, Bruce, *The Early Versions of the New Testament* (New York, 1977).

Miletto, Gianfranco, 'Die *Hebraica veritas* in s. Hieronymus', in Helmut Merklein, Karlheinz Müller, and Günter Stemberger (eds.), *Bibel in jüdischer und Christlicher Tradition. Festschrift Johann Maier* (Frankfurt, 1993), 56–65.

Millar, Fergus, *The Roman Near East, 31 BC–AD 337* (Cambridge, 1993).

Mirri, Luciana, *La vita ascetica femminile in san Girolamo* (Rome, 1992).

—— 'Girolamo e la lectio divina', in Enzo Bianchi and Benedetto Calati (eds.), *La lectio divina nella vita religiosa* (Magnano, 1994), 107–24.

Miscellanea Geronimiana: Scritti varii pubblicati nel XV centenario dalla morte di San Girolamo (Rome, 1920).

Mohrmann, Christine, 'Considerazioni sulle *Confessioni* di Sant'Agostino, iii: La lingua e lo stile delle *Confessioni*', *Convivium*, NS 2 (1959), 129–39.

Mohrmann, Christine (ed.), *Vita di Antonio*, Vite dei Santi, i (Milan, 1974).

Moine, Nicole, 'Melaniana', *RecAug*, 15 (1980), 3–79.

Mommaerts, T. S., and David Kelley, 'The Anicii of Gaul and Rome', in John Drinkwater and Hugh Elton (eds.), *Fifth-century Gaul: A Crisis of Identity?* (Cambridge, 1992), 111–21.

Moreschini, Claudio, 'Gerolamo e la filosofia', in Aldo Ceresa-Gastaldo (ed.), *Gerolamo e la biografia letteraria* (Genoa, 1989), 45–62.

—— and Giovanni Menestrina (eds.), *Motivi letterari ed esegetici in Gerolamo. Atti del convegno tenuto a Trento il 5–7 dicembre 1995* (Brescia, 1997).

Morin, Germain, 'Un écrit méconnu de s. Jérôme: la 'Lettre à Présidius' sur le cierge pascal', *RBén*, 8 (1891), 20–7.

—— 'La Lettre de saint Jérôme sur le cierge pascal: réponse à quelques difficultés de M. l'abbé Duchesne', *RBén*, 9 (1892), 392–7.

—— 'Pour l'authenticité de la lettre de s. Jérôme à Présidius', *BALAC*, 3 (1913), 52–60.

Morton Braund, Susanna, *The Roman Satirists and their Masks* (London, 1996).

Mouterde, Réne, and Antoine Poidebard, *Le Limes de Chalcis: organisation de la steppe en Haute Syrie romaine* (2 vols., Paris, 1945).

Mratschek, Sigrid, *Der Briefwechsel des Paulinus von Nola. Kommunikation und soziale Kontakte zwischen Christlichen Intellektuellen* (Göttingen, 2002).

Müller, Hildegund, 'Der älteste Brief des heiligen Hieronymus. Zu einem aktuellen Datierungsvorschlag', *WS*, 111 (1998), 191–210.

Munier, Charles, 'Divorce, remariage et pénitence dans l'Église primitive', *RSR*, 52 (1978), 97–117.

Murphy, Francis X., 'Melania the Elder: A Biographical Note', *Traditio*, 5 (1947), 59–77.

—— (ed.), *A Monument to St Jerome: Essays on Some Aspects of His Life, Works and Influence* (New York, 1952).

—— 'St Jerome: The Irascible Hermit', in Murphy (ed.), *A Monument to St Jerome: Essays on Some Aspects of His Life, Works and Influence* (New York, 1952), 3–12.

Nadjo, Léon, and Élisabeth Gavoille, (eds.), *Epistulae antiquae*, i. *Actes du Ier colloque 'Le genre épistolaire antique et ses prolongements'* (Université François-Rabelais, Tours, 18–19 Sept. 1998) (Louvain-Paris, 2000).

—— and —— *Epistulae antiquae*, ii. *Actes du IIe colloque 'Le genre épistolaire antique et ses prolongements européens'* (Université François-Rabelais, Tours, 28–30 Sept. 2000) (2 vols., Louvain-Paris, 2002).

Nagel, Peter, *Die Motivierung der Askese in der alte Kirche und der Ursprung des Mönchtums* (Berlin, 1966).

Nauroy, Gérard, 'Jérôme, lecteur et censeur de l'exégèse d'Ambroise', in Yves-Marie Duval (ed.), *Jérôme entre l'Occident et l'Orient, XVIe*

centenaire du départ de saint Jérôme de Rome et de son installation à Bethléem. Actes du colloque de Chantilly, Sept. 1986 (Paris, 1988), 173–203.

Nautin, Pierre, 'La Date du *De viris inlustribus* de Jérôme, de la mort de Cyrille de Jérusalem et de celle de Grégoire de Nazianze', *RHE*, 56 (1961), 33–5.

—— 'Études de chronologie hiéronymienne (393–397), i. Le Livre de Jérôme contre Jean de Jérusalem', *REAug*, 18 (1972), 209–18.

—— 'L'excommunication de saint Jérôme', *AEHE V*, 80–1 (1972–3), 7–37.

—— 'Études de chronologie hiéronymienne (393–397), iii. Les Premières Relations entre Jérôme et Paulin de Nole', *REAug*, 19 (1973), 213–39.

—— 'Études de chronologie hiéronymienne (393–397), iv. Autres lettres de la période 393–396', *REAug*, 20 (1974), 251–84.

—— *Origène: sa vie et son œuvre* (Paris, 1977).

—— 'La Date de la mort de Pauline, de l'épître 66 de Jérôme et de l'épître 13 de Paulin de Nole', *Augustinianum*, 18 (1978), 547–50.

—— 'La Date des commentaires de Jérôme sur les épîtres pauliniennes', *RHE*, 74 (1979), 5–12.

—— 'L'activité littéraire de Jérôme de 387 à 392', *RThPh*, 115 (1983), 247–59.

—— 'Le Premier [*sic*] échange épistolaire entre Jérôme et Damase: lettres réelles ou fictives?', *FZPhTh*, 30 (1983), 331–44.

—— 'La Lettre de Paule et Eustochium à Marcelle (Jérôme, Ep. 46)', *Augustinianum*, 24 (1984), 441–8.

—— 'La Liste des œuvres de Jérôme dans le *De viris inlustribus*', *Orpheus*, NS 5 (1984), 319–34.

—— 'Hieronymus', *TRE*, 15 (1986), 304–15.

—— 'La Lettre *Magnum est* de Jérôme à Vincent et la traduction des homélies d'Origène sur les prophètes', in Yves-Marie Duval (ed.), *Jérôme entre l'Occident et l'Orient*, XVIe centenaire du départ de saint Jérôme de Rome et de son installation à Bethléem. Actes du colloque de Chantilly, Sept. 1986 (Paris, 1988), 27–39.

—— 'Le *De Seraphim* de Jérôme et son appendice *ad Damasum*', in Michael Wissemann (ed.), *Roma renascens. Beiträge zur Spätantike und Rezeptionsgeschichte. Festschrift Ilona Opelt* (Frankfurt, 1988), 257–93.

Nenci, Giuseppe, 'Onasus Segestanus in Girolamo, *Ep.* 40', *RFIC*, 123 (1995), 90–4.

Neuschäfer, Bernhard, *Origenes als Philologe* (2 vols., Basle, 1987).

Newman, Hillel, 'Between Jerusalem and Bethlehem: Jerome and the Holy Places of Palestine', in Alberdina Houtman, Marcel Poorthuis, and Joshua Schwartz (eds.), *Sanctity of Time and Space in Tradition and Modernity* (Leiden, 1998), 215–27.

Newman, Hillel, 'Jerome's Judaizers', *JECS*, 9 (2001), 421–52.

—— 'How Should We Measure Jerome's Hebrew Competence?', in Andrew Cain and Josef Lössl (eds.), *Jerome of Stridon: His Life, Writings and Legacy* (Aldershot, 2009), Chap. 10.

Nistler, Johanna, 'Vettius Agorius Praetextatus', *Klio*, 10 (1910), 462–75.

Norton, M. A., 'Prosopography of Pope Damasus', *Folia*, 4 (1950), 13–31; 5 (1951), 30–55; 6 (1952), 16–39.

Nuvolone, F., 'Notulae manuscriptae', *FZPhTh*, 26 (1979), 243–56.

Oberhelman, Steven, 'Jerome's earliest attack on Ambrose: *On Ephesians*, Prologue (ML 26: 469D–70A)', *TAPhA*, 121 (1991), 377–401.

—— *Rhetoric and Homiletics in Fourth-century Christian Literature* (Atlanta, Ga., 1991).

O'Brien, Mary, *Titles of Address in Christian Latin Epistolography to 543 AD* (Washington, DC, 1930).

O'Donnell, James J., 'The Authority of Augustine', *AugStud*, 22 (1991), 7–35.

—— (ed.), *Augustin: Confessions* (3 vols., Oxford, 1992).

Oliensis, Ellen, *Horace and the Rhetoric of Authority* (Cambridge, 1998).

Oort, Johannes van, Otto Wermelinger, and Gregor Wurst (eds.), *Augustine and Manichaeism in the Latin West: Proceedings of the Fribourg-Utrecht Symposium of the International Association of Manichaean Studies* (Leiden, 2001).

Opelt, Ilona, *Hieronymus' Streitschriften* (Heidelberg, 1973).

—— 'Hieronymus' Leistung als Literarhistoriker in der Schrift *De viris illustribus*', *Orpheus*, NS 1 (1980), 52–75.

—— *Die Polemik in der Christlichen lateinischen Literatur von Tertullian bis Augustin* (Heidelberg, 1980).

—— 'Origene visto da san Girolamo', *Augustinianum*, 26 (1986), 217–22.

—— 'S. Girolamo ed i suoi maestri ebrei', *Augustinianum*, 28 (1988), 327–38.

—— 'Aug.*Epist.*, 27* Divjak: ein Schreiben des Hieronymus an Bischof Aurelius von Karthago', *Augustiniana*, 40 (1990), 19–25.

Otten, Willemien, 'Augustine on Marriage, Monasticism, and the Community of the Church', *ThS*, 59 (1998), 385–405.

Palanque, Jean-Remy, 'St Jerome and the Barbarians', in Francis X. Murphy (ed.), *A Monument to St Jerome: Essays on Some Aspects of His Life, Works and Influence* (New York, 1952), 173–99.

—— *Le Diocèse de Marseilles* (Paris, 1967).

Paoli, Elmore, 'Autour de Paula (347–404): Subsidia prosopographica', *ZPE*, 103 (1994), 241–9.

Paredi, Angelo, 'S. Gerolamo e s. Ambrogio', in *Mélanges Eugène Tisserant, Studi e Testi 235* (Vatican City, 1964), 183–98.

Patrich, Joseph, *Sabas, Leader of Palestinian Monasticism. A Comparative Study in Eastern Monasticism, Fourth to Seventh Centuries* (Washington, DC, 1995).

Penco, Gregorio, 'Il concetto di monaco e di vita monastica in Occidente nel secolo VI', *StudMon*, 1 (1959), 7–50.

Penna, Angelo, *Principi e carattere dell'esegesi di s. Gerolamo* (Rome, 1950).

Perago, Fernando, 'Il valore della tradizione nella polemica tra s. Agostino e Giuliano d'Eclano', *AnnNap*, 10 (1962), 143–60.

Perrin, Michel-Yves, ' "Ad implendum caritatis ministerium": La place des courriers dans la correspondance de Paulin de Nole', *MEFRA*, 104 (1992), 1025–68.

Perrone, Lorenzo, 'Sulla preistoria delle *quaestiones* nella letteratura patristica. Presupposti e sviluppi del genere letterario fino al IV sec.', *AnnSE*, 8 (1991), 485–505.

—— 'Monasticism in the Holy Land: From the Beginning to the Crusaders', *POC*, 45 (1995), 31–63.

—— 'Perspectives sur Origène et la littérature patristique des *Quaestiones et Responsiones*', in Gilles Dorival and Alain le Boulluec (eds.), *Origeniana Sexta*, Origen et la Bible: Actes du Colloquium Origenianum Sextum, Chantilly, 30 Aug.–3 Sept. 1993 (Leuven, 1995), 151–64.

—— 'The Mystery of Judea (Jerome, *Ep.* 46): The Holy City of Jerusalem between History and Symbol in Early Christian Thought', in Lee Levine (ed.), *Jerusalem: Its Sanctity and Centrality to Judaism, Christianity, and Islam* (New York, 1999), 221–39.

Pétré, Hélène, *Éthérie: journal de voyage. texte latin, introduction et traduction* (Paris, 1948).

Pharr, Clyde (ed.), *The Theodosian Code and Novels and the Sirmondian Constitutions* (Princeton, NJ, 1952).

Philippart, Guy (ed.), *Hagiographies: histoire internationale de la littérature hagiographique latine et vernaculaire en Occident des origines à 1550* (2 vols., Turnhout, 1994).

Pietri, Charles, 'Concordia apostolorum et renovatio urbis (Cult des martyrs et propagande pontificale)', *MEFRA*, 73 (1961), 275–322.

—— *Roma christiana: recherches sur l'Église de Rome, son organisation, sa politique, son idéologie de Miltiade à Sixte III (311–440)* (2 vols., Paris, 1976).

—— 'Le Mariage chrétien à Rome', in Jean Delumeau (ed.), *Histoire vécue du peuple chrétien* (Toulouse, 1979), 105–31.

—— 'Damase, évêque de Rome', *Saecularia Damasiana. Atti del convegno internazionale per il XVI centenario della morte di Papa Damaso* (Vatican City, 1986), 31–58.

Pizzolato, Luigi, 'La *consolatio* cristiana per la morte nel sec. IV. Riflessioni metodologiche e tematiche', *CCC*, 6 (1985), 441–74.

Plinval, Georges de, 'Recherches sur l'œuvre littéraire de Pélage', *RPh*, 8 (1934), 9–42.

—— *Pélage: ses écrits, sa vie et sa réforme* (Lausanne, 1943).

Plumer, Eric, *Augustine's Commentary on Galatians. Introduction, Text, Translation, and Notes* (Oxford, 2003).

Poinsotte, Jean–Michel, 'Hieronymus poeta (ep. 108, § 33)', in Louis Holtz and Jean-Claude Fredouille (eds.), *De Tertullien aux Mozarabes: mélanges offerts à Jacques Fontaine, à l'occasion de son 70ᵉ anniversaire, par ses élèves, amis et collègues* (2 vols., Paris, 1992), i. 211–21.

Polman, A. D. R., *The Word of God According to Augustine* (London, 1961).

Préaux, Jean-Georges, 'Procédés d'invention d'un sobriquet par saint Jérôme', *Latomus*, 17 (1958), 659–64.

Pricoco, Salvatore, 'Motivi polemici e prospettive classicistiche nel De viris illustribus di Girolamo', *SicGymn*, 32 (1979), 69–99.

—— '*Egredere de terra tua*: La fortuna di Gen. 12.1 nella prima cultura monastica', in Louis Holtz and Jean-Claude Fredouille (eds.), *De Tertullien aux Mozarabes: mélanges offerts à Jacques Fontaine, à l'occasion de son 70ᵉ anniversaire, par ses élèves, amis et collègues* (2 vols., Paris, 1992), i. 119–31.

Prinzivalli, Emanuela, '*Sicubi dubitas, Hebraeos interroga*: Girolamo tra difesa dell'*Hebraica veritas* e polemica antigiudaica', *AnnSE*, 14 (1997), 179–206.

Pronberger, Nicolaus, *Beiträge zur Chronologie der Briefe des hl. Hieronymus* (Amberg, 1913).

Rackett, Michael, 'What's Wrong with Pelagianism?: Augustine and Jerome on the Dangers of Pelagius and his Followers', *AugStud*, 33 (2002), 223–37.

Radicke, Jan, 'Die Selbstdarstellung des Plinius in seinen Briefen', *Hermes*, 125 (1997), 447–69.

Rapp, Claudia, *Holy Bishops in Late Antiquity: The Nature of Christian Leadership in an Age of Transition* (Berkeley, Calif., 2005).

—— 'Holy Texts, Holy Men and Holy Scribes: Aspects of Scriptural Holiness in Late Antiquity', in William Klingshirn and Linda Safran (eds.), *The Early Christian Book* (Washington, DC, 2007), 194–222.

Raspanti, Giacomo, 'Aspetti formali dell'esegesi paolina dell'Ambrosiaster', *AnnSE*, 16 (1999), 507–36.

—— 'San Girolamo e l'interpretazione di *Gal.* 2.11–14', *REAug*, 49 (2003), 297–321.

Rebenich, Stefan, *Hieronymus und sein Kreis: Prosopographische und sozialgeschichtliche Untersuchungen* (Stuttgart, 1992).

—— 'Jerome: The *vir trilinguis* and the *Hebraica veritas*', *VChr*, 47 (1993), 50–77.

—— 'Hieronymus und Evagrius von Antiochia', *StudPatr*, 28 (1993), 75–80.

—— 'Asceticism, Orthodoxy and Patronage: Jerome in Constantinople', *StudPatr*, 33 (1997), 358–77.

—— 'Der Kirchenvater Hieronymus als Hagiograph: Die *Vita s. Pauli primi eremitae*', in Kaspar Elm (ed.), *Beiträge zur Geschichte des Paulinerordens* (Berlin, 2000), 23–40.

—— *Jerome* (London and New York, 2002).

—— 'Inventing an Ascetic Hero: Jerome's *Life of Paul the First Hermit*', in Andrew Cain and Josef Lössl (eds.), *Jerome of Stridon: His Life, Writings and Legacy* (Aldershot, 2009), Chap. 1.

Rebillard, Éric, 'A New Style of Argument in Christian Polemic: Augustine and the Use of Patristic Citations', *JECS*, 8 (2000), 559–78.

Rees, Bryn, *Pelagius: A Reluctant Heretic* (Suffolk, 1988).

—— *Pelagius: Life and Letters* (2 vols., Woodbridge, 1991).

Refoulé, J., 'Datation du premier concile de Carthage contre les Pélagiens et du *Libellus fidei* de Rufin', *REAug*, 9 (1963), 41–9.

Regnault, Lucien, *La Vie quotidienne des pères du désert en Égypte au IVe siècle* (Paris, 1990).

Reynolds, R. E., 'An Early Medieval Mass Fantasy: The Correspondence of Pope Damasus and St Jerome on a Nicene Canon', in Peter Linehan (ed.), *Proceedings of the Seventh International Congress of Medieval Canon Law* (Rome, 1988), 73–89.

Rice, Eugene, *Saint Jerome in the Renaissance* (Baltimore, Md., 1985).

Ridderbos, Bernhard, *Saint and Symbol: Images of Saint Jerome in Early Italian Art* (Groningen, 1984).

Rivet, A. L. F., *Gallia Narbonensis: Southern France in Roman Times* (London, 1988).

Rocca, Giancarlo, *L'Adversus Helvidium di san Girolamo nel contesto della letteratura ascetico-mariana del secolo IV* (Berne, 1998).

Roda, Sergio, 'Polifunzionalità della lettera *commendaticia*: teoria e prassi nell'epistolario Simmachiano', in F. Paschoud (ed.), *Actes du Colloque pour le 1600e anniversaire du débat autour de l'Autel de la Victoire, Genève 1984* (Paris, 1986), 177–202.

Rondet, Henri, 'Le Symbolisme de la mer chez saint Augustin', Congrès international augustinien, *Augustinus Magister* (3 vols., Paris, 1954), ii. 691–711.

—— 'Essais sur la chronologie des *Enarrationes in Psalmos* de saint Augustin', *BLE*, 61 (1960), 11–127; 258–86; 65 (1964), 110–36; 68 (1967), 180–202; 71 (1970), 174–200; 77 (1976), 99–118.

Rougé, Jean, 'La Navigation hivernale sous l'empire romain', *REA*, 54 (1952), 316–25.

—— *Recherches sur l'organisation du commerce maritime en Méditerranée* (Paris, 1966).

Rousseau, Philip, *Ascetics, Authority, and the Church in the Age of Jerome and Cassian* (Oxford, 1978).

—— *Pachomius. The Making of a Community in Fourth-century Egypt* (Berkeley, Calif., 1985).

—— ' "Learned Women" and the Development of a Christian Culture in Late Antiquity', *SO*, 70 (1995), 116–47.

—— 'Jerome's Search for Self-identity', in Pauline Allen, Raymond Canning, and Lawrence Cross (eds.), *Prayer and Spirituality in the Early Church* (4 vols., Brisbane, 1998–2006), i. 125–42.

—— 'Jerome on Jeremiah: Exegesis and recovery', in Andrew Cain and Josef Lössl (eds.), *Jerome of Stridon: His Life, Writings and Legacy* (Aldershot, 2009), Chap. 6.

Russo, Daniel, *Saint Jérôme en Italie. Étude d'iconographie et de spiritualité (XIIIe–XVe siècle)* (Paris, 1987).

Saecularia Damasiana. Atti del convegno internazionale per il XVI centenario della morte di Papa Damaso (Vatican City, 1986).

Sághy, Marianne, '*Scinditur in partes populus*: Pope Damasus and the Martyrs of Rome', *EME*, 9 (2000), 273–87.

Saint Martin et son temps. Mémorial du XVIe centenaire des débuts du monachisme en Gaule 361–1961 (*Studia Anselmiana*, 46) (Rome, 1961).

Salzman, Michele, *The Making of a Christian Aristocracy: Social and Religious Change in the Western Roman Empire* (Cambridge, Mass., 2002).

Saulnier, Christine, 'La Vie monastique en Terre Sainte auprès des lieux de pèlerinage (IVe s.)', *MHE*, 6 (1983), 223–48.

Savon, Hervé, 'Les Intentions de saint Ambroise dans la préface du *De officiis*', in Michel Soetard (ed.), *Valeurs dans le stoïcisme, du portique à nos jours. Textes rassemblés en hommage à Michel Spanneut* (Lille, 1993), 155–69.

—— 'Saint Ambroise a-t-il imité le recueil de lettres de Pline le Jeune?', *REAug*, 41 (1995), 3–17.

Savramis, Demosthenes, *Zur Soziologie des byzantinischen Mönchtums* (Leiden, 1962).

Schatkin, Margaret, 'The Influence of Origen upon St Jerome's Commentary on Galatians', *VChr*, 24 (1970), 49–58.

Schmitz, P., 'La Première communauté de vierges à Rome', *RBén*, 38 (1926), 189–95.

Schwind, Johannes, 'Hieronymus' Epistula ad Innocentium (epist 1)—ein Jugendwerk?', *WS*, 110 (1997), 171–86.

Scourfield, J. H. D., 'A Literary Commentary on Jerome, Letters 1, 60, 107', dissertation (Oxford, 1983).

—— 'Jerome, Antioch, and the Desert: A Note on Chronology', *JThS*, NS 37 (1986), 117–21.

—— *Consoling Heliodorus: A Commentary on Jerome, Letter 60* (Oxford, 1993).

Seligman, Jon, and Rafa Abu Raya, 'Dwelling Caves on the Mount of Olives (Et-Tur)', *Aliqot*, 40 (2000), 123–38.

Serrato Garrido, Mercedes, *Ascetismo Femenimo en Roma. Estudios sobre San Jerónimo y San Agustín* (Cadiz, 1993).

Shackleton Bailey, D. R., *Cicero's Letters to Atticus* (7 vols., Cambridge, 1965–70).

Shanzer, Danuta, 'The Anonymous *Carmen contra paganos* and the Date and Identity of the Centonist Proba', *REAug*, 32 (1986), 232–48.

—— 'The Date and Identity of the Centonist Proba', *RecAug*, 27 (1994), 75–96.

—— 'Jerome, Tobit, Alms, and the *Vita aeterna*', in Andrew Cain and Josef Lössl (eds.), *Jerome of Stridon: His Life, Writings and Legacy* (Aldershot, 2009), Chap. 7.

—— and Ian Wood, *Letters and Selected Prose of Avitus of Vienne* (Liverpool, 2002).

Shaw, Teresa, *The Burden of the Flesh: Fasting and Sexuality in Early Christianity* (Minneapolis, 1998).

Shepherd, Massey, 'The Liturgical Reform of Damasus I', in Patrick Granfield and Josef A. Jungmann (eds.), *Kyriakon. Festschrift Johannes Quasten* (2 vols., Münster, 1970), ii. 847–63.

Sherwin-White, A. N., *Letters of Pliny: A Historical and Social Commentary* (Oxford, 1966).

Sieben, Hermann-Josef, 'Israels Wüstenwanderung (Num 33) in der Auslegung des Hieronymus und des Origenes. Ein Beitrag zur Geschichte der Spiritualität und der origenistischen Streitigkeiten', *Th&Ph*, 77 (2002), 1–22.

Sivan, Hagith, *Ausonius of Bordeaux. Genesis of a Gallic Aristocracy* (London, 1993).

Skeb, Matthias, *Epistulae: Paulinus von Nola* (2 vols., Freiburg, 1998).

Smith, Alfred, 'The Latin Sources of the Commentary of Pelagius in the Epistle of St Paul to the Romans', *JThS*, 19 (1918), 162–230.

Sogno, Cristiana, *Q. Aurelius Symmachus: A Political Biography* (Ann Arbor, Mich., 2006).

Souter, Alexander, *A Study of Ambrosiaster* (Cambridge, 1905).

——*Pelagius' Expositions of Thirteen Epistles of St Paul* (3 vols., Cambridge, 1922–31).

——*The Earliest Latin Commentaries on the Epistles of St Paul* (Oxford, 1927).

Spinelli, G., 'Ascetismo, monachesimo e cenobitismo ad Aquileia nel IV secolo', *AAAD*, 22 (1982), 273–300.

Stade, Walter, *Hieronymus in prooemiis quid tractaverit et quos auctores quasque leges rhetoricas secutus sit* (Rostock, 1925).

Stancliffe, Clare, *St Martin and his Hagiographer* (Oxford, 1983).

Starr, Raymond, 'The Circulation of Literary Texts in the Roman World', *CQ*, 37 (1987), 213–23.

Steinhausen, J., 'Hieronymus und Laktanz in Trier', *TZ*, 20 (1951), 126–54.

Steinmann, Jean, *Saint Jerome and His Times* (Notre Dame, Ind., 1959).

Stemberger, Günter, *Juden und Christen im Heiligen Land* (Munich, 1987).

——'Hieronymus und die Juden seiner Zeit', in Dietrich-Alex Koch and Hermann Lichtenberger (eds.), *Begegnungen zwischen Christentum und Judentum in Antike und Mittelalter. Festschrift für Heinz Schreckenberg* (Göttingen, 1993), 347–64.

Sterk, Andrea, *Renouncing the World Yet Leading the Church: The Monk–Bishop in Late Antiquity* (Cambridge, Mass., 2004).

Steur, Pieter, *Het karakter van Hieronymus van Stridon bestudeerd in zijn brieven* (Nijmegen, 1945).

Stewart, Columba, *Cassian the Monk* (Oxford, 1998).

Stoico, Giuseppe, *L'Epistolario di san Girolamo: Studio critico-letterario di stilistica latina* (Naples, 1972).

Stowers, Stanley, *Letter Writing in Greco–Roman Antiquity* (Philadelphia, 1986).

Sugano, Karin, *Das Rombild des Hieronymus* (Bern, 1983).

——'Marcella von Rom. Ein Lebensbild', in Michael Wissemann (ed.), *Roma renascens. Beiträge zur Spätantike und Rezeptionsgeschichte. Festschrift Ilona Opelt* (Frankfurt, 1988), 355–70.

Sutcliffe, Edmund, 'The Name Vulgate', *Biblica*, 29 (1948), 345–52.

Swan, Laura, *The Forgotten Desert Mothers: Sayings, Lives, and Stories of Early Christian Women* (New York, 2001).

Taylor, Joan, *Christians and the Holy Places: The Myth of Jewish–Christian Origins* (Oxford, 1993).

Tchalenko, Georges, *Villages antiques de la Syrie du nord* (Paris, 1953).

Testard, Maurice, *Saint Jérôme, l'apôtre savant et pauvre du patriciat romain* (Paris, 1969).

——*Saint Ambroise: Les Devoirs* (2 vols., Paris, 1984–92).

—— 'Jérôme et Ambroise. Sur un "aveu" du *De officiis* de l'évêque de Milan', in Yves-Marie Duval (ed.), *Jérôme entre l'Occident et l'Orient*, XVIe centenaire du départ de saint Jérôme de Rome et de son installation à Bethléem. Actes du colloque de Chantilly, Sept. 1986 (Paris, 1988), 227–54.

—— 'Les Dames de l'Aventin, disciples de saint Jérôme', *BSAF* (1996), 39–63.

—— 'Démétrias, une disciple de saint Jérôme, et la *sollicitudo animi*', *BSAF* (1999), 238–56.

Thraede, Klaus, *Grundzüge griechisch-römischer Brieftopik* (Munich, 1970).

Tibiletti, Carlo, 'Immagini bibliche nel linguaggio figurato di s. Girolamo', in Aldo Ceresa-Gastaldo (ed.), *Gerolamo e la biografia letteraria* (Genoa, 1989), 63–79.

Trapp, Michael, *Greek and Latin Letters. An Anthology, with Translation* (Cambridge, 2003).

Trigg, Joseph, *Origen. The Bible and Philosophy in the Third-century Church* (Atlanta, Ga., 1983).

Trisoglio, Francesco, 'La personalità di san Girolamo attraverso l'epistolario', *ScC*, 120 (1992), 575–612.

—— 'Note stilistiche sull'epistolario di Girolamo', *VetChr*, 30 (1993), 267–88.

Trout, Dennis, 'Augustine at Cassiciacum: *Otium honestum* and the Social Dimensions of Conversion', *VChr*, 42 (1988), 132–46.

—— 'The Dates of the Ordination of Paulinus of Bordeaux and of his Departure for Nola', *REAug*, 37 (1991), 237–60.

—— *Paulinus of Nola. Life, Letters, and Poems* (Berkeley, Calif., 1999).

—— 'Damasus and the Invention of Early Christian Rome', *JMEMS*, 33 (2003), 517–36.

Urbainczyk, Theresa, *Theodoret of Cyrrhus: The Bishop and the Holy Man* (Ann Arbor, Mich., 2002).

Vaccari, Alberto, 'Le Antiche vite di s. Girolamo', *Scritti di erudizione e di filologia* (2 vols., Rome, 1958), i. 31–51.

Veltri, Giuseppe, 'L'ispirazione della LXX tra leggenda e teologia. Dal racconto di Aristea alla *veritas hebraica* di Gerolamo', *Laurentianum*, 27 (1986), 3–71.

Verboven, Koenraad, *The Economy of Friends. Economic Aspects of Amicitia and Patronage in the Late Republic* (Brussels, 2002).

Vescovi e pastori in epoca teodosiana. In occasione del XVI centenario della consacrazione episcopale di s. Agostino, 396–1996 (Rome, 1997).

Vessey, Mark, 'Jerome's Origen: The Making of a Christian Literary *Persona*', *StudPatr*, 28 (1993), 135–45, repr. in his *Latin Christian Writers in Late Antiquity and their Texts* (Aldershot, 2005).

Vessey, Mark, 'Conference and Confession: Literary Pragmatics in Augustine's *Apologia contra Hieronymum*', *JECS*, 1 (1993), 175–213, repr. in his *Latin Christian Writers in Late Antiquity and their Texts* (Aldershot, 2005).

—— 'From *cursus* to *ductus*: Figures of Writing in Western Late Antiquity (Augustine, Jerome, Cassiodorus, Bede)', in Patrick Cheney and Frederick de Armas (eds.), *European Literary Careers. The Author from Antiquity to the Renaissance* (Toronto, 2002), 47–103.

—— *Latin Christian Writers in Late Antiquity and their Texts* (Aldershot, 2005).

—— 'Jerome and the Jeromanesque', in Andrew Cain and Josef Lössl (eds.), *Jerome of Stridon: His Life, Writings and Legacy* (Aldershot, 2009), Chap. 17.

Villela, J., 'Los corresponsales hispanos de Jerónimo', *SEJG*, 41 (2002), 87–111.

Vincent, Hugues, 'Bethléem: le sanctuaire de la Nativité', *RBi*, 45 (1936), 544–74; *RBi*, 46 (1937), 93–121.

Violardo, Giacomo, *Il pensiero giuridico di san Girolamo* (Milan, 1937).

Viscido, Lorenzo, *Atteggiamenti ironici nell'epistolario geronimiano* (Salerno, 1978).

Vismara, Giulio, *L'audientia episcopalis* (Milan, 1995).

Vogels, Heinrich, 'Ambrosiaster und Hieronymus', *RBén*, 66 (1956), 14–19.

Vogüé, Adalbert de, 'La Règle du Maître et la lettre apocryphe de saint Jérôme sur le chant des Psaumes', *StudMon*, 7 (1965), 357–67.

—— 'La *Vita Pauli* de saint Jérôme et sa datation: examen d'un passage-clé (ch. 6)', in *Eulogia: mélanges offerts à Antoon A. R. Bastiaensen à l'occasion de son soixante-cinquième anniversaire* (Steenbrugge, 1991), 395–406.

—— *Histoire littéraire du mouvement monastique dans l'antiquité* (6 vols., Paris, 1991–2003).

Volgers, Annelie, and Claudio Zamagni (eds.), *Erotapokriseis. Early Christian Question-and-Answer Literature in Context. Proceedings of the Utrecht Colloquium, 13–14 October 2003* (Leuven, 2004).

—— 'Ambrosiaster: Persuasive Powers in Progress', in Annelie Volgers and Claudio Zamagni (eds.), *Erotapokriseis. Early Christian Question-and-Answer Literature in Context. Proceedings of the Utrecht Colloquium, 13–14 October 2003* (Leuven, 2004), 99–125.

von Campenhausen, Hans, *Tradition und Leben. Kräfte der Kirchengeschicht: Aufsätze und Vorträge* (Tübingen, 1960).

—— 'Die asketische Heimatlosigkeit im altkirchlichen und frühmittelalterlichen Mönchtum', *Tradition und Leben: Kräfte der Kirchengeschichte. Aufsätze und Vorträge* (Tübingen, 1960), 290–317.

—— *Lateinische Kirchenväter* (Stuttgart, 1960).

von Moos, Peter, *Consolatio. Studien zur mittellateinischen Trostliteratur über den Tod und zum Problem der Christlichen Trauer* (4 vols., Munich, 1971–2).

Vööbus, Arthur, *History of Asceticism in the Syrian Orient* (2 vols., Leuven, 1958).

Walker Bynum, Caroline, *Holy Feast and Holy Fast: The Religious Significance of Food to Medieval Women* (Berkeley, Calif., 1987).

Walsh, Peter (ed. and trans.), *Augustine: De bono coniugali; De sancta virginitate* (Oxford, 2001).

Ward, Benedicta (trans.), *The Sayings of the Desert Fathers: The Alphabetical Collection* (Kalamazoo, 1984).

Weber, Robert (ed.), *Biblia Sacra iuxta Vulgatam Versionem* (Stuttgart, 1983).

Weichert, Valentin, *Demetrii et Libanii qui feruntur ΤΥΠΟΙ ΕΠΙΣΤΟΛΙΚΟΙ et ΕΠΙΣΤΟΛΙΜΑΙΟΙ ΧΑΡΑΚΤΗΡΕΣ* (Leipzig, 1910).

Weingarten, Susan, *The Saint's Saints: Hagiography and Geography in Jerome* (Leiden, 2005).

Welten, P., 'Bethlehem und die Klage um Adonis', *ZPalV*, 99 (1983), 189–203.

Wermelinger, Otto, *Röm und Pelagius: die theologische Position der römischen Bischöfe im pelagianischen Streit in den Jahren 411–432* (Stuttgart, 1975).

White, Carolinne, *The Correspondence (394–419) between Jerome and Augustine of Hippo* (Lampeter, 1990).

——— *Christian Friendship in the Fourth Century* (Cambridge, 1992).

Wickham, Lionel, and Caroline Hammond Bammel (eds.), *Christian Faith and Greek Philosophy in Late Antiquity: Essays in Tribute to George Christopher Stead* (Leiden, 1993).

Wiesen, David, *Saint Jerome as a Satirist: A Study in Christian Latin Thought and Letters* (Ithaca, NY, 1964).

Wikenhauser, Alfred, 'Der heilige Hieronymus und die Kurzschrift', *TQ*, 29 (1910), 50–87.

Wilken, Robert, *The Land Called Holy: Palestine in Christian History and Thought* (New Haven, Conn., 1992).

Wilkes, John, *Dalmatia* (London, 1969).

Wilkinson, John, 'Christian Pilgrims in Jerusalem during the Byzantine Period', *PEQ*, 108 (1977), 74–101.

——— *Jerusalem Pilgrims before the Crusades* (Warminster, 2002).

Williams, Megan Hale, *The Monk and the Book: Jerome and the Making of Christian Scholarship* (Chicago, 2006).

Williams, Wynne, *Pliny: Correspondence with Trajan from Bithynia (Epistles X)* (Warminster, 1990).

Wisniewski, Robert, '*Bestiae Christum loquuntur*: ou des habitants du désert et de la ville dans la *Vita Pauli* de saint Jérôme', *Augustinianum*, 40 (2000), 105–44.

Wissemann, Michael (ed.), *Roma renascens. Beiträge zur Spätantike und Rezeptionsgeschichte. Festschrift Ilona Opelt* (Frankfurt, 1988).

Yarbrough, Anne, 'Christianization in the Fourth Century: The Example of Roman Women', *ChHist*, 45 (1976), 149–65.

Yoyotte, Jean, 'Les Pèlerinages dans l'Égypte ancienne', in Anne-Marie Esnoul, et al. (eds.), *Les Pèlerinages* (Paris, 1960), 17–74.

Zeiller, Jacques, 'Saint Jérôme et les Goths', *Miscellanea Geronimiana. Scritti varii pubblicati nel XV centenario dalla morte di San Girolamo* (Rome, 1920), 123–30.

—— 'La Lettre de saint Jérôme aux Goths Sunnia et Frétela', *CRAI* (1935), 238–50.

Zelzer, Micaela, 'Zur Sprache des Ambrosiaster', *WS*, 4 (1970), 196–213.

—— '*Plinius Christianus:* Ambrosius als Epistolograph', *StudPatr*, 23 (1989), 203–8.

—— 'Zur Komposition der Briefsammlung des hl. Ambrosius', *StudPatr*, 18 (1990), 212–17.

—— 'Der Brief in der Spätantike: Überlegungen zu einem literarischen Genos am Beispiel der Briefsammlung des Sidonius Apollinaris', *WS*, 108 (1995), 541–51.

Ziolkowski, Jan, 'Classical Influences on Medieval Latin Views of Poetic Inspiration', in Peter Godman and Oswyn Murray (eds.), *Latin Poetry and the Classical Traditio: Essays in Medieval and Renaissance Literature* (Oxford, 1990), 15–38.

Zovatto, Paolo, 'Paolo da Concordia', *AAAD*, 5 (1974), 165–80.

General Index

280 *General Index*

leftSaint-Mesmin, Abbey of 16 n. 12
Salvina 134, 158, 159, 195 n. 118, 212
Scientia Scripturarum 62
Scipiones 36
Seneca 4, 208
Septuagint 65, 128 n. 114
Sextus Claudius Petronius 160 n. 158
Sidonius Apollinaris 4, 19, 220 n. 1, 227
Siricius, Pope 105, 117, 136–7
Sixtus V, Pope 1
Slaves 117–18
Sofronius 109
Solitude 30, 70, 73, 146 n. 91, 154
Solomon 170 n. 13, 192–3, 219
Sophronius 101 n. 12
Stridon 1, 45 n. 9, 48, 121
Suetonius 18
Sulpicius Severus 11, 129 n. 2, 155–8,
     167
Sunnia 210
Symmachus 4, 19, 211
Synesius of Cyrene 27 n. 58, 220 n. 1
Synkrisis 192–3
Syria 8, 15, 22, 25, 34–5, 37–8, 44, 104,
     146, 155
Syriac, Jerome's knowledge of 31 n. 72,
     193 n. 114

Terence 45 n. 8
Tertullian 3 n. 10, 52, 61
Theodora 212
Theodoret 25, 220 n. 1
Theodosius, monk 20–1, 25, 30–1, 210
Theodosius I, emperor 115–17, 188 n.
     91
Theophilus, bishop 210, 217, 227
Toxotius 36
Trajan, emperor 18
Tranquillinus 217
Travel
  by land 123, 127, 184, 189–90
  by sea 92, 123, 125, 184

Trier 45 n. 9, 186 n. 87, 199
Turpilius 28
Typology
  Asella as desert anchorite 72
  Blesilla as Christlike figure 75
  Desert as new Eden 20
  Jerome as Jonah 137
  Jerome as Moses 162, 165
  Jerome as St. Paul 162 n. 163
  Jerome's disciples as great women of
     Bible 133
  Jerome's enemies as Pharisees 119
  Jovinian as Epicurus 136, 138
  Paula as Melania 142 n. 76
  Rome as Babylon 126–8

Ursinus 47

Valentinian I, emperor 114–15, 199
Valentinians 33
Vallarsi, Domenico 16 n. 13
Venerius 151
Vergil 45 n. 8
Vessey, Mark 70–1
Vettius Agorius Praetextatus 47–8, 77
Vigilantius 179, 210, 214
Vincent of Lérins 136 n. 42
Vincentius 49, 125, 125 n. 102
Virginity and virgins 72–4, 76, 94–5,
     100, 104, 108–9, 111–12, 124,
     130, 140, 149, 152, 158–66, 214,
     215
Vitalis 170 n. 11, 219
'*Viva vox*' 190–1
Vogels, Heinrich 62
Vogüé, Adalbert de 164

Widowhood and widows 35–6, 73–6,
     101, 109, 111, 133–4, 158–60,
     215
Wiesen, David 130
Work ethic, monastic 24–5

Index of Ancient Sources